D0895353

TRUST ON TRIAL

TRUST
——— ON ———
TRIAL

*How the Microsoft Case Is
Reframing the Rules of Competition*

RICHARD B. McKENZIE

*Graduate School of Management
University of California, Irvine*

PERSEUS PUBLISHING
Cambridge, Massachusetts

Many of the designations used by manufacturers and sellers to distinguish their products are claimed as trademarks. Where those designations appear in this book and Perseus Publishing was aware of a trademark claim, the designations have been printed in initial capital letters.

Copyright © 2000 by Richard B. McKenzie

A CIP record for this book is available from the Library of Congress.
ISBN 0-7382-0331-9

Perseus Publishing is a member of the Perseus Books Group.

Find us on the World Wide Web at http://www.perseuspublishing.com

Perseus Publishing books are available at special discounts for bulk purchases in the U.S. by corporations, institutions, and other organizations. For more information, please contact the Special Markets Department at HarperCollins Publishers, 10 East 53rd Street, New York, NY 10022, or call 1-212-207-7528.

Text design by Jeff Williams
Set in 11-point Minion by Perseus Publishing Services

First printing, March 2000

1 2 3 4 5 6 7 8 9 10—03 02 01 00

For Gary Byrne

CONTENTS

Preface   IX

The Nation's Major Antitrust Laws   XIV

1   From Railway Time to Internet Time   1

2   Monopoly Mantra   27

3   Little Linux   49

4   Digital Predation   67

5   Digital Switching   83

6   Innovative Thinking   115

7   Mud Farming   141

8   Politics 101   165

9   Politicizing Antitrust   191

10 Antitrust Ironies   217

    Appendix I   231

    Appendix II   235

    Notes   241

    Index   273

PREFACE

TRAINS ARE A GRACIOUS WAY TO TRAVEL long distances and at the same time be able to watch the ever-changing landscape of forests and distant towns go by. Trains are slow but steady, cramped for sleeping but comfortable. There is no better experience than to see a snow-capped peak drift by a train's window while sipping on a glass of wine.

Trains are a throwback to an earlier era when life moved at a slower pace. Indeed, trains force life onto their schedule; they are often late and sometimes break down in the middle of nowhere. And they demand that life move at their speed; they chug along.

So it was when my family decided to see a part of the world at eye level at the speed of a train, traveling from Los Angeles to Seattle. Why that trip? It was there, and we also knew the end of the trip would be highlighted with views of spectacular volcanic mountains, Mount Shasta, Mount Rainier, Mount Saint Helens, and Mount Hood.

I make note of the train trip because it combined pleasure with work on this book. Remarkably, the experience straddled two distinct eras, one that operated at the slow pace of "railway time" and the other that operated at the demanding pace of "Internet time." How strange it was to be moving along at the speed of a bygone era while sitting at a lounge-car table rapidly tapping out a portion of a chapter on a laptop that had more power than many mainframe computers two decades earlier. All the while, I could keep tabs on office calls with a cell phone.

On that trip, each time I booted up my Toshiba laptop with its familiar "Intel Inside" logo on the side of the screen, the familiar multicolored flag of the Microsoft Corporation came up. I was able to do things there on the train that people a century before could not possibly dream about. Even a generation before, people had to be tethered to a mainframe computer to do what I was doing on the go, much to the credit of Intel, Toshiba, and Microsoft—and, it goes without saying, to a host of inventive people who work for those companies and to those who went before them at any number of other high-tech firms. I was also able to work with a laptop that several years before would have cost some multiple of what I paid for the one I had.

The Windows operating system, which rendered the other laptop parts productive, may have accounted for a mere forty-five dollars of the laptop's price, a much lower price for a more powerful product than previous versions that came installed on earlier laptops.

I was not alone in my effort to work while sightseeing. There was another writer across the way, an author of children's books typing away with much the same hardware and the exact same software as mine. She, too, saw the Microsoft flag when she booted up, as did virtually everyone else who used a laptop on the train.

How odd it was to reflect that at the time of our train trip the Microsoft Corporation was embroiled in the legal fight of its short life with the federal government. The federal Department of Justice had charged the company with being a monopoly and abusing its monopoly power in violation of the country's antitrust (or anti-monopoly) laws. The government's position was fully endorsed by the presiding federal judge in his "Findings of Fact," made public just as this book was being finalized in early November 1999.

There on the train the children's book author and I were writing away, all very cheaply, efficiently, and voluntarily. I could not help but ask myself, was there evidence on that train of an oppressive monopoly at work? Were the government's lawyers working with the interests of the authors on board that train at heart? If they prevailed in the court's final decision on the "Conclusions of Law," to be handed down later, would we really be able to work even more cheaply and efficiently and have even more and better choices as to computer systems we might use on future train rides? I had to wonder again what was really afoot in a courtroom a transcontinental flight and a time warp away.

When, several years ago, I first heard of the government's charge that Microsoft is a "monopolist," I was a little skeptical but accepting. After all, I knew Microsoft Windows operating system came preloaded on at least nine of every ten computers containing Intel microprocessors sold in the country, if not the world. Microsoft may not be the proverbial "single seller" (one way of defining monopoly), but it was darn close.

The more I read about the case, however, the more I began to question the government's case. Monopolies are expected to charge "high" prices, but Windows 98 doesn't seem to cost all that much—no more than other available operating systems. In addition, the record shows that more often than not, when Microsoft has entered a software market—for example, the browser market—software prices have gone down, not up.

Monopolies are supposed to be in the business of restricting production in order to raise their prices and profits. Microsoft stands accused of trying to extend its market dominance by charging the lowest of all prices for its browser Internet Explorer—nothing! Monopolies are not supposed to have competitors and are supposed to be protected by insurmountable barriers to entry. But there are at least a dozen and maybe two dozen *existing* operating systems for computers. Moreover, at their digital cores, operating systems are nothing more than strings of *1*'s and *0*'s, which can be reproduced endlessly all over the world—hardly the making of a lasting barrier to entry, *if* Microsoft were to operate as a monopoly.

The more I investigated the case, the more I realized that a lot of the government's arguments did not make a lot of economic sense. Its claim that there was "no commercially viable competitor" to Microsoft's operating system (a claim that the trial judge accepted using almost the same words) did not square with the fact that other operating systems, including IBM's OS/2, do exist, but they may not be commercially viable because Microsoft's product is cheap—in other words, because Microsoft does not charge monopoly (i.e., high) prices. The government's conclusions about Microsoft's alleged monopoly practices did not match well with its premises about how software markets work or with the available evidence on the impact of Microsoft's business strategies on software prices. Indeed, at times the government seemed to do nothing more than throw out charges—for instance, Microsoft has impaired software innovation—without offering a shred of supporting evidence. As the trial proceeded, the government lawyers scored numerous points with the press in their skilled attempts to discredit defense witnesses, but they left unchallenged critical evidence about the consequences of Microsoft's pricing practices.

The more I followed the case, the more evident it became that it is not about Microsoft's monopoly practices at all. Rather, it is for the most part about Microsoft's extraordinary competitiveness, which Microsoft's market rivals—Netscape, Oracle, IBM, and Sun Microsystems, among others—have never liked, mainly because Microsoft has hampered their growth and constrained their market shares and prosperity. Sure, like most industry leaders, Microsoft has some power—which some might call "monopoly power"—to raise prices without seeing sales evaporate, but that is not the issue in the case. The substantive issue is whether Microsoft has the ability to manipulate its prices and maintain its market leadership over the long haul and has, on balance, systematically used its pricing and market power to the detriment of consumers. If Microsoft has abused its market power, this was nowhere evident on that train trip.

Supposedly, the Microsoft case is about how a new start-up, Netscape, developed a better browser, Navigator, than the then existing browser, Mosaic (developed at the University of Illinois), and had plans to cooperate with Sun Microsystems to develop a new computer platform that would threaten Microsoft's monopoly in operating systems for desktop and laptop computers—only to have Microsoft use its supposed monopoly position to seek to "crush" poor little Netscape by giving away its browser, Internet Explorer.

But the story can be seen as a different drama entirely, one that has been largely overlooked in the media, and obscured by all the attention given to the judge's findings. This story will be told here. It is a story of how Microsoft beat its rivals handily in the desktop operating system market and then began to invade the rivals' stronghold, the server market. The rivals formed a consortium to beat Microsoft with a reorganization of industry assets. When the consortium fell apart, the rivals went to Washington to press their political contacts to do what they couldn't do: throttle Microsoft's competitive advance by way of an antitrust suit.

After Judge Jackson handed down his Findings of Fact in November 1999, it became clear that many of Microsoft's harshest critics, like Scott McNealy, head of Sun Microsystems, wanted nothing less than to have Microsoft thoroughly hobbled with draconian government-enforced remedies, such as the following:

- Require Microsoft to price its software products uniformly and openly
- Break up Microsoft into several companies, or "Baby Bills"
- Force Microsoft to give up or auction off its property rights to its source code for Windows
- Even deny Microsoft the right to use its "huge" cash reserves to buy other firms and extend its influence in the software industry, or even other industries

What these critics seem to want is not simply to make Microsoft obey the same laws that they have to obey, but in reality to quash Microsoft as the viable competitive force it has been. In no small way, they seem intent on breaking the economic back of Microsoft and the market position of its crown jewel, Windows, even though their proposed remedies might be more troublesome for consumers than Microsoft has ever been—which many observers were beginning to realize as this book went to press. The critics probably could not be more pleased with the trial outcome. For years to come Microsoft will have its competitive hands tied: with the federal antitrust case, if it is not settled and instead goes the appeals route, or, failing that, very likely with extensive regulations as well as a plethora of class-action lawsuits. Seven such lawsuits had already been filed as this book went to press, brought by rapacious lawyers who see a gold mine in Microsoft's great corporate wealth that can be tapped and possibly drained with the help of the country's legal system.

At a number of points in the past, the validity of antitrust enforcement has been questioned by economists and others. As it turns out, the Microsoft case has once again drawn into question the social and economic value of antitrust enforcement. It has resurrected old arguments about "predatory pricing" and "exclusionary contracts" that two or three decades ago were repeated by antitrust lawyers without embarrassment but have since been largely discredited by an avalanche of legal scholarship. The case has also shown how the aggressive pricing and marketing strategy by a firm faced with "network effects" can be misinterpreted by legal experts who see as "predatory" strategies that by and large are normal responses of a profit-making firm to the particular conditions of its market.

Finally, and perhaps most important, the Microsoft case has shown—and not for the first time—how politics can taint the antitrust enforcement process. The sad truth about the case is that Microsoft would not likely now be in the legal straits it is in if it had not been so competitive and if it had curried more favors with politicians in Washington—made more payouts—over the years. As a consequence, more than Microsoft is now on trial: trust in antitrust enforcement is on trial. This is the rest of the story told here.

My concern in writing this book is not the health and well-being of Microsoft and its cofounder, Bill Gates, or anyone else who works for Microsoft. I have no financial tie to the company and have never had one. I've never worked for Microsoft, either as an employee or as a consultant and will never do so. I've never received a fee from the company and do not own any of its stock. My concern in writing this book is with the rightness—or wrongness—of the government's arguments, regardless of the corporate target. I take up the case because I have become convinced that the government and judge haven't made their case of monopoly wrongdoing and that the proposed remedies would exact an unnecessary toll on the American economy for the benefit of Microsoft's rivals. I also take up the case because antitrust enforcement should attack monopolists, not aggressive competitors. And I don't think we should allow antitrust enforcement to bend with the political winds in Washington, D.C.

In writing this book, I am indebted to a number of people. I must express special thanks to my former colleague in the Economics Department at the University of Mississippi, William Shughart, who read the entire manuscript with great care and made many valuable suggestions for improving it. I am also indebted to Fred McChesney, a professor at the Northwestern University Law School, who read and critically evaluated important legal portions of the book. As usual, my good friend Dwight Lee, a professor of economics at the University of Georgia, provided long hours of discussion on important issues that have arisen in the case, helping me to straighten out the arguments. I am also indebted to Jacqueline Murphy and Kate Scott, my editors at Perseus Books, and my wife, Karen McKenzie, for numerous suggestions for improving the flow of the words. My student assistants Ji Lee Kim and Young Kim Lee provided important research assistance. Finally, I am indebted to the Earhart Foundation and the Lynde and Harry Bradley Foundation for the support they provided to the project over the past two years.

I've had the good fortune over the last several years of getting to know Gary Byrne, one of the most perceptive investment and policy analysts I've ever met. Over the course of numerous long bike rides, he and I have settled many of the world's most pressing problems (at least to our satisfaction), and have also worked out many of the arguments in my most recent books, including this one. For being a good friend and providing many valuable comments on the manuscript, I am pleased to dedicate this book to him.

Richard McKenzie
Irvine, California
December 5, 1999

THE NATION'S MAJOR ANTITRUST LAWS

The U.S. government's antitrust policy was ostensibly designed to improve market efficiency by reducing barriers to market entry, breaking up monopolies, preventing monopolies from being formed in the first place, and reducing the gains from companies conspiring to restrict production or raise prices. Its foundation is three major laws, which have been subsequently amended by Congress and modified by court decisions: the Sherman Act, the Clayton Act, and the Federal Trade Commission Act.

THE SHERMAN ACT—1890

The Sherman Act was passed in 1890, after a series of major corporate mergers. It contains two critical provisions. The first, Section 1, declares illegal "every contract, combination in the form of trust or otherwise, or conspiracy, in restraint of trade or commerce among several states or with foreign nations." The second, Section 2, declares that "every person who shall monopolize, or conspire with any other person or persons to monopolize any part of trade or commerce among the several states, or with foreign nations, shall be guilty of a misdemeanor." In short, the first section outlaws any form of cooperative behavior that restrains competition; the second outlaws monopolization or any attempt to acquire monopoly power. Violations may be subject to both criminal and civil penalties. The Sherman Act is enforced exclusively by the U.S. Department of Justice.

The Clayton Act—1914

Because the Sherman Act did not specify what constituted unfair and unethical business practice, and because the courts generally took a very narrow view of what constituted restraint of trade and commerce, Congress passed the Clayton Act in 1914. The Clayton Act listed four business practices deemed illegal if their effect "may be substantially to lessen competition or tend to create a monopoly." Both the Justice Department and the Federal Trade Commission enforce the Clayton Act, Section 2, which outlaws price discrimination, or the use of price differences not justified by cost differentials to lessen competition or create a monopoly. This provision was intended to prevent firms from cutting prices below cost in a particular geographical region in order to drive competitors out of the market. Railroads and national chain stores were allegedly involved in such "predatory competition."

The Clayton Act also forbade tying contracts and exclusive dealerships. A tying contract is an agreement between seller and buyer that requires the buyer of one good or service to purchase some other product or service from the same producer. For example, if IBM tried to force buyers of home computers to purchase only IBM software, its purchase and sale agreement with customers might be considered a tying contract. An exclusive dealership is an agreement between a manufacturer and its dealers that forbids the dealers from handling other manufacturers' products. As long as other manufacturers' products are sold in the same area, however, manufacturers may organize exclusive dealerships covering designated territories, as is common in the automobile industry.

Section 7 of the Clayton Act forbids a merger, the acquisition by a firm of its competitors' stock or physical assets, if the effect of the merger is to reduce competition substantially. However, the act applies only to horizontal mergers, the joining of two or more firms in the same market. Merger law enforcement was strengthened considerably by the Celler-Kefauver Act, passed in 1950, which brought vertical mergers, the joining of two or more companies that perform different stages of the production process, within the Clayton Act's reach.

Finally, the Clayton Act declared interlocking directorates illegal. An interlocking directorate is the practice of having the same people serve as directors of two or more competing firms. If the same people direct competing firms, share information, and agree on policies that effectively reduce industry output, they may constitute a de facto monopoly. Section 8 of the Clayton Act prohibits such arrangements if they "substantially reduce" competition. This provision of the law has never been actively enforced, however.

THE FEDERAL TRADE COMMISSION ACT—1914

The original purpose of the Federal Trade Commission Act, passed in 1914, was to thwart "unfair methods of competition" among firms. The act empowered the Federal Trade Commission to investigate cases of industrial espionage, bribery for the purpose of obtaining trade secrets or gaining business, and boycotts. In 1938, the Wheeler-Lea Act expanded the commission's mandate to cover "unfair or deceptive acts or practices" that harmed customers, including the sale of shoddy merchandise and misleading or deceptive advertising. The Clement Institute case of 1948 established that the FTC may bring charges under the FTC Act against any business practice that would also constitute an offense under the Sherman Act.

TRUST ON TRIAL

⚖ CHAPTER 1 ⚖

From Railway Time to Internet Time

THE LAST QUARTER OF THE TWENTIETH CENTURY was remarkable for its technological and economic progress. During those twenty-five years, any number of new household and business devices—including videocassette recorders, answering machines, cordless phones, camcorders, cellular phones, and CD players—spread rapidly through American homes and businesses.

But nowhere was progress more evident than in personal computing. At the start of the 1970s, no American home had a personal computer, for one good reason: the personal computer had not yet been developed. Back then, if people needed computing power, they had to make a trek to a computer center with boxes of punch cards in hand. Over the last quarter century, the personal computer advanced from a primitive box that could do very little to a machine that today has far more power than one of the mainframe computers in use when personal computers were first introduced in the mid-1970s.

The history of personal computing was written by many very smart people, all of whom were building on each other's good ideas and hard work. However, that history was in no small way pressed forward at an ever-faster pace by developments at the Microsoft Corporation, which just happened to be founded at the start of the last quarter of the twentieth century and which is today the world's premier software company, dominating many of the markets it has entered and developed. What is remarkable today, at the start of the twenty-first century, is that the Microsoft Corporation finds itself under legal assault by the federal government, plus nineteen states. Why have the federal government and the states undertaken this legal attack? Is success being punished? Has politics played a role? What will be the consequences?

1

The antitrust suit that the Department of Justice brought against the Microsoft Corporation in the spring of 1998 is important in its own right. It involves substantive legal issues, such as whether Microsoft is a monopolist and has acted like one. It also involves intriguing courtroom dynamics, if not drama, as the legal and financial power of the federal government are tested by an aggressive American corporation determined to beat the odds and win the case. In early November 1999, U.S. District Court Judge Thomas Penfield Jackson handed down one of the strongest declarations of monopoly wrongdoing in the history of antitrust prosecutions.

On the surface, it's the Justice Department against Microsoft, but behind the courtroom scenes there has been a good deal of political maneuvering by other major American corporate high-tech combatants—Sun Microsystems, Oracle, Netscape, IBM, and America Online, to name just a few—who would like nothing better than to see their market rival, Microsoft, get its comeuppance in the court of law. The case is also a human interest story that involves the wealthiest man in the universe, Bill Gates, pitted against a covey of other bigger-than-life luminaries—Sun's Scott McNealy, Oracle's Larry Ellison, and Netscape's Jim Clark and Jim Barksdale—who are also extraordinarily wealthy business leaders with egos as big as their bank accounts. They have made no secret of what they think of Bill Gates and Microsoft. In no small way, they see the trial as the only way they have to play out their fondest dream, which is to humble the "Menace from Redmond" (Microsoft's headquarters are in Redmond, Washington).

But the importance of the case extends far beyond the particulars of the courtroom and the industry personalities who awaited the trial judge's final decision, his "Conclusions of Law." This is because more than Microsoft has been on trial in the courtroom. The efficacy of antitrust law enforcement has been on trial. The Microsoft case has been the first large-scale antitrust proceedings of the digital age; it has tested the appropriateness of new economic concepts such as "network effects," "tipping," "path dependency," and "lock-ins" and has forced us to ask whether nineteenth-century antitrust law, combined with twentieth-century enforcement norms, are applicable to twenty-first-century problems of business organization. It has also been a case in which competitors, via political pressure, have once again used the antitrust laws not to fight monopoly, but to throttle an aggressive competitor. The ultimate outcome of the case, which could go to the Supreme Court if a settlement is not reached, could affect the way business is done for decades to come.

FROM SMOKESTACKS TO MICROCHIPS

By practically all accounts, we live and work in an world radically different from that of the last quarter of the nineteenth century, the world in which the economic and political forces were taking shape that later led to the country's code of antitrust laws. At the turn of the nineteenth century, the icons of even advanced economies like that of the United States were horse-drawn plows and belching smokestacks. The plows represented the dominant but shrinking sector of the economy, agriculture, where in the United States over 40 percent of the gainfully employed labor force still worked, with little mechanized farm equipment. The smokestacks represented the expanding industrial sector of the economy, where as yet less than 20 percent of the American workforce labored in dank, dusty, and dirty conditions that would not be tolerated today.

In this earlier era, *real capital*—not the money kind financiers talk about, but the tangible kind that represents man-made means of production—largely consisted of real, material objects such as concrete and steel, formed into ever-expanding superstructures, plants, that could extend practically the length of whole towns. The bigger the plants and the more they smoked, the more powerful and more prosperous the economies were, or so local chambers of commerce were inclined to claim with the pictures they proudly printed in their promotional brochures.

In this earlier era, markets in different parts of the country and world were far more separated than they are today, meaning that many markets did not overlap extensively; the phenomenon of large numbers of competing firms moving fluidly among markets did not exist. Competition was restricted by many mundane factors, not the least of which was the cost of firms changing their product mixes and shifting their locations. Geography may have been the more pressing restriction on production, given the expense of transporting products by road, rail, and ship. For much of the first half of the twentieth century, business gurus could smartly repeat what was widely believed to be the three most important factors in doing business—"Location, location, location"—implying that physical position in markets was crucial to earning above-competitive rates of return.

At that time, when people wrote about the "American economy" or the "French economy" or any other national economy, it was clear what they meant, since production and distribution chains covering more than one country were not well integrated. The reasons? Business integration was costly. The means of communicating with far-flung suppliers were limited, as was the ability of firms to monitor their distant suppliers, distributors, and buyers.

Everywhere production largely involved the creation of real stuff (like food or housing) made from real stuff (such as cloth or wood) at a real cost that faithfully obeyed an economic dictum that had been known for a century or more, the "law of diminishing returns." Under diminishing returns, as every undergraduate business major learns, the cost of production invariably rises (at least when production expands beyond some undefined level). At that time (and, in some industries, even today) diminishing returns imposed a check on how much of any market any given company could profitably serve. As a company sought to expand its market share, production costs would rise, which would tend to choke off the economic rationale for further expansion.

Granted, a century ago, competition among firms became progressively more intense as technology evolved, production costs fell, and firms could more readily move their goods and their plant and equipment across invisible market boundaries. But by today's standards, movement was still sluggish and costly. At best, firms could move their goods at the pace of rail traffic, which was maybe the breakneck speed of sixty miles an hour. Firms that wanted to move their plants to more profitable locations could do so, but they had to close their plants in one place and open plants in other places—after more concrete was poured and more steel girders were formed and erected.

Clearly, production at the turn of the nineteenth century proceeded at a faster pace than had ever before been known, but business still operated on what can now be dubbed "railway time." Just as clearly, most producers did not see themselves as actual or potential competitors to their counterparts in different parts of the country, much less the world.

Accordingly, firms that formed and passed their initial market tests of producing a product consumers wanted could relax, somewhat assured that they could continue operations with modest changes made at the speed of "railway time" for a decade or more. They could expect to pass their businesses down to their children, who would pass them on to the grandchildren. Workers who started careers in a local plant could with reasonable confidence anticipate retiring in the same job. "Railway time" in this earlier era may have been demanding by the historical standards of the day, but a century later the pace of change seems to be one that only snails could appreciate.

This book on the Microsoft antitrust case begins with a brief description of economic conditions at the turn of the nineteenth century because those were the conditions under which the core of the nation's antitrust laws, the Sherman Act, passed in 1890, was devised. In that time it might have been reasonable for legislators at the state and federal levels to fear the growth of trusts, or monopolies, that would have enduring market power. In that earlier time, the terms "market share" or "market dominance" may have been meaningful because "markets" were more or less distinct and identifiable and may even have had enduring qualities. People expected the markets of the future to have much the some look and feel as markets then. Potential competition was costly (or more costly than now), given the limited mobility of capital across national borders and across product lines. Perhaps it was reasonable for governments to want to closely monitor the extent of competition in markets and to take corrective action, because the revitalization of competition, where it had been suppressed by mergers or cartels through natural market movements, might be slow in coming. Perhaps it was reasonable to assume that the government could orchestrate antitrust policy with some expectation of doing it right, because it could see the future of markets with reasonable clarity by observing what existed then.

In this book I do not advocate eliminating antitrust enforcement altogether. But I do question the wisdom of a return to antitrust activism at a level never before seen, in which I see the threat of the country's software industry's being extensively regulated under the guise of antitrust enforcement. With the help of issues raised in the Microsoft case, the book does carry an important message for those who believe that nineteenth-century antitrust law needs to be and should be enforced with the same vigor that it always has been. That message is simply that times have changed—dramatically.

Production has changed. Agriculture is now a trivial part of the national economy, especially in terms of employment (less than 3 percent). Industrial employment today represents a smaller share of the employed labor force than when the Sherman Act was passed. The employment growth sector at the turn of the twenty-first century is services. And production of both goods and services takes place on a global scale, so much so that it is hard to identify products as "American made" or "French made." Products are made in parts everywhere. And they are made and re-made on production cycles that are measured in a few months, not in the years it used to take.

Products have changed. Sure, we all still buy a lot of things, but the value of the things we buy today, from cars to clothes, exceeds the value for the materials used to a far greater extent than it once did. And then so much of what we buy does not consist of things at all. We buy services—from diet plans to pay-per-view movies—where much of the value comes from very little that is material. Or the services are computer programs or databases in which the "material" is limited to the electrons that are transmitted through wires and the disks they are stored on. In a real sense goods have become "immaterial" or "unreal," a point that the business management guru Tom Peters drove home by noting in one of his seminars, "Welcome to a world where, in the words of one executive I know, 'If you can touch it, it's not real.' I don't know about you, but that's a tough concept for an old (me) civil engineer (me, again) to get." Perhaps more important, because technology and market conditions are changing so rapidly, manufactured products are constantly under revision, which means that many goods that will appear in markets a year or two from now will have only faint resemblance to the goods that are on the market today. And don't forget, commerce is shifting relentlessly to the Internet.

Long-standing economic dictums have changed or have had to be seriously revised. For much of this century, economists could faithfully repeat to their students the law of diminishing returns (or, more descriptively, decreasing returns to scale) as if there were no exceptions. They could also say with confidence that as products become more abundant in markets, their market values are bound to decline. For some products—most notably software—old expected relationships between the quantity produced and the cost of production have clearly been broken. Indeed, the cost of producing additional units of some products—again, software—may have evaporated altogether, given that additional units can be duplicated by electronic means at virtually zero cost. As the Justice Department and economic theorists have argued with reference to the Microsoft case, for some products the law of diminishing returns may never kick in within the scope of the market. Moreover, as some products—those called "network goods," a term I will discuss in later chapters—become more abundant, their value to consumers increases, not decreases.

The nature of capital has changed, as I have argued at length in previous books. Much capital is no longer stuff, which is difficult and costly to transport. The principal capital of many firms has become *brainpower* (education and the creative skills of their employees), *good ideas*, and *information*, all of which are highly mobile, meaning they can be shipped around the globe at the touch of a few keys on a computer keyboard and at the cost of a long-distance telephone call. It is now widely recognized that the growing mobility of capital has thrown firms through a time warp, forcing them to do business at a substantially higher pace; this new speed has, appropriately, been dubbed "Internet time": the Net will likely be the medium on which a growing share of business will be conducted.

Governments have changed. Over the past hundred years, governments around the world have grown dramatically in their influence over the economy (although their power may have slipped in recent years owing to the growing mobility of capital). As a consequence, an array of special interest groups stand ready to manipulate, via a variety of payments to politicians, governmental powers in hot pursuit of their own personal gain at the expense of the public. Escalating campaign contributions from business is a symptom of this. With the growing competitiveness of the national and world economies, it is all too tempting for special interest groups to use whatever governmental powers they can tap to abate some of the growing competitive pressures they might feel.

All of these changes imply that over the past hundred or so years, the economy has gone through a metamorphosis of major proportions. In this new economic universe we now inhabit, which the technology writer George Gilder calls the "microcosm," millions of people already go to work and opportunities abound, unchecked by former material constraints, because the critical resources in this universe, ideas, "are not used up as they are used," as Gilder writes. In the microcosm, the economic burdens of matter decline, and "space and time expand as size and power drop. In the age of the microcosm, the inventive inputs of producers launch a spiral of economic growth and productivity at steadily declining cost in every material domain: land, energy, pollution, and natural resources." Coming up with an icon for this new age is tough, because the best icon would be a "virtual icon," something that is unreal. But maybe the microchip will do.

None of these market changes, in and of themselves, imply that the nation's antitrust laws should be scrapped, but they certainly do require that we—Justice Department officials, judges, and citizens—think much longer and harder than in the past about the efficacy of antitrust actions, given that the speed of business has shifted from "railway time" to "Internet time." Antitrust doctrine is unavoidably grounded in the proposition that its enforcers can identify "products" and "markets" and can say with some certitude that this or that firm has a "monopoly," has exploited its "monopoly powers," and will continue to be able to do so for some time to come.

Can such decisions be rendered with the same certitude that was once possible? There are good reasons to doubt this, no matter how much confidence judges' decisions reflect.

To improve the workings of the economy, the antitrust enforcers must also be able to predict the contours of markets into the distant future and, on the basis of what they know about future market conditions, take appropriate and timely legal action today that will improve, not worsen, competitive market conditions both today and in the future. All the while, the enforcers must avoid taking actions at the behest of disgruntled competitors against targeted rivals whose greater business skills have elevated them to a position where they have the *appearance* of trusts or monopolies. These changes represent a serious challenge to antitrust law. All of the requisite conditions for effective enforcement have radically changed from what they once were, and the rate of change can only be expected to increase, so that making predictions about future market conditions will be all the more difficult and fraught with the potential for policy error. The shift from "railway time" to "Internet time" over the past hundred or more years raises important questions:

- If markets have become more fluid, as capital has become more mobile, should market forces be expected to correct problems that might arise from trusts exercising their powers? Should we expect antitrust enforcement to be conducted ever more judiciously and more reluctantly?
- If problems of trusts are ever evident, should we expect appropriate antitrust action to be taken in a timely manner? After all, it is doubtful that government, including the legal system, will ever be able to operate on "Internet time" or "at the speed of business."
- Have old ways of identifying trusts, with reference to market shares and market dominance, become outdated, especially now that markets are much more amorphous than they once were, both in terms of what products are actually covered by any defined market and in terms of their fluidity?
- If antitrust enforcement is pursued with the same vigor it once was, might the enforcement process be subject to corruption by politics, given the private gains that can be had by competitors from antitrust action and the ability of competitors to share the gain from enforcement with cooperative politicians?

The Microsoft case is important because an examination of the issues raised in the trial will allow us to answer, albeit tentatively, these kinds of questions, as well as permit us to explore the strictly legal issue of whether Microsoft is in violation of any antitrust law. As readers will quickly realize, this book takes a dim view of the Justice Department's charges and Judge Thomas Penfield Jackson's Findings of Fact. Not because Microsoft is a high-tech angel whose every business practice is commendable. Hardly. The Microsoft business record may be no more commendable than that of any other high-tech firm. Microsoft may or may not have always abided strictly by the terms of its contract; Sun Microsystems has charged in one lawsuit that it has not (Microsoft denies Sun's charge). Microsoft may or may not have attempted years ago to undermine the credibility of an alternative operating system, DR-DOS; the company that developed it, Caldera, claims that it did (Microsoft denies Caldera's allegation). These are the kinds of issues that need to be settled in court, not here or in the press.

There is no point in denying that Microsoft has some market power. It clearly does. So do a lot of other firms. But there is no reason to believe that Microsoft's market power rises to the level of a monopoly that must be corralled by antitrust laws. I take an even dimmer view of the Justice Department's ability to fashion remedies that will actually make Microsoft's markets work better in terms of improving the welfare of consumers, as distinct from making life easier and more prosperous for Microsoft's competitors who have pressed for the Justice Department to take up the case. To understand the positions taken, we need first to take a look at the accused. Later, we can look carefully at the economic foundations of the Justice Department's case and Judge Jackson's findings.

"GODZILLA FROM REDMOND"

The Microsoft Corporation is an economic juggernaut. A substantial majority of all new computers sold each year are preloaded with the Windows operating system, and more than a hundred million personal computers around the globe, when they are booted up each morning, fly the famous Windows multicolor flag as the first image on the screen. Microsoft now sells four out of every five packages (often called suites) of "productivity applications," such as word processing, spreadsheet, database, presentation, calendar, and Internet browser programs. Not surprisingly, it is the world's largest software company. (IBM is a close second.)

The company is also a major provider of e-mail and Internet access services and entertainment, education, and reference software, as well as an ever-expanding library of electronic content. Its Internet portal, MSN, is one of the most heavily visited sites on the World Wide Web, although it is dwarfed by Yahoo! and America Online. Moreover, the company is aggressively extending its financial tentacles into practically every corner of the booming computer, telecommunication, and entertainment industries, most notably Internet browsing, e-commerce, interactive television, and wireless communications.

Many readers might view these observations as the highlights of a major American business success story, but the lawyers in the Antitrust Division of the U.S. Department of Justice (led by Assistant Attorney General Joel I. Klein), the attorneys general from nineteen states, and Judge Jackson beg to differ—and strongly so. They see Microsoft in much more sinister terms. To them, Microsoft's dominance in software markets must mean only one thing: the company is a monopoly that has systematically sought to fortify and extend its monopoly powers with a variety of unfair, anticompetitive business practices. For example, according to the Justice Department, Microsoft has tried to snuff out market rivals with "predatory" prices on its software products and with restrictive contracts with buyers and suppliers that exclude rivals from competing on an equal footing. Moreover, if Justice Department lawyers are to be believed, Microsoft tried to collude with a key market rival, Netscape, for the purpose of dividing up two critical software markets, operating systems and browsers, in order to further insulate its market powers from erosion by superior products. It is interesting to note that because of its business practices, Microsoft's critics charge the company with being a "monopolist" and simultaneously "a ruthless, cutthroat competitor."

I begin this book with one important point of agreement with the Justice Department lawyers: Microsoft employees do more than simply write computer code for given programs on a daily basis. Their lines of code have a more profound effect on their industry and, indeed, the entire world economy than the lines of code written by the hordes of programmers at other software companies. The 30 million-plus lines of code those Microsoft programmers have written for the Windows operating system set basic standards for how the world's personal computers work by themselves and with each other. Other programmers are constantly adjusting their code writing to what the programmers at Microsoft do.

The 30 thousand-plus relatively youthful Microsoft employees scattered throughout the world, of whom half are concentrated at the company's headquarters outside Seattle, are literally creating, and recreating, the playing field on which the rest of us play our games and do our work. Microsoft programmers who wrote code years ago have shaped the future we all have come to know as the current state of the personal computer world. Few doubt they will, for years to come, continue to shape the future we cannot now imagine. Therein may lie the source of both the considerable admiration and the resentment that Microsoft engenders with relative ease.

Any firm that achieves Microsoft's economic prominence surely deserves admiration, especially when the substantial risks the company's founders faced years ago are recognized. Back then, it took more than brains and long hours to do what the Microsoft founders have done; it took a lot of self-confidence and guts. And make no mistake about it, Microsoft's success was not guaranteed, especially since it faced serious competitive threats from firms as ingenious as Apple, which created the first graphics-based operating system, and as established as IBM in all aspects of the mainframe and personal computer industry.

When the first version of OS/2, the operating system jointly developed by IBM and Microsoft, was released in 1987, key computer industry columnists were betting that OS/2, not Windows, would eventually dominate the market for operating systems. Why? Microsoft was then a growing but still not thoroughly tested upstart that had only recently introduced the first version of Windows, a fairly primitive product that did not generate rave reviews from either the trade press or consumers. IBM's OS/2 was viewed by some analysts back in the late 1980s as a technically superior system, and it had IBM's established brand name behind it, as well as a more established sales and service network. After IBM and Microsoft parted ways on OS/2 in 1989 and subsequently developed their operating systems OS/2 and Windows independently, one columnist for *PC Magazine* concluded back in the winter of 1992, "I expect that OS/2 will not only succeed but will take a lot of wind from Windows' sails in the process. I think OS/2 is the odds-on favorite to replace DOS as the dominant desktop operating system. ... I see a big change toward OS/2 and away from Windows over the next year." No two ways about it, Microsoft won a hotly contested operating system derby, and it beat some tough competition and some tough odds.

At the same time, it is altogether understandable why some observers may now see Microsoft as the proverbial "800-pound Gorilla," or as the "Godzilla from Redmond"—an entity capable of molding the economic future of hundreds of millions of people around the globe and perhaps of perpetuating its own economic empire as it demolishes competitors and throttles much progress for the rest of the economy, unless it is somehow fettered. After all, Microsoft succeeded where others failed. That observation can all too easily be converted to the claim "It was Microsoft's fault," or, worse yet, "Microsoft could not have beaten back competitive challenges from such formidable rivals fair and square."

When Microsoft asks in its ads, "Where do you want to go today?" many readers very likely see the question as disingenuous: they fear that Microsoft knows where it plans to take them. No doubt many computer buyers, suppliers, and users feel anxious when their futures are so inextricably tied to the *evolution* of technology, a force largely outside their own control, one possibly controlled by people whose motives might not always be the most noble. No one—not the Justice Department's lawyers, nor Microsoft's staunchest defenders—knows exactly how technology will evolve over the coming years. At the same time, no one doubts that Microsoft's motivation for remaining an integral player in the technological evolution is an old and honorable one (or dishonorable, depending on perspective): Profit. Certainly Microsoft has made, and continues to make, a lot of money. In its fiscal year ending in June 1999, Microsoft had close to $8 billion in profits on sales of nearly $20 bilion, a return on sales of 39 percent, the highest of any major American corporation.

What is remarkable about Microsoft is that it is far from being the largest American company in terms of sales or physical plant or employees. In 1999 its gross revenues of nearly $20 billion were less than one seventh those of a company as pervasive as Wal-Mart and slightly about one fifth those of a company as old and established as General Electric. Microsoft's economic clout must derive from something other than its sales, or else its market evaluation would not be so high. Microsoft's market capitalization (or the total market value of its stock) at the start of 1999 was over $360 billion, the highest market cap of any U.S. corporation, five times Wal-Mart's market cap, and twice GE's. By late 1999, Microsoft's market cap was close to $480 billion (it topped $500 billion in midyear). Microsoft is now worth far more than the sum of its parts, given that its market value in November 1999 was seventeen to eighteen times its book value, the price of its assets on its balance sheet. Clearly, Microsoft "owns" something—a lot—that is not reported on its books. Therein may also lie another source of the critics' and the Justice Department's anxiety: Microsoft's wealth is intangible and elusive, yet apparently rock solid as far as investors are concerned. Is Microsoft's wealth related to its "market power"?

Amazingly, Microsoft has risen to its current economic prominence in less than a quarter century. No American company has ever been so successful in such a short time, which is all the more reason why Microsoft and its founding CEO Bill Gates may be so widely admired—as well as scorned and feared. Again, people want to know—understandably: Has Microsoft played fair?

Many consumers and business people seem to think so. Though the Justice Department doesn't have one good thing to say about Microsoft in its complaint and seems to suggest that Microsoft does consumers little good, no one should lose sight of the fact that millions of people *voluntarily* buy Microsoft's products, and choose those products over existing rivals' products. Even if Microsoft has the market power the Justice Department says it has, which is subject to serious dispute, its powers are severely circumscribed. Microsoft doesn't have the power of coercion that, say, the Internal Revenue Service has. People buy personal computers with Windows in spite of the fact that they could buy computers with Apple's operating system or IBM's operating system (or other computers with several other non-Windows operating systems). Also, consumers buy Microsoft Word in spite of the fact that they could purchase Corel's WordPerfect or IBM's Ami Pro. Tens of millions of people will freely admit that they buy Microsoft products not because they were forced to do so, but because they are "better" (not perfect, but better, as *they* define better) and often less expensive.

As Microsoft's legal problems with the Justice Department are recounted, it should be remembered that the *Financial Times* of London's 1998 survey of business executives and opinion leaders ranked Microsoft as the second most admired company in the North Atlantic business world, behind GE. In early 1999, *Fortune* magazine ranked Microsoft as the third most respected American company, behind GE and Coca-Cola, mainly for its talented new hires and financial soundness. Its *Fortune* ranking is well deserved, given that in spring 1999, Microsoft had virtually no debt. It also had close to $22 billion in cash reserves and little need for additional plant and equipment, the usual stuff of business investment in the earlier era of industrial capitalism. In the fall of 1999, *PC Magazine* once again ranked Microsoft at the very top of one hundred "most influential" technology firms in the country, attributing the company's continuing preeminence in the listing to its "ability to adapt to the Internet."

In November 1999, the publicity surrounding the antitrust case had made little apparent dent in Microsoft's standing. The *Wall Street Journal* reported the results of a survey (undertaken by Harris Interactive, Inc.) of over 5,000 people in the technology industry: Microsoft was ranked number one among the country's most prominent technology companies, and was noted especially for its financial performance, vision, leadership, and workplace environment. It should be little wonder that at the end of 1999 Microsoft won the "Millennium Award" for technical innovation from *PC Magazine UK*.

In spite of all the good things that are said about the company, Microsoft is clearly a company that many people love to hate. Bill Gates, renowned for being a college dropout and the richest person in the world, is a CEO whom newspaper cartoonists and late-night humorists delight in caricaturing. And Gates is an easy target. He seems to have the demeanor not of an established business executive but of a very bright nerd, subject to fits of rocking in place, who seems better suited to a college classroom or a computer lab than to the head of a board-room table. Few ordinary Americans can fathom how any human being could actually *earn* Gates's vast fortune. No one else in history has ever earned so much (not even the best of entertainers and pro basketball players). Did he accomplish what he has on the up and up?

Both Microsoft and Bill Gates have become the butt of so many jokes and snide and hostile commentaries that literally dozens of Internet Web sites are devoted to keeping surfers posted on the latest humor and criticism. If you don't like Gates, there's a Web page where you can—virtually—punch him in the mouth and knock out a couple of his teeth in the process (http://www.well.com/user/vanya/bill.html). At another site, you can download a video of Bill Gates being hit in the face with a cream pie on a trip to Brussels in 1998 (http://www.bitstorm.org/gates/), an assault for which the Belgium offenders a year later were fined a measly eighty-eight dollars.

There are over a dozen Web sites where you can get hour-by-hour estimates of Gates's net worth, for example, http://web.quuxuum.org/~evan/bgnw.html. In early March 1999, Gates's Microsoft stock alone was worth an estimated $70 billion; he owned more than 476 million, 19.12 percent, of all Microsoft shares, which at the time were selling for $146.25 a share. Two hours later, he had lost what most Americans would consider an outlandish fortune, $400 million—all in the course of a morning's work. Two days later, his net worth was up a couple of billion. Two months later, in May, his net worth was up $5 billion. In early September 1999, he was worth slightly more than $88 billion, after his wealth had peaked at over $100 billion during the previous July, a fact that caused a *New York Times* reporter to write that "it would take an American earning the approximate median income—$50,000 a year—two million years to equal it. Or, to put it another way, it would take two million Americans earning the median income to raise the same sum in a single year."

Bill Gates has no doubt learned not to sweat such small changes in his portfolio. But then, Gates has probably also learned to keep his focus on the real prize, the long-term trend in his net worth, which is up. When Microsoft went public in March 1986, Gates's interest in the company was worth a mere $139 million. This means that his net worth has escalated at a compound annual rate of over 65 percent. Put in more human proportion, since 1986, Gates's wealth has risen by an average of more than $200 each and every second—more than $744,000 each hour or $535 million each month.

WHY MICROSOFT?

Such financial calculations may be interesting and add context, but they are hardly worthy of the focus of a whole book. Microsoft is the focus of this book because of the much larger issues revolving around Microsoft that in many ways make the case illustrative, even though the company itself is incidental. Those larger issues are whether or not, or the extent to which, nineteenth-century antitrust laws can be applied with tolerable fairness to digital-age companies. These companies don't fit the mold for industrial age firms that existed at the turn of the nineteenth century, when antitrust legislation was signed into law. A further issue is whether consumers—not Microsoft's competitors—will benefit from the antitrust prosecution. As discussed in detail in later chapters, there are serious concerns that Microsoft is being picked on. The nation's antitrust enforcement process has been politicized, and the prosecutorial powers of the federal government are being used by market rivals to throttle their more efficient and more aggressive competitor.

It seems that Microsoft needs some independent assessments that it can't buy, because of the presumption that any defense it buys is tainted; it does appear that in the courts, the company hasn't gotten the defense it deserves and that can be marshaled. At the beginning of the trial, in the fall of 1998 and winter of 1999, Microsoft and its executives and defense lawyers were being hammered in the press and the courts for being a monopoly, which is presumed to be an obvious fact, and for exercising market-crushing powers to the detriment of its rivals and consumers. Many of these attacks have been mounted by well-meaning people who have some of the facts right, but it is also clear that many of the critics' underlying arguments are fatally flawed.

As of November 1999, Microsoft stood accused of being a monopolist that has abused its market position. By spring 2000, the court may have ruled that the company has violated the antitrust laws. But if the Justice Department wins such a legal victory, it should not be construed as a determination that Microsoft's actions have in fact been anticompetitive or anticonsumer—or monopolistic. As I will argue in detail in a later chapter, being found in violation of the antitrust laws and acting like a monopolist are two separate matters that can be easily confused simply because "monopoly" and "antitrust" are everywhere used in tandem in the government's case. A firm's competitiveness should not be throttled by the fear that its actions will be construed by legal authorities as anticompetitive and that it will be subject to heavy legal penalties. Given the complexity of high-tech markets and their likely even greater complexity in the future, we all have to worry that the Justice Department doesn't really know what it is doing, because it can't know very much about the future that will continue to unfold from the interactions of hundred of millions of people around the country and the globe.

Make no mistake about it, there is a detectable dark side to the media and legal assaults on Microsoft that are mean-spirited, even vicious. This book takes up the case because so much of the government's legal strategy seems to be intended, first, to demonize both the company and its founder, and then, to hope that its own speculations about market power will carry (as they have carried) great weight with the public as well as with Judge Thomas Penfield Jackson, who is presiding over the trial. If the Justice Department lawyers' intentions were to stick solely to the merits of the case, theatrics in the courtroom and on the steps of the courthouse after each court session would be of little consequence. However, the theatrics seem to be central to the Justice Department's strategy, which explains why the prosecuting lawyers time and again played the video of Bill Gates's deposition, especially the parts that showed him giving delayed responses to their questions, and why they have made such a point of putting their own spin, at the close of each day, on what was and was not said in court. The Justice Department's spin seemed to play well with the media, as the *Wall Street Journal* and other major publications have acknowledged.

I also suspect that a healthy portion of the criticisms against Gates and company emerges from old sources—envy and greed. Envy shows up all too frequently in commentaries that, for example, juxtapose comments on Gates's vast fortune with comments about how the Justice Department is justified in taking Gates to court for antitrust violations because he earned his wealth by being "fiercely competitive." The conclusion: "Fiercely competitive does not quite cut it as a modus operandi for becoming the richest person in the world. Luck, the ungovernable role of circumstance, has had its way with this man, and the disparity between intention and chance is one source of the mystifying air that seems to surround him." The demagoguery involved in such commentaries is as damnable and wrongheaded as it is common. Antitrust laws should never be used to harass firms for building fortunes or for being "fiercely competitive."

As the case moved forward and the prospects of Microsoft's defeat loomed ever larger, the state attorneys general started talking openly about how much money their states might extract from Microsoft, because the fines in the various states could range from $2,000 in Kentucky to $100,000 in New York "per incident." If an "incident" is defined as any purchase of Windows, that "would be millions and millions of dollars" for the state treasury, one attorney general figured with obvious glee. The public should know that there is a good reason state attorneys general look to the potential payoff from the case, because in many states their offices are nothing short of profit centers; they need to look for legal gold mines.

I simply don't believe that envy and greed should ever fuel or guide policy debates or legal actions. And Microsoft's critics should not be allowed to mask their envy and greed behind flawed arguments.

One aim of criticisms and legal actions against Microsoft seems to be to weaken an aggressive market competitor, Microsoft, for the benefit of other rivals, by forcing Microsoft to undertake expensive legal and public relations defenses. A coalition of Microsoft's market rivals that have become so tightly unified in their "Get Microsoft" campaign that they actually have their own acronym, NOISE, for Netscape, Oracle, IBM, Sun Microsystems, and Everyone else. Though the public might believe that antitrust suits originate solely within the halls of the Justice Department, that is not always true. All too often Justice Department suits are brought at the behest of the market rivals of the accused company, supported by the rivals' representatives in Congress. This should cause one to pause and ask, "What is the objective of the suit, to strengthen competition or to lessen it?"

Unfortunately, antitrust suits are as often used to hobble aggressive competitors as they are to constrain monopolies. The NOISE group has not only actively supported the suit, it has done worse: it has campaigned in a variety of media and political forums to press the Justice Department to take up the case. This alone can undermine citizens' trust in the aims and fairness of antitrust enforcement.

The Justice Department has proposed that Microsoft be forced to place an icon for Netscape's Internet browser, Navigator, on the Windows desktop, all free of charge. This remedy is sought even though Netscape could buy such a placement from Microsoft and, if not Microsoft, from the computer manufacturers, who have the right to sell such icon placements to firms like Netscape. If the desktop is some of the most valuable "real estate" available in the information age economy, the proposed remedy sounds like a "virtual land grab." Similarly, proposals to hobble Microsoft by breaking it up will likely raise, not lower, software prices, all for the benefit of Microsoft's competitors.

In theory, a company that is a monopoly causes higher prices by restricting output. Microsoft's record doesn't fit that mold. Indeed, as a growing body of research is showing, when Microsoft has entered a market, the prices of software products in those markets have tended to fall. Now Microsoft stands accused of seeking to radically expand its market by giving away its browser. If the government were simply interested in thwarting monopoly power, its efforts might be better directed at Apple Computers. Historically, Apple has attempted to charge higher prices for its computers and software by not licensing its operating system. But there is probably a good reason Apple has been spared an antitrust assault: its flawed strategy of refusing to license its operating system means that Apple is not worth very much.

There are good reasons for believing that Microsoft and Gates have been under legal attack simply because they have not been playing an old, well-worn political game, expertly played by other major American firms, that of coughing up contributions for a host of political campaigns. Before the antitrust suit was filed, Microsoft was contributing only minor sums to campaign coffers and was spending meager amounts maintaining an inconsequential lobbying office in the nation's capital. Regrettably, it has learned it must pay the political piper. It has since substantially beefed up its political presence in Washington, D.C.

Why? A convincing argument can be made that Microsoft is now trying to buy off the political muggers. No one should want the courts to be used as a vehicle for padding the pockets of politicians. Mounting an independent assessment of the economics underlying the Microsoft case might—just might—help cool the jets of political operatives who would otherwise see legal suits, and the accompanying distortions of evidence and arguments, as a way to threaten those who don't play their political game—as a hidden means for political fundraising.

More important, this independent review of the Microsoft case has been undertaken to help the public better understand how markets, especially markets in information goods, work over stretches of time to benefit consumers at the expense of market rivals. Many of Microsoft's market strategies are consistent with the actions of an aggressive competitor seeking to outsmart, outproduce, and outsurvive its rivals, who are also trying to do exactly the same things.

The Justice Department seems to think that Microsoft's dominant market position and pricing and contract strategies can only be explained as those of a big, bad, abusive monopolist. Yet sound logic runs counter to the Justice Department's arguments. Contrary to what the Justice Department and its supporting cast of expert witnesses have relentlessly argued, Microsoft's actions can also be explained as competitive outcomes, given key market attributes—production and demand economies and network effects—that even the Justice Department acknowledges are intrinsic to the software industry.

This is not to whitewash the role Microsoft has played in the American economy. The history of Microsoft is filled with mistakes in the way it has treated people, inside and outside the firm. Microsoft executives have not always been on their best behavior. Some seem to have poor manners. They have written e-mails in which they used some fairly inflammatory language—for example, calling for a "jihad" and "browser war" against their major competitor in the Internet browser market, Netscape, comments that Microsoft doesn't contest. But much the same could be said about Microsoft's rivals. Indeed, one of the founding technicians and key strategists at Netscape, Marc Andreesen, is renowned for being brash and suggesting that Netscape intended to effectively bury Microsoft, rendering it "a mundane collection of not entirely debugged device drivers." Similarly, Netscape chairman Jim Clark also tagged Microsoft as the "Death Star" because Netscape's network-based operating system would, he thought, make Microsoft's Windows obsolete. Scott McNealy, head of Sun Microsystems, is reported to have hired a marketing director for the express purpose of "killing Digital and IBM."

Perhaps it's important as we review the charges and countercharges relating to the Microsoft case to remember an observation made by Daniel Lyons, a writer for *Forbes* magazine: "Everybody plays rough in Silicon Valley. They bundle weak products with bestsellers, give away freebies, bad-mouth rivals and use standards and alliances to favor friends and punish foes." "Rough play," however, was never intended to be an antitrust offense; "rough play" can be beneficial for consumers, for it might be a way to refer to a firm's competitiveness. It should be acknowledged that there are some forms of human behavior that simply can't be rectified by antitrust laws.

Microsoft has not been kind to rivals it has seen as a threat. Indeed, it seems to have tried to bury a few, most notably Netscape, which will be considered at length in this book, but also other firms, such as Caldera, which has pursued its own private antitrust case against Microsoft. Caldera charged that Microsoft attempted to undermine the public's confidence in Caldera's DR-DOS by introducing error messages that would come up when DR-DOS was running with Windows. This did happen, but only in a beta, or test, version of Windows that was not marketed. Caldera also claims that Microsoft integrated MS-DOS in its Windows graphical interface in order to destroy DR-DOS, which Caldera says Microsoft saw as a major threat, and by giving computer makers favorable per copy prices if they would pay that price for each computer (or processor) shipped, regardless of whether the computer was shipped with MS-DOS, Windows, or some other operating system.

Similarly, IBM charges that Microsoft used its market power in 1995 to dramatically raise the licensing fee it charged IBM for each copy of Windows, solely because IBM insisted on competing with Microsoft in the operating system market. Supposedly, IBM insisted on installing OS/2 and its newly acquired Lotus SmartSuite along with Windows 95 on its personal computers, which Microsoft didn't like. Garry Norris, the IBM executive in charge of the Windows contract negotiations, testified in court, "On several occasions, I remember several specific occasions that I was told IBM can have Compaq's deal when it quits competing. I was told, 'As long as you're competing with Microsoft, you will suffer in the market in terms of prices, terms and conditions, marketing support programs, and technical support programs.' " He explained that Microsoft was "definitely worried about SmartSuite being given away and eating into their 'Office Heartland.' "

According to Norris, Mark Baber, a now-retired Microsoft executive, added, "Where else are you going to go? This is the only game in town." Then, according to Norris, Microsoft held up finalizing the contract with IBM until a few minutes before the actual release on August 24, 1995, causing IBM to lose a mountain of sales. Microsoft then hiked IBM's licensing fee for Windows several dollars above the price given Compaq.

If Norris's recollections of the contract negotiations and Microsoft position are accurate, it would appear that Microsoft might in this instance have been in violation of the country's antitrust laws. Frankly, however, I can't hope to assess in this book the IBM executive's veracity or the accuracy of his memory. All that can be done is to point out that Microsoft has denied the charges and stresses that IBM had been given favored pricing treatment. Microsoft claims that the contract negotiations stalled because of IBM's delay in conceding to Microsoft's demand for an audit of IBM royalty payments on past IBM Windows sales, which Microsoft at the time believed had been understated. Norris has acknowledged that the royalty dispute was settled by IBM's paying Microsoft $30 million in additional royalties, which seems to suggest that Microsoft had reason to call for the audit. When Baber was asked by the *New York Times* whether he had made the "only-game-in-town" comments Garry Norris attributed to him, he told the paper, "Absolutely not—it's not in my character to say some things like that." Microsoft introduced documents that showed that if any such discussions ever occurred, they did not lead to IBM's being penalized for installing Lotus SmartSuite and Netscape Navigator at no cost to consumers on its computers.

These he said/she said questions must be settled in court; the court must assess the relevance of the evidence and testimony and the credibility of the witnesses. I can't say who is lying or whose memory is failing. Both parties have market reasons to lie, which is why I will note what they say. Granted, in almost all of these cases of wrongdoing, the trial judge's Findings of Fact support the government's contentions. However, you can imagine that Microsoft takes issue with the judge's Findings and very likely will appeal the case, which means the ultimate decision on the legal meaning of these Findings may not be known until the case has worked its way to the Supreme Court. Stay tuned.

What I can do, and will do, is assess whether Microsoft's business strategies and market outcomes are more consistent with the expected behavior of a monopolist or a competitor, given market conditions as described by the Justice Department and endorsed by Judge Jackson.

IMPORTANT QUESTIONS

I don't ever wish to deny that Microsoft has some market power to affect price through its control of production of key software products. Practically all American firms have market power to one extent or another, and they use the power they have to one degree or another. No firm of any consequence in this country or, for that matter, the world meets the requirements for the absence of market power under a market structure economists call "perfect competition." This is understandable because perfect competition is a classroom model of market behavior, or a means economists use for thinking about markets and for making tentative predictions concerning the consequences of changes in markets. It was never intended to describe real-world markets with any reasonable degree of accuracy. All real-world markets, in other words, are necessarily imperfect by the standards of perfect competition. And no company should be judged by idealized conceptual standards. Companies should be judged by more realistic standards, like whether improvements in market structure are possible. Accordingly, this study of the case is guided by several key questions:

- Can Microsoft's business practices be explained by the market conditions that it faces, as described by the Justice Department and accepted by the judge, or are its practices those of a monopolist behaving badly?
- If Microsoft is a monopolist, has it actually exercised its market power? If it has, has its exercise of that power reached a level that is or should be construed as illegal under the nation's antitrust laws? In other words, has Microsoft's exercise of market power harmed consumers, or just Microsoft's competitors?
- Would the world today have been a better place if Microsoft had never existed or had adopted other business practices?
- If there have been abuses of market power, are there ample market forces in the software industry to correct any significant and systematic abuse of that power?
- Even if there is some abuse, do we really want to correct the abuse with the forms of government interventions the Justice Department and others have proposed? If we do, should we ask whether the remedy—government tinkering with markets and the design of software—might be worse than the problem?

As the trial evolved, it became progressively more apparent that the Justice Department and the nineteen states supporting the Justice Department's suit had pursued their case with little or no understanding of what they might do if they won. As this book went to press, there was a transparent rift emerging between the Justice

Department and the nineteen states over what remedy they would seek and how remedies would impact Microsoft and software markets in general. All the while, as calls to punish Microsoft escalated, consumers' interests (as opposed to the personal stakes of the people involved in the remedy negotiations) seemed to be set aside, and it seemed to be forgotten that consumer welfare will be affected by any punishment meted out to Microsoft. Shouldn't we expect more of the antitrust process?

To put it bluntly, there are fundamental inconsistencies between the Justice Department's description of the software markets and its claims that Microsoft's business practices should be construed as those of a monopolist, in violation of long-established antitrust principles. Also, it is likely that any legal remedies under consideration would benefit Microsoft's rivals at the expense of American and world consumers. For example, a breakup of Microsoft into three distinct companies, as has been proposed, will likely raise the prices consumers have to pay, not lower them.

No matter how the case is ultimately settled, historians of the future will likely look back on the trial as one of the landmark cases of both the twentieth and twenty-first centuries. The Justice Department accused Microsoft of using its presumed monopoly power to destroy existing competitors in the operating systems and Internet browser markets and to prevent new competitors from entering those markets, a position endorsed by the judge. In so many words, the Justice Department and judge effectively claim that Microsoft has amassed much of its vast wealth not from excellence in the development and marketing of its products, but from raw market power, guile, and gall. Microsoft has not, the Justice Department and judge claim, been playing by the competitive market rules that supposedly everyone else has been obeying. The analysis of the case presented in this book leads us to the opposite conclusion: if Microsoft had tried to act like a monopolist over the last decade or more, it would not be the force that it is today in the world's software market. And Bill Gates would not be nearly so wealthy.

Microsoft's Defense in Disarray

As this book was begun, in the winter of 1999, the first trial, United States v. Microsoft Corporation, which was taking place in the U.S. District Court for the District of Columbia, had reached its midpoint. The Justice Department had completed presenting its accusations, along with the testimony of supporting witnesses. Microsoft's lawyers were seeking to mount a defense. Matters got worse for Microsoft's legal defense team as the Justice Department lawyers scored crucial points at almost every turn. The *Wall Street Journal*'s chief technology columnist called Microsoft's courtroom strategy a "disaster." A seemingly unending parade of legal analysts on television news programs scoffed at Microsoft's defense team for being unwilling to concede that the company was a "monopoly," which, supposedly, is a widely accepted fact.

In his videotaped testimony, Bill Gates was shown to be forgetful, at times agitated, and apparently unaware of what transpired at key meetings with his top executives. Microsoft's key supporting economic witness, the MIT economist Richard Schmalensee, had been thoroughly embarrassed with the government's lead attorney's presentation of apparent contradictions between what Schmalensee had said about how markets work in his sworn affadavit and what he had said in his earlier academic writings. His credibility with the press also seemed to suffer when the prosecuting attorney got him to concede that computer manufacturers would not be able to switch very quickly from Windows to other operating systems because of customer demand for Windows, contrary to what he seemed to be arguing in his lengthy written statement.

As the trial proceeded, television commentators openly wondered why Microsoft, with its vast wealth and influence, could not buy a better defense. Few legal observers were willing to give Microsoft an even chance of winning this first court battle. Jake Kirchner, a columnist for *PC Magazine*, summed up Microsoft's court position during the spring 1999 trial recess: "Microsoft and its executives have been thoroughly humiliated in the process. The government has ripped apart the testimony of just about every Microsoft witness, frequently using their own subpoenaed e-mails to contradict their prepared materials and in-court statements." He goes on to suggest that the Justice Department's lawyers have "done an admirable job of making the Microsoft corporate hierarchy look like incompetent con artists at best—and liars and thieves at worst."

Toward the end of the trial phase in late June 1999, the *New York Times* reporter Joel Brinkley agreed with Kirchner's assessment: "Most of the points in the courtroom drama went to the Justice Department and the 19 states." Even Microsoft's attorney William Neukom acknowledged that "the government has put on a great performance," but was quick to add that the government's case was "fluff, legally." The judge clearly didn't agree. In anticipation of Microsoft's legal defeat, class action suits were being filed in courts across the country with the idea that they would be pursued as soon as Microsoft's defeat was recorded; the lawyers' claim was that whole classes of consumers they represented had suffered damages from Microsoft's abuse of its monopoly powers and deserved compensation. In addition, various commentators and groups, assuming the defeat was all but certain, had begun to debate legal remedies. The Software and Information Industry Association, made up of 1,400 technology industry firms (including Microsoft), audaciously began calling for the breakup of Microsoft into three separate firms, or "Baby Bills," a play on the "Baby Bells" that resulted from the breakup of AT&T into one long-distance carrier and several smaller companies. They also recommended that Microsoft be forced to divulge—free of charge—the source code for Windows, something that Microsoft's competitors have coveted for years. The group's reasoning was that breaking up Microsoft and forcing it to give up its source code would eliminate the continuing need to have the Justice Department monitor the competitiveness of the software industry. The proposed remedies would also "effectively cure—once and for all—the competitive crisis plaguing the software industry."

CONCLUDING COMMENTS

A hundred or more years ago, the threat of monopoly might have been greater than it is today because of the limited variety of resources available within given markets. A firm might conceivably corner the market on a given resource—for example, iron or bauxite ore—for which there were no available or nearby substitutes, and then restrict production with the intention of increasing its prices and profits. In such a case it might have been quite difficult for other firms to devise substitutes in any reasonable amount of time.

Is the fear of such a monopoly justified as we move into the new millennium, especially in software markets? Microsoft likes to characterize itself as a software or Internet company whose main products are "digital" in nature, a claim not many industry observers, even those in the Justice Department and the trial judge, would dispute. If the characterization is tolerably accurate, it follows that Microsoft's main products can be represented as very long sequences of *1*'s and *0*'s, which, when you think about it, are not likely to be a source of vast and enduring monopoly power, since *1*'s and *0*'s can be duplicated in various arrangements without end by practically anyone with a few good ideas on how the *1*'s and *0*'s should be arranged. What is remarkable is how many people in today's world economy—hundreds of thousands, if not millions—are hard at work trying to come up with alternative, competitive rearrangements of those two digits.

Granted, there is a great deal more to developing successful software than linking up sequences of *1*'s and *0*'s, but the point remains that entry into the software market will not be choked by a lack of the basic resource. Moreover, with so many people seeking to enter virtually all software markets, we should not be surprised if any firm's dominance of an identified software market is at best temporary, most likely stretching over a few years and certainly no more than a decade or two. The firm's market dominance is likely to be cut short if it mistakenly equates its market dominance with monopoly power and thinks it can live the quiet life of the monopolist.

Even Microsoft feels compelled to rearrange its digits as frequently as it can, mainly because, as Bill Gates has observed, "In three years, every product my company makes will be obsolete. The only question is whether we will make them obsolete or somebody else will."

Yet, in this world of rapid change that runs according to Internet, not railway, time, the government has sought to take Microsoft to court on the grounds that the company has managed to corner the market on a formula that at its digital core consists of various sequences of *1*'s and *0*'s. Although it has a copyright to a particular, extra long sequence of *1*'s and *0*'s, the number of combinations of potentially productive *1*'s and *0*'s must be extraordinarily large, if not infinite. These observations about the ultimate resource foundation of any category of software do not prove that Microsoft is not in violation of the country's antitrust laws, but they certainly are intriguing. Before we buy in to the Justice Department's and judge's claims, we should pause and reflect, "In this digital age, could Microsoft really have done what it has been accused of doing, monopolized its markets and then exploited them to the extent that the Justice Department claims? Could it continue to do so for as long as the judge imagines?" If it has done that, it has pulled off an amazing feat, given the worldwide abundance of *1*'s and *0*'s and the ease with which, in Internet time, various sequences of *1*'s or *0*'s can be shipped to all points on the globe. If Microsoft is the monopoly it is supposed to be, then it must have every intention of continuing to exploit hordes of consumers, many of whom are sophisticated buyers for large transnational corporations, and it must have the capacity to prevent the hordes of programmers around the globe from coming up with their own strings of *1*'s and *0*'s. Is it really believable that a single firm in the digital age could pull that off?

The answer the Justice Department and judge want us to believe challenges plausibility, although, as will be seen, it cloaks its claims in new digital age theories that will be assessed. Nevertheless, the thrust of the case starts with five main claims:

First, following well-worn twentieth-century antitrust enforcement norms, monopoly power is largely determined by market share (especially with regard to major industries that are national in scope and critically important to the health of the national economy) and by barriers to entry. A sufficiently high market share thus can be equated with monopoly.

Second, special characteristics of software markets—"scale economies" in production and "network effects" in demand—impose barriers to entry that permit the dominant (or monopoly) firm to impose its will on market participants, consumers and computer producers.

Third, since Windows is installed on more than 90 percent of personal computers, there is no commercially viable alternative, and there are scale and network barriers to entry. Hence, Microsoft is a monopolist.

Fourth, if a firm has monopoly power in one market—for example, operating systems—it can use that power to dominate and monopolize other markets—for example, Internet browsers—and then use the extended dominance in other markets to protect its original monopoly position.

Fifth, Microsoft has used its monopoly power to extend its market dominance to Internet browsers and thus to protect its operating system monopoly in four main ways:

1. Microsoft has engaged in illegal "predatory" (zero) pricing against its market rival Netscape with the intent to destroy any existing or potential threat to its operating system market.
2. Microsoft has illegally tied Internet Explorer to Windows for the purpose of restricting Netscape's distribution of its browser, Navigator, and Netscape's ability to develop an alternative operating system platform.
3. Microsoft has illegally developed exclusionary contracts that have required computer manufacturers and Internet service providers to promote and distribute only Internet Explorer, thereby once again choking off competition from Netscape.
4. Microsoft has harmed consumers, by restricting consumer choice (which would be greater with both Internet Explorer and/or Navigator programs on their personal computers' hard drives and both icons on the desktop) and by impairing innovation in the software industry.

In the next chapter, we will be concerned mainly with the issue of Microsoft's monopoly status in the operating system market. Following chapters will deal with the other more detailed charges.

This book obviously takes a very dim view of the legal claims against Microsoft. Microsoft doesn't fit the mold of a pernicious monopoly that has been systematically undercutting consumer welfare by the broad sweep of its market strategies. Any consumer harm that may have occurred when Microsoft integrated its browser with Windows has very likely been outweighed by consumer gains in other areas of its activities.

Again, we can acknowledge that Microsoft has made some mistakes in how it has developed, marketed, and priced its products. But mistakes and bad manners do not necessarily make for the systematic exercise of monopoly power that should be corralled by an antitrust suit. If they did, few companies—even Microsoft's accusers—would be immune from antitrust prosecution. The *PC Magazine* columnist Jake Kirchner was probably right to chastise the Microsoft defense team for not handling the government's attacks more deftly in court, but he was also right when he added a note of caution for those who had deduced that Microsoft's ultimate legal defeat was assured: "[D]espite the public thrashing suffered by Microsoft in the Washington courtroom, it's not clear to me that the government has proved its case. There really hasn't been a smoking gun introduced into evidence. The embarrassing e-mails for the most part have been just that—embarrassing. They really haven't shown anything beyond what we already knew: Microsoft fights with no holds barred." And it should be noted that on the same day Judge Jackson handed down his Findings of Fact in the Microsoft case, another judge reminded everyone in a private antitrust lawsuit against Intel that the "Sherman Act does not convert all harsh commercial actions into antitrust violations."

Microsoft has made a lot of money, as fully noted. However, this is no reason to cast Microsoft as either the devil incarnate nor as an angel on the wing. More realistically, Microsoft is an aggressive but constrained competitor. Again, the Microsoft case is taken up here not because of deep concern for Microsoft per se, but rather because the economic and legal principles that run through the case could have broad application to many other American firms, especially those in the emerging high-technology and information industries. From the perspective developed in this book, it would be a shame if Microsoft were penalized for its market strategies, mainly because such a conviction would have a broadly chilling effect on American competitiveness in the emerging information age.

⚖ CHAPTER 2 ⚖

Monopoly Mantra

THE ANTITRUST CASE AGAINST MICROSOFT is grounded in nineteenth-century thinking about monopoly, combined with twentieth-century enforcement norms. Justice Department officials start with a declaration that Microsoft is a monopoly. The word "monopoly" is loaded, implying a single seller with market power and serious guilt of market wrongdoing—because any single seller will naturally do what it can do if there are impenetrable barriers to entry. If the Justice Department officials and Judge Thomas Penfield Jackson are to be believed, Microsoft's monopoly—its "single-seller" market status—is self-evident. One statistic seems to say it all: Microsoft's Windows operating system is installed on more than nine tenths of all personal computers with Intel-compatible processors.

Market dominance necessarily translates into latent, if not kinetic, monopoly power. Moreover, according to Justice Department officials and the judge on the case, Microsoft is doing what any good monopolist should be expected to do: illegally exploiting its market power in various ways to its own advantage and to the detriment of existing and potential market rivals and, more important, consumers.

U.S. Attorney General Janet Reno affirmed her department's starting assessment that Microsoft is unquestionably an exploitative monopoly at the December 1997 press conference where she announced the Justice Department's suit against Microsoft: "Microsoft is unlawfully taking advantage of its Windows monopoly to protect and extend that monopoly." According to the attorney general and everyone else at the Justice Department involved in the case, this means that all active monopolies are bad for business and consumers, and the Justice Department's antitrust suit against Microsoft will, if successful, produce gains for the American public. "We took action today [in the courts]," Ms. Reno boasted, "to ensure that consumers will have the ability to choose among competing software products." She clearly sees the case as a morality play, on a par with old grade-B western movies in which the good guys wearing white hats were always pitted against the bad guys wearing black hats.

The attorney general was echoing a widespread public sentiment. It has become commonplace for reporters, columnists, scholars, and computer industry analysts to use terms like "monopoly" or "near monopoly" to describe Microsoft, as if the firm's monopoly status is an established fact, not one open to debate in a court of law or in other public forums. The presumption seems to be that if a refrain is repeated with sufficient frequency, then the truth of the claim is established.

Many of Microsoft's media critics and political accusers have felt at ease applying their rhetorical skills in condemning Microsoft and Bill Gates. Indeed, the condemnations of Microsoft's supposed unfettered market power have given rise to increasingly shrill media attacks, fortified with what seems to be a campaign of vilification by name-calling and guilt by association. *New York Times* columnist Maureen Dowd has minced few words in her denunciation of Gates as a "rich spoiled brat" who has not yet realized a "grim truth": "People hate Microsoft even more than they hate the Government." Gary Reback, a Silicon Valley antitrust lawyer, mused to *The New Yorker*, "The only thing the 'Robber Barons' did that Bill Gates hasn't done is use dynamite against their competitors." The real "grim truth" might be that Gates is no more spoiled than Dowd, or that being spoiled has nothing to do with the matter of Microsoft being a monopoly. Furthermore, the supposed robber barons of the late nineteenth and early twentieth centuries—for example, John D. Rockefeller—did not always deserve this derogatory label (an issue that will be considered later in the chapter).

No wonder Jacob Weisberg, a Microsoft employee, lamented in his article for the electronic magazine *Slate*, "A few months ago, everyone I met seemed to think that working for Microsoft was a pretty cool thing to do. Now, strangers treat us like we work for Philip Morris."

Before we take up the Justice Department's specific charges against Microsoft, we need to ask a question that is as easily overlooked as it is important to the case: Is Microsoft really the kind of pernicious monopoly it has been made out to be?

MICROSOFT, THE MONOPOLIST

The Justice Department's chant "Microsoft is a monopolist" has taken on a rhetorical life of its own, drawing support from unexpected quarters. The former Republican presidential candidate Bob Dole, who once defended Microsoft against Justice Department action but who now lobbies against Microsoft for other computer software companies, accepts the legal action as necessary. He declared in the *Los Angeles Times*, "Microsoft's goal appears to be to extend the monopoly it has enjoyed in the PC operating system marketplace to the Internet as a whole and to control the direction of innovation." Without Dole's, and others', acceptance of the monopoly mantra, there is no monopoly power to extend to the browser market, no evil intent on Microsoft's part to give away its browser by integrating it into Windows, and no illegality.

The *Wall Street Journal* reporter and television commentator Alan Murray announced on the front page of the *Journal*, "Microsoft *is* a monopoly" (emphasis in the original). This is so, Murray tells us, repeating nearly verbatim the Justice Department's position, because Mr. Gates has managed to win near-total control of the most valuable real estate in business today: "His Windows operating system has become almost the sole entry point to cyberspace." It may appear to many that "entry points into cyberspace" are not subject to duplication, and so such a declaration strongly implies that Microsoft's market position amounts to a "choke point" or a "stranglehold" on market rivalry (these words were used by other Microsoft critics and Justice Department lawyers).

New York Attorney General Dennis Vacco summed up the concern of the nineteen cooperating attorneys general that Microsoft's product development strategies are evidence of monopoly power: "It would be unfortunate if one company were allowed to control access to the Internet in violation of the antitrust laws, restricting consumer choice and stifling competition before it has a chance to develop." This statement appears to be an assertion that "sole entry point" is tantamount to *controlling* access to the Internet, which is not necessarily the case at all.

Clearly, if Microsoft has become "the sole entry point," it follows that there is "no viable competitive alternative," or so the Justice Department reasons in its initial complaint against Microsoft, and Judge Jackson concurred in his Findings of Fact. Why is that true? Because, according to the Justice Department, computer manufacturers attest that "it is a commercial necessity to preinstall Windows on nearly all of their PCs. Both OEMs [original equipment manufacturers] and Microsoft recognize that they have no commercially viable substitutes for Windows, and they cannot preinstall Windows on their PCs without a license from Microsoft."

The Justice Department quotes the computer manufacturer Micron's executive Eric Browning as saying, "I am not aware of any other non-Microsoft operating system product to which Micron could or would turn as a substitute for Windows 95 at this time." The Hewlett-Packard executive John Romano affirmed that "absolutely there's no choice." The Gateway executive John Von Holle concluded that "we don't have a choice" and that greater competition in the operating system market "would drive prices lower." In the rebuttal phase of the trial, the Justice Department's chief economic consultant, Franklin Fisher, argued that Microsoft's monopoly position in operating systems is the reason that Microsoft can charge "superhigh prices" and earn "supernormal profits." Similarly, the former judge Robert Bork argues that Microsoft's monopoly position is self-evident because the "company's profits are among the highest of any American business. Its own financial statements show a profit margin of about 47%. Though profit levels are viewed by some as ambiguous indicators of monopoly power, this profit margin is so high that many commentators would think it raises a strong inference of monopolistic pricing."

The Justice Department's claim that Microsoft is a monopoly is crucially dependent on proving Microsoft's market dominance in operating systems for personal computers. Fisher explains the tie between market dominance and monopoly power: "Monopoly power is a substantial degree of market power," or the ability of a firm "(a) to charge a price significantly in excess of competitive levels and (b) to do so over a significant period of time." Fisher believes his definition is consistent with "the oft-cited legal definition of monopoly power as 'the power to control prices or exclude competition,' " which he equates with "the absence or ineffectiveness of competitive constraints on price, output, product decisions, and quality." He then suggests that the "relevant market" can be defined as that "candidate market" in which the firm can raise its price above competitive levels without fear of loss of its market to new entrants.

Fisher points out that Microsoft dominates sales of operating systems in the Intel-compatible personal computer market and that its dominance is protected by "barriers to entry" in the form of "economies of scale in production," "network effects," and "switching costs" (concepts that will be explored at length in later chapters). These barriers to entry in the market for Intel-compatible operating systems give Microsoft the ability to earn "supra-normal profits" by charging higher than competitive prices. Hence, "Microsoft possesses monopoly power in the market for operating systems for Intel-compatible desktop personal computers. There are no reasonable substitutes for Microsoft's Windows operating system for Intel-compatible desktop PCs. Operating systems for non-Intel-compatible computers are not a reasonable substitute for Microsoft's Windows operating system" because there would be high costs to switching to non-Intel-compatible computers like Mac and Unix. Like the Justice Department, Fisher backs up his monopoly claim by deferring to the testimony of several computer industry executives who argued that they have no choice but to install Windows in the computers they sell.

Frederick Warren-Boulton, the chief economic consultant for the state attorneys general, develops a similar line of argument—from the consistency in the structure of the arguments made by Warren-Boulton and Fisher it is clear that their testimonies were coordinated. However, Warren-Boulton more explicitly develops the pricing implications of Microsoft's supposed monopoly power. He argues that the absence of viable competitors in Intel-compatible operating systems means that Microsoft doesn't have to worry about raising its price or using its economic weight in other ways. Moreover, he adds that the market demand for operating systems is derived from the demand for personal computers: the greater the demand for personal computers, the greater the demand for operating systems. According to Warren-Boulton, the cost of the operating system represents on average 2.5 percent of the price of personal computers (and at most 10 percent for very inexpensive personal computers), so "even a 10 percent increase in the price of the OS [operating system] would result at most in a 1 percent increase in the price of even inexpensive PCs. Given the cost to users of switching to another [operating system] platform, such a small increase in the price of the PC platform would not be expected to result in a large reduction in the demand for PCs, and thus the PC operating system." This implies, he maintains, that the "price elasticity [responsiveness of buyers to a price change] of derived demand for PC operating systems must be *very low* for at least a significant price range above the competitive price for PC operating systems. . . " (emphasis added). "Very low" has been italicized because those two words speak directly to the issue of whether or not Microsoft's prices can more aptly be characterized as "competitive" or "monopolistic." There are two reasons:

First, it is clear that what Warren-Boulton meant by "very low" was that the demand, within range of the going price, for Windows is not only inelastic (as opposed to elastic), but *decidedly* inelastic, meaning that within the relevant price range, consumers would be very unresponsive to a price change. Under the demand for any good, we would expect that a price increase will lead to a reduction in quantity sold, and vice versa. However, an "inelastic demand" is one under which any given percentage increase in the price will lead to a smaller percentage reduction in quantity, and vice versa. This implies that no profit-maximizing monopolist would ever choose to sell its product at a price that is in the inelastic range of its demand. This is because the monopolist could raise its price and increase its revenues, given that the percentage reduction in the quantity sold would be less than the percentage increase in the price. The reduction in sales would also translate into a reduction in cost, albeit a very modest reduction in the case of software. A price increase in the inelastic range of demand simultaneously increases revenues and lowers cost, and thus increases profits. Accordingly, a monopolist would continue to raise its price so long as its profits rose. Put another way, it would continue to raise the price at least until its demand was no longer "inelastic," or the price elasticity were no longer "very low."

Hence, economists are fond of deducing that monopolists will always produce where the demand is "elastic." This means that Warren-Boulton is really admitting that Microsoft's prices are not those that would likely be charged by the kind of monopoly he attests Microsoft is.

Second, by describing the price elasticity of Windows demand as "very low," Warren-Boulton is also suggesting that Microsoft's price for Windows is very likely far below the monopoly price. This is because the so-called "coefficient" of the price elasticity of demand facing any firm (the ratio of the percentage change in the quantity to the percentage change in the price, which is what Warren-Boulton really must have had in mind when he used "very low") varies from something that is "very low" (close to zero) at a very low price to something that is "very high" (all the way to infinity) at very high prices. Even a monopolist with a very low (if not zero) marginal cost of production would never price its product where the price elasticity is "very low." Again, this is because a very low elasticity implies that a price increase will increase profits. A monopolist would never charge a zero price. Hence, the testimony of Warren-Boulton, the economist for the states, contradicts (or at least is at odds with) that of Fisher, the economist for the Justice Department: A monopolist facing a "very low" elasticity of demand could not, at the same time, be charging "supernormal prices." The two descriptions simply can't both be true. Indeed, Judge Richard Posner, who is also a distinquished professor of law and economics in his own right (in November 1999 he was appointed by Judge Jackson to mediate settlement talks), has argued that an inelastic demand at the current price is good evidence of the absence of monopoly power.

Warren-Boulton admits that Microsoft's current pricing doesn't appear to be designed to maximize profits (which seems to also contradict Fisher's claim that Microsoft earns "superhigh profits"). However, he insists that any current loss of profits from charging low prices (and even suffering some current increase of costs) are intended to build and protect Microsoft's market power, which can lead to higher prices in the future. We have to wonder how he knows that prices will be higher in the future, given that for years Microsoft had controlled over 90-plus percent of the operating system market (as the Justice Department wants to define the market) and doesn't seem to be willing to exploit its supposed current monopoly position. Why does Warren-Boulton, or Franklin Fisher, think that Microsoft has to have even more dominance before it acts like the monopolist it is accused of being?

Microsoft's giving away its browser, either separate from Windows or integrated into Windows, could be a predatory action, but it also could be a competitive action. Any firm that is dominant in a software market isn't likely to want to give up its dominance, especially if there are substantial economies of scale in production and network effects in demand, as the Justice Department, Warren-Boulton, Fisher, and Judge Jackson all maintain is true of the software industry. With those conditions in place concerning its operating system, if Microsoft loses market share for its operating system, then it could anticipate problems in keeping its applications network intact, which could mean its market share could spiral downward as a new market entrant makes sales and those sales lead to more and more applications being written for the new operating system. Competition requires that producers meet the competition, and new competition *could* come from the use of Netscape as a platform for the operating system. One of the more fundamental problems with the government's case is that it interprets anything Microsoft does as being the actions of a monopolist. If Microsoft had the monopoly power the Justice Depart-

TABLE 2.1   Microsoft's Actual and Projected Percentage Share of the Intel-based Operating System Market (figures compiled by International Data Corporation)

Operating System[1]	Year[4,5,6]										
	1991	'92	'93	'94	'95	'96	'97	'98	'99	2000	'01
Microsoft[2]	93	92	93	93	90	94	95	95	95	95	96
IBM OS/2	0	3	3	4	7	3	3	3	3	3	3
UNIX[3]	0.2	0.2	0.2	0.1	0.1	0.1	0.1	0.1	0.1	0.1	0.1
Other Intel	7	4	4	3	3	2	2	2	2	2	2

[1] Operating systems used in single-user client and PC operating environment.

[2] Includes Microsoft 16-bit and 32-bit Windows and MS-DOS.

[3] Intel-based UNIX operating

[4] Market shares may not total 100% due to rounding off.

[5] The market shares for the years 1997–2001 are forecasts.

[6] Worldwide

SOURCE: U.S. Department of Justice, Antitrust Division Web site, at: http://www.usdoj.gov/atr/cases/exhibits/1.pdf.

ment says it has, then it would not have to give away its browser, or hold its prices down to what are supposedly "predatory levels."

THE RELEVANCE OF MARKET SHARE

Like his colleague Fisher, Warren-Boulton bolsters his argument with supporting quotes from executives of computer firms who attest to Microsoft's monopoly position, and suggests that the executives' claims should be given credence, since "Microsoft's worldwide share of shipments of Intel-based operating systems has been approximately 90 percent or more in recent years," an observation fully accepted by the judge as fact. Fisher refers to the Government's exhibit 1, shown here as Table 2.1. This table shows Microsoft's share of sales of all Intel-based operating systems for personal computers, as determined by industry surveys done by the International Data Corporation. The table shows that Microsoft had 93 percent of the Intel-compatible operating system market in 1991 and 95 percent of that market in 1997, the latest year for which data were available. In 1997, IDC was forecasting that Microsoft would more or less hold its market share for operating systems through 2001.

What should we make of these arguments? First, we must point out that a claim that a firm's market share is in and of itself indicative of the firm's monopoly power should be summarily dismissed. Such a claim is bogus but, admittedly, deceptively appealing. The Justice Department offers no evidence that the claim has practical merit, other than in the testimony of computer executives that they don't have a "viable" alternative to Windows, which *seems* to suggest that Microsoft has control over price and, therefore, significant monopoly power.

It's true that basic microeconomics textbooks often teach that a monopolist is a "single producer" that is capable of restricting output, raising its prices above competitive levels, and imposing its will on buyers. If a monopoly is so defined, the Justice Department apparently deduces that a firm that has a high percentage of all market sales might be construed as an "almost monopoly" or "near monopoly." Having framed the argument this way, the Justice Department and other critics seem to take rhetorical license by suggesting in a roundabout way that being an "almost monopoly" is like being "almost pregnant." You either are or you aren't, so let's just say that Microsoft is a monopolist and not waste words because everyone knows that Microsoft is perfectly capable of acting like a monopolist. The basic difficulty with this line of argument is a point that most respectable economics textbooks make: namely, a firm can sell every unit there is to be sold in a market—have 100 percent of the market—but still be forced to act like a competitor. In other words, it must price and develop its product as though it actually had market rivals *because the firm has to fear the entry of potential competitors.*

For example, it appears that a company called Signature Software has 100 percent of the market for a program that allows computer users to type their letters and e-mails in a font that is derived from their own handwriting. In spite of its total domination of its market, the firm prices its software very modestly, simply because the program can be duplicated with relative ease. At one time, Netscape almost totally dominated the browser market, and it should have known that it would never be able to price its product *as if* it were a monopolist. Why? Because as the cofounder of Netscape, Jim Clark, admits in his book, *Netscape Time,* it took his company and a band of seven young programmers from the University of Illinois only four months to write the first version of Navigator from scratch. At the time, twenty other firms had paid licensing fees for the Mosaic browser technology to the University of Illinois (where it had been developed) via a firm called Spyglass, and one of those potential competitors—Microsoft—turned out to be a bit more than a "potential" competitor.

Indeed, some firms with high market shares might act more like competitors than other firms in markets where they have much smaller market shares. The reason is that the threat posed by potential competitors in a highly concentrated market can be more constraining than the competitive threat of actual competitors in less-concentrated markets. Microsoft may act more like a competitor, in spite of its 90-plus percent market share of the operating system market, than do other firms like General Electric and Wal-Mart that have much lower market shares in their respective markets. This is because, as will be shown, a number of actual competitors can exist and a few people with good computers could become competitors.

The government also asserts that a sufficiently high market share can be equated with "monopoly" and implies the existence of no "commercially viable alternative." Yet this assertion is clearly self-contradictory. If a firm has less than 100 percent of the market, it follows that there are commercially viable alternatives. We all concede that there might be *few* commercially viable alternatives in a given market because of natural or legal barriers to entry, or because of malicious anticonsumer behavior on the part of the dominant producer. This is what the Justice Department and judge seem to want the public to accept in the Microsoft case. However, there may also be few commercially viable alternatives because the dominant producer has developed its product to such a high level yet priced its products so low that more producers are unable to make their operating systems commercially viable.

Ask yourself whether IBM's operating system OS/2 would be commercially viable if Microsoft were to raise its price for Windows ten- or even a hundred-fold. This would certainly be within the realm of plausibility if Warren-Boulton's estimate of the "very low" elasticity of demand for Windows were correct. You can imagine that IBM and owners of other operating systems would be delighted and would work hard to ensure that consumer responsiveness to the Windows price hike was substantial.

Obviously, Microsoft has *some* control over its price. Within limits, it can choose to raise its price for Windows and still expect to sell a large number of copies, at least in the short run. It can influence its profits by juggling price and sales. Does that mean it necessarily charges more than the "competitive price," as the Justice Department, its economists, and Judge Jackson suggest? It depends on how you define "competitive price." If "competitive price" means the price that would be charged under market conditions that textbooks call "perfect competition," in which competitors have no choice whatsoever over the price they charge, then it is clear that Microsoft is very likely charging more than competitive prices.

However, "perfect competition" is an unrealistic pricing standard—perfection, no less!—that rigs the argument against Microsoft. "Perfect competition" requires *numerous* producers selling an *identical* product and having *zero* costs of entry and exit, which means that no one firm has any control at all over the price it charges, mainly because the output of any one firm can be easily replaced by production from all the other existing producers or new entrants. Obviously, no real-world market mirrors the conditions of perfect competition, nor could those pristine market conditions ever be duplicated, especially in markets where extensive scale economies and network effects exist.

All markets are, to one degree or another, "imperfectly competitive," meaning that the firms in them have *some* choice over the prices they charge, but their choices are constrained. If by "competitive price" the government has in mind the price that would be charged in an imperfectly competitive market, it seems certain that the Justice Department and judge do not really know whether Microsoft's prices are above its competitive standard. The government gives no evidence that it knows what that standard is, and there is good reason for that: the information is nowhere available in the halls of the Justice Department or the courthouse or anywhere else, which means that legal institutions are extraordinarily poor substitutes for markets in establishing "competitive prices."

The problem is that it is very hard for anyone to say what constitutes a high or low (monopolistic or competitive) price for an operating system. Judge Jackson tries to extricate himself from this legal box by musing about how a Microsoft study found that a Windows upgrade could be sold profitably at $49, but the price of $89 was chosen because it was the "revenue-maximizing price." But is the revenue-maximizing price a monopoly price? Only if you start with the presumption that Microsoft is a monopolist. Firms that face substantial competition can also have a "revenue-maximizing price" that is highly constrained and in line with the competition.

What do we know about Microsoft's pricing? Well, first we know that the judge is not being totally forthright in his declaration that Microsoft charges $89 for Windows upgrades and his use of that price as a marker for a presumed "monopoly price." This is because upward of 90 percent of all copies of Windows are sold with new computers, and it is revealing to note that Microsoft sells Windows 98 to large computer manufacturers under licensing agreements at between $40 and $60 per copy, which seems to be in line with what the judge seems to think is the base-line competitive price. Microsoft's average revenue per copy of the various versions of Windows (95, 98, and NT) was $73 in 1998. Such prices don't seem like "superhigh prices," given the complexity of Windows and the up-front investment Microsoft had to make to develop the program and maintain its worldwide distribution and support system, and it doesn't seem all that out of line with the pricing standard set by the judge.

Indeed, one of the government's economists suggested that the current price of Windows is not all that far removed from the "competitive level." Moreover, you can't judge Microsoft's prices by looking at how profitable those prices appear to be today, and we say that for a couple of reasons.

First, the government makes no allowance in the normal calculation of Microsoft profits for the risks assumed years ago. Some of the current profitability has to be seen as a payoff for past risks. Years ago, when the founders of Microsoft contemplated building their operating system market, they must have assumed that eventually, if they were successful in dominating the market, the payoff would be great. Otherwise, they may not have been willing to take the risks. From the perspective of the past, the prospects of today's profits would rightfully have had to be discounted greatly by the real possibility that profits would never be reaped. Seen this way, the profits today look more reasonable. When considered in terms of the risks taken years ago (and properly discounted for the risks), the profits (back then) were not expected to provide much more than a competitive rate of return. If the present value of today's profits back then was substantially above that of alternative investments, then one would have expected far more software firms to try to enter the market than actually did. Microsoft's profits today may be far greater than they expected years ago, but that doesn't mean that Microsoft is a monopolist. It may mean nothing more than Microsoft, and Gates, got lucky.

If Microsoft's prices are substantially above true competitive levels, meaning other firms could and would be willing to make do in the market with much lower rates of return on their investments, then it seems that all the Justice Department has to do is alert producers to the profitable opportunities available for entering Microsoft's markets and undercutting Microsoft prices. Granted, the Justice Department claims that the "special economics" of "network effects" prevent firms from being able to enter Microsoft's markets. But such a response has a hollow ring. As we'll see in Chapter 3, people in the computer industry are not so dumb that they will stay with a firm over the long haul if it promises to charge "superhigh prices" now and forever, if one or more other firms offer to provide the product for less and to stick with the lower price into the distant future. At the foundation of the Justice Department's case is the assumption that people operating in markets are downright stupid. Only the people in the Justice Department and their hired expert witness seem to be smart enough to detect superhigh prices when they see them.

Second, Judge Bork suggests that Microsoft's considerable profitability would necessarily point to a "strong inference of monopolistic pricing." No such inference—not even a weak one—can be drawn. Even Judge Bork argues in his classic treatise on the ills of antitrust enforcement, *The Antitrust Paradox*, that the profitability of a firm is "utterly ambiguous." This is because the profitability of Microsoft's prices today can be attributed to the fact that Microsoft has lower production, distribution, and service costs than its potential rivals, because it has a larger "network." Under such circumstances, we might expect Microsoft to do what any other self-respecting profit-maximizing producer might be expected to do— charge a price that is profitable but still below the prices that potential rivals with higher costs could afford to charge. Such a price would be competitive *and* highly profitable. Certainly, no other competitor could meet it, and given supposed economies of scale and network effects, it would be lower than if the market were somehow more segmented than it is. With this price consumers would also be better off than if Microsoft were removed from the market and replaced by any other producer.

SCALE ECONOMIES AND MONOPOLY POWER

The Justice Department contends that Microsoft has monopoly powers because its market dominance in the operating system market is protected by high barriers to entry in the form of certain economies of scale and network effects, which reinforce each other. This, says the Justice Department, gives it a "natural monopoly," which occurs when a company becomes the single producer in the market because only one firm can produce at the lowest possible cost. Though "certain economies of scale" sounds as though there is something special about the operating system market, all the Justice Department seems to mean is that the cost of reproducing an operating system falls precipitously after the first copy is produced. There are substantial development costs for any computer program as complicated as Windows—and Microsoft does indeed spend hundreds of millions of dollars on developing the first copy of any version of Windows—but those costs are basically up-front costs, what economists call "sunk costs," which are costs that can't be affected by how many copies of the program are sold. The reason: They've already been incurred and can't be changed.

The additional cost to Microsoft of the second and each succeeding copy of the program is by all accounts fairly low, though it isn't zero. In the case of preinstalled software, it costs perhaps a few pennies for computer makers to transfer a copy of Windows or any other program from their central servers to the hard drives of new personal computers. The computer manufacturers bear these costs, along with the cost of the backup copy of Windows typically shipped with a new computer (and a fee paid to Microsoft). When Microsoft sells copies of Windows in retail stores, the marginal cost of each copy is still no more than the few dollars it costs to burn an additional copy of Windows onto a compact disk, package it, send it through the distribution channels, and sell it to consumers at retail outlets like CompUSA or Wal-Mart. Thus, with CD copies, there are unavoidable materials and handling costs. Moreover, Microsoft does incur some support and service cost each time a copy of Windows is sold no matter how it was bought, whether through the computer manufacturer, over the Internet, or at a retail outlet. Judge Jackson has noted that computer makers' contracts stipulate that they are supposed to cover the support costs for their machines, including support costs on Windows. However, this does not mean that Microsoft does not incur support costs; it has higher support costs for computer makers. These costs can translate into a lower price that Microsoft can charge computer makers for Windows, and this would be true for a monopolist, which makes bogus the judge's claim that Microsoft has no incentive to control support costs for computer makers.

I don't know what the marginal cost of reproducing a copy of Windows is, and there is no way to find out. I was unable to get this information—I asked for it— but it's confidential, understandably, because such cost information can be valuable to competitors. It is practically certain that the Justice Department lawyers don't have any better fix on the marginal cost of copies of Windows than anyone else outside Microsoft. Some of the costs reflect an assessment of market risk that is unknowable by external observers because such costs are subjective, dependent upon actually being involved in the risk-taking investment process. Justice Department lawyers and I were not involved in that risk-taking process in years gone by, and we won't be involved in it in years to come.

Economists often judge the monopoly power of a firm by the extent to which the price of the product is above marginal cost. The greater the gap between the marginal cost of production and the price, they argue, the greater the monopoly power. It can be readily conceded that the price of Windows, whether $40 or $89, is very likely substantially above the full marginal cost of each copy of Windows as an electronic file of lines of code, which makes Microsoft's operating system very profitable. However, no software firm can long ignore development costs and price its product solely in line with the "marginal cost" of each electronic file. The firm wouldn't stay in business for long. Even if the marginal cost is really zero, or near zero, we would expect the price to be much higher than that just so the firm can cover its development costs. Clearly, the costs associated with the duplication of a string of electronic code is not all that matters in program pricing. Let's compare the company Red Hat, which manufactures and distributes the Linux operating system. In late 1999 Red Hat was selling retail copies of its latest version of the Linux operating system for $80. (Linux is, by all accounts, a more difficult program to set up and use than Windows.) Red Hat paid nothing for the operating system, so presumably it is not charging for the program. What it is charging for is the documentation and the support the company provides. This suggests that maybe much of the price of Windows is unrelated to the direct cost of producing each electronic file copy.

Also, the price of Windows seems to be low—in fact, substantially below what Microsoft could and would charge if it had the vast monopoly power the Justice Department and judge claim it has. In addition, the prices of Windows upgrades, in current and real dollars, have gone down as Microsoft's market dominance has expanded (see Table 2.2), not exactly what one would expect if Microsoft's market dominance translated into monopoly power, as the Justice Department has argued.

During the 1990–98 time period, as Microsoft's market dominance rose, what happened to its price for Windows? In May 1990, the retail list price was $100. That price rose to $130 in April 1992, only to fall from that by 16 percent, to $109, by the middle of 1998. The real (inflation-adjusted) price went from $129 in May 1990 to $155 in April 1992 and then back down to $111 in mid-1998, a 28 percent drop in the six-year period. The street price of Windows went from $95 in current dollars and $103 in real dollars in 1995 to $88 in current dollars and $90 in real dollars by mid-1999, a decline in real terms of 13 percent.

The current and real dollar street prices of the complete operating system had similar declines, as can be seen in Table 2.3. During the last half of 1990, the average real (mid-1999) price of a complete version of Windows 3.0 was $225; at the start of 1995 Windows 3.1 cost $126; in July 1995 Windows 3.11 was launched

TABLE 2.2   Windows Upgrade Prices 1990–98, Current and Real (mid-1999) Prices

Date Launched	Retail Price of Upgrade (current $)	Retail Price of Upgrade (mid-1999 $)	Street Price (current $)	Street Price (mid-1999 $)
5/22/90 (Windows 3.0)	$100 *	$129	NA	NA
4/6/92 (Windows 3.1)	130 *	155	NA	NA
2/15/94 (Windows 3.11)	110 *	125	NA	NA
8/24/95 (Windows 95)	109	118	$95	$103
6/25/98 (Windows 98)	109	111	88	90

* Includes MS-DOS upgrade.
SOURCE: Author's calculations, based on data from Microsoft, CompUSA, and chumbo.com.

TABLE 2.3   Windows Average Street Prices 1990–98, Current and Real (mid-1999) Prices

Date	Current Price*	Real Price*
5/90–12/90 (Windows 3.0) [†]	$177	$225
1/91–12/91 [†]	154	188
1/92–3/92 [†]	152	180
4/92–12/92 (Windows 3.1) [†]	138	163
1/93–12/93 [†]	122	141
1/94–1/95 [†]	112	126
2/95–7/95 (Windows 3.11) [†]	167	182
8/95–12/95 (Windows 95)	167	182
1/96–12/96	136	144
1/97–12/97	110	134
1/98–6/98	104	106

* To nearest dollar; † Includes price of MS-DOS.
SOURCES: Microsoft, various computer retailers, and author's calculations.

with a jump in the average real street price to $182 (with a free upgrade to Windows 95 when it appeared). In August 1995 Windows 95 appeared at a street price of $182, only to fall to $106 during the first half of 1998. This means that the average real price of Windows fell by more than half—or precisely 53 percent from 1990 to 1998.

The top half of Figure 2.1 plots the real price of Microsoft's operating system from 1990 to 1998; the bottom half shows Microsoft's market share for operating systems for Intel-based personal computers for 1991 through 1999, as presented by the government in its exhibit 1. If there has been a trend in Microsoft's market share, it has been upward, but modest, going from 93 percent market share in 1991 to 95 percent in 1999. What is more striking is the downward trend in the real price of Microsoft's operating systems, not exactly what would be expected of a monopolist taking advantage of its presumed growing monopoly market share. Granted, Microsoft radically raised its price from $126 to $182 when it introduced Windows 95 (version 3.11), but the lower part of the graph indicates why it likely began lowering its price thereafter: its market share took a significant dive.

Also, the data in Table 2.2 and Figure 2.1 are warped against Microsoft. The changes in "real prices" in Table 2.2 understate consumer gains from Windows, mainly because there have been significant enhancements in Windows with each new version (see Table 2.4).

Moreover, the current and real prices for Microsoft business applications and Microsoft Office have also fallen, often more than the prices of competitors' products. For example, compare the current and real prices of Microsoft Word with WordPerfect, and Microsoft Excel with Lotus 1–2–3 (Table 2.5). In real dollars, the price of Word fell by 55 percent between 1991 and 1998 while WordPerfect fell by only 32 percent. The price of Microsoft's Excel fell by 51 percent during the same period while the price of Lotus 1–2–3 fell by 32 percent.

If Microsoft is charging "superhigh prices" for its operating system, then so are its competitors. A November 1999 inspection of prices at local computer superstores revealed that Microsoft was charging $89 retail for a Windows 98 upgrade; IBM was charging $110 for OS/2; Apple was charging $85 for Mac 8.0; Red Hat was charging $80 for its Linux 6.0 version (with documentation and service); and Sun was charging $430 for its Solaris operating system.

The Justice Department probably draws attention to the substantial economies of scale in the production of operating systems because it is a way of suggesting that Microsoft is a "natural monopoly," a firm that becomes the single producer in the market because only one firm can produce at the lowest possible cost. This line of analysis has an honorable history in economic theory. If a market subject to substantial scale economies is divided among two or more producers, each producer's costs are higher than they would be if only one firm sold to the entire market. For example, each one of four firms producing 25,000 units of a good will have higher per unit costs than if one of the four firms produced all 100,000 units.

In such an environment, if several firms are producing the good, their costs and prices must be higher than they need to be. Hence, any one of the firms can lower its price, take over a larger share of the market, and lower its production costs. One

FIGURE 2.1   Microsoft's operating system: market share and real price, 1990–99

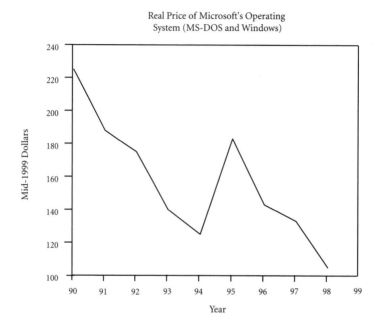

Real Price of Microsoft's Operating
System (MS-DOS and Windows)

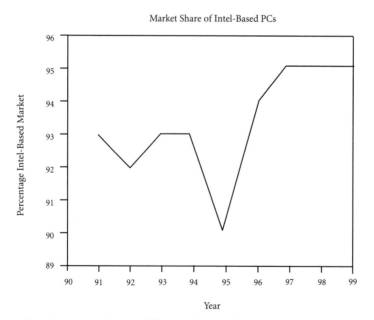

Market Share of Intel-Based PCs

SOURCE: Data for top panel from Table 2.3. The data for bottom panel from Table 2.1.

TABLE 2.4   New Features Added to Windows, 1990–98

Date Launched	Enhancements
May 22, 1990 (Windows 3.0)	New system font; 3D scroll bars; command buttons and icons for graphical user interface; program manager, file manager, and control panel; new memory-management system; desktop accessories such as CardFile, Windows Write, Recorder, and Solitaire; and a full-color painting program.
April 6, 1992 (Windows 3.1)	StartUp program launcher; improvements to user interface; improved speed and reliability, including better memory management; improved file manager; better SMARTDrive disk cache, and improved print manager; ability to restart MS-DOS applications without exiting Windows; setup hardware analysis; advanced power management; multimedia functionality; and improved network support.
February 15, 1994 (Windows 3.11)	Improved setup, use, and maintenance for networking; integration with server-based systems; and improved functionality and 32-bit performance.
August 24, 1995 (Windows 95)	Improved graphical user interface, including Start button, Taskbar, and Windows Explorer; long file names; shortcuts; multitasking; dial-up networking; Internet technology; compatibility with applications for DOS and Windows 3.x, as well as 32-bit applications; and greater hardware compatibility and system reliability.
June 25, 1998 (Windows 98)	Faster launching of applications; more efficient file system; USB support; Web-based WebView user interface; complete Internet integration; self-maintenance; increased reliability and improved troubleshooting; supports multiple monitors; better and faster 3D graphics, improved game support; and Web TV support.

SOURCE: Microsoft Corporation.

TABLE 2.5   Street Prices of Windows Applications and Competitors' Applications in 1991 and 1998, in Current and Real Dollars (pre-1991 data unavailable)

	Current Dollars			Real (mid-1999) Dollars		
			Percentage			Percentage
	1991	1998	Change	1991	1998	Change
Microsoft Word	$274	$146	-47	$334	$149	-55
WordPerfect	269	219	-19	328	223	-32
Microsoft Excel	266	156	-41	325	159	-51
Lotus 1–2–3	373	259	-31	455	264	-32

SOURCE: Microsoft, Metro Computing, and author's calculations.

producer—a so-called monopolist—will likely survive the competition and will do so more or less "naturally"—hence, the term "natural monopolist."

Some version of the natural monopoly argument was certainly covered in the economics textbooks studied by the Justice Department lawyers and the judge. Nevertheless, there are obvious problems in applying the natural monopoly argument to the operating system market. The supposed scale economies in this market may not be as great as they think. The reason is now an old one: viable producers of operating systems other than Microsoft exist today. Indeed, I count at this writing nineteen producers of operating systems—IBM, Oracle, Sun, Apple, AT&T, Hewlett-Packard, NeXT, Xerox, Wang, Be, Linux, DEDC, Psion, Data General, Compaq, 3COM, Geos, FreeBSD, and GEM—and I've probably missed some, including a number of versions of Unix. Almost certainly other operating systems and platforms will emerge. There is every reason to believe that one of the reasons AOL bought Netscape was (once the Microsoft antitrust trial is over) to combine Navigator with applications such as word processors, spreadsheets, calendars, etc., supplied by AOL or other non-Microsoft companies, that work with any operating system, thus creating an alternative to the Intel-Windows computing environment.

None of these existing or prospective producers has a large market share now, but that is the point: a large market share may not be important to prosper (well, it might be important to prosper as much as Microsoft has). A large market share is obviously not as critical for actual survival in the operating system market as the Justice Department and Judge Jackson believe.

The viability of other producers in the operating system market is important because it suggests that scale economies may not be the "high" barrier to entry that they have been made out to be. There are no market entry barriers for existing firms; they are already in the market and don't have to enter. The fact that scale economies do not extend to the entire market suggests that Microsoft must compete with its smaller rivals in the market and with potential rivals not yet in the market but who could enter the market on a far smaller scale than Microsoft and possibly compete effectively—if (and this is a very important if) Microsoft acts like a monopolist, and restricts production and market share in order to raise its price.

The Justice Department and judge want the public to believe that Microsoft has achieved its dominant position solely because of some factor like scale economies that is outside its direct control and is totally a consequence of the technology of production in operating systems, which is unaffected by what Microsoft does. The existence of smaller firms creating operating systems undermines this argument in an important but unnoticed way: if firms smaller than Microsoft are able to survive, if not prosper, then it appears that something other than independent technology forces are at work. Just maybe Microsoft's dominant position is attributable to what Microsoft has done right by consumers, or more right than other firms would have done if they had been in Microsoft's dominant position. Consumers, computer manufacturers, programmers, and everyone else in the personal computer markets are not automatons, marching in lock-step to Microsoft's orders to buy Microsoft products. They make their purchases in the good old-fashioned way—voluntarily, after evaluating the alternatives.

The Justice Department and the judge don't admit what economists have known for at least three decades: scale economies do not by themselves amount to a barrier (natural or otherwise) to entry and, hence, do not protect a natural monopolist's dominance of the market. If scale economies are in any sense natural, any producer can develop them. If the "natural monopolist" tries to behave like a monopolist by restricting production, it will elevate its price above competitive levels *and* increase its per unit production costs (because of the smaller sales and production scale). The firm might then earn monopoly profits, but only for a short time, because other firms can supplant the established firm that acts monopolistically. How? By charging a lower price, grabbing the established firm's market share, and achieving the fabled scale economies.

Judge Jackson has staked much of his Findings of Fact on the claim that Microsoft enjoys market protection from competition by what he calls the "applications barrier to entry" into the operating system market. Supposedly, other firms can't compete with Microsoft because there are so many applications, perhaps 70,000, written for Windows that they constitute a barrier, one that "would make it prohibitively expensive for a new Intel-compatible operating system to attract enough developers and consumers to become a viable alternative to a dominant incumbent in less than a few years."

Wait a minute. First, a "few years" is not a long time, and what happens after a few years can make a big difference to how a dominant firm interested in its stock price will price its product. Second, nothing is "prohibitively expensive" to venture capitalists or established firms like IBM or AOL if they are convinced—or as confident as the Justice Department lawyers and judge—that Microsoft is charging monopoly prices and will continue to do so into the distant future. Third, it is not at all clear that a viable competitor needs anywhere near 70,000 applications to survive. The overwhelming majority of computer users use just a handful of office applications, which suggests there is a very big market out there for an operating system that focuses on users with limited needs. The judge himself notes that Apple has far fewer than 70,000 applications and seems to be doing reasonably well, at least in terms of the devotion of its customers.

Some Justice Department officials and the presiding judge seem to think that raising the required funds to enter the software/operating system market on a sufficient scale to achieve the requisite scale economies would be a barrier to entry. Only big, bad, powerful Microsoft has sufficient market clout to produce operating systems. In this thinking, the Justice Department officials fall into an old error: the assumption that a large amount of investment funds is difficult, if not impossible, for other potential market entrants to raise. If the established "natural monopolist" is behaving competitively, it would indeed be difficult to raise a lot of money because there would be no ability on the part of the new entrant to supplant the established producer by entering with a lower price.

If, on the other hand, the established producer is acting like a true monopolist ("natural" or otherwise), as Microsoft stands accused of doing, there is a good chance for a new firm to supplant the established firm, the natural monopolist, by entering with a lower price. There is every reason to believe that the new firm could raise the funds that are needed to achieve the scale economies, even if the needed funds are large, as might be true in the operating system market. In that scenario there would be plenty of profits to be made, and many investors who would like to fill Bill Gates's shoes by being a party to a market takeover. If individual investors can't raise enough money for the takeover, there are plenty of large firms within and outside the computer and software industry—from IBM to General Electric to Rockwell International to Dell Computers to Sun Microsystems to America Online—that could easily raise the financial capital to build and sell a better operating system. But this requires that the established firm, Microsoft, act like a monopolist. If no one is able to raise the required funds, it is strong evidence that the established dominant producer is acting sufficiently competitively that there are not enough profits to be made from a takeover to induce enough people to mount one.

In other words, the costs of takeover are too great, or too risky, or investors have something better to do with their funds. The replacement of the established dominant producer with a new producer could therefore be construed as an inefficient redeployment of resources.

Finally, economists have long known that the term "natural monopolist" is a gross misnomer. A natural monopolist is not necessarily a monopolist at all. A natural monopolist can be in as competitive a market as any other firm in any other market. The natural monopolist simply has the benefit of decreasing production costs, nothing more, and this allows it to serve the whole market more efficiently than if more producers were dividing up the market. A firm that emerges as the sole producer of a product subject to extensive scale economies could just as correctly be dubbed a "natural competitor," implying that it is the sole survivor of an intense competitive process. For a company to be a genuine monopolist, there must be other barriers to market entry than scale economies.

Concluding Comments

In his classic treatise *The Antitrust Paradox*, Robert Bork cites approvingly the UCLA economist Harold Demsetz's observation that "*we have no theory that allows us to deduce from the observable degree of concentration in a particular market whether or not price and output are competitive*" (emphasis in the original). Bork was also right to conclude that "high rates of return are consistent with other factors besides restriction of output, primarily superior efficiency, so that if these debatable correlations [for example, that high rates of return imply monopoly] could be made to stand up, they would prove nothing of interest to antitrust policy," because—it cannot be stressed too often—they are "utterly ambiguous." And Bork was right on target when he stated repeatedly throughout his book that "antitrust should not interfere with any firm size created by internal growth." Judge Jackson and the legal scholars at the Justice Department would have served the country well, and saved Microsoft, as well as taxpayers and consumers, a lot of money, if they had gone back and reread Judge Bork's seminal work.

Instead, the government's case convinced Judge Jackson, who in no uncertain terms found that "Microsoft enjoys monopoly power in the relevant market" because "viewed together, three main facts indicate that Microsoft enjoys monopoly power. First, Microsoft's share of the market for Intel-compatible PC operating systems is extremely large and stable. Second, Microsoft's dominant market share is protected by a high barrier to entry. Third, and largely as a result of that barrier, Microsoft's customers lack a commercially viable alternative to Windows." The judge is patently wrong on all counts, which will become even more apparent as we go through the arguments of the next two chapters.

CHAPTER 3

Little Linux

TIME IS CRUCIAL TO ANTITRUST PROCEEDINGS. If the time span looked at by antitrust lawyers is short enough, then almost all firms have some degree of control over price. In the very short run, buyers may know of few alternatives to the particular goods they buy. Suppliers are unable to develop many new substitutes and make buyers aware of new, more attractive alternatives. Hence, firms might understandably reason that they can, in the short run, hike their prices without causing many of their customers to desert them. They can use price as a means of padding their profits—but only in the short run. Sooner or later, however, the power of the firms to hike their prices is bound to deteriorate as more and more substitutes come onto the market and as more and more buyers become aware of the available substitutes.

There are two important rules to remember: first, the higher the price—the closer the price is to the monopoly level—the greater incentive firms have to develop substitutes and the greater incentive buyers have to incur the cost of searching for substitutes. Second, the more time suppliers and buyers have to respond, the greater the anticipated response, which implies that the greater the time, the less profitable price hikes will be (and the more likely price decreases will be profitable).

Time is a constant in one sense: an hour is an hour. But it is also true that in the digital age, the "long run" has been rapidly collapsing toward the "short run," and the speed with which buyers and suppliers can respond to profitable opportunities has been quickening. In no small way, time is being compressed by the pace of change, so much so that we've had to invent new terms to capture the essence of the new time frame. "Internet time" is now commonly used, but Jim Clark, the cofounder of Netscape, shows his company allegiance in his preference, "Netscape time." What is that? It is, according to Clark, "life lived in a blur, like top-action photography speeded up to the point where individual events can't be clearly separated and understood."

Clark exaggerates, but his point is well taken. Time has changed. Which makes it particularly intriguing that as we entered the era of "Netscape time," the Justice Department, with the encouragement of Netscape and other companies in the digital economy, has chosen to initiate a new period of antitrust activism whose center-piece is the case against Microsoft. You might think that time itself would punish firms so bold as to price their products as if the pace of change, and the ability of suppliers and buyers to respond to price hikes, had not changed. In fact, it just might be that "Netscape time" has already seriously eroded the need for antitrust activism—if there ever was a demonstrated need for it in this decade. It looks as though a variety of market forces might be making the Justice Department's case against Microsoft irrelevant.

But never mind, the trial judge, Thomas Penfield Jackson, remains convinced that nothing much can happen in telecommunications, computers, and software markets over what he seems to believe is a long time, a "few years" or "several years," the time frame within which he is convinced that Microsoft will be able to maintain its relentless monopoly grip on the computer industry. What is really interesting about the Microsoft case is that if it is not settled, there is a good chance that the judge will be proved wrong long before the case is brought to a close in the court system. Indeed, relentless technological forces and market changes have been at work even as the judge has been taking the lawyers through their courtroom paces.

These forces suggest that even if Microsoft has indeed abused its market position by taking more from than it has given to computer manufacturers, Internet service providers, and application software providers, then we don't necessarily need the kind of legal remedies Judge Jackson might fashion—for example, breaking up Microsoft or requiring behavioral changes that might lead to onerous and continuous regulatory oversight by a government body or the court system. The market might be expected to mete out its penalties on Microsoft far more effectively and in more timely fashion than anything the court or Justice Department might devise.

DOING THE IMPOSSIBLE

The Justice Department has never bought the argument—and Judge Jackson has indicated that he does not buy it—that time is a factor in its case or that Microsoft has to be concerned about "potential competition" in a "long run" that may be getting shorter. Indeed, the Justice Department and the judge seem to have blinders on and see the world in static terms. In spring 1998, when the Justice Department filed its suit, its investigators and experts looked only at the actual competition in an operating system market that was being served only by Microsoft and declared there was no competition—zero, nada. They also claimed that there was no competitive threat to Microsoft on the economic horizon other than Netscape. Even a year later, in early June 1999, the Justice Department's economist Franklin Fisher still maintained in the rebuttal phase of the trial that just because there are unknown future threats "doesn't prevent Microsoft from having monopoly power today." As late as

November 1999, Judge Jackson declared without equivocation that "there exists no commercially viable alternative [to Windows] to which [customers] could switch in response to a substantial and sustained price increase or its equivalent by Microsoft."

Yet there is at least one viable alternative on the horizon. The Justice Department and court do not acknowledge that their case has been seriously undermined by an operating system, Linux, that in 1998 was little known outside communities of computer geeks. As the case progressed, the Justice Department lawyers and Fisher did not notice—at least, they gave no indication that they had noticed—that little Linux was coming on strong in the operating system market. Indeed, Linux's share of the server operating system market (a server is a computer that provides a service to other computers on a network) grew from under 7 percent in 1997 to over 17 percent by the end of 1998. And that percentage understates its true market share, for only *sold* units were counted, and Linux is often downloaded free from the Web. Linux's market share of sold operating systems continued to expand in late 1999. Granted, the court found that most copies of Linux are currently used by servers, not by desktop computer users. But *if Microsoft were to try to price Windows with all the monopoly power the Justice Department and court say it has,* Linux would certainly be used more heavily by desktop computer users (it is already being used by them). And if, as the court declares, "there exists no commercially viable alternative [to Windows] to which they could switch in response to a substantial and sustained price increase or its equivalent by Microsoft," why hasn't Microsoft imposed on consumers a "sustained price increase or its equivalent"? Maybe the answer lies in the threat of competition over the next "few years" that the Justice Department and court don't acknowledge.

Linus Torvalds, the original developer of Linux, noted with pride in *Business Week* in early 1999, "Suddenly, Windows NT [Microsoft's server operating system] isn't the thing taking over everything." Linux's invasion of the operating system market was expected to expand rapidly through 1999 and beyond. The International Data Corporation estimated in 1999 that commercial shipments of Linux for use in business computer servers would expand by a compounded annual rate of 25 percent from 1999 through 2003. Computer manufacturers—most notably, IBM, Dell, Compaq, Sun Microsystems, Hewlett-Packard, and DEC—had begun offering Linux as an alternative operating system for servers. By mid-1999, users could even get a Linux version of Corel's WordPerfect. Germany's Star Division had by mid-1999 converted its entire office suite of business applications to Linux, and IBM was developing a Linux version of its Lotus Notes. One of the factors holding the Linux operating system back has been the absence of games written for it, but now, Loki, a small Tustin, California, software company, has begun eliminating that deficiency with the introduction, in late 1999 and early 2000, of a series of games written for Linux.

More important, in spite of Linux's not being user-friendly— setting up a personal computer for Linux might take two days (according to Red Hat, a prominent Linux source)—there were in 1998, 15 million Linux users around the world, a tripling of 1997 figures for retail sales. Retail sales continued to grow substantially during the first half of 1999, in part because the retail price of Linux was even lower than Windows (actually, it could be downloaded from the Web for free, but users wouldn't get documentation and service); Linux was considered more reliable; and it was sometimes faster, which might have caused the sales jump. According to speed tests, Linux might be as much as 50 percent faster than Windows NT on the typical desktop computer used by one person.

At the start of 1999, retail versions of Windows 98 were easily outselling Linux in the country's largest computer superstores. By May of that year, the two operating systems were neck and neck, and in some outlets Linux was beating Windows 98 hands down. This turnaround in Linux's (and Microsoft's) retail sales fortunes caused *Business Week*'s technology columnist, Stephen Wildstrom, to admit that at the start of 1999, he had thought it would be "years before Linux was ready for ordinary folks, since it was way too difficult to install and use." By mid-1999, he had to state, "Boy, was I wrong," because Linux's installation and interface had been made far more user-friendly by versions developed by Caldera and Red Hat.

More important, Linux's rapid advance severely challenges the Justice Department's and the court's most fervent claim, that Microsoft's market position is indomitable. That is no longer true, if it ever was. Not only does Microsoft need to worry about "unknown future threats," to use Fisher's words; but the threat is real today, although no one should expect Fisher and his colleagues at the Justice Department to concede that point.

Interestingly, as Franklin Fisher gave his courtroom testimony about Microsoft's market invincibility, one of the country's largest computer superstore chains was ordering the same number of copies of Linux as of Windows 98 and Mac OS 8. The International Data Corporation was no longer putting Linux in its "other" category of operating systems. It had given Linux its own category and was making individual sales forecasts for Linux as it has always done for Windows and other major operating systems.

If, in the last half of 1999, Justice Department officials and the judge had wanted to see whether Linux was a "commercially reasonable alternative" to Windows, all they would have had to do was visit their local CompUSA or Micro Center or Frye's (as I did) and look at the often equal shelf space devoted to Linux and Windows 98, and then take a look at the floor space devoted to the various "flavors" of iMac computers and the Mac operating system. They would have quickly realized that Linux was for real and that the Mac was back.

Instead, the judge kept his head buried deeply in legal sand and was able to write forcefully, "By itself, Linux's open-source development model shows no signs of liberating that operating system from the cycle of consumer preferences and developer incentives that, when fueled by Windows' enormous reservoir of applications, prevents non-Microsoft operating systems from competing." How such a conclusion can be offered as a "finding of fact" makes even casual observers of the computer market shake their heads in disbelief.

⚖

There is an interesting story behind the emergence of Linux, especially the version of the story told by the company called Red Hat, which is marketing Linux. That story included the fact that major key supporters of the government's case against Microsoft are investors and board members of important Microsoft competitors, including Oracle, Netscape, Sun, and IBM. The Silicon Valley venture capitalist John Doerr's company also has a financial stake in several firms supporting the government's case. These investors are hardly listening to the judge for investment advice.

But the really interesting story in operating systems for servers (and possibly eventually desktops) may be the totally free operating system known to techies (but so far, no one else) as FreeBSD. Yet, FreeBSD runs the one thousand servers used by the world's busiest Web site, Yahoo!, which has 80 million visitors a month, as well as by the multitude of servers used by Hotmail, a free e-mail server owned by, would you believe, Microsoft. In fall 1999, BSD also ran on 15 percent of all servers connected to the Internet and its market share was growing along with Linux's. Microsoft needs to worry all right, not so much about its future standing in court as its future standing in the market.

Of course, Microsoft's market position cannot be assessed on the basis of its current retail sales performance vis-a-vis that of other companies in different markets. And the server and desktop markets are fairly separate—though not totally: many people use several versions of operating systems on their desktops for technical reasons (I do). But even though the vast majority of all copies of Windows sold are installed on new computers, the continuing growth in retail sales of Linux and FreeBSD refutes a very important aspect of the Justice Department's suit: the much lauded "scale economies" and "network effects" are not, after all, the impenetrable barriers to entry that the Justice Department has made them out to be. Moreover, the operating system market is far more fluid and subject to unanticipated changes in short periods of time than the Justice Department has asserted. Otherwise, how could "little" Linux, or unknown FreeBSD, beat up on Microsoft so badly in such a short time? How could Mac make the comeback that it has?

After all the evidence was taken in the trial, Joel Klein, the assistant attorney general for antitrust, stepped before the reporters on the courthouse steps and declared once again that Microsoft remained a "serious, serious problem." He then added, "If you think that Microsoft's operating system monopoly is going to go away in two or three years, then we shouldn't have brought the case. But I obviously don't believe that. What this case is about is protecting innovation to make a dynamic industry even more dynamic and innovative."

Do you really think that people in high offices in Washington know what the market will look like in two to three years when so many did not anticipate—could not have anticipated—the advent of Linux just a year before the assistant attorney general and the judge made their pronouncements? The case is really about whether Klein, Jackson, or anyone else can know the future of technology. The fact is that that future will evolve gradually but relentlessly from the trillions of ongoing interactions of millions of people around the world. In a world that runs on Internet time, some things are just not knowable for people in high offices to make the kinds of predictions they would like to make. In today's technological world, "two or three years" is a lifetime for many products, including operating systems.

ONGOING DYNAMIC CHANGE

The recent success of Linux and Mac operating systems are clear indications that the industry is already dynamic. But if more evidence is needed, there is plenty of such evidence of dynamism that the Justice Department and Court have tried to sidestep or dismiss. There's good reason to believe that America Online has Microsoft on its radar screen. AOL has developed a customer base—20 million at last count—that offers it a ready-made foundation for creating an alternative computer platform, for many programmers will see AOL's customer base as worthy of serving with applications designed for any operating system AOL chooses. AOL's server system will allow it to deploy network computing, which means that programs and disk space can be rented on a per-use basis or for a monthly charge, much as cell phone systems are rented today. AOL bought Netscape in the fall of 1998, just after the Microsoft trial began, which means that AOL now has the necessary browser technology to make network computing a reality, if it chooses to go in that direction and if Microsoft prices its products so high that network computing becomes commercially viable. By the time this book is published, in spring 2000, AOL may have a TV-based network computing appliance, AOL TV, that will allow its customers to use AOL on their TVs, possibly without ever booting up Windows.

Larry Ellison, the chairman and CEO of Oracle, complains all the time about Microsoft, the software bully, but also admits that Oracle has never been bullied. When pressed on a talk show to talk about Oracle's future, Ellison indicated that Microsoft might not be the serious problem both he and Klein had made it out to be:

Well, let's look at the facts. Right now, the fastest-growing segment of my industry is the Internet. Of the ten largest consumer Web sites, all ten of them use the Oracle database. In the ten largest business-to-business Web sites, nine of the ten use Oracle. None of them use Microsoft. Every single Web portal, things like Lycos, Excite, Yahoo!, all use Oracle. None use Microsoft. Microsoft's been in the database business for a decade and they continue to lose. They've been losing share to us at a faster and faster rate over the last several years. In fact, we dominate. We almost have a Gates-like share in the Internet and it's the Internet that's driving the business.

Sun Microsystems' CEO, Scott McNealy, also seems to see a bleak future for Microsoft. In an interview in January 1999, McNealy noted:

We added in Netscape and AOL as distribution channels, getting Java 2 into the tens of millions of disks that AOL sends out, so that the world is going to be littered with Java 2, just on the desktop. Then you add in what's going on in Personal Java and Java Card and Java on the server, and all of a sudden we have a very, very interesting, stable volume platform that gives any developer for the telco or ISP community a virus-free, object-oriented, smart-card-to-supercomputer scalable, down-the-experience-curve platform that allows you to interoperate with every kind of device you can imagine.

In August 1999, McNealy announced that Sun Microsystems had bought out the German software company Star Division with the intent of putting its business applications, all written for Linux, on Sun's central servers so that copies of all of the applications could be downloaded free of charge. Then in September, McNealy announced Sun's second major push (the first push two years earlier had been a failure) to establish its own brand of network computing, the $499 "Sun Ray." It was billed as an alternative platform for corporations, a "desktop appliance" that would allow workers to connect to their companies' networks and work off the central server's operating system and collection of stored programs and files, including the applications from Star Division. McNealy's intent is to rent computer power that can be tapped from anywhere in the subscribing company.

The likely viability of Sun's efforts to establish network computing as an alternative to desktop computing has been supported by a little-known Florida-based software firm, Citrix, which has developed a means of adapting personal computer programs so that they can run on servers, and then separating the computing functions that are done on central servers from what the user sees on the monitor. Citrix plans to charge for the rental of the office software on a per-unit-used basis. This should bring about a radical reduction in TCO—"total cost of ownership"—the big bugaboo of personal computing for firms. The cost of the hardware—personal computer itself—is a minor share of firms' TCO; the major share of TCO is the cost of servicing the computers and upgrading the programs. Under network computing, high TCOs will be a thing of the past, or so the promotions go. According to Mark Templeton, Citrix's CEO, his company has found that a firm now requires on average one system administrator for every 50 users. With Citrix's system, a company will only need one administrator for every 500 to 700 users.

Does anyone seriously believe that McNealy and Templeton don't have designs on Microsoft's operating system and business applications market? You won't convince Sun and Citrix that Microsoft is the impregnable software fortress the Justice Department and court claim it is.

If it were, why would a firm like Sun buy Star Division? Why go to the pain and expense of developing network computing? Just so McNealy could "stick it" to his nemesis, Bill Gates? Maybe so, in part. As will be seen, McNealy has not kept his disdain for Gates a secret. But that can't be the whole story. I suspect McNealy, a savvy business entrepreneur, has soberly and realistically appraised the business opportunities involved. If he hasn't, the financial market is an unforgiving taskmaster, and investors can be expected to drop Sun in favor of companies whose CEOs do not allow their personal feelings to influence their business decisions.

The efforts of such as McNealy and Oracle's Larry Ellison may only be the beginning of a broad-based replace-Windows movement among computer and software manufacturers. In late October 1999, Dell, Gateway, and Compaq were all readying personal computers that shifted the focus of computing from the desktop to the Web. Moreover, dozens of firms demonstrated "network (information) appliances" at the fall 1999 Comdex in Las Vegas, and many of these Internet appliances allow users to send e-mails, surf the Internet, and undertake network computing, without Windows. No wonder computer insiders have begun to talk glibly about the "post-PC era."

The *Wall Street Journal*'s legal columnist, Holman Jenkins, has observed, "Microsoft built us a common platform by committing itself to a big, bulky, backwards-compatible Windows, and now it's stuck with a platform too big and bulky to be useful for a new generation of devices. These gadgets will run happily on any number of narrowly targeted, code-light operating systems, as long as they speak the common language of the Internet. Even Mr. McNealy predicts Windows will have less than 50% of the market by 2002—that is, in 'two or three years.'" Yet with blinders in place, the judge in the case insists that Microsoft cannot possibly be expected to feel the market heat from its presumed monopoly ways for the next "few years."

No one can be sure how computing will evolve in the near or long term. The desktop computing system may prevail in spite of forays by competitors. Then again, network computing might seriously erode the desktop market, or desktop and network computing might share the market that Microsoft now has practically to itself. Perhaps the new Internet strategy that Microsoft announced in September 1999, dubbed DNA (for distributed Internet applications)—which will make the Web, not desktop computers, the focus of its company efforts—will enable the company to grow with Web-based business as it grew with desktop-based business.

It bears repeating that the future of computing is highly unpredictable because so much information about what will happen is not now known and is unknowable by those who care to make predictions. Future events will unfold in response to a multitude of actions taken by people in the computer industry who are scattered throughout the world and who have information that no one else has. What we do know is that the Justice Department and the judge have no better idea of where the industry will be than we do. We also know that a lot of people in the computing industry stand ready to take advantage of profitable opportunities that will arise as soon as any established, dominant firm stumbles—or falls victim to the presumption, held dear by the Justice Department and the court—that with current market dominance comes sustainable monopoly power.

MICROSOFT, A HIDEOUT FOR MODERN-DAY ROBBER BARONS?

As noted at the start of Chapter 2, the newspaper columnist Maureen Dowd did what so many Microsoft critics have done in one way or another: she compared the great wealth of Bill Gates to that of John D. Rockefeller, stated that Rockefeller was a robber baron, and then deduced that Gates is some modern-day reincarnation of a nineteenth-century robber baron. The critics want to pin the robber-baron label on Gates by juxtaposing his name and company, Microsoft, with Rockefeller's name and company, Standard Oil. Both have been involved in major antitrust suits of their respective eras, for supposedly similarly bad monopoly practices.

Should Gates be miffed at being associated with Rockefeller and Standard Oil? Not according to recent scholarship. The economists Donald Boudreaux and Burton Folsom have recently argued that the association of the two cases "is unjust not because Gates' Microsoft is *different* from Rockefeller's Standard Oil. Rather, it is unjust precisely because Gates' Microsoft is *similar* to Standard Oil in its effectiveness at promoting consumer welfare." It's true that Rockefeller controlled close to 90 percent of the oil market throughout the 1880s (Gates has a similar percentage of the Intel-based operating system market today), but did Rockefeller act like a monopolist during the decade? Boudreaux and Folsom say, emphatically, no. The company achieved its high market share in part by innovating (finding ways of extracting 300 by-products from crude oil) and by lowering its prices—not increasing its prices as practicing monopolies are expected to do. The authors point out:

> Under Rockefeller, Standard Oil plowed its profits into bigger and better equipment, and as volume increased, he hired chemists and developed 300 by-products from each barrel of oil. They ranged from paint and varnish to dozens of lubricating oils to anesthetics. As for the main product, kerosene, Rockefeller made it so cheaply that whale oil, coal oil, and, for a while, electricity lost out in the race to light American homes,

factories, and streets. "We had vision," Rockefeller later said. "We saw the vast possibilities of the oil industry, stood at the center of it, and brought our knowledge and imagination and business experience to bear in a dozen, in twenty, in thirty directions."

In the process, as Standard Oil dominated the market in the 1880s, the price of oil went from 9.125 cents per gallon in 1880 to 7.375 cents per gallon in 1890 to 5.91 cents per gallon in 1897, a decline of 35 percent between 1880 and 1887. Were his prices "predatory," intended to wipe out his competitors for the purpose of charging higher prices later, as he was charged with doing? If they were intended to be predatory, Rockefeller never got to see the upside of his falling prices. The falling oil prices did wipe out a bunch of producers, and they might have thought that Rockefeller practiced predation for predation's sake. In reality, the so-called robber baron seemed to believe that the mantra of his company should be "Do well by serving the consumer well." Boudreaux and Folsom cite Rockefeller's letter to his partners in the mid-1880s: "Let the good work go on. We must ever remember we are refining oil for the poor man and he must have it cheap and good." He said in another letter: "Hope we can continue to hold out with the best illuminator in the world at the *lowest* price."

When Rockefeller refused to invest heavily in the Texas oil boom and was slow to switch from kerosene to gasoline production, Standard Oil's market share started falling and was down to 67 percent in 1911, when the government filed an antitrust suit and broke up the company.

This brief review of the Rockefeller record will hardly deter many of Microsoft's harshest critics as they try to establish guilt by association with icons of antitrust history. Nevertheless, the evidence of Rockefeller's real record must be set out because it might give open-minded readers reason to pause before they accept claims that a high market share or charges of antitrust violations are conclusive proofs of monopoly. The history of antitrust enforcement is replete with miscarriages of justice.

EQUAL ANTITRUST JUSTICE FOR ALL

To be candid, I don't like the government's case against Microsoft at the most fundamental of levels partially because it does disservice to the concept of "equal justice for all": that everyone will be held to the same legal standard. But Microsoft and Netscape have never been held to the same legal standard. Microsoft stands accused of predatory pricing, because it has given away its Internet browser. Netscape did the same thing years ago, killing off the then existing browser standard, Mosaic.

The Justice Department, court, and Microsoft's critics seem to consider Microsoft a special case because Windows has become an "essential facility," something on the order of a single bridge that connects an island to the mainland. This concept seems to be intended to advance their argument beyond the simple claim that Microsoft is a monopolist. The argument might be made that the owners of the bridge should be regulated in ways that other firms on the island or mainland are not. The bridge is a "choke point" that controls the flow of people and commerce.

The problem with the analogy of Microsoft to a bridge is that in the case of a bridge, the geography of the island and mainland may preclude altogether the construction of other bridges. That is not the case in the operating system market. The landscape in "cyberspace" is hardly like the landscape associated with two land masses with a channel of water running between them. The landscape in cyberspace is multidimensional. Indeed, the landscape is created as program developers do their work. All kinds of bridges have and can be constructed between people and computers, especially since, as pointed out at the end of the first chapter, programs are nothing more than sequences of *1*'s and *0*'s that can be arranged and rearranged into an infinite number of alternative sequences. As noted in the previous chapter, at least nineteen alternative "bridges," or operating systems, exist, as does the potential for many others to be developed, which means that Windows is just not "essential" in the same way that the bridge is. IBM's OS/2 is also available for use as a "bridge." Nor does Windows have the control over the flow of commerce that the bridge has. Thus, claims that Microsoft is an essential facility should be viewed as nothing more than a rephrasing of the claim that Microsoft is a monopolist.

THE JUSTICE DEPARTMENT'S NEED FOR MICROSOFT TO BE A MONOPOLIST

Acceptance of the Justice Department's claim that Microsoft is a monopolist is critically important to the case. However, even if Microsoft were a monopolist, the case would not be solid. Merely *being* a monopoly is not a crime. The government must show that monopoly power either has been achieved illegally (through anticompetitive means, which the Justice Department has never alleged) or is used illegally to thwart competition to the detriment of consumers. Only then would the courts design remedies. This means that the government has to show that Microsoft's actions have been harmful to consumers, not just to competitors.

Long before we arrive at that point, however, it must first be shown that Microsoft is a monopoly. If Microsoft is not a monopoly, and has never been one, Microsoft's actions can't be in violation of the antitrust law, and the government's antitrust case totally falls apart. No wonder the Justice Department and court would like its claim that Microsoft is a monopolist to be accepted as an article of received antitrust faith. No wonder it repeats the "Microsoft is a monopolist" mantra every chance it gets.

A presumption about Microsoft's monopoly status has a tremendous effect on how its actions are interpreted. Once it is accepted that Microsoft is a monopoly, it is all too easy for the courts and everyone else to interpret any of Microsoft's market strategies—for example, its low prices and contract restrictions—as anticompetitive. If the claim is not accepted, Microsoft's actions might be viewed as competitive. The Justice Department has chosen to sue Microsoft for the simple reason that it has accepted the monopoly mantra, which means it cannot imagine (or does not want anyone else to imagine) that Microsoft's actions have any conceivable competitive justification.

For example, if you believe that Microsoft is a monopolist, then you will interpret its browser giveaways as the actions of a monopolist, not of a competitive marketer. No sane monopolist would do such a thing, unless it had some devious intent, for example, to protect and extend its monopoly powers. Hence, the price, which is zero in a give-away, has to be termed "predatory," a price intended to wipe out competitors so that a higher price can be charged with impunity at a future point in time.

If, on the other hand, you do not believe that Microsoft is a monopolist (for all the reasons enumerated above), Microsoft's give-away can be viewed as a common-sense response to actual competitive pressures. Microsoft must charge virtually zero for its browser because it must fend off competitors who it fears can erode its dominance in the market for operating systems by way of a similar browser give-away. This is especially the case if production exhibits supply-side and demand-side scale economies, because such economies can work to the advantage of new entrants.

Judge Jackson catalogues at great length in his Findings of Fact Microsoft's efforts to get computer manufacturers and Internet service providers to adopt and distribute Internet Explorer. If you believe the monopolist mantra, these might be seen as the actions of a monopolist to exclude Navigator and to prevent the breakdown of what the judge calls the "applications barrier to entry" (those 70,000 Windows applications), which Judge Jackson sees as protecting Microsoft from competition. But this so-called applications barrier to entry may have been the consequence of Microsoft's competitive behavior, when it offered users a compelling deal years ago (and continues to do), which caused programmers to write their 70,000 applications for Windows.

By the way, no programmer was forced to write Windows applications. The Windows programmers could have written for Apple or IBM if these operating systems had offered the prospect of a more competitive network than Microsoft. One of the benefits of the Microsoft Windows network is that Microsoft stands as the manager of the standards for the network. Though all members of the network most likely want to garner the benefits of the network, some might not like all demands that the standards manager imposes on them. Indeed, it is a sure bet that network members disagree on many particulars in the standard, just as some people prefer the

Apple desktop to the Microsoft desktop. Indeed, programmers grumble all the time about how "low tech" Windows is (which suggests that disagreements on standards abound). Nevertheless, all are held together in the network because of the consistency across all users that the manager brings to the standard. If Microsoft tried to accommodate the interests of everyone, including the preferences of some for a system tailored to all of their individual needs and wants, you can imagine that Windows would be a mess.

So it is with the inclusion of Internet Explorer in Windows. As the judge found, there are no doubt some users who might prefer Windows without Internet Explorer and there may be some computer manufacturers who prefer to offer their customers the option of two versions of Windows, one with and one without Internet Explorer. (We concede the judge's point that the inclusion of Internet Explorer soaks up hard-disk space, a presumed user "harm." But for Window Millennium, which should be available by the time this book is published, we are only talking about seventeen cents' worth of disk space at the current price of hard drives!) The real question here is: Are there potential efficiency gains from Microsoft's requiring all computer manufacturers to take Windows with Internet Explorer? The answer is clearly yes. Such a standard can contribute network benefits, and programmers know that a lot of people actually do want their browser integrated into Windows, for all kinds of reasons the judge never acknowledges. For example, users don't have to deal with two programs and two service support systems.

But there is an even more important reason Microsoft might want to press computer manufacturers, Internet service providers, application writers, and users to accept Windows with an integrated browser, and all of these people might, on balance, want Microsoft to apply pressure: the integration of the browser can hold off the breakup of the network, which can mean a loss to everyone of the network benefits that are so dear to the heart of the Justice Department and court's analysis of software markets. It is evident that Microsoft, the network manager, saw in the Internet in general and Netscape in particular a serious threat to the viability of its network. The judge has decided that at every turn Microsoft was working only for the interest of its investors. Microsoft might indeed have been working for the interest of its investors but may also have simultaneously benefited its network members. The network members—even those who were pressed to adopt and distribute Internet Explorer— may have wanted to have everyone pressed to adopt and distribute Internet Explorer. By having a browser with Windows, the network members got the benefits of knowing that their network would not be easily undermined, fragmented, and dispersed among competing networks—the net result of which could be a loss of network benefits (as well as the loss of the prospects of having 70,000 applications to choose from). From this perspective, the inclusion of the browser in Windows and the press to get it adopted and distributed as widely as Windows can be seen as a competitive (not a monopolistic) move against alternative computing platforms.

MICROSOFT'S GREATEST COMPETITION: ITSELF

The Justice Department's case and the court's Findings of Fact are grounded in the kind of nineteenth-century market analysis that is based on a simple count of producers in the market. The Justice Department and court think that Microsoft has little or no competition. That's because it ignores everyone producing an operating system other than Microsoft, and therefore declares the count is one. In doing that, it has overlooked the fact that Microsoft faces serious competition from an unsuspected source: itself.

Microsoft faces a competitive dilemma when it considers upgrading Windows: If Microsoft changes the basic code in Windows so much that new versions are no longer compatible with old versions, it raises the specter of leaving its valuable network behind and of giving potential rivals a chance to pick off part of its customer base. Many application programmers will understandably reason that if they have to rewrite their own applications, perhaps from scratch, to fit the radically new version of Windows, they might as well consider rewriting their programs for some other operating system. Many buyers will also conclude that they might as well consider moving to a new operating system. Both buyers and programmers will want Microsoft to maintain the network as much as Microsoft does and, therefore, will want Microsoft to do what will come naturally to Microsoft under the circumstances of the network it has created: Make sure that any new version of Windows is broadly compatible with applications written for the old version.

However, this means that Microsoft must trade one competitive threat (developers of alternative operating systems) for another (competition with itself): Every time Microsoft introduces a new "backward-compatible" version of Windows, the new version must compete with the existing stock of old versions of Windows—because old versions of Windows installed on computers around the world do not evaporate when the new version is released. Unfortunately for the Justice Department's case against Microsoft, any existing version of Windows is a highly durable good. This means that consumer responsiveness to price in Microsoft's market is elevated not only by the existence of network effects, but also by the ability of the tens of millions of Microsoft's customers to stay with old versions of Windows. This means that Microsoft must work hard at holding switching costs down, which means holding prices down and minimizing the retraining costs.

As a matter of fact, only 16 percent of Intel-based personal computer users had by 1999 upgraded to Windows 98, according to IDC, a computer industry statistics keeper. Slightly more than two fifths of all users stayed with Windows 95, and a fifth of all users were still using versions of Windows and DOS that Microsoft stopped selling in the early 1990s. Microsoft, a monopolist that can impose its will on all others? It seems to have a tough time reselling to many of its own users!

The University of Chicago professor of law and economics Ronald Coase, a Noble Laureate, wrote a celebrated article years ago in which he pointed out that even a monopolistic producer of a durable good would charge a competitive price for its product. Why? Because no sane person would buy all or any portion of the durable good at a price above the competitive level. He used the example of a monopoly owner of a plot of land. If the owner tried to sell the land piecemeal, he would have to lower the price on each parcel until all the land was bought, which means the owner would have to charge the competitive price: the price where the demand for the land and the supply of the land come together. It might be thought that the sole owner of land would be able to restrict sales and get more than the competitive price. However, buyers would reason that if the monopoly owner eventually wanted to sell the remaining land, it could only be sold at less than the price of land already sold, which means the buyers who bought the land at the high price would suffer a loss in the market value of their land. This means that the buyers would wait to buy until the price came down, but then the owner would sell nothing at the monopoly price, and would only be able to sell the land at the competitive price.

Although Coase's thesis was founded on land, a good more durable than Windows, the argument remains applicable. It suggests that the durability of Windows is one reason Microsoft must seek prices lower than the monopoly price. In addition, Microsoft has to charge even lower prices just to ensure that users of old versions will *consider* switching to the new version. The Coase analysis helps explain why the price of Windows is as low as it is ($40 to $60 per copy for computer manufacturers, $89 for retail customers). Microsoft has to charge such low prices because it has to compete aggressively with itself, just like the sole land owner who contemplates selling off parcels of land to competing buyers. Microsoft must give Windows users a good reason to actually make the switch to the new version.

The Justice Department wants the court to believe that Microsoft had no good business reason to integrate Internet Explorer into Windows 98—other than to be predatory against Netscape. There's one very good reason Microsoft must do something like integrate an important new feature—for example, an Internet browser—every time it comes out with a new version of Windows: it must give its customer base—its network—a good reason to spend even a modest sum of money for the new version. When Microsoft was contemplating the construction of Windows 98, it was obvious to just about everyone in the computer industry, including people at Netscape and Microsoft, that the Internet would play an important role in the future of computing. Microsoft had to move aggressively toward making Windows useful in the emerging Internet world and thereby give its customer base a reason to move to Windows 98. Microsoft also had to give its customers a good reason not to move toward rival operating systems that could easily emerge.

The court stresses that Microsoft's monopoly power is self-evident from the fact that when it brings out a new version of Windows, it raises the price of old versions.

"In a competitive market," Judge Jackson writes, "one would expect the price of an older operating system to stay the same or decrease upon the release of a newer, more attractive version." The judge once again succumbs to industrial-era economic thinking: that "old goods" left in inventory should be sold off at the highest price possible, which usually means at a substantial discount. However, copies of Windows are not kept in inventory. They actually don't exist until the point of sale and are transferred to new computers electronically. There is a good reason Microsoft raises the price of old versions of Windows to the price of the new version: it wants to move its existing and prospective network members to the new and improved version and the new and improved network, which can have network benefits as programmers can reduce their attention to old versions. Again, what can be seen as a move of a monopolist against its users can actually be a benefit for everyone involved in the network, which is all the more reason for us to ask: Do we really want the Justice Department and the courts deciding on software content and pricing strategy when they obviously don't understand the market forces they are observing at work?

MICROSOFT'S MARKET SHARE

Virtually every news article on Microsoft repeats a familiar refrain: Microsoft is a monopolist because 90 percent or more of all personal computers sold come equipped with the Windows operating system. We've noted that the 90 percent market share figure comes from the government's case and relies on a 1997 study undertaken by the International Data Corporation. As can be seen in Table 2.1, the correct figure for 1997 is 95 percent.

Fortunately for the Justice Department, but unfortunately for Microsoft, many media reports on Microsoft's market share fail to note what has already been mentioned but needs to be reemphasized here, that Microsoft's often-cited percentage share of the market applies to a fairly narrow definition of the computer market, namely, only those Intel-compatible personal computers that have Intel microprocessors (or compatible microprocessors) and are used by single individuals. This is a fraction of the total market for operating systems. As the Hudson Institute economist Alan Reynolds has correctly observed in the *Wall Street Journal*, this definition of the market is grossly misleading, if not fraudulent, because it does not cover many personal computer purchases that most people would presume are covered in the rubric "personal computers."

For example, it does not cover purchases of Apple computers, which accounted for 9.6 percent of all personal computer sales in the fourth quarter of 1998. Thus, Windows could have been loaded on no more than 90.4 percent of all personal computers. Why are Apple computers not included in the "market"? The answer is that iMac and other Apple computers are not Intel-compatible. Hence, the growing popularity of iMacs will never have an impact on Microsoft's Intel-compatible "market share," as the Justice Department computes it. As Reynolds observes, "[E]ven if Apple grabbed half the market, Microsoft's share of Intel-based computers would be unaffected," which means that Apple's recent resurgence in sales would leave the Justice Department unfazed. Microsoft would still have more than 90 percent of the market.

Reynolds goes on to point out that the Justice Department's chosen definition of the market also necessarily excludes Sun Microsystems' work stations, many of which operate much like personal computers and use Sun's Solaris operating system, which can run on Intel-based machines. The reason? They are, generally, networked, hence, not "single-user clients." Using a more reasonable definition of the market would result in a smaller market share for Microsoft than is reported. Personal computers equipped with Microsoft's Windows NT operating systems are also not counted as part of Microsoft's market share because NT is normally used on servers. If all server computers were included, then surely Microsoft's market share would fall, because Microsoft only has a third of the network computer business.

Finally, Microsoft's market share also does not include the sales of handheld computers (for example, the Palm Pilot) or sub-notebooks (for example, Psion and IBM's WorkPad), even though some of them have keyboards and the computing capacity to run many of the same business, personal finance, games, and e-mail programs as Windows 98. Microsoft Windows CE, a stripped-down operating system for handhelds and subnotebooks, only has 25 percent of that market.

The projections for Microsoft's market share through 2001 will also likely be lower than what is reported in Table 2.1. Those projections were done in 1997, before sales of the Linux operating system jumped radically in 1998, to nearly 3 million copies; it also has been estimated that millions of copies of Linux have been downloaded free of charge via the Web.

No one knows Microsoft's exact market share for all personal computers operating in the world. What we do know is that its market share is significantly less than the often-quoted 90 percent (or the 95 percent cited by the Justice Department). The 90-percent figure seems intended more to score public relations/legal points than accurately to describe the magnitude of Microsoft's influence in its markets. Citing data from the Software and Information Industry Association, Reynolds estimates that Windows 95 and 98 ran on only two thirds of all home computers. He concludes, "Exhibit One [Table 2.1] is normally expected to be the most powerful evidence a prosecutor can muster. If that's true in this case, Microsoft's shareholders deserve reimbursement for legal expenses [incurred by Microsoft in its defense]."

CONCLUDING COMMENTS

As I hope I have made clear, much of the Microsoft case is founded on the pervasive use of a single word, "monopoly." In Chapter 1 and this chapter, we have sought to understand what "monopoly" means in both economic and legal terms. When the actual meaning of the word is examined, Microsoft doesn't appear to be the monopoly it has been made out to be. Microsoft's pricing policies don't seem to be those of a monopolist, and it certainly doesn't have the market share that has been claimed. In highlighting this point in the *Wall Street Journal*, Alan Reynolds has probably done more to undermine the government's case than all of Microsoft's lawyers combined.

Reynolds has acknowledged that Microsoft has a substantial share of the personal computer operating system market. At the same time, he has also flat-out declared that the Justice Department's case is flawed at its core. Contrary to the Justice Department claims, Microsoft obviously has substantial competition. The competitive threat exists *today*. Other software firms may have a third or more of the personal computer market. They are already in the market, so obviously there are no barriers to entry for those firms. The fact that Linux, written by a college student, could enter Microsoft's market and then expand to over 15 million users in a few short years when Microsoft supposedly controlled over 90 percent of the operating system market would seem to suggest that Microsoft is not the big bad monopoly after all. Judge Jackson's fabrication of the overarching "applications barrier to entry" behind which Microsoft works its monopolistic will is, when examined closely, dubious at best. A truly superior computing platform really doesn't need tens of thousands of applications to make it viable. For the vast majority of computer users, a dozen or so will do. And applications programmers would gladly flock to a truly superior system sold at a lower price. However, it has to be added that any firm that seeks to challenge Microsoft's Windows platform should understand that it will need to make the challenge with a truly superior platform sold at a more attractive price than the cost of Windows and the attendant applications. That would not be a tough go if Microsoft were intent on acting long into the future like a monopolist.

⚖ CHAPTER 4 ⚖

Digital Predation

THE JUSTICE DEPARTMENT WANTS TO HAVE its legal cake and eat it, too. It wants to make sure that the courts and public believe that Microsoft's good fortune is largely attributable to the intrinsic nature of Microsoft's market and the company's anticompetitive business practices, not to anything it may have done right, like make better business decisions and produce superior programs for eager buyers. Apparently the Justice Department hopes that if nothing is said about the value of Microsoft's products, which consumers freely choose to buy, its claim that Microsoft has illegally sought to maintain and extend its "monopoly" will be accepted as fact. The Justice Department's courtroom tactics may help it win the case, but they certainly undermine the credibility of antitrust enforcement, which is supposed to be about even-handed treatment under the law, not about winning for winning's sake.

And it does appear that the Justice Department just wants to win. But it would like to do so without carrying its claims about modern digital markets to their logical conclusions. If it did, its case would be undermined. If there is something really new about the digital age, it is the so-called "special economics" of digital products that challenge old ways of thinking about monopoly.

BUILDING BETTER DIGITAL MOUSETRAPS

Nowhere in its arguments does the Justice Department come close to commending Microsoft for anything, and Judge Jackson uses only a couple of paragraphs of the 61,000 words in his Findings of Fact to acknowledge Microsoft's contributions. But this is understandable, from their point of view. To spend more time on Microsoft's contributions to users and programmers and vendor welfare could throw into question the whole case, which is anchored on the proposition that Microsoft has engaged in digital predation against its competitor, not that it has succeeded so wildly because its products simply are preferred by consumers.

The truth is that there is much to commend Microsoft for. Windows is hardly a perfect operating system, but few software programmers aspire to perfection, especially when tens of millions of lines of code are involved. Actually, no one programmer at Microsoft can understand the entire program, which makes the fact that it works without too many bugs all the more miraculous. Despite the bugs, all technical reviews rate Windows as a pretty darn good operating system, perhaps better than all the others. It is recognized that Windows seeks to provide compatibility across machines made by thousands of computer manufacturers, all with variations on the personal computer design, which is a huge challenge. Windows' high market share speaks volumes about what a lot of people think about its relative merits.

If Microsoft were an abusive monopoly, as claimed, then you might think the abuse would show up in inferior products across the board. At least, we should expect that the quality of Microsoft's products would fall as its market dominance has risen. But this simply has not happened. In fact, the opposite has occurred.

The economics professor Stan Liebowitz of the University of Texas–Dallas and Professor Stephen Margolis of North Carolina State undertook a survey of how well Microsoft products fared in reviews by major computer publications when compared with its major competitors. Their conclusion is that Microsoft has achieved its success in "the old-fashioned way—with better products." In the 1986–96 period, there were 38 reviews in major computer magazines that compared Microsoft's personal computer version of its spreadsheet program, Excel, with its major competitor, Lotus 1–2–3. Twenty-eight of the reviewers gave Excel a higher rating than Lotus. Only one gave Lotus a higher rating than Excel (the remaining reviewers rated the two programs more or less equal).

In word processing the situation is similar. When DOS was the dominant operating system, WordPerfect was the dominant word-processing program and won most of the comparison reviews. After the introduction of Windows in 1985, however, WordPerfect began to falter badly, mainly because it was late to market with a Windows version. In the late 1980s Microsoft prodded WordPerfect to develop a Windows version, but when it did appear—late—it was full of frustrating bugs, causing many users (like me) to switch to Word. Between 1992 and 1996, Microsoft's Word came out ahead of WordPerfect in 16 of 30 reviews that compared various word-processing programs; WordPerfect was rated the top program in only two reviews (the remaining reviewers rated the two word-processing programs more or less equal).

Liebowitz and Margolis also found that in areas of its business where Microsoft did poorly in comparison reviews, it also did poorly in the market. For example, Microsoft's personal finance program, Money, was rated better than Intuit's Quicken in only 6 percent of the reviews in the 1992–96 period, and Money remains a minor player in that market.

Microsoft's application prices have also fallen over the years. The price of Excel has fallen by 80 percent since 1986, and most of the price reduction came *after* Excel began to outshine Lotus 1–2–3 in the reviews, according to Liebowitz and Margolis. The price of word-processing programs rose by 35 percent from 1986 to 1990, when WordPerfect dominated reviews. But when Microsoft's Word began to dominate reviews, prices began to fall, leaving the price of word-processing programs in 1997 at a quarter of their 1990 level.

The Justice Department and court may think that Internet Explorer has rapidly gained market share *solely* because of Microsoft's dominance in operating systems or because of Microsoft pressure sales tactics, but the logic of such an assessment is hardly impregnable. This is because Internet Explorer's market share has risen as its performance has improved. Internet Explorer's improved performance is clearly evident in the growing number of "editor's choice awards" it received between 1995 and 1998 from major computer publications, for example, *PC Magazine, Computer Shopper,* and *InfoWorld*—far more than Netscape Navigator. When version 1.0 of Internet Explorer was released in 1995, it was not the choice of any of the thirteen major computer publication surveys. Versions 1.0 and 2.0 were never used by more than 10 percent of Internet surfers. Yet version 3.0, which was released in the third quarter of 1996, was the choice of a quarter of the thirteen publications and was tied with Netscape in half of the publications. After this, Internet Explorer began to gain market share, rising to 30 percent of users by the third quarter of 1997. Version 4.0, which was released in the fourth quarter of 1997, was the choice of 73 percent of the computer publications and was tied with Netscape Navigator in the remaining publications. These facts were presented in court by Microsoft's expert witness, Richard Schmalensee, and the Justice Department never contested them, but the court chose to ignore them.

In early 1999, the chief technology columnist for the *Wall Street Journal,* Walter Mossberg, commended Microsoft for introducing a new version of Internet Explorer, 5.0, which "puts it once again ahead of Netscape in the continuing browser wars." Similarly, the *New York Times* praised Microsoft for taking the lead in the "technical race with Netscape" with the introduction of Internet Explorer 5.0, which is actually a simpler program than version 4, and takes up one half the disk space.

We understand why the Justice Department doesn't bubble over with commendations for the many good reviews Microsoft has received on its products, including Internet Explorer. The Justice Department understands its legal bind: if it graciously commends Microsoft for doing anything right, it might suggest that Microsoft has been innovative and attentive to market demands—in fact, to consumer needs and wants that underlie market demands. Microsoft's market dominance might—just might—have been achieved on the merits of its products, not monopoly power. That is something the Justice Department doesn't want to concede. If

Microsoft has achieved great success by serving consumer needs in the past, then perhaps its efforts to integrate Internet Explorer into Windows was another smart business decision, one that is in consumers' best interests. In other words, the integration of Internet Explorer into Windows for free might not be predatory at all, in the legal sense. In a general way, all competitive actions could be called predatory: they are designed by a competitor to take the market shares of rivals. But the term has a specific legal meaning: the actions must be intended to destroy market rivals by pricing below cost and to acquire monopoly power. Lowering prices to meet or beat competition is not legally predatory.

Instead, to build its grossly one-sided case against Microsoft, which much of the press has dutifully passed on to the public as truth that is not subject to challenge, the Justice Department has asked its expert witnesses whether they saw any consumer benefits in the integration of the browser and operating system. The answers of most of the Justice Department witnesses were basically that they saw absolutely no such consumer benefits. But when we are speaking of programs as complicated and multifaceted in their potential benefits as Internet Explorer and Windows, how can any witness, no matter how expert, speak for more than a hundred million computer users around the world? Furthermore, benefits are necessarily subjective—for example, to many consumers the technical advantages of having a browser tightly integrated into Windows may be considerable, for these consumers might want their browser to have the same look and feel as their word processor. Can an expert declare this benefit to be nonexistent or irrelevant? Dare we allow the government and its experts to speak for all of the world's consumers? That is exactly what the Justice Department has asked the courts to permit them to do.

The Justice Department argued that having a browser integrated with the operating system introduces, for some firms, an unwanted security risk, for an employee might accidentally download and spread a computer virus throughout the firm. Even though Judge Jackson accepted the security argument in his Findings, he did press the security issue with one of the government's witnesses, Edward Felten, the head of the Secure Internet Programming Laboratory at Princeton University. Felten responded by noting that firms' computer administrators might worry that "your less-trained users might accidentally introduce a virus or something like that—you might well choose not to have browsers on your users' computers in order to prevent that means of spread of viruses." It is well known that there are dozens of ways to guard against viruses—for example, the erection of firewalls—that do not require tampering with Windows itself, and surely computer administrators are sufficiently competent to develop guards of their own.

Maybe some people do want an operating system without a browser, but who is in a better position to know this and to make relevant decisions, Edward Felten or Bill Gates? The Justice Department—by way of the courts—or consumers? These questions are of more than academic legal interest, for either way, some computer users' interests will be frustrated. If Microsoft gets its way, computer users with security problems might be less happy than they would otherwise be. If the Justice Department gets its way, computer users who want the benefits of an operating system with an integrated browser will be disappointed. Who is to say which group should be served?

The court could rule that Microsoft should be required to offer two operating systems, one with and one without a browser—in fact, Judge Jackson's Findings of Fact suggest that he might be considering this as a remedy—but this seems to be a solution that doesn't need to be imposed by a court. Sufficient demand for both operating systems would mean that both groups of consumers are willing to more than cover Microsoft's added costs of providing two products. If this were the case, surely Microsoft would be willing to do so. No one has ever accused Microsoft of not tapping potential profits. (Of course, the group not wanting the browser would have to be willing to accept the impairment of some features, like HTML help.)

By requiring the two operating systems, the court would introduce all the problems and lost benefits of network fragmentation discussed in the last chapter, and it would add an unneeded rigidity into the operating system market, for there would undoubtedly be some form of regulatory oversight by the government. Moreover, it would make it all the more difficult and costly for potential rivals to threaten Microsoft's market position. If legal principles are (or, rather, should be) applicable to all, then presumably newcomers to the operating system market would also be required to provide two types of their own operating systems.

In presenting its case, the Justice Department, however, repeatedly tried to argue on both sides of the browser issue. So it was on the integration issue. In the morning court session on June 10, 1999, Professor Felten said that Microsoft had done wrong by having Internet Explorer integrated with Windows. This was after the Justice Department had long argued that Internet Explorer was not really all that tightly integrated into Windows and could be easily removed, as Professor Felten had thought he had demonstrated. The Microsoft legal team showed the court that Professor Felten's program did not actually remove Internet Explorer; it only "hid" it, which meant the browser could still be used after it was supposedly removed, as demonstrated in court, very likely to Professor Felten's chagrin. And there is no question that Windows and Internet Explorer will be one unified, fully integrated operating system with the release of Windows Millennium in 2000.

What is distressing (if not maddening) about the Justice Department's and court's line of argument is that the claim is made that it is "bad" for the browser to be integrated with the operating system, but then it is also claimed that the browser is not really integrated and can be easily removed. If the latter is true—if the browser can be easily removed—why worry about the supposed security risk that was brought up in court? It seems that computer administrators who are truly concerned about the added security risk of having a browser on employee machines could easily remove the browsers, or even pay Microsoft or Professor Felten to remove them—or the computer administrators could even buy one of the other available operating systems that do not have the same security risks.

These computer administrators would incur added costs. However, if they don't incur those costs, someone else will. The other computer users who want an integrated browser will suffer the added costs of having to install a browser and the lost benefits of integration. Meanwhile, Microsoft's overriding goal ought to be to minimize the costs to all consumers, because that is how it can make the most profits.

Whether one product (a program) is sold bundled with another product (the operating system) will very likely depend on how commonly the two products are used together by consumers. When few consumers buy both products, then there is little advantage for the products to be sold together, and there is one good reason for leaving them unbundled: consumers have more flexibility in the combinations of goods they buy. However, when practically everyone buys both products, then there are good reasons for selling them as one product, especially when there are production economies: the bundling can save the consumer the time and trouble, and possibly added expense, of buying the products separately and making two installations.

There are other examples of the same kind of thinking. Several years ago, e-mail was not widely retrieved by travelers when they were on the road, and modems were almost always sold as an add-on to laptops. People could buy their laptops with or without modems. Now that e-mail retrieval has become common among travelers, laptop manufacturers have understandably begun manufacturing their laptops with built-in modems. The built-in modems are smaller, lighter, and better suited for particular parts of the laptops. Consumers get the added advantage of having a card slot freed up for other uses. Some consumers may never use the modem that is built in to their laptops, which means they have paid good money for which they will get no benefit. But if no laptop manufacturer is willing to sell laptops without modems, we've got to believe that it is cheaper for them to bundle the modem with the laptop than it is for them to incur the higher production costs of providing a line of laptops sans modem. This leads to the conclusion that laptop buyers, even those who will never use their modems, are better off by not having to choose between laptops with and without modems. This is the kind of market logic that is challenging the efficacy of modern-day enforcement of antitrust laws. If the enforcers can't get their thinking straight, and are pursuing unreasonable enforcement of outmoded ideas, how can we expect genuinely reasonable, efficiency-enhancing enforcement?

The same logic as that of the modem applies directly to Internet browsers and the operating system. Back in what now seems the dark ages of the Internet—say, in the mid-1990s—when the Web was fairly small and people did little browsing, there were few economies to be gained from integrating the browser with the operating system. All people needed back then was an operating system that controlled the hard drive and other devices in the computer box. Now, networks are expanding in all directions. People talk freely of networks, or computers linked together, as one big integrated computer and of the "worldwide hard drive." At the close of the century, nearly half of all computer users browse the Web to some extent. Nearly everyone connected with the computer industry predicts, along with *PC Magazine*, that "networking will be simultaneously invisible and ubiquitous." Accordingly, with Web browsing expected to rise dramatically over the next few years, people need an operating system that can work as easily within the Web as within the box. It makes far less sense today, and will make progressively less sense as browsing escalates, to leave the browser as an add-on, especially when including the browser adds little or nothing to the cost of the operating system package, and when the operating system is expected to operate as well outside the computer box as in it. (The court argued that browsers soak up hard-disk space, but this is truly a trivial cost consideration.)

Because Microsoft's browser is integrated with the operating system, Windows users get the added advantage of being able to have access to information wherever it is located, of having an improved Windows platform from the added support for HTML and HTTP, and of knowing that Microsoft has an incentive to make sure that the browser works well with the operating system. Otherwise, Microsoft will have to incur added support costs. Okay, the judge is right to point out that the support cost for Windows with or without Internet Explorer is incurred by the computer manufacturers because of their licensing agreement with Microsoft. However, he is wrong to suggest that Microsoft doesn't consider the support cost that computer manufactures have to incur with Windows. As the judge also recognizes, computer manufacturers often operate on thin profit margins, which is all the more reason that they would bargain to have Microsoft lower its price or give on some other contract margin in return for their taking Windows and having increased support costs, and this would be the case even if Microsoft were a monopolist charging monopoly prices.

The Justice Department obviously wanted to show that a host of Microsoft's market strategies can only be interpreted as those of a dominant firm behaving very badly, or exploiting its unearned privileged market position. The claim of the Justice Department's lead attorney, David Boies, and prosecution witnesses that there are *no benefits* whatsoever to be derived from integrating the browser into the operating system reflects unbelievable sciolism and arrogance. But they hope the courts and the public will accept one of their central tenets: Microsoft's contract restrictions, its integration of its browser with Windows, and its low, zero, or even negative prices for any of its software products have one overriding purpose—to destroy any and all rivals, actual or potential.

However, one of the reasons the Justice Department brought the case is that it accepted the argument that Netscape was seeking to devise a new computer platform that would combine Navigator with the Java programming language into a Web-based operating system that could run on any personal computer, regardless of whether it was running Windows. This seems to mean that even Netscape and Sun see a real market potential for a computer platform that integrates a browser into a larger programming scheme, which is what Microsoft seeks to do. So what if Microsoft invades the market that Netscape and Sun see as potentially very large? That's not monopoly, played out through digital predation. That's the prevention of monopoly. No, more accurately, it's competition at its finest, although Netscape and Sun might not agree, for obvious reasons. The Justice Department should not be in the business of protecting markets from invasion under the guise of thwarting monopoly.

THE SPECIAL ECONOMICS OF SOFTWARE

With the Microsoft case, the Justice Department seeks to update antitrust enforcement and to bring it into the digital age with two strategic lines of argument that, admittedly, have a good deal of legal and public relations sex appeal. First, the Justice Department argues that the software market is special in that its production is engulfed with economies of scale and its market is awash with network effects that ensure that a single software producer will naturally tend to dominate a product category, like operating systems. Moreover, the operating system that comes to dominate may not, because of the nature of networks, be superior to other products that already exist in the market or could exist if the dominant producer were not in such a favorable market position. In other words, Microsoft has become the world's largest software producer because of "network effects," not because its products are valuable to consumers around the world.

Second, as noted in Chapter 2, the Justice Department asserts that market dominance is tantamount to monopoly power. It then reasons that many of Microsoft's actions—low, zero, and negative prices and restrictive contracts—can be seen as the work of a monopolist, especially because several juicy, apparently incriminating e-mails written by Microsoft executives over the years that were found among the gigabytes of e-mails that Microsoft's executives have written appear to support the government's case. And it is evident that Judge Jackson was fully persuaded on every point.

Clearly, network effects impact the evolution of software markets in several potential ways. First, as the Justice Department and court argue, network effects *may* lead to domination of the market by a single company, especially if economies of scale are ever present in production. It may also be true that a firm that comes to dominate a network market *can* have monopoly power, especially if it is protected from competitors' entry into the market by "barriers to entry," which the Justice Department claims to be the case. Keep in mind that Microsoft is not yet the *single producer* of anything, which suggests that network effects do not appear to be all that matters in software markets. Network effects tend to give producers a strong incentive to suppress prices and maintain them at a level below what they would be in the absence of network effects. This is because a suppressed price for an operating system can increase its immediate sales, which can give rise to more applications being written for the operating system, which in turn can increase the future demand for and sales of the operating system. The revenue lost from the currently suppressed price can be recouped from future sales (which might be able to be made at higher prices).

The incentive to suppress prices can be even stronger for a dominant firm in the operating system market that also has an array of other software products that tend to work together, or are complementary in use. This is because such a dominant producer understands that if it lowers the current price of its operating system, more copies of the operating system will be sold along with more personal computers, which can give rise to more sales of applications, many of which will be sales by the dominant producer with the array of software products. Indeed Judge Jackson fully recognizes this line of argument in his Findings of Fact:

> It is not possible with the available data to determine with any level of confidence whether the price that a profit-maximizing firm with monopoly power would charge for Windows 98 comports with the price that Microsoft actually charges. Even if it could be determined that Microsoft charges less than the profit-maximizing monopoly price, though, that would not be probative of a lack of monopoly power, for Microsoft could be charging what seems like a low short-term price in order to maximize its profits in the future for reasons unrelated to underselling any incipient competitors. For instance, Microsoft could be stimulating the growth of the market for Intel-compatible PC operating systems by keeping the price of Windows low today. Given the size and stability of its market share, Microsoft stands to reap almost all of the future rewards if there are yet more consumers of Intel-compatible PC operating systems.

In other words, the Justice Department's and the court's own network-effects argument is a major reason Microsoft's low, zero, and even negative prices should not be construed as predatory, and its below-zero prices should not be construed as "bribes" that Microsoft must make to buyers to get them to take its products, as Franklin Fisher indicated in his court testimony. They are simply what would be expected of any successful company that seeks to take advantage of network effects. The relevant business model is one followed by lots of firms in the software industry: free software leads to ubiquity, which leads to profits from sales of add-ons, upgrades, and advertising. In short, though the Justice Department and the court show that they can use some high-minded-sounding jargon relating to modern economics, the application of the concept of network effects in modern antitrust enforcement is shaky at best.

Second, it can be shown why markets submerged in network effects are not likely to be markets where inferior products will hold their dominant position for long in the face of competition from superior rivals. Any dominance is very likely temporary at best, especially if the dominant firm acts as the Justice Department assumes it can and will act, like a monopolist.

Yes, these conclusions are intriguing. Let's look at another example of network effects.

THE NATURE OF TELEPHONE NETWORKS

Pick up any introductory economics book, and you will find a lengthy discussion of the demand for a normal good. A normal good is one whose value to anyone is unaffected by how many other people are consuming it—say, a particular candy bar, like Snickers. The author will explain that the quantity of candy bars purchased will be related to its price and a number of other considerations such as weather, income, and the prices of other goods. The lower the price of the candy bar, the more will be bought. This inverse relationship between price and quantity is such a revered concept in economics that it is called a law: the law of demand. In markets for normal goods, it is reasonable to conclude that the more abundant the good becomes, the lower the good's market value.

Nothing will be said by the author of the economics textbook about how the benefits received by any one candy bar buyer depend upon how many other people have bought them. The benefit that one person gets from eating a candy bar is not materially affected by how many other people buy them. People just buy and consume candy bars independent of one another, and couldn't care less about how much other people enjoy their candy bars.

This is not true with "network goods," goods that exhibit network effects. With network goods, the benefits one person receives from buying the good are intrinsically related to how many other people buy the good. A network good has one defining feature: The greater the number of buyers, the greater the benefits all buyers receive. The Justice Department economic consultant and long-time MIT professor of economics, Franklin Fisher, describes a network effect as "a phenomenon in which the attractiveness of a product to customers increases with the use of that product by others."

Network effects are best understood in terms of telephone systems that actually form networks, that is, are tied together with telephone lines (as well as microwave dishes and satellites). No one would want to own a phone or buy telephone service if he or she were the only phone owner. There would be no one to call. However, if two people buy phones, each person has someone to call, and there are two pairwise calls that can be made: A can call B, and B can call A. As more and more people buy phones, the benefits of phone ownership escalate geometrically, for there are progressively more people to call and even more possible pairings. If there are three phone owners, six calls can be made: A can call B or C, B can call A or C, and C can call A or B. If there are four phone owners, there are 12 potential calls; five phone owners, 20 potential calls; 20 phone owners, 380, and so forth. If the network allows for conference calls, the count of the ways calls can be made quickly goes through the roof with the rise in the number of phone owners. It's important to remember that the benefits buyers garner from others joining the network can rise just from the potential to call others; they need not ever call all of the additional joiners. Each phone owner may not expect to call every business in the country, but each still gains some benefit from having the opportunity to call any of the businesses that have phones.

Accordingly, the demand for phones can be expected to rise with phone ownership. The benefits from ownership go up as more people join the network. Hence, people should be willing to pay more for phones as the count of phone owners goes up. Some of the benefits of phone ownership are said to be "external" to the buyers of phones because people other than those who buy phones gain by the purchases. A concrete example: When a writer buys a phone, the author's editor gains from the author's purchase—though the editor pays nothing for the author's phone. For that matter, everyone who has a phone gains more opportunities to call as other people buy phones, or as the network expands. The gains that others receive from the author's or anyone else's purchase are external to the author, hence are dubbed "external benefits"; they are also called "network externalities."

In passing, it needs to be noted that networks tend to turn basic economic propositions on their head. In classic economic theory it is a law that as a good becomes scarcer, its market value increases. In networks, just the opposite is true: as the good becomes more abundant, its value increases.

A phone company faces two basic problems in building its network. First, the company has the initial problem of getting people to buy phones, given that at the start the benefits will be low. Second, if some of the benefits of buying a phone are external to the buyer, each buyer's willingness to buy a phone can be impaired, because each buyer should not be willing to pay a price that reflects value to others besides the buyer. This implies that production will be curbed because of the external effects.

How does the phone company solve this chicken-or-egg problem and build the network? One obvious solution is for the phone company at the start to underprice or subsidize phones or, at the extreme, to give the phones and service away, or even to pay people to have phones installed in their houses and offices. Once the network starts building and people see the value of being part of it, then the company can raise its price to match market demand.

THE NATURE OF SOFTWARE NETWORKS

In principle, the network effects of operating systems are similar to those in the telephone industry, but of course the details differ. When it comes to computers, the network consists not of a system of telephones and lines, but of the computer, the operating system, and the applications (such as games, word processing, spreadsheets, etc.). The software developer trying to create a network may face more difficult problems than the telephone company, for the software developer must somehow get the computer users on one side of the market and the application developers on the other side to build the network more or less together.

Few people other than computer nerds are likely to buy an operating system for which no applications are available. If a producer of an operating system is only able to get a few consumers to buy and use its product, the demand for the operating system may be highly restricted, because few applications producers will write for an operating system with a very limited number of users, hence offering few potential customers. As the number of people using the system increases, however, the number of applications written for the operating system can be expected to grow too. Why? Because there are more potential sales and more profits to be made from applications. If more applications are written for the operating system, then more people will want to buy and use the operating system—which can lead to a snowball effect: more sales, more applications, and even more sales in an ever-expanding array of people connected to the operating system by way of the invisible network.

As in the case of telephones, some of the benefits of purchase of the operating system and applications are external to the people who buy them. People who join the operating system network increase the benefits of all previous joiners, given that they have more people with whom they can share computers, data, or manuscripts. All joiners have the additional benefit of knowing that a greater number of operating system users can increase the likelihood of more applications from which they can choose. However, as in phone purchases, when the benefits are external, potential users have an impaired demand for buying into the network. The greater the external benefits, the greater the buying resistance, or willingness to cover the operating system cost.

The network may grow slowly at the start, because both computer users and programmers might initially be skeptical that any given operating system will be able to become a sizable network and provide the "external benefits" that a large network can provide. However, as with phones, for the software/operating system network abundance—not scarcity—can imply greater value.

As the network for a given operating system grows, more and more people begin to believe that the operating system will become sizable, if not dominant, which means that the network can grow at an escalating pace. According to the Justice Department and network effect theorists, as the network grows, there can be a hypothetical "tipping point" beyond which the growth in the market for the operating system takes on a life of its own—it will grow at an ever-faster pace *because* it has grown at an ever-faster pace. (No evidence has been offered in support of this tipping-point theory.) People will buy the operating system because everyone else is using it, which can mean that the self-accelerating growth in buyers of one operating system can translate into the contraction of the market share for other operating systems. According to the Justice Department, after the tipping point has been reached, the firm's eventual market dominance—and monopoly power—is practically assured.

This discussion might have relevance to the history of the dominance of the Apple and Microsoft operating systems. Before the introduction of the IBM personal computer, Apple was the dominant personal computer, running the CP/M operating system. However, in 1981, IBM and Microsoft went to market with the DOS operating system, naming their systems (which were identical) PC-DOS and MS-DOS, respectively. At that time, 90 percent of programs ran under some version of CP/M. CP/M's market dominance was likely undermined by two important factors: First, CP/M was selling at the time for $240 a copy; DOS was introduced at $40. Second, the dominance of IBM in the mainframe computer market could have indicated to many buyers that some version of DOS would eventually be the dominant operating system. In addition, Apple refused to unbundle its all-in-one computer system: it insisted on selling its own operating system together with its hardware, the Macintosh computer, at a price inflated by the restricted availability of Apple machines and operating systems.

Microsoft probably came to dominate Apple for two reasons: first, Bill Gates appears to have understood the special economics of networks far better than Steve Jobs and John Sculley, Apple's founder and president, respectively, early on in the history of personal computing. In 1981, Gates, just twenty-six, rhetorically asked in a talk at a conference, "Why do we need standards?" and then answered his own question perceptively, "It's only through volume that you can offer reasonable software at a low price." Admirably frank, he added, "Standards increase the basic machine that you can sell. . . . I really shouldn't say this, but in some ways it leads, in an individual product category, to a natural monopoly: where somebody properly documents, properly trains, properly promotes a particular package and through momentum, user loyalty, reputation, sales force and prices, builds a very strong position with that product." That seems to be a very rough, early statement of the network snowball that the Justice Department says could develop in software.

In mid-1985, Bill Gates wrote John Scully, then head of Apple, suggesting that Apple license the Mac operating system and interface technologies to others, including Microsoft. Gates advised Scully on the network benefits of licensing the operating system: licensing could expand support from independent developers, which was necessary for any computing firm, even IBM, if the technology was to achieve critical mass and become the standard in personal computing. Further-more, licensing would help reduce the risk of corporate buyers who feared that if they bought Apple products, they would be "locked into the Mac for reasons of price and choice." Gates also indicated that Microsoft would work aggressively with Apple to make the Mac technology the personal computing standard.

Gates took his own advice and steered Microsoft onto a radically different path from Apple's when it came to the dissemination of its operating system: he un-hooked DOS and Windows from the computers themselves. First, Microsoft got IBM to agree to allow it to license MS-DOS to other manufacturers, and then it did license MS-DOS to all comers, in the expectation that the competition among com-puter manufacturers on price and other attributes of personal computers would spread the use of computers—and, not incidentally, Microsoft's operating system. The expected "abundance" of MS-DOS and PC-DOS systems led to an even greater demand for such systems, and to a lower demand for Apple systems. Many people started joining the Microsoft network, presumably because they felt that any poten-tial inferiority in the technical capabilities would be offset by the benefits of the greater size network—and not necessarily because they thought MS-DOS or Win-dows was a superior operating system to Apple's. Sometime in the late 1980s or early 1990s (possibly with the release of Windows 3.0 in 1990) there supposedly was a "tipping point" for Microsoft that caused Windows to take off and sent Apple into a market-share tailspin.

WHEN AN ENTRY BARRIER IS A BENEFIT

Regardless of how the network forms, what is important to remember is that con-sumer value and demand builds with the network's expansion. This means that even if the price of the operating system is raised in the future, it does not follow that the price charged should necessarily be construed as monopoly pricing. This is because the consumers of the operating system are getting more value with the greater future demand and higher price—even in competitive markets prices could be expected to rise with greater consumer value and demand. Put another way, the higher price of the operating system after the network has taken shape can be well below the monopoly price.

In addition, there is a potential, even necessary, connection between the initial and future prices that are charged. If the producer of an operating system can raise its price in the future with the development of the network, then it has all the more incentive to lower the initial price. Why? By lowering its initial prices, it can more rapidly and completely develop the network and gain the benefits of the higher fu-ture price, and recover any lost revenue from the initial low price. What is intrigu-ing about network economics is that consumers might even have an interest not only in low initial prices but also in higher prices later, when the network is formed.

This is the case because consumers can reason that the dominant firm that is able to raise its future prices will have a greater incentive to build the network rapidly with low initial prices, and the consumers can appreciate the fact that they gain from the rapid development of the network as well as from the lower initial prices. They get a bargain if they buy early.

In his Findings of Fact, Judge Jackson makes a great deal out of the "applications barrier to entry." As noted, he reasons that the tens of thousands of software programs written for Windows makes market life tough for all of Microsoft's competitors. Maybe so. When he acknowledges that Microsoft doesn't necessarily charge a monopoly price and may be charging low prices because of the potential network effects, he still finds a way to condemn Microsoft for all the good that it is doing for consumers: "By pricing low relative to the short-run profit-maximizing price, thereby focusing on attracting new users to the Windows platform, Microsoft would also intensify the positive network effects that add to the impenetrability of the applications barrier to entry." What the judge and the lawyers at the Justice Department don't seem to understand is that what the judge sees as a barrier to entry is also a considerable real benefit for consumers: consumers have an interest in Microsoft's maintaining its network of applications, and this could be true even *if* Microsoft is able to raise its prices in the future. And the *if* is important because future competition, and the threat of future competition, could hold Microsoft's prices in check for a long time to come, as it seems to have done to date. No wonder that while the Justice Department and court were condemning Microsoft for being an abusive monopoly, three quarters of Americans polled continued to have a favorable view of Microsoft. Why? They see the world from a radically different, more benign perspective, and they even seem to understand the consumer consequences of network economics better.

CONCLUDING COMMENTS

The concept of network effects is central to the government's case against Microsoft. But actual network effects are hardly sufficient for Microsoft to be charged with being a monopoly, or acting like one. As I have pointed out, a monopolist raises its profits by restricting production to raise prices. However, to be a *real* monopoly, one that can actually generate above-competitive-level profits, somehow the competition has got to be barred from the market, or else profit-hungry firms will invade the putative monopolist's domain, increasing market supply and defeating his goal of making "monopoly profits." As will be seen in the next chapter, to bolster its case, the government has introduced into the trial new concepts that amount to novel sources of entry barriers that can deter competition, namely "switching costs" and "lock-ins."

⚖ CHAPTER 5 ⚖

Digital Switching

IN CONVENTIONAL ECONOMIC THINKING, a monopoly was thought to exist when there were identifiable barriers to entry into a firm's market. The barrier could be a result of natural conditions: a firm could buy up all of a known resource that was critical to the production of the good. Or the barrier might originate with the government: the government could give a company exclusive rights to sell a product or service in given markets. This was the case with electricity distribution and first-class mail delivery. Until recently, no one could set up a power distribution system in most areas of the country without government approval (deregulation of electric power distribution has begun in limited areas around the country). And the U.S. Post Office still is the only entity that can deliver first-class mail to our mailboxes (private delivery services, faxes, and e-mails have eroded the value of the Post Office's monopoly).

When it comes to software markets, however, such external barriers to market entry are hard to find. As was pointed out very early in the book, there is no important resource critical to the manufacture of software that can be cornered. After all, the "critical" resource amounts to sequences of *1*'s and *0*'s, which are abundant. Software markets have been renowned for being free of government intrusion. Hence, the Justice Department, to make its charge of monopoly stick, must have other forms of entry barriers in mind. Instead of external barriers, the Justice Department posits the existence of internal barriers such as "switching costs" and "lock-ins." Do these market factors indeed represent the high barriers to entry the Justice Department and court have made them out to be?

SWITCHING COSTS AND LOCK-INS

The Justice Department has argued, and the court has concurred, that the dominance Microsoft now enjoys in the operating system market can be equated with monopoly power because of the presumed existence of "high switching costs" and "lock-ins." These are said to work in the following fashion: once people have adopted the operating system, along with the accompanying computer hardware, and have learned how to use a particular set of applications, there are presumed costs of switching to other operating systems. To switch, people have to buy a different operating system and maybe different computer equipment, as well as learn new applications with new instructions and a different look and feel. They might also have to retool and retrain their computer service providers, or switch providers altogether. Thus, switching costs result in consumers' being locked in to one line of products, to some extent.

Assistant Attorney General Joel Klein introduced "switching costs" into his argument by first repeating his position that Microsoft was convinced that it could not win the browser war on the basis of the relative merits of Internet Explorer. He then quoted Microsoft's Megan Bliss and Rob Bennett, who had written in an e-mail that the way to increase Internet Explorer's share of the browser market was by "leveraging our strong share of the desktop": "[I]f they get our technology by default on every desk, then they'll be less inclined to purchase a competitive solution." The Justice Department's chief economic consultant, Franklin Fisher, gave more details on how switching costs are connected to network effects in his testimony for the government: "Where network effects are present, a firm that gains a large share of the market, whether through innovation, marketing skill, historical accident, or any other means, *may* thereby gain monopoly power. This is because it will prove increasingly difficult for other firms to persuade customers to buy their products in the presence of a product that is widely used. The firm with a large market share *may* then be able to charge high prices or slow down innovation without having its business bid away" (emphasis added). Fisher added later: "As a result of scale and network effects, Microsoft's high market share leads to more applications being written for its operating system, which reinforces and increases Microsoft's market share, which in turn leads to still more applications being written for Windows than for other operating systems, and so on."

Thus, according to Judge Thomas Penfield Jackson, Microsoft is a monopoly because there are now 70,000 applications written for Windows, far more than for any other operating system; further, Microsoft is protected by an "applications barrier to entry" that "make[s] it prohibitively expensive for a new Intel-compatible operating system to attract enough developers and consumers to become a viable alternative to a dominant incumbent in less than a few years."

The government's and court's position on the role of switching costs has been widely accepted in the media. For example, the editors at *The Economist* have summed up the network effects–switching costs–lock-in line of argument very neatly in their retort to Microsoft's supporters:

"Network" effects, in which the value of a product depends on the number of users, occur in many high-tech markets—just as they did in earlier industries such as railways and telephones. These effects hugely increase the risk that one firm may dominate a particular market, probably not forever but certainly for a significant amount of time. True, the products may change, often substantially. But such are the barriers to entry, arising from large installed bases that are locked into a particular technology and from control over distribution, that [a] dominant firm can still remain entrenched.

The Justice Department, by suggesting that the operating system market is beset with network effects that can cause a firm's market share to build on itself, is effectively suggesting that Microsoft's current market dominance has been a consequence of economic forces outside the company's influence; in fact, Microsoft set out to garner the benefits of network effects before they were widely understood as such. If Microsoft's market position can be viewed as a product of blind forces of nature or technology, then it might be rightfully deduced that Microsoft has itself achieved virtually nothing in its own behalf, but is the beneficiary of historical accident. Seen this way, the Justice Department's threat to force Microsoft to put Netscape's icon on the desktop would not be violating any property rights Microsoft may have justly earned, because Microsoft is seen to have no justly earned property rights to the market value of the desktop real estate.

One of the real problems with the Justice Department's argument (which the court has accepted) is that, contrary to the impression left by all the talk about how network effects build on themselves, network effects just don't happen. They do not exist as a part of "nature" or "technology"—they exist because someone or some firm has caused them to exist. Neither telephone networks nor software networks fall from the sky like manna from heaven. Someone must conceive of the network and then build it. Someone must also think of ways to overcome the initial chicken-or-egg dilemma: How does a network firm get customers to buy its operating system when there are no application programs written for it, and how does the firm get program developers to write programs when there are no buyers of the operating system?

The operating system buyers and applications programmers must emerge more or less together, and the process must be coordinated, encouraged, and directed by someone, or some firm. And it should be understood that creating the network is likely to be very expensive, because of buyer and developer resistance. It is also likely to require a substantial up-front investment on the part of someone, or some firm, to overcome the resistance—Microsoft, for example.

As a matter of history, Microsoft has spent a fortune on developing its operating system and application networks. In recent years Microsoft has spent more than $1 billion annually on improving Windows and about $500 million annually on cultivating its network of buyers and suppliers. Programs need to be developed, but so must networks of developers, and they must be kept up-to-date on how the networks' software is evolving. Microsoft continues to spend several billions of dollars a year on researching the boundaries of software development, maintaining and building its customer base, and working with applications developers.

Recognition of the substantial costs of building and maintaining a network calls into question efforts on the part of Microsoft's critics to assert that Microsoft's profits are extraordinary. It also calls into question the Justice Department's efforts to take away without compensation the network any firm has created, or some of the property the company has created—even if the taking of property involves only a few square inches on the desktop that is given to another firm such as Netscape for the purpose of displaying its icon. The taking of property also could come in the form of a breakup of Microsoft so that a part of the network—say, the operating system—would no longer benefit from the development of other parts of the network, such as applications, and vice versa. There is no mention in the Justice Department's proposed remedies of compensation for Microsoft, partly because Microsoft's investment in the desktop and in the entire Windows program is never spoken of as Microsoft's property. The case thus represents a largely unrecognized assault on a firm's property rights in its technology and network, which were earned as a consequence of a substantial up-front investment. Do we really want antitrust laws to be used for a virtual land grab?

By arguing that networks are beset with "high switching costs," the Justice Department and court are effectively saying that Microsoft's market dominance is protected by an *internal* barrier to entry, which like all barriers restricts entry. Switching costs reduce competition, lower consumer choice, and enable the dominant producer to raise its prices. The Justice Department argues that with high switching costs, the dominant producer doesn't have to worry about its customers switching in response to a higher price. Frederick Warren-Boulton, the lead economist for the nineteen state attorneys general, reasons that computer users "become 'locked in' to a particular operating systems [sic]," which implies a barrier to entry and expansion for existing competitors. He adds, "The software 'lock-in' phenomenon creates barriers to entry for new PC operating systems to the extent that consumers' estimate of the switching costs are large relative to the perceived incremental value of the new operating system."

The higher the switching costs, the Justice Department asserts, the more the dominant producer can raise its price without fear of the customers switching to existing or new competitors. The customer is locked in. By introducing the specter of "lock-ins," the Justice Department is seeking to suggest that the switching costs are so high that switching is extremely difficult, if not impossible, thus presumably fortifying its argument that Microsoft has substantial monopoly power. Fisher concedes that "market forces and developments can erode monopoly power based solely on network effects," but that is precisely why, according to Fisher, Microsoft felt compelled to engage in "predatory pricing," to wipe out Netscape as a potential alternative software platform for running personal computers.

Is that the case? Before people accept these arguments, they should consider whether Microsoft's pricing strategy is consistent with the dictates of a market entrenched in network effects. If the economics of networks dictate zero or below-zero prices, Microsoft's price for its browser is not necessarily predatory, contrary to the Justice Department's claim that predation is the only conceivable explanation of Microsoft's pricing decisions.

Predatory Pricing in Networks

For normal goods associated with the "old" industrial era—washing machines or candy bars, for instance—zero or below-zero prices seem to have no economic basis. Industrial goods always involve costs for materials and labor, if nothing else. The old adage that you can't get something for nothing (or no cost) is valid. Hence, a good sold for a zero price appears to be nonsensical, if not downright stupid. Production costs would be incurred with nothing in the way of revenues. The Justice Department probably views Microsoft's zero and below-zero prices as predatory because the lawyers haven't been able to shake the economic mind-set of an earlier industrial era, the one that gave rise to antitrust laws. This means that the Justice Department and court don't really understand the pricing implications of its own network-effects theory.

The Justice Department argued without qualifications in its filing of facts with Judge Jackson that Microsoft business practice, including its pricing strategy, "makes sense only if there is a monopoly to protect." The phrase "only if" communicates that the Justice Department is absolute in its position. Yet the Justice Department couldn't possibly believe what it is saying, because this position is at odds with its characterization of the software markets. Indeed, at the time it wrote its assessment of the facts of the case, there was at least one article available, presented at a conference organized by an anti-Microsoft think tank and funded by anti-Microsoft firms, that carefully explains why zero and below-zero pricing are rational for a network firm in a business subject to network effects that is *not* trying to protect a monopoly position.

If the operating system market is controlled by network effects to the extent suggested by either the Justice Department or the court, it follows that any firm in that market can build its network by suppressing prices at the start. An artificially suppressed price can give buyers an incentive to purchase the operating system or browser or any application for which network effects are important. The firm has an incentive to suppress its price because it understands that a suppressed price will have a series of desirable mutually reinforcing consequences: a lower price for the operating system now can increase the number of buyers in the future, which can give rise to more applications being written, which in turn can give rise to more buyers of the operating system—and then even more applications, even more buyers, and so on. Any firm in a network market must also worry that some other firm will do the same thing.

The firm can also reason that consumer demand will rise as consumer benefits escalate with the expansion of the network. The firm can further reason that with the increase in future demand it will be able to recover some of the lost revenues by charging a low or zero price initially and by charging higher prices in the future as market demand rises. The firm can make what is really an up-front investment in the network partially through its expenditures on enlisting buyers and application developers, but also partially through its low initial price. The firm may not actually be able to raise its price in the future to monopoly levels because of the threat of potential competitors, but such potential competitive threats will increase the firm's willingness to lower its price initially to build the network.

Notice that the firm has an incentive to artificially suppress its price all the way to zero (and even beyond), depending on the extent of the network. It is willing to do that because it can anticipate higher prices in the future with the rising market demand. Notice also that if the firm raises its price in the future, the higher price is not necessarily a sign of monopoly power, which is the ability to raise prices above a level that will yield a return that is above a competitive rate of return in the long run. The firm may be raising its price to a reasonable level from the low price it started with in the full understanding that it was too low for long-run viability.

Buyers should not necessarily mind the initial low price followed by a higher price in the future. Buyers can see that the artificially suppressed initial price is required to get the network going, just as the distribution of free samples of a new product is often a good way to attract new customers. They can also understand that as the network grows, consumer benefits and demand grow. In the future, they may be paying a higher price, but they also are getting more benefits. In fact, the higher future price can be a better deal than the initial low or zero price. Why? Because for network goods, consumer demand rises with the development of the network effects. This is in fact a fundamental contention of the Justice Department and court. The ratio of the benefits to price can be higher with the higher future price than with the lower initial price. This is especially true if the quantity of the product bought and sold rises over time.

In addition, there is a potential, even necessary connection between the initial and future prices that are charged. If the producer of an operating system can raise its price in the future with the development of the network, then it has all the more incentive to lower the initial price. Why? By lowering its initial prices, it can more rapidly and completely develop the network and gain the benefits of the higher future price (and to recover any lost revenue from the initial low price). What is intriguing about network economics is that consumers might even have an interest in not only low initial prices but also higher prices later when the network is formed.

This is the case because consumers can reason that the dominant firm that is able to raise its future prices will have a greater incentive to build the network rapidly with low initial prices, and the consumers can appreciate the fact that they gain from the rapid development of the network as well as from the lower initial prices.

It's not clear why the Justice Department is concerned with Microsoft's zero price for Internet Explorer. When Netscape introduced Navigator in late 1994, it gave it away via the Internet. Later, in 1995, it began charging $49 for copies sold at retail stores, but still gave Navigator away when it was downloaded from the Web. Microsoft introduced Internet Explorer with a zero price in August 1995 for much the same reason Netscape introduced Navigator at a zero price: *Network effects are real; they exist.* Each firm sought to use a zero price to help build its network, and market dominance, as well as to take advantage of the economies of scale in production.

When Microsoft's market share began to rise, Netscape responded by lowering the price of Navigator to $39 in 1997, and then back to zero in January 1998. That would seem to be a competition story, not a monopoly one: prices didn't rise; they fell.

We also don't see why anyone would be concerned about a firm's instituting below-zero prices, meaning the firm pays buyers to "purchase" its product. There is nothing magic about any price. It can simply make more economic sense to both the firm and the buyers to charge one price (below-zero) instead of another (zero or above-zero). Which price is best depends upon the exact nature of the network effects and production costs or the extent of economies of scale. The greater the anticipated network effects and scale economies, the lower the initial price should be.

The Justice Department and court don't know the exact nature of the browser market. I surely don't, and the Justice Department and court don't offer any evidence that they know very much other than that there are network effects and scale economies. One thing is certain: in an environment of pervasive network effects, low, zero, or below-zero prices are not necessarily predatory. The Justice Department accepts network effects, yet has made no attempt to show that Microsoft's low, zero, and below-zero prices are predatory, or are inconsistent with its network theories or are anticonsumer. (They may indeed be contrary to the interests of Microsoft's market rivals.) All the Justice Department and court can do is speculate as to what Microsoft might do with price in the future.

The Justice Department's legal argument has two separate parts. The first part involves the claim that Microsoft has monopoly power that has emerged from network effects and scale economies and that is supported by high switching costs and lock-ins. The second part amounts to the totally separate claim that Microsoft's zero and below-zero prices are "predatory" simply because there is no visible (to the Justice Department) business or economic justification for them. But the Justice Department *itself* provides the justification for zero or below-zero prices in the first part of its case.

Microsoft actually has an incentive over and above the incentive built into network effects to keep its operating system and browser prices very low and to constantly upgrade them with additional features such as an integrated calculator or a game or browser. This is true because Microsoft has a vast array of applications and Internet services—it is in fact dominant in the applications and operating system markets. The price of its operating system will affect the number of computers sold and the number of application packages and Internet services sold. If Microsoft suppresses the price of Windows and integrates a browser into it, then more personal computers will be sold, along with more applications. Microsoft's dominance in the operating system and application markets means that the benefits of the price reductions and browser integration are not all "externalized," or passed off to other application producers. Some of the benefits generated in the computer and software markets from the lower prices for the operating system and the integration of the browser are garnered by Microsoft through a greater demand for its applications and Internet services, which can cause Microsoft to charge higher prices for its other products, and this in turn can offset any losses it might have incurred from the suppressed price for the operating system and the integration of the browser.

Following this line of reasoning, it is altogether understandable why Microsoft might want to pay another firm to adopt its browser as the recommended browser on its portal, making the price below zero. Assistant Attorney General Klein made special note of how Bill Gates passed the word among the executives at Microsoft through the e-mail system that he had offered to pay Scott Cook, the founder of Intuit, $1 million to switch browsers, which Klein sees as "paying some customers to take IE [Internet Explorer]." Microsoft says this was never contemplated, much less offered. Franklin Fisher maintained in his direct testimony, "A predatory anti-competitive act is one that is deliberately not profit maximizing, save for supranormal profits to be earned because of the effects on competition." Such a declaration supports Fisher's earlier unqualified assertion that "Microsoft's [predatory] actions as to price are not profit-maximizing in themselves but are profitable only because of their adverse effects on competition." This conviction led Fisher into asserting that any price below the short-run profit-maximizing price is necessarily "predatory." But as we have seen, a zero or below-zero price can make perfect business and economic sense to Microsoft, contrary to what the Justice Department maintains. Microsoft could easily recover the $1 million allegedly offered to Intuit on the sale of other products and services.

We should expect the Justice Department and court to update and upgrade its thinking to the digital age, if it intends to bring the full force of the federal government down on any firm, costing it a small fortune.

THE RIVALS' GAINS

Though zero and below-zero prices don't hurt consumers, it is altogether understandable why Microsoft's market rivals don't like such prices. Those are pretty tough pricing standards for any firm to compete with. Moreover, Microsoft's rivals may not be able or want to justify meeting Microsoft's prices. However, just because market rivals can't or don't want to meet the competition from a firm with a product line-up like Microsoft's is not a good reason to conclude that Microsoft has predatory intentions. Microsoft need not be charging a zero price for its browser because it is ignoring its cost structure and intends only to wipe out Netscape at great cost, after which it will act like a monopolist. It may understand that it can't ever act like a monopolist. Microsoft could be charging the price it does because of network effects and because of how the sale of one product affects the sales of other products. If other producers can match Microsoft's prices, then so be it. That's competition, the way markets should work. If Microsoft ever operates like a monopolist, as claimed, then other producers should see Microsoft's market strategy as an opportunity to take over its dominant position in an array of products. After all, as noted, digital products at their core are nothing more than sequences of *1*'s and *0*'s, which are in abundant supply the world round.

Having said that, we can also understand why Microsoft's competitors want the firm hobbled with antitrust charges and legal expenses. Such added expenditures drive up Microsoft's costs, which means they reduce the incentive Microsoft has to suppress its prices and extend its network. If Microsoft holds its prices down, it runs the risk of expanding its network and incurring heavy legal expenses. From this perspective, legally assaulting firms for being dominant in network markets is surely a clever, albeit legal, means of forcing the dominant producer to raise its prices—and of allowing the dominant producers' rivals to raise their prices, as well as gain market share. It is interesting that such use of the nation's antitrust laws can force anticompetitive pricing by all firms in the market, an outcome contrary to the ostensible intent of antitrust laws.

Similarly, we can understand why Microsoft's rivals want Microsoft to be broken up into constituent parts, or so-called "Baby Bills." Such a breakup reduces the gains the company can receive from suppressing the price of the operating system and integrating the browser. Such a breakup will make life easier for Microsoft's competitors because it encourages Microsoft to raise its prices. The breakup should also translate into higher prices for the products and services of the so-called "Baby Bills" and also of Microsoft's market rivals. Throughout its arguments, the Justice Department talks eloquently about the need to maintain consumer "choice" in the operating system and browser markets. However, make no mistake about it: if the Justice Department is right when it claims that software markets are swimming in network effects, it follows that the "choices" consumers will have if the Justice Department gets its way will be more expensive than they are now.

SWITCHING COSTS AS A LIMIT TO MONOPOLY POWER

The prevalence of high "switching costs" is crucial to the Justice Department's case. Given that, we might expect the Justice Department and court to present some real numbers on the actual extent of these costs. But the Justice Department has never offered any solid numbers, and there's been no other convincing evidence that the switching costs are as great as the Justice Department suggests or that switching costs are any greater for software products than for any number of other products, for example, automobiles. Certainly there are some switching costs, but are they high or low? This is a critical issue. If the switching costs are considered "low," Microsoft's potential monopoly power is very limited.

The jury is still out on the existence of lock-ins. Clearly, in the brief time personal computers have been around, lock-ins have been short-lived at best. Over the past two decades, the personal computer industry has gone through a progression of operating systems, first CP/M, then Apple, followed by MS-DOS/PC-DOS, and now Windows. As these words are written, it appears that the operating system market may be moving back, albeit marginally, to Apple and then over to Linux, although the move is modest at this point.

Indeed, the Justice Department and its chief economic consultant don't appear to be of one mind on the ability of switching costs to protect monopoly power. Franklin Fisher acknowledges that "in the absence of anti-competitive conduct, market forces and developments can erode monopoly power based solely on network effects." This is why, in Fisher's view, "Microsoft felt it necessary to take the actions discussed below with respect to Java and Internet browsers." The "actions" Fisher had in mind were the contract restrictions and predatory pricing that are the heart of the Justice Department's charges against Microsoft.

Again, the Justice Department wants to have the argument both ways. It wants the court to believe that switching costs are high, which gives Microsoft monopoly power. Simultaneously it charges that Microsoft has used anticompetitive tactics to stifle competition, suggesting that switching costs might not be as high as claimed.

It seems likely that America Online (AOL) believes that it is possible to get people to switch computer platforms. It probably bought Netscape because it saw the prospect of using Netscape's Navigator along with Java as a new platform for an operating system. Scott McNealy at Sun Microsystems doesn't believe that lock-ins are airtight, or else why would he be so dedicated to establishing network computing as an industry standard? In addition, it appears that with advances in computer technology, the operating system might well become irrelevant, which is what Netscape's Marc Andreesen seemed to have in mind when he predicted, as noted earlier, that Windows would eventually be reduced to "a mundane collection of not entirely debugged device drivers."

I question the switching-cost and lock-in theories because they tend to ignore the costs that monopoly pricing can impose on consumers long into the future. They also seem to be grounded on the belief that consumers are at the mercy of some big bad giant called Microsoft and that there is no one or no firm out there other than the Justice Department willing to protect or help them. But if Microsoft were operating like a monopolist, it follows that there would be monopoly profits to be made by someone else willing to enter the monopolized market and charge a price that is marginally below Microsoft's. Any number of firms—from IBM to Red Hat to Dell to General Electric to a host of foreign firms—should be willing to help buyers and application developers with their switching costs in a variety of ways, for example, through subsidized prices or through payments to cover retraining costs.

Why would they do that? The short answer is that these firms could then build their own networks. Microsoft's monopoly strategies would ensure that the new firms' switching-cost investments would be a paying proposition.

Again, the Justice Department can't have it both ways: claim that there are high switching costs and at the same time claim that Microsoft is exploiting its monopoly position in a variety of ways (for example, by imposing monopoly prices on buyers and/or by imposing uncompensated costs through its contract restrictions on application developers). If there are high switching costs, the monopoly costs Microsoft imposes on buyers and application developers lower the *net* cost of switching. Warren-Boulton was right when he noted almost in passing that "the software 'lock-in' phenomenon creates barriers to entry for new PC operating systems to the extent that consumers' estimate of the switching costs are large relative to the perceived incremental value of the new operating system." It can't be stressed enough that any firm that acts like a monopolist, or even is expected to act like one, dramatically hikes the costs of *staying with* the monopolist, necessarily increasing the "perceived incremental value of the new operating system" and increasing the likelihood of switching occurring.

For example, if a buyer must incur $20 to switch to another operating system but Microsoft imposes long-run monopoly costs of staying with Windows of $20 (in present discounted value terms), there are no net costs of switching. In the long run buyers would be no worse off if they switched than if they stayed with Windows.

Okay, Microsoft might not *fully* exploit its monopoly position. It might impose only $18 of monopoly/staying costs. The buyer would be $2 worse off by switching to another operating system. But notice Microsoft is making $18 in monopoly profits. Some other firm can reason that it can cover the buyer's net switching costs of $2 and make the investment a paying proposition, given that it can offer its operating system on better terms and take a major share of Microsoft's monopoly profits of $18 per copy sold. Clearly, Microsoft can protect itself by reducing its monopoly/staying costs: the lower the monopoly/staying costs Microsoft imposes on consumers, the less likely buyers are to switch. Indeed, if the switching costs are truly modest, then Microsoft's monopoly power to exploit buyers in uncompensated ways would be equally modest, and we might anticipate Microsoft acting *as if* it faces no switching costs and has no monopoly power for a simple reason: it knows it has a good thing going, and the greater the monopoly/staying costs it imposes on buyers, the greater the risk it will lose its "good thing" in the long run.

But wait a minute, Microsoft only charges $89 retail for an upgrade on Windows (and it charges much less for new versions of Windows on new computers). If there really are *high* switching costs of the sort that the Justice Department claims exist, then you might think that the switching costs would be far greater than $89. (If you took the Justice Department's claims seriously about absolute lock-ins, you might think the switching costs for individuals would be thousands of dollars and for firms would be hundreds of thousands of dollars, if not unlimited.) But then, why isn't Microsoft charging far more than it is, if the switching costs are as high as claimed and Microsoft doesn't have to worry about actual competitors or the threat of entry. Once again, the Justice Department and court can't have it both ways: either switching costs are not as high as the Justice Department and court think or Microsoft doesn't have the monopoly power to raise its price. The threat of competition must be more real than the Justice Department pretends. Otherwise, why charge the public only $89 and computer manufacturers only $40?

I make these arguments not because I am oblivious to the fact that Microsoft makes a lot of money. Microsoft is very profitable. I suspect, however, that the company's unusual profitability is related to the fact that it has developed a means of producing superior products at better prices that other firms can't match. That's not the politically correct thing to say in many circles, but it certainly has the ring of greater truth than the Justice Department's assertions. If other firms—for example, IBM—could do better than Microsoft, we would expect them to do it, and Microsoft would be history.

Again, it can be agreed that some of Microsoft's profits might come from its being able to take advantage of switching costs, but we can't see that the switching costs are all that substantial when prorated over the long term, say ten years. If the Justice Department is right concerning the nature of network effects and the emergence of a dominant firm, then how would the world be improved by replacing Microsoft with some other firm, such as Netscape, which would have the same motivation to exploit the extant switching costs, modest or otherwise, that Microsoft now has? If the Justice Department believes its own description of the software markets—that they are mired in economies of scale and network effects—then it is hard to see why it thinks that thwarting Microsoft's dominance and supplanting it with Netscape's would be an improvement in the welfare of Americans and others. The Justice Department and court claim to want to promote consumer choice, and, they claim, there is little consumer choice in markets with extensive network effects. Thus, increasing consumer choice would require a division of the market, but it would also lead to higher production costs and lower network benefits for buyers.

Market Dominance and Antitrust Laws

If antitrust laws are used to benefit a firm's competitors, they will have perverse market effects that are hardly in accord with the ostensible intentions of the framers of the country's antitrust laws. Such use of antitrust laws can give rise to higher, not lower, prices. However, it is also true that if antitrust laws were enacted and enforced with the intent of throttling a true monopolist in markets with pervasive network effects, they can have the paradoxical effects of increasing the dominance of the dominant producer. This is a problem for the Justice Department and court, given that they have based their arguments against Microsoft on the claim that market dominance is a good indicator of monopoly power. The reasoning is straightforward.

A firm in a market where network effects and extensive economies of scale abound can reason that it needs to suppress its price in order to build its network of buyers and application developers. However, if there are extensive switching costs, buyers and application developers have to fear that if the firm becomes dominant and actually acquires monopoly powers, it can be expected to eventually take advantage of its market position, raising prices and lowering product quality. In short, the firm can give consumers benefits through lower prices today and take more than what it gives today through higher monopoly prices in the future. On balance, over time, buyers and developers can be worse off.

The network firm may not be able to make a credible commitment that it will be a "good guy" in the future and not take advantage of its future monopoly position. As it struggles at the start to build its network, the firm will not have the required reputation that its word is truly binding. In addition, buyers and developers can reason that if the firm ever acquires monopoly powers in the future but fails to exploit them, the firm's profits and stock prices will be lower than they could be. Some smart investor will see the suppressed price, profits, and stock price as an opportunity to buy the firm; jack up its prices, profits, and stock prices; and then sell out with a handsome capital gain.

Given this monopoly threat, buyers and developers will resist joining the network, which means that in order to overcome buyers' and developers' fears and get them to join, the firm must suppress its prices by more than it would otherwise. Accordingly, not being able to make a credible commitment can be expensive to the firm, and it can deny buyers and developers the benefits of an expanded network.

You can now see why the firm, along with its buyers and developers, would have an interest in the existence of antitrust laws and of a third-party enforcer like the Justice Department or the Federal Trade Commission. With antitrust laws on the books, the third-party enforcer—the Justice Department—can make the firm's commitment credible. The firm can say, in so many words, to its buyers and suppliers, "Look, you may not believe me, but the Justice Department will enforce the law and will ensure that I will not act monopolistically in the future." To the extent that the Justice Department can make its own credible commitment to seek out *only* monopolistic behavior, then the Justice Department can increase the demand for joining the network. This means, ironically, that the network firm can become more dominant than otherwise *because* of the existence of the antitrust laws and their likely enforcement.

Put another way, with antitrust laws and effective enforcement and with the expanded demand generated by network effects, the firm can achieve any given level of dominance with a price that is less suppressed than it would otherwise be. This means also that antitrust laws can cause prices to be higher than they would otherwise be.

For a couple of good reasons, this outcome—greater firm dominance with a higher price than otherwise—is not contrary to the interests of consumers: first, there are more benefits to consumers and applications developers from the expanded network than would otherwise exist. Second, they get the security that the firm's prices will not be raised to monopoly levels in the future.

This line of argument is grounded in the presumption that the antitrust laws are used properly, to thwart monopoly. If they are used to thwart competition (and the ability of firms to take advantage of network effects and scale economies), the enforcement (of the wrong thing) can have a perverse effect. This is because people who join the network can reason that the future benefits of the network will be curbed by the government's actions to undo the dominance of the dominant network producer, and thereby eliminate the benefits of the would-be larger network that could be developed at lower cost because of the scale economies.

Supposed Inefficiency of "Path Dependency"

The Justice Department and court have some theoretical support for its argument that people can be "locked in" to a network—or, rather, to Windows or Word or Internet Explorer. The argument is grounded in the proposition that once the network is established, no one person by himself or herself has an incentive to move to another network. This can be the case even when the other network and products around which the network forms is superior. It might be the case, the Justice Department and court could argue, that the Apple operating system is "superior" to Windows. And each Windows user might agree when asked to judge the relative merits of the two operating systems. The argument is then extended to suggest that the only reason people stay with Windows is that Windows has the larger network—and the greater array of applications and opportunities for collaborative work with other Windows users. Apple *would be* the better system *if* it had the same size network, and all of the associated applications and network users. However, each Windows user can be expected to decide, individually, not to move to Apple because he or she can reasonably conclude that his or her shift, taken by itself, will have no consequential impact on the expansion of the Apple network.

According to Justice Department strategists and network theoreticians, the market can "fail" in the sense that a superior outcome can be conceptualized, but the market does not move toward this superior outcome, toward "improvement." The market failure in networks is much the same as the market failure where pollution is concerned: no one may like the consequences of the polluting that everyone in a given community does collectively (say, by driving to work in the morning), but each polluter individually does not have the requisite incentive to refrain from polluting or correcting the pollution problems of others. Phil Lemmons, the editorial director of *PC World*, summarizes the "network externality" problem this way: "Most of us aren't using our PCs to fight political battles; we're just following the path of least resistance. How many consumers will be so noble to go to the extra trouble to make sure that there is diversity in software choices [for example, by personally switching from Windows to Linux]? Very few."

The network externality argument then reduces to the issue of "path dependency" on a problem of market outcomes being determined by how products are initially developed. Networks, it is said, are "path-dependent." Once a "path," a certain product standard, is adopted, other people will be obliged to join the network. Once the network gains "critical size," or the "tipping point" is achieved, the network will have a life of its own, virtually assuring market dominance of one firm. At the point where all network participants are supposedly locked in to the established network by the logic of the absence of benefits of anyone shifting to a superior product, the dominant network firm can work its monopoly will without fear of being supplanted even by a superior product.

The Justice Department and court apply this logic to Windows and maybe to other Microsoft applications. What they fear is that Microsoft can use its monopoly powers in Windows, which come from networks, path dependency, switching costs, and lock-ins or any combination thereof, to become the dominant monopoly producer in browsers. Microsoft can then raise prices and/or control the quality of browsers in the future. The Justice Department also argues that in the absence of antitrust constraints on Microsoft, "consumers will be deprived of their choice of browsers and consumers and the public will be deprived of the benefits of competition during the pendency of this action." Here, the Justice Department seems to be concerned with the prospects that Windows and Internet Explorer will remain the only viable choices for consumers.

Two questions must be raised before the Justice Department's arguments are accepted. First, are there important examples of path dependency that fortify the Justice Department stance? Second, is it possible for a monopoly to extend its monopoly power from one product line to another?

The path dependency–lock-in theory has gained wide support among many academics and policymakers partially because economic theoreticians and historians have been able to point to two concrete examples of the supposed wrongs of path dependency and lock-ins. The classic, widely cited example of path dependency and lock-ins is the "QWERTY" keyboard, which takes its name from the sequence of keys on the far left of the top row of most keyboards.

According to economic historian Paul David, this arrangement was first developed and adopted in the 1860s only because it minimized the prospect of the keys jamming as their arms moved toward the paper. Apparently this arrangement was adopted by one typewriter manufacturer after another, not because it was the best arrangement of keys, but because it had become established as the standard. Manufacturers became further locked in to the QWERTY keyboard after touch-typing, developed in the 1880s, became widely taught thereafter. David writes, "The occurrence of this 'lock in' as early as the mid-1890s does appear to have owed something also to the high costs of software 'conversion' and the resulting *quasi-irreversibility of investments* in specific touch-typing skills" (emphasis in the original).

Supposedly, the QWERTY key arrangement is now widely used on computer keyboards, not because QWERTY is better than all potential alternatives but because of the lock-in of the key arrangement, thought to be a historical accident. According to this view of keyboard history, "Competition in the absence of perfect future markets drove the industry permanently into standardization *on the wrong system*—where decentralized decision making subsequently has sufficed to hold it."

The legend—and it has proved to be just that—doesn't stop there. In 1932, August Dvorak and W. L. Dealey developed a keyboard (referred to as the Dvorak, or DSK, keyboard) that has, according to David, "long held most of the world's records for speed typing." Moreover, experiments by the Navy supposedly showed that the greater productivity from the Dvorak keyboard could more than cover the cost of the required retraining.

The Dvorak keyboard has never gotten a toehold in the keyboard market. Why? The advocates of the concept of lock-in argue there are high switching costs for typists who are used to the QWERTY keyboard; they would have to learn another key arrangement. Typewriter manufacturers have never switched to Dvorak because it did not make good business sense, since their keyboard would not appeal to existing typists. Computer keyboard manufacturers adopted the QWERTY key arrangement because they had no other choice, for no typists, who were potential computer customers, would buy keyboards with the new key arrangement, in spite of its supposed superiority. The author of the QWERTY story imagined that "there are many more QWERTY worlds [in which an inferior standard is adopted by historical accident] lying out there in the past, on the very edges of the modern economic analyst's tidy universe; worlds we do not yet fully perceive or understand, but whose influence, like that of dark stars, extends nonetheless to shape the visible orbits of our contemporary economic affairs."

The implication for the Microsoft case is obvious. If the QWERTY story is true, it is plausible that the operating system market might be one of those "dark stars" that has become visible, because tens of millions of computer users are similarly locked in to Windows, even though there might be a superior operating system (such as some combination of Netscape's Navigator and Sun's Java programming language) waiting in the wings of modern technology to be adopted. However, the superior system doesn't have a chance of making it in the market because each Windows user does not, by himself or herself, have the requisite incentive to make the switch. Unless large numbers of people make the switch more or less together, a single user of a new system may have a technically superior system that has few applications written for it.

Fortunately for consumers and unfortunately for the case against Microsoft, the QWERTY story is a good story that has taken on a life of its own but is not grounded in the facts of keyboard history. The University of Texas–Dallas economics professor Stan Liebowitz and the North Carolina State University economics professor Stephen Margolis did what a lot of QWERTY storytellers should have done long ago: they went back and researched the history of keyboards and found that much of the evidence on the supposed superiority of the Dvorak keyboard was from Dvorak's own studies, which were poorly designed. Even then, Dvorak's own "evidence was mixed as to whether students, as they progress, retain an advantage when using the Dvorak keyboard, since the differences seem to diminish as typing speed increases." The claimed benefits from the Navy study are similarly disputable, and other studies found substantial retraining costs, leading Liebowitz and Margolis to conclude that "the claims for the superiority of the Dvorak keyboard are suspect."

Even if it were proven that the Dvorak keyboard were superior to the QWERTY keyboard, the future gains from making the switch (in present discounted-value terms) must be greater than the current costs incurred before it can be said that the "wrong" keyboard continued in use. If the cost of switching were greater than the gains to be gotten from the switch, switching would constitute a net societal loss, as well as a loss for employers and/or typists. Liebowitz and Margolis argue that though Paul David made provocative claims, he never proved his point.

The Liebowitz-Margolis finding is altogether understandable. If a new keyboard were *substantially* more efficient than the established keyboard, it's hard to see why the new keyboard wouldn't be adopted. Granted, some individual typists might be resistant to making the switch without some outside help. But if the keyboard were substantially superior, then, as pointed out earlier in this chapter, it follows that the manufacturer should have ample incentive to cover some of the typist's switching costs, perhaps by providing retraining. Companies that hire large numbers of typ-ists or computer users would also have ample incentives to buy the new keyboard. They could prorate the retraining costs over a large number of employees from whom they could garner substantial productivity improvements. Their investment in retraining could be expected to have an immediate upward impact on their com-pany's stock price, given that market watchers would expect the productivity im-provement to improve the company's long-term profit stream. If the company's executives were not sufficiently wise to make the retraining investment, then surely there would be entrepreneurs outside of the firm who would understand that they could buy control of the company at a low price, change company policies on things like keyboards, and then sell the company at a higher price.

Another similar legend has grown up around how the VHS format for videocas-sette tapes and recorders came to overshadow the Betamax format, which was sup-posedly the markedly superior format of the two. The Betamax format may actually be technically superior to the VHS format (we are unwilling to judge), but the VHS format has always had one big advantage over Betamax that counts for more than greater technical attributes such as a clearer picture: A whole movie could be recorded on a VHS tape, which was not possible on the Betamax. VHS became the adopted format because it better met the needs of the growing home movie rental and sales business.

From both fact and conceptual arguments, the presumption that some combina-tion of path dependency, network effects, switching costs, and lock-ins protect net-work firms is wrong, or, at the very least, not proven. If Microsoft were protected to the same extent (and for the same reasons) as the QWERTY keyboard and VHS, then we all might easily concur. However, such agreement could mean that Mi-crosoft doesn't have much in the way of long-term market protection.

Surely, we all might imagine that there is an operating system out there that is *marginally* superior to Windows and that switching costs might cause people to re-sist switching, but it doesn't follow that it always makes sense for people to switch to the superior system. The superior system would have to be sufficiently superior to the existing system to more than cover the switching costs. Any system that has ben-efits (in present-value terms) that are greater than the switching costs is bound to be adopted, because making the switch makes too much business sense to too many people. Unlike the classic example of externalities, in which no one has an incentive to correct the problem, there are market solutions to network externalities, another term for network effects. If Microsoft is acting like a monopolist, the switch makes even greater business sense, and should be viewed as virtually an irresistible temp-tation for those who have an economic interest in engineering the switch to actually do so.

But all of this is in fact saying nothing special about the operating system market. Markets for a variety of goods and services have switching costs, and new entrants have to find ways of overcoming such costs. New hamburger restaurants have to overcome customer inertia that might be related to a new restaurant's lack of reputation for good food and clean restrooms. Banks that wish to operate on-line have the problem of overcoming people's resistance to doing their banking on a computer.

But businesses have been creative in finding new ways to cover the switching costs. New restaurants will often cut their prices below cost, or pass out coupons that have the same effect. A variety of businesses have offered cash payments or discounts for each on-line transaction made. In 1998, Chase Bank advertised that it would pay on-line customers $25 for each of the first five on-line transactions they made. In 1999, after it set up its auction Web site, Amazon.com offered book customers a $10 gift certificate on their first auction purchase. Similarly, Drugstore.com offered its first-time customers a $20 discount on any order (even for products that cost $20, making the products free). If switching to another product brings efficiency improvements that mean greater profits for new firms, network effects may be "external" to buyers, but those network externalities can be "internalized" by entrepreneurial firms. Justice Department action is unnecessary to maintain consumer choice.

NETWORK EFFECTS AS A THREAT TO MICROSOFT

The Justice Department presents network effects as if they were an unmitigated blessing for the dominant producer and to no one else. The argument is that network effects provide protection for a monopolist such that it can comfortably hide behind the switching cost of changing to a new product. That's not really the case, and Microsoft executives know it, which is one reason the company is constantly upgrading all of its programs and not sitting back and enjoying its success, as we would expect a monopolist to do. The fact of the matter is that network effects represent a competitive threat to any firm that seeks to survive for long and, accordingly, has an eye on its stock price.

In markets for conventional goods, if a firm lowers its price (and if nothing else happens in the market), more of the good will be bought. How much more depends upon consumer responsiveness to price changes, or to the demand "elasticity," to reintroduce a bit of economic jargon. The producer of a conventional good need not think much about how the quantity bought today will influence how much more may be bought tomorrow, next week, or next year. Sales do not materially build on themselves over time, because there are no network effects. The responsiveness of consumers of a conventional good to a price change up or down will likely be greater in the long run than the short run. This is because consumers have more time to adjust their purchases among goods over longer periods of time, gradually substituting more and more of the good whose price has fallen for other goods.

Consumer responsiveness to a price change on network goods can be similarly greater in the long run than the short run because of the potential for substitution among goods. However, there is an additional reason why the long-run consumer responsiveness (and the elasticity of demand) for network goods will be higher than that for conventional goods; it can be summed up in two words: network effects. In the case of network goods, a lower price can spawn greater sales today, but as time goes by, those greater current sales can give rise to even greater future sales as sales build on sales, as people seek to move to the dominant firm and take advantage of the network effects. Hence, the long-run responsiveness of consumers (or their elasticity of demand) can be quite high.

It has been long recognized in microeconomic theory that this relatively greater consumer responsiveness can impose a binding constraint on the monopoly powers of the network firm—Microsoft—and the Justice Department and court should know this. When Frederick Warren-Boulton testified that the "price elasticity of derived demand for PC operating systems must be very low for at least a significant price range," he was clearly thinking in terms of conventional goods of the industrial era, not the network goods of the digital age. He based his deductions on prior comments about how the price of the operating system to computer makers "averaged about 2.5%," causing him to suggest that a "10% increase in the price of the OS [operating system] would result at most in a 1% increase in the price of even inexpensive PCs," thus causing consumers to be very unresponsive to the price of the operating system. Warren-Boulton is no doubt right—for the *short run*, for the reason he gives, mainly switching costs. If the network firm, Microsoft, tries to raise its price, the consumer short-run response might not be immediately all that great, which would result in a rise in the firm's short-run revenues and profits. (If a firm raises its price by 10 percent, but sales decline in the short run by, say, 1 percent because consumers are unresponsive in the short run, then its short-run profits will naturally rise as short-run revenues rise and short-run costs fall with fewer sales.)

However, raising the price to a higher level and holding it there can be myopic, given the prospects of network effects that Warren-Boulton and everyone associated with the Microsoft prosecution believe are rampant in software markets. Lower sales in the short run can give rise to even lower sales tomorrow or next month, which can give rise to even lower sales next year. That's the nature of network effects working in reverse. The result can be that profits can rise in the short run but fall over the long term, especially when people expect the price to be held to its monopoly level, and it is the long-run stream of profits that will govern the firm's stock price, which in turn will determine a firm's pricing policy for its product. This means that a price increase currently can, in the presence of substantial network effects, translate into a lower stock price.

Once again, the Justice Department wants to have it both ways. It can't claim that the operating system (or any other software market) is controlled by substantial network effects and then pretend that consumer responsiveness (or the elasticity of demand) will be low for all time. The fact of the matter is that substantial network effects translate into a significant curb on any monopoly power the dominant network firm, Microsoft, might have.

And the dominant firm's monopoly powers are necessarily constrained by another factor that the Justice Department doesn't appear to recognize: the network effects are available to all comers. The dominant network firm has to worry at all times that if it raises its price, some other firm will take that pricing strategy as an opportunity to move into the market with a lower price (and some expenditures to overcome the switching costs), and allow the resulting network to build on itself, to the detriment of the once-dominant firm.

Apple Computers may at one time have thought it could extract additional short-run profits by restricting sales of both its operating system and its computers. Apple's restrictive strategy was a market opening for Microsoft, which exploited it to the hilt, just as the theory suggests some firms would. The result is what we have today, the personal computer market dominated by Microsoft, which followed an open (or "let you") licensing strategy. Apple is today a minor player because it followed a closed (or "got you") licensing strategy, which it thought would be its road to riches.

Put another way, Microsoft's dominance today may be ascribed as much to what Apple (and others) did wrong as to what Microsoft did right. If Microsoft and Apple had swapped market strategies years ago, the Justice Department might be suing Apple today, not Microsoft. That prospect contains a sad commentary on the nation's antitrust enforcement policy. The Justice Department and court are attacking market success, not market failure.

Warren-Boulton believes that Microsoft is protected from entry in the face of monopoly pricing because each potential new supplier can be expected to reason that the resulting competition between itself and Microsoft "would likely result in a decrease in prices, further reducing the profitability of entry to the would-be entrant. Entry into head-to-head operating system competition with Microsoft thus would be time consuming, risky, and costly; profiting from such entry would be at best very uncertain and long in coming." Warren-Boulton's argument has an appealing ring, so long as you overlook the fact that Microsoft's customers (especially those in charge of information technology systems in firms) might be as smart as the lawyers at the Justice Department and so could hire economists like Warren-Boulton, or Franklin Fisher, to alert them to the long-term monopoly prices Microsoft presumably charges and to how the cost of staying with Microsoft would likely exceed their switching costs. You might think that armed with such knowledge from such informed sources, Microsoft's customers would be eager to switch to and stay with any new entrant offering equal quality software products selling for less than the monopoly price that Microsoft presumably charges. Given how relatively cheap operating systems are, you might even think that many customers, especially corporate customers, would be willing to buy the new entrant's competing operating system, even though they planned to continue using Microsoft's operating system. Such a purchase would send a clear message to Microsoft: "Act like a monopolist, and my company is prepared to switch."

DIGITAL OPPORTUNISM

All businesses, regardless of their industries, have to worry about their buyers and suppliers who might behave *opportunistically*, that is, take advantage of their particular bargaining position—and no doubt about it, many firms will not think twice about taking every opportunity at their disposal to gain at the expense of the people they deal with. What are some of the ways a firm can behave opportunistically? Suppose a firm buys a specialized piece of manufacturing equipment—say, a metal casting machine—because another business customer has agreed to buy some specified volume of a metal part at a price that makes the equipment purchase profitable. Suppose also that the equipment is so specialized that there is no resale market for it. Without some form of protection (for example, a tightly worded contract), the firm that buys the equipment has set itself up for what economists understandably call a "holdup," a form of opportunistic behavior. After the equipment has been bought, the parts buyer can demand a lower price that might make the equipment purchase unprofitable—but so what? The company has already bought the equipment and can't use it for any other purpose. As in real holdups, the firm must concede to the demands of the parts buyer.

The Justice Department and court have basically argued that Microsoft has in identifiable cases behaved opportunistically. That may be true, but it doesn't mean that the basis of Microsoft's actions is its monopoly power. The reason for the opportunistic behavior could be bad manners, lack of ethics, bad judgment, and miscalculations. Any firm could fall prey to the attraction of opportunistic behavior. The court might, however, believe that Microsoft's opportunism is much more widespread than the opportunism of other computer and software industry firms, and the judge does spill a lot of ink in his Findings of Fact, trying to show that Microsoft's opportunism has been evident in much, and perhaps all, of its business dealings.

Some of the court's examples of supposed opportunism seem to be more legal padding than anything else. For example, it cites the time in 1995 when Intel began to develop software to work with its microprocessors and to compete with Microsoft's products. According to the court, Microsoft pressured Intel to terminate its software project by threatening to stop supporting Intel chips as it had in the past. Is this opportunism from a monopolist? The court thinks so, but it might very well be the kind of bargaining that should be expected by firms that form strategic alliances even when everyone involved in the bargain is in a competitive market. Microsoft's pressure on Intel may be seen as nothing more than one party's (Microsoft's) insisting that the other party (Intel) live up to their previous bargain to specialize their work. The bargaining can also be interpreted as the actions of a network manager trying to hold the network together, for the benefit of everyone involved, producers (Intel as well as Microsoft, given that Intel would not have to worry about Microsoft going into the chip business) and consumers (computer manufacturers and users).

The court also includes examples of wrongdoing on Microsoft's part that may indeed have been properly characterized in the Findings of Fact as opportunistic behavior on Microsoft's part but that did not work. For example, the court notes that RealNetworks' streaming media software was a potential threat to the Windows platform. In its efforts to put the breaks on RealNetworks' software development for multiple computer platforms, Microsoft supposedly bought VXtreme, a streaming media company, to use as a bargaining chip to get RealNetworks to limit its software development to programs that run on top of Windows in exchange for Microsoft's agreement to promote RealNetworks' streaming media with Internet Explorer. Sounds like a good old-fashioned quid pro quo: you do something for me and I'll do something for you. Obviously, Microsoft didn't have sufficient monopoly power to force RealNetworks to accept the deal, which it didn't accept.

Other examples of wrongdoing are included in the Findings of Fact that could be interpreted in ways other than the pernicious actions of a monopolist. We must be wary of accepting carefully crafted examples that seem to be credible monopoly explanations but aren't. The history of antitrust enforcement is replete with seemingly plausible monopoly stories that have been successfully used in court for decades, but that on serious scholarly reflection have been found to be dead wrong (as the former federal judge Robert Bork has argued in excruciating detail in his classic work on antitrust law).

For example, the court notes that in 1995, Microsoft offered AOL a place on the desktop—some of the most "valuable real estate" in the world, according to many industry observers—if AOL would make Internet Explorer its preferred browser. Is this really evidence of a monopoly at work? If so, on the part of Microsoft or AOL, or both? Again, the deal seems for all the world to be nothing more than two businesses trading assets. If the desktop is valuable real estate that Microsoft was clearly instrumental in creating, and Netscape had absolutely nothing to do with its creation, should Microsoft not be allowed to use its assets in bargains with AOL or any other firm, just as Netscape could be expected to use its assets?

If being AOL's preferred browser was so valuable to Microsoft, as the court and Netscape seem to think, it stands to reason that Netscape could have used its substantial resources to pay AOL the required price for making Navigator its preferred browser. This might not have been so much a case of Microsoft acting opportunistically as it was a case in which Netscape put less value on a deal with AOL than did Microsoft, or else Netscape could and would have outbid Microsoft for the right to be AOL's preferred browser.

The court goes on to note, "Microsoft actually paid AOL a bounty for every subscriber that it converted to access software that included Internet Explorer instead of Navigator." So what? Netscape could have done likewise. There is nothing in this deal that prevented Netscape from competing. Okay, Microsoft is a very profitable company with a lot of business wealth, but it is not going to pay more for access to AOL's subscribers than it is worth, and that worth was available to Netscape, especially if it intended to become the next Microsoft, as its founders claimed it could be with the development of an alternative computer platform. Netscape could have made a bid for preferential treatment by AOL and financed the deal in any number of ways, not the least of which is a loan against future earnings from having the deal with AOL. As it was, the AOL space went to the highest valued user, Microsoft.

Both the Justice Department and court have argued that software markets are beset with switching costs, which make it difficult for new firms to enter the market and accumulate the requisite customer base to make entry profitable. But then the court in effect denounces Microsoft for having paid AOL "$500,000 plus 25 cents up to $1 million for upgrading 5.25 million subscribers by April 1997." The court saw the deal as a one made by a deep-pocket monopolist trying to prevent the distribution of a rival product. But it could also be seen as the result of one competitor, Microsoft, outbidding another, Netscape, for a valuable piece of property, AOL's subscribers. Surely, Microsoft's bid didn't preclude Netscape from bidding more, and it seems as though the terms of the deal were well within Netscape's ability to top, if Netscape had seen AOL's property as being more valuable than Microsoft did. The deal could also be seen as a way for a competitor—in this case, Netscape—to overcome switching costs, a presumed source of market inefficiency. Through this type of deal, Microsoft effectively showed the court how the problem of switching costs in moving from Navigator to Internet Explorer could be overcome. But the court chose to see the deal as counterproductive—in spite of the fact that the court recognized that AOL also chose Internet Explorer because it had technology that Navigator did not have at that time.

The judge goes on to stress that Microsoft lowered its price on Windows to computer makers that agreed to promote Internet Explorer. Again, so what? Netscape could have competed with Microsoft by offering computer makers a fee for promoting Navigator that was greater than the reduction in the price of Windows that Microsoft offered. That's how competition among competitors works; you outbid everyone else, and that seems to be what Microsoft did—it outbid Netscape.

Then the judge faults Microsoft for providing a Web-based technology to Internet access providers: the providers could download Internet Explorer if they distributed copies of Internet Explorer to their customers. Twenty-five hundred

Internet access providers made the download. Again, this seems to be a smart move on the part of a firm that was acting competitively and was intent on dominating the browser market more aggressively and competitively than Netscape. But the judge chides Microsoft for having pressed the Internet access providers who made the download to live up to their obligations to distribute Internet Explorer. Yet any firm, competitor or monopolist, has the right to ensure that its customers live up to their agreements.

The court also found that Microsoft pressured IBM to stop installing on its own personal computers IBM software, OS/2 and SmartSuite, that competed directly with Microsoft's applications, Windows and Office Suite. Because IBM would not concede to Microsoft's demands, "IBM (along with Gateway) paid significantly more for Windows than other major OEMs (like Compaq, Dell, and Hewlett-Packard) that were more compliant." The way the episode is constructed, you might think that IBM was worse off than other computer manufacturers that got lower prices, but that is not necessarily the case. It is only natural for a firm like Microsoft that sells an array of software products to offer discounts on Windows to firms that are willing to promote Microsoft's applications. What Microsoft gives up on the price of Windows, it makes back on sales of other applications. Through discounts on Windows, Microsoft effectively shares with computer makers some of its profits on application sales that the computer makers encourage. It's a win-win arrangement. IBM didn't take the discount deal, presumably because it figured that it would make more money on the sale of its own software than it would gain from a Windows discount. In short, by not taking the discount deal, IBM was not harmed; it was better off than it otherwise would have been. IBM's only complaint may be that Microsoft didn't offer enough of a discount.

Throughout the Findings of Fact, the judge constantly seems to suggest that anything bad that happens to any software firm should be attributable to Microsoft's impenetrable "applications barrier to entry." For example, the court finds that "IBM's inability to gain widespread developer support for its OS/2 Warp operating system illustrates how the massive Windows installed base makes it prohibitively costly for a rival operating system to attract enough developer support to challenge Windows."

The judge simply doesn't understand the full history of the operating system wars. If he did, he would understand that IBM made several critical mistakes in its promotion of the OS/2 applications network. For instance, according to the *Byte* magazine columnist Jerry Pournelle, IBM sought to make money off its software development kit, charging as much as $600. Meanwhile, Microsoft was passing out a software development kit free of charge to anyone remotely connected with programming work. In addition, IBM made the twin mistakes of not adequately coping with the growth in CD-ROMs and of not incorporating Internet access technology in its operating system. On the other hand Microsoft was aggressive on both technology fronts, plus any number of others, not the least of which is the resources devoted to encouraging its programmers' network. Pournelle concluded after reading Judge Jackson Findings of Fact, "In other words, the story told in this judgment is flat wrong: IBM didn't lose because of Microsoft's dominance; it lost because it didn't take the competition seriously. I am reminded of Aesop: The fox, chided for failing to catch a rabbit, said, 'I was only running for my dinner. The hare was running for his life.' Microsoft, an unimportant company much smaller than IBM when this competition began, was running for its life. In doing so, it ended up eating IBM's dinner."

Of course, other examples of opportunistic actions that the court highlights as monopolistic could be cited. But the court's labeling of an action as one by a monopolist acting opportunistically doesn't necessarily mean that it is any such thing. We can easily imagine that many software business dealings involve similar deals by all sorts of firms.

There are two episodes the court cites in its Findings of Fact that, if they were true, would indeed look like Microsoft's rank opportunism at work and would be troubling, even for Microsoft defenders. Yet once again, the cases are not as simple as the court makes them look.

In the Findings of Fact, Judge Jackson relates the Justice Department's claim that in late spring and summer of 1995, Netscape needed technical information—the API, or application program interface (technically, the "remote network access application program interface")—from Microsoft in order to finalize the development of a new version of Navigator for Windows 95. According to the court, Microsoft wanted Netscape to enter into a "special relationship" with it under which Netscape would allegedly have been required to suppress its competitive intentions against Windows. Netscape refused to do this, and Microsoft did not release the needed API to Netscape until October, causing Netscape to "postpone its release of its Windows 95 browser until substantially after the release of Windows 95 (and Internet Explorer) in August 1995. If this did happen as described, then Microsoft seems to be guilty of obstructing competition.

Was it? Microsoft argues that it introduced evidence in court, evidence that was not challenged by the Justice Department and was not acknowledged in the Findings, showing that through both the Microsoft Development Network and the Web, Netscape had access to all the technical information it needed to complete its browser development. Microsoft maintains that Netscape's claim on this issue was totally fabricated out of whole cloth.

The second case involved Apple Computer. The court found that in 1996 Apple was shipping Internet Explorer with the Apple operating system, but was also preinstalling Netscape Navigator as the default browser. In 1997, Apple's market share was falling and its market fortunes looked bleak; any indication that Microsoft might drop the development of Office for the Mac could lead to a major loss of market confidence that could seal Apple's fate. According to the court, Microsoft threatened to terminate development of Mac Office unless Apple made Internet Explorer the default browser, removed any other browser from the desktop and placed it in a folder, and encouraged Apple employees to use Internet Explorer.

Supposedly, Gates called Steve Jobs to ask how they might break the news on the termination of Microsoft's development of Mac Office, and after this call Apple conceded to Microsoft's demands. One could argue that Microsoft should be free to use its development resources in any way it chooses in order to get its way, but that would seem to be a legal stretch. Even if such threats by Microsoft were legal—and their legality does seem suspect—they still appear opportunistic, if not ruthless. If such threats were indeed made, an argument could be advanced that Apple had no reason to believe back in the eighties that the continued development of Mac Office in the late 1990s would be conditioned on new, unexpected, seemingly unrelated events like the advent of the Internet and Apple's acceptance of Internet Explorer as its favored browser.

However, Microsoft tells the story a different way. It contends that it showed in court that its concerns about the continued development of Mac Office arose out of a cross-patent dispute that began back in 1993 and was still unresolved in 1997. In 1993, Apple accused Microsoft of infringement of numerous Apple patents and demanded $1.2 billion in unpaid royalties, plus a variety of other concessions. Microsoft also fervently maintains that it was reconsidering its continued development of Mac Office because of the Apple's shrinking market share and precarious financial conditions. There would be no reason for Microsoft to incur the costs of developing Mac Office if Apple was not expected to survive. Microsoft and Apple settled the dispute in August 1997. There were three main conditions of the settlement: (1) Microsoft would provide Apple with a $100 million royalty payment for the cross-patent license. (2) Microsoft would invest $150 million in Apple. (3) Microsoft would continue the development of Mac Office. For its part of the technology agreement, Apple agreed to make Internet Explorer Apple's default browser. Seems like a pretty good deal for Apple, and at the time, Steve Jobs publicly lauded it.

Even if the Netscape and Apple episodes had been accurately described by the court, it does not follow that the best remedy against Microsoft's opportunism would be one fashioned by the courts. Opportunistic behavior has feedback effects in markets. If Microsoft has been acting opportunistically, it will likely learn (as it may be learning) that the people with whom it deals are smart enough to expect that the company will probably act opportunistically again in the future. These smart people will take precautions to guard themselves against Microsoft's expected opportunism. Even monopolies intent on making as much money as possible can't impose costs on the firms with which they deal without having to incur those costs embedded in lower prices they can extract. This will be especially true for computer manufacturers, which, the judge insists, operate on such low margins that "just three calls from a consumer can erase the entire profit that an OEM earned selling a PC system to that consumer."

Granted, such market-imposed remedies may take time in coming and may not be as precise or severe as some Microsoft critics might like. But the shortcomings of real-world market remedies for opportunism must be measured against real-world government-imposed remedies. These may be even slower in coming, may be far more severe than necessary, and may be tainted with the political demands of Microsoft competitors. Their interest may be not to punish Microsoft for past wrongdoings but to throttle Microsoft in order to enrich themselves. While evaluating remedies for what appear to be troublesome cases, we must remember that Microsoft categorically denies that events happened as described and has a pile of documents to support its position. The court, in its blanket acceptance of the Justice Department's position, has dismissed these. This means the case is very likely far from over. Stay tuned.

Digital Harm

Both the Justice Department and court understand that in order for any ruling or remedy to stick, they must ultimately show that Microsoft has materially harmed consumers, and the court does identify areas of consumer harm throughout its Findings of Fact. Most of the identified forms of harm—for example, Microsoft's having given away its browser to maintain its monopoly position—have been dealt with directly or indirectly in this and earlier chapters. One of the more important forms of identified harm is how Microsoft's behavior has stifled innovation in software markets; the next chapter will be devoted to this issue.

Many of the other identified forms of harm are stunning for their seeming triviality. For example, the court finds that consumers who do not want a browser or who prefer Navigator may not want the Internet Explorer integrated into Windows because it will soak up their computer's hard-disk space. The judge makes a big deal out of this issue on a couple of occasions, which suggests he hasn't checked the prices of hard drives lately. A megabyte of space on commonly used hard disks on new computers can cost as little as one cent. Internet Explorer adds as little as a couple of dozen megabytes to Windows 98, so the cost of this supposed harm to the consumer is truly trivial, less than the cost of a first-class stamp. With Windows Millennium, the next version of Windows 98, the cost of the hard-disk space for the fully integrated browser components will be down to 17.5 cents!

But it should be added that there might be no net harm even to computer users who do not want Internet Explorer on their operating systems. These users will get the benefits of other features of Windows—embedded applets, for instance—that they want but that other users prefer not to have on their hard drives (applets are small programs like calculation, disk compression, and fax programs). Basically, all consumers share the cost and gain the benefits of a wide offering of components, with a net gain to practically all. Sure, each consumer suffers a hard-disk cost for the unwanted components, but he or she gains greater benefits of desired components at a lower cost than otherwise.

Another consumer harm identified by the court was that having a browser integrated into an operating system slows down some computer functions. Maybe so, but the change in speed is so slight that that it is not likely to be perceptible to the overwhelming majority of users. Furthermore, once again there is a gain for consumers: having an integrated browser can speed up other computer functions for all users, for Web links can be embedded in applications and launched from them.

The court suggests that having an integrated browser can impose security risks for some computer users, especially in businesses, as well as introduce unwanted bugs that add to user support demands. There are technical but relatively easy ways to solve many of these problems for a substantial majority of users.

Granted, not all of such identified problems can be solved for all users, but no one should expect Microsoft, or any other software firms, to provide programs that are perfect for each customer's needs, so that every user, or group of users, gets only what they want. No doubt there are consumers who would prefer a version of Windows without games, WordPad, and the calculator (just to minimize the wasted hard disk space and maximize computers speeds of all users). Imagine if Microsoft tried to tailor versions for individuals or groups—the numerous versions of Windows would undoubtedly add to all the problems that the court now thinks are everywhere evident in the operating system market: consumer "frustration," "confusion," and "increased technical support costs."

Clearly, an operating system is and will always be a "bundle" of attributes. Someone has got to decide exactly what bundle of attributes should be offered, but such product development decisions are necessarily a judgment call. Microsoft may not always have made the best calls for all consumers, but do the judge and lawyers in the Justice Department really think that they could make better calls over time than the people at Microsoft?

There are plenty of solid reasons to doubt this, even if Microsoft were the monopolist it has been made out to be. There would be few competitive market pressures on the Justice Department or the courts to make better calls in terms of the costs and benefits of product development decisions. Moreover, their calls would likely be guided to a significant extent by politics, which has problems of its own, especially when the judgment calls can favor one interest group (Microsoft's competitors) over another (Microsoft), a subject that is taken up later (in Chapters 7–9). If having two versions of Windows—one with and one without Internet Explorer—would suffice in this case, it probably could have been settled long ago. But that solution would not satisfy many of Microsoft's competitors. Just think: if consumers across the board were given their preferred options at what the court believes would be zero cost, the two-browser remedy would make Microsoft even more competitive in its markets, and would make competing with Microsoft all the more difficult. That is not an outcome sought by the industry backers of the antitrust suit. As a consequence, you can bet that they will be pressing the Justice Department to seek remedies that in some way hobble Microsoft's competitiveness. This is the only outcome that would justify their investment in pressing the case.

CONCLUDING COMMENTS

I have made no attempt in this and the previous chapter to be sympathetic to Microsoft as a company. I don't care about what happens to Microsoft anymore than I care about what happens to any other company that comes under Justice Department antitrust scrutiny. Microsoft is just another company, one in which I have no personal or financial stake. What I do care about is not allowing the goal of winning a case to throttle logical thought. If the Justice Department wants to introduce relatively new economic concepts like network effects and switching costs, then fine. But it shouldn't extend the logic only so long as it suits an antitrust suit.

In one regard in this chapter I have actually tried to be sympathetic to the Justice Department's case and the court's Findings of Fact. I have accepted their major tenet that the operating system and browser markets are subject to prevalent network effects and switching costs. Scale economies and network effects may indeed contribute to a firm's becoming the dominant producer, as the Justice Department and court have argued. However, I have insisted that it does not follow from this that the dominant firm has monopoly power of the kind that has been claimed or that a "superior" product is prevented from taking over the market.

It has also been stressed that in markets where network effects are prevalent, low, zero, and even below-zero prices are indicative of competitive behavior, not monopoly behavior. Also, contrary to what the Justice Department and court maintain, switching costs and lock-ins do not constitute an impenetrable barrier to market entry for a dominant firm acting like a monopoly and therefore do not provide protection from those potential rivals who can find creative ways of covering people's switching costs. Indeed, in a network world, if the dominant firm tries to act like a monopolist, it is all the easier for rivals to take over its market position.

Finally, I have also discussed several key episodes of what the court construes as Microsoft monopolistic misconduct, but that I would term opportunistic. I showed that most of these episodes have legitimate business interpretations. In these episodes, Microsoft may stand wrongly accused. More important, legally contesting the identified practices might very well have a chilling effect on the competitiveness of other firms. Several of the episodes—two, to be exact—are questionable, perhaps reasonably clear violations of the antitrust laws (which an appellate court may have to settle). If those episodes are ultimately ruled to be violations, however, it may be that the remedy is obvious: Restrict Microsoft's opportunism. However, at this writing it is generally believed that the imposition of behavior restrictions won't work without constant court monitoring. If this position is adopted and a more serious, structural remedy is fashioned such as a breakup of the company, for example, it may do more harm to consumer welfare than Microsoft has done. Fortunately, as indicated, markets—especially fast-moving ones—have a way of penalizing opportunists in a far more effective and timely way than maybe the legal system has: they impose costs on the offending opportunists, regardless of whether they are monopolists or competitors.

⚖️ CHAPTER 6 ⚖️

Innovative Thinking

THE MOST REMARKABLE CHARACTERISTIC of the information age is that innovation has proceeded at a pace never before experienced. The Dallas Federal Reserve's chief economist, Michael Cox, and the *Dallas Evening News* reporter Richard Alm, astute observers of the pace of change, have noted that "before the advent of steam power in the early 1800s and electricity a few generations later, they [our ancestors] produced important innovations: paper, plows, printing presses, sails, sextants, telescopes, windmills, smelting furnaces, and architectural arches, to name a few of the most important." But then Cox and Alm lament, "It took them some 6,000 years to do it."

Throughout the last hundred or so years, major innovations—from automobiles (invented in 1886) to airplanes (1903) to the Internet (1991)—have been introduced in ever greater numbers and have spread through the citizenry at ever faster speeds. It took automobiles nearly a hundred years to become a universal fixture in the American way of life, and air travel three quarters of a century. But it's taken the Internet less than a decade to spread to over a third of the American population.

Whereas less than three decades ago products like automobiles and mainframe computers had life cycles that extended over years, products like laptops and cell phones now commonly have life cycles numbered in months. The shortening life cycle is nowhere more evident than in software, where major upgrades may occur every year or so, with minor upgrades more or less continuous.

One of the reasons for the rapid pace of innovation in the software industry is that much of the resource constraints of the old industrial era have evaporated. Today, innovations in software come from carefully rearranging sequences of *1*'s and *0*'s in programs. Slight changes in those sequences can translate into major improvements in computer performance.

THE INNOVATION CLAIMS

In spite of the evidence of the quickening of the pace of change, the Justice Department and court are adamant that Microsoft, with its monopoly power, has been able to harm consumers in part by impairing innovation, not just of a particular firm like Netscape, but broadly, in the whole software industry. Assistant Attorney General for Antitrust Joel Klein argued in his original May 1998 complaint that Microsoft's practice of giving away Internet Explorer and then bundling it with Windows and its practice of developing "exclusive dealing contracts" with computer manufacturers "deter innovation, exclude competition, and rob customers of their right to choose among competitive alternatives." In two separate places in his Findings of Fact of November 1999, Judge Thomas Penfield Jackson concurred strongly with Klein's assessment: "Although Microsoft's campaign to capture the OEM [original equipment manufacturer] channel succeeded, it required a massive and multifarious investment by Microsoft; it also stifled innovation by OEMs that might have made Windows PC systems easier to use and more attractive to consumers." And "Microsoft's past success in hurting such companies and stifling innovation deters investment in technologies and businesses that exhibit the potential to threaten Microsoft. The ultimate result is that some innovations that would truly benefit consumers never occur for the sole reason that they do not coincide with Microsoft's self-interest."

How does this happen? Klein reasons that by seeking to crush Netscape, Microsoft has impaired the "incentive of Microsoft's competitors and potential competitors to undertake research and development, because they know that Microsoft will be able to limit the rewards from any resulting innovation." Consequently, he asserts, Microsoft's practices impair the ability of its competitors and potential competitors to obtain financing for research and development and to successfully market their products. The judge concurs.

Klein's claim has been repeated by any number of other Microsoft critics in and out of court. For example, Thomas Lenard, a researcher for the Progress and Freedom Foundation, which is supported by Microsoft's industry critics, argued in one of the foundation's policy papers that the mere existence of a competitive browser was "extremely threatening" to Microsoft, mainly because the Java-Navigator development environment can run on "numerous" operating systems. (Java is a programming language developed by Sun Microsystems that allows applications written in it to run on any processor—a personal computer, Macintosh, network computer, or even a cell phone.) Consequently, it is clear to Lenard that "Microsoft has a clear incentive to destroy the 'cross-platform compatibility' characteristic of Java." Lenard and many others accept as fact that Microsoft has yielded to the monopoly incentives it faces; according to them, it follows that "Microsoft's practices pose an additional burden on potential competitors and diminish the likelihood that innovators will attempt to enter markets where Microsoft is dominant."

THE NETSCAPE EXPERIENCE

Before we accept the critics' arguments, we need to get the facts straight. First and foremost, Netscape was never actually *crushed* by Microsoft. Indeed, Netscape was bought lock, stock, and programs by America Online in November 1998, less than four and a half years after it was founded. At the time the deal was struck in November 1998 the "price" was $4.3 billion in AOL stock, but the rapid appreciation of AOL stock meant the deal was worth $10 billion to Netscape shareholders by the time it was finalized in the spring of 1999.

It's possible that Netscape's market value might have been much higher had Microsoft not entered the browser market. It is true that Netscape's stock price shot up in the first few months after the company went public in August 1995, only to fall when Microsoft introduced Internet Explorer and then rapidly upgraded the program. But it is still important to recognize Netscape's final sale price, because it suggests that the rewards for creating a browser company that expands into other software markets, as Netscape did, remain substantial. This suggests that innovation in the browser or any other market might not have been impaired in any systematic way. In fact, after all is said and done, the Netscape experience might have elevated the rate of innovation because it elevated the *perceived* rewards.

Make no mistake about it, innovation is dependent on the motivation provided by *expected* rewards, after the potential rewards have been properly discounted by the risks that the innovation would not be received. For example, if a firm estimates that an innovative product might generate $1 million in profits when successful, but only has a one-in-ten chance of doing so, the firm will base its research and development work on the assumption that the *expected* reward will be $100,000. This is the case because it will lose on nine of the ten innovations, earning the $1 million only once, which means the average profit per attempt will be one tenth of $1 million.

In the spring of 1994, when Netscape's cofounders, Jim Clark and Marc Andreesen, first met to discuss forming a joint venture, the risk of their venture's not paying off was substantial, quite irrespective of what Microsoft did. Indeed, we have to wonder whether Clark and Andreesen (both of whom moved on in 1999 to new startup firms) believed way back in 1994 that they would create over the next four and a half years a company that would be worth what Netscape was sold for. It's doubtful. Probably they, like Gates, were rewarded beyond their wildest dreams. And it is also possible that other innovators could look at the full sweep of Netscape's history, including the competitive troubles it encountered from Microsoft, and take from it a great deal of inspiration to search for the next "big idea" in software.

According to Jim Clark's story of Netscape's formation and development, he and Andreesen were at first puzzled over what they would do together, until Andreesen hit upon the idea of developing a "Mosaic killer," a browser that would be much better and faster than Mosaic, which was by far the most widely used browser in 1994. Once they decided on creating a "Mosaic killer," they went into the browser business fully aware that when Gates decided to react to Netscape's success, it would be "with ferocity." Indeed, Clark says that he and Andreesen fully understood that, as they put it, "Gates was like the evil Lord Sauron in J. R. R. Tolkien's fable *The Lord of the Rings*, whose all-seeing eye searched ceaselessly for any threat to his tyranny." Yet he and Andreesen took the risk they did with some eagerness, mainly because the potential rewards were so high. Also, they probably understood that Gates and Microsoft was not an unmitigated negative when they estimated the potential return on their investment, for Microsoft might buy Netscape out. In fact, Clark reports that he offered Microsoft an equity interest in Netscape in the fall of 1994, plus a seat on its board, in order to bring in some much needed investment funds. Even if Gates lived up (maybe it should be "down") to their expectations, the expected payoff could still be substantial for what was anticipated to be a fairly small investment by Clark and Andreesen.

Apparently they were right in their calculations. Both sides of their investment equation—the gains and costs—came to fruition in a remarkably short period of time. Even with Microsoft eventually dominating their market, the increase in their personal net worth amounted to hundreds of millions of dollars each.

Would Clark and Andreesen have undertaken their joint venture in 1994 had they known what their experience over the next four years would actually be? The Justice Department appears to have concluded that Clark and Andreesen would not have done what they did. That's hardly likely. But even if the two had been deterred, it's also very likely that any number of other entrepreneurs, even if they could have known the full record of Netscape's future success and problems, would likely have jumped at the chance. As Clark tells the story, the programmers who joined Netscape at the start worked night and day on Navigator in part because they feared that other programmers in other startups might be doing the exact same thing: trying to come up with a "Mosaic killer."

COMPETITION TO INNOVATE

The Justice Department charges that if Microsoft had not entered the browser market, the incentives and rewards accruing to Netscape would have been far greater than they turned out to be—that the price of Netscape's stock would have followed a higher path on stock markets over its short life than it did. However, the Justice

Department has not attempted to show that the price of Netscape's stock would have followed any other path than the one it did. Given the government's firm charge that Microsoft harmed Netscape and, because of that harm, has impaired innovation and hurt consumers generally, this is not a trivial, merely academic issue. There are statistical procedures the government surely knows about—government economists use them all the time—and could have used to support its position. But it chose not to use them and present the documentation in court, maybe for a very good reason: the evidence doesn't match up with the government's strong charge.

Admittedly, it's hard to show what would have been if a certain thing had or had not happened. But then this means that the Justice Department and court really don't know what would have happened to the incentives to innovate had Microsoft not been around. The government's charge amounts to pure speculation, which seems like a poor foundation for a serious charge of consumer harm in order to make its broader antitrust case stick. What we do know is that Netscape's market life would not likely have been a comfortable one even if Microsoft had not entered its market. By the time Microsoft bought the rights to use the Mosaic browser technology from its developer, Spyglass, in early 1995, Spyglass had licensed the technology to twenty other firms, and any one of these could well have entered the browser market had Microsoft not done so, and these other firms might have cut into Netscape's market share as fast as or even faster than Microsoft did.

The point is that Netscape had no intention of making life easy for Spyglass; they intended to "kill" every version of Mosaic available by making Navigator substantially better than the others, and then giving it away. Similarly, several of these other firms that had licensed the Mosaic technology would have certainly been more active competitors had Microsoft not been as active as it was.

In addition, by Jim Clark's own admission, it only took him, Andreesen, and six other recent University of Illinois computer science graduates who had developed Mosaic while in college four months to write the code for Navigator from scratch. In fact, Clark is open on the subject of how easy it is to write such computer programs: "In comparison [to industrial age goods], the manufacture of software is no big deal. The idea, the design, and the engineering are all done in the same place, by the same people. The basic materials are laughably cheap. No spot-welding robots need apply. All you need is a good brain and an okay computer (though some people have managed surprisingly well by reversing those adjectives)." This means that without Microsoft around, there very likely would have been a host of entrants into the browser market, especially if Netscape had done what it wanted to do, sell its browser at a significant price and garner even more profits than it did. These other entrants would have jumped through all sorts of Internet hoops to get a part of Netscape's action.

Gates was probably right when he concluded as early as the fall of 1994 that because of the economics of producing browsers—they were unbelievably easy to duplicate—there would be no money to be made in browsers by anyone, so Microsoft might just as well go ahead and give its browser away.

Mind you, Microsoft did have an extra competitive incentive to give away its browser, as the Justice Department claimed: Microsoft understood that in the then projected expansion of the Internet world, any operating system with a browser included would be seen by buyers as superior to an operating system without one. The combination of Navigator and Java was definitely a competitive threat to Windows not only because it could be used on a variety of computer platforms, but because, unless Microsoft reacted by developing a browser technology and tying it to Windows, the Netscape-Java development environment would be seen as superior to Windows and could eventually replace it.

Did Microsoft act as a monopolist by trying to protect its Windows turf? Not at all. Monopolists are companies that restrict output to raise prices. The Justice Department has never presented any evidence that Microsoft has done that. All it has ever accused Microsoft of doing is lowering its price (to zero and below) for the purpose of expanding its market. In the process, Microsoft actually innovated, producing a browser that was better reviewed than Netscape's. These are classic competitive—not monopolistic—responses.

Would the Internet market have experienced more or less innovation in the browser or any other software market if Microsoft had stayed on the sidelines? The answer is certainly not as clear as the Justice Department lawyers, the court, Lenard, and other Microsoft critics seem to think. First, it needs to be stressed that because Microsoft entered the browser market, Netscape probably was spurred to innovate more rapidly than it would have done otherwise. It probably upgraded its browser faster and more extensively than otherwise, and then, because of the Microsoft threat, it probably looked more aggressively for other software products that it could produce and that would be outside Microsoft's market purview.

Second, because of the Netscape-Microsoft market rivalry, Microsoft was spurred to innovate at a faster pace than it might have chosen had Navigator never been developed. And to win what became known as the "browser war," Microsoft and Netscape probably upgraded their innovation plans each time the other came out with a "new and improved version." The result today is that the Mosaic browser technology was all but scrapped early in the browser war, and both Navigator and Internet Explorer are probably far better than either would have been without the other. What is remarkable is that from this competitive struggle, consumers got something, a browser, that is basically free, and this has resulted in many other innovative Web-based products being created and then given away. Indeed, in one of the very few tips of his legal hat to Microsoft in his entire Findings of Fact, Judge Jackson observed, "The debut of Internet Explorer and its rapid improvement gave Netscape an incentive to improve Navigator's quality at a competitive rate. The inclusion of Internet Explorer with Windows at no separate charge increased general familiarity with the Internet and reduced the cost to the public of gaining access to it, at least in part because it compelled Netscape to stop charging for Navigator. These actions thus contributed to improving the quality of Web browsing software, lowering its cost, and increasing its availability, thereby benefitting consumers."

What more could the Justice Department and court want, assuming that they are doing what they are supposed to be doing—working for consumers—not working for specific competitors like Netscape? Understandably, the founders of Netscape wanted the company to be worth more than it was when it sold out to AOL, but the Justice Department's and the court's role in enforcing antitrust laws is not to protect or enhance the wealth of particular firms. Their role should be to increase the wealth of consumers by encouraging competition that could cause the demise of some companies.

THE MICROSOFT THREAT?

Does Microsoft's mere existence, backed up by the threat of Gates's "all-seeing eye" that searches "ceaselessly for any threat to his tyranny," deter innovation? Frankly, Microsoft could be deterring some innovations by people outside Microsoft, those that Microsoft could easily duplicate and sell at lower prices, of which the browser might be one, but then there is no real reason we should have an economy that encourages innovations where they are not needed, or where the innovators are not likely to be the most cost-effective producers. At the same time, Gates's "all-seeing eye" could also be encouraging other innovations. This is because Microsoft stands as an additional buyer for innovative software products, adding to their market demands and to their sales prices—and, hence, to others' incentive to innovate.

Given Microsoft's ability to market and distribute software products, it is very likely that it can outbid many other existing competitors for innovative products. As a consequence, Microsoft's market superiority could be an important spur to all sorts of innovations, not a factor undercutting the returns to innovation, as the Justice Department seems to believe. More innovators than otherwise could do their thing in anticipation of reaping the rewards of a Microsoft network and a Microsoft buyout. As pointed out, Clark and Andreesen checked out Microsoft as a buyer of an equity share of Netscape in late 1994, so it is likely that the thought of doing just that crossed their minds six months earlier, when they were contemplating the establishment of Netscape.

Jim Clark worries that if entrepreneurs seek only to be bought by Microsoft, they "won't want to do things the elegant, interesting way, but merely the Microsoft way." There is really nothing in the opportunity of a Microsoft buyout that prevents people from doing "elegant" (but presumably not highly profitable) things. They can still do that, if they wish. But they will not reap the prospect of a higher return that can come from a Microsoft buyout; they will have to be satisfied with the personal reward of having done what they, not Microsoft, wanted to do. But who's to say whether doing something the "elegant" way or the Microsoft way is more innovative? What we do know from Clark's own book, *Netscape Time,* is that Clark and Andreesen's primary goal from the start was not so much to do the "elegant" thing; it was to produce a "Mosaic killer" that would make the founders one whale of a lot of money, and they accomplished this in spades.

Without hesitation Clark adds at one point in his book that "if Microsoft owns the browser as well as the operating system, there will be no Yahoo!, no Infoseek, no Excite, just Bill standing at the gate, pointing out where he wants to go. Microsoft will be the one and only 'portal' [Web entry point]." Such hyperbolic argumentation, which has been common in the Microsoft debate, can be judged on its own merits. In spite of Microsoft's owning the browser and operating system, Yahoo!, Infoseek, and Excite do exist! Microsoft is hardly the only Web portal—there are tens, if not hundreds, of thousands—and Microsoft is not, at this writing, widely known for its portal prowess.

Network Effects, Again

We must remember that software markets are subject to network effects, and this also goes for browser software. This means that the number of programs written with a given browser depends on how many people are using the browser, or are expected eventually to use it. A market fragmented among several browsers can be a market that potentially limits the development of innovative products.

The Justice Department has staked its case on the idea that innovation has been stifled by Microsoft's market tactics, especially its aggressive push to make its technology the market standard. But the opposite may in fact be the case. Microsoft's mere existence, and the competitive threat it posed to other browser companies, could have had exactly the opposite effect. It may be that back during the browser war, innovators anticipated that Microsoft would be the eventual winner and that its browser would be fully integrated with Windows. This may have spurred innovators to innovate related Internet software and Web sites more rapidly than they otherwise would have, saving some time and development costs in the process, which means more resources may have been available for the development of additional software and Web innovations. It may very well be that in spite of any difficulties Netscape might have confronted, the Web is more fully developed today than it would have been had Gates never seen the emergence of the "Internet tidal wave" (the phrase Gates used in a May 1995 memo to Microsoft executives).

This line of argument is the same kind of speculation about past history that the Justice Department and court have undertaken. But that is the point. The Justice Department and court present their claims regarding Microsoft's impact as if they were proof positive of the antitrust charges it has leveled against Gates and company. Yet the arguments about Microsoft's impact on innovation can just as easily go the other way—and very likely do. There may have been net consumer gains from Microsoft's existence, mainly because Microsoft has provided relatively cheap software that works on a multitude of computer platforms, which can now be used to produce any number of innovative products—for all we know, Navigator was created on a computer running Windows.

STIFLING SUPERIOR PRODUCTS

What is remarkable about the Microsoft case is that the Justice Department and court dare to claim solemnly that Microsoft, the presumed monopolist, has been able to stifle the development of an alternative computer platform, which would have combined Netscape's Navigator with Sun's Java. Moreover, this new platform, according to the Justice Department and court, could have been superior to Windows with or without Internet Explorer, had Microsoft not quashed Netscape with "predatory" prices and all the rest.

This argument doesn't make a great deal of sense unless you assume that Justice Department lawyers and the court are a lot smarter than a lot of other people around the world, including those who are a lot closer to the computer market and have financial stakes in it. Microsoft is not capable of destroying new age software products in the same way that industrial-era products could be destroyed—say, by blowing them up or terminating production. Navigator still exists on maybe a quarter of all personal computers, and really can't be destroyed by Microsoft. It can still be used by any firm or combination of firms (for example, AOL, which now owns Netscape and Sun) that thinks it can put together a computing platform, including a browser, that is superior to Windows.

If Microsoft had been acting like a monopolist before the development of Navigator and Java, and was expected to continue to operate like one into the distant future, Navigator with Java could have easily entered Microsoft's market and taken it over, especially since the Navigator-Java combination had the presumed advantage of operating on several computer platforms. Computer buyers—especially corporate buyers—are not likely to stay with a firm that is expected to continue to operate like a monopolist when there is a superior, lower-priced alternative available. As noted in an earlier chapter, switching costs should not be much of a barrier to switching, especially for large corporate buyers, if the firm truly operates like a monopolist. Moreover, the Justice Department has speculated that the Navigator-Java combination would substantially lower the cost of switching. (Of course, the Justice Department might be wrong on this.) And to hear Netscape and Sun tout the benefits of their platform, no one would have to switch from Windows anyway. Computer users can use Netscape-Java on top of Windows or any other platform.

What about the scenario that Microsoft could act like a competitor when threatened and then like a monopolist when it has beaten the competition. Smart buyers are not likely to be fooled for long. These buyers could easily see Microsoft's strategy of being an "intermittent monopolist," which necessarily means it would still over time be giving its users a worse deal than they could get with some other operating system. If Microsoft acted like an intermittent monopolist the incentive of buyers to switch to a truly superior, lower-priced operating system would still be there.

THE SUPERIORITY OF NAVIGATOR-JAVA?

This all leads to an important question: Would a combination Navigator and Java platform actually have been superior to Windows? More generally, would a cross-platform operating system necessarily be superior to a single-platform operating system? The answer is not at all clear. Technical experts have raised some questions about the relative speed of programs written with Java, mainly because Java works "on top" of other operating systems and there is an extra layer of code, which can slow down computers.

Like all business endeavors, software programs involve a host of tradeoffs, and in order to enable a program to operate on several platforms, the Navigator-Java–based programs might have to give up advantages that a single-platform program would not have to give up, for example, the advanced operating system features that have been written into new versions of Mac or Windows. In addition, the Navigator-Java development environment was to be plotted with the idea that applications would run through the Web, off a central server, which means that the operating speed of the applications will be significantly influenced by the bandwidth of the connecting network and the amount of other Internet traffic at the time of use by someone wanting to write a document or develop a spreadsheet.

This arrangement might turn out to be superior in speed, features, and price to the Windows-based desktop systems people use today, but the point is that the superiority of Navigator-Java for the broad sweep of computer consumers targeted by Microsoft has yet to be proved. The fact that Navigator-Java has never emerged as a commercially viable platform alternative may not be attributable to Microsoft's monopoly power at all, but rather to the superiority of the Windows platform.

If the Navigator-Java development environment were indeed superior and preferable to current users, Netscape and Sun would not have given up on it, even with a zero price for the browser, and there would be no need for the Justice Department to charge Microsoft with being a monopolist, and for the court to so rule. If Navigator-Java were a real improvement and could be sold in combination at a lower price than Windows with Internet Explorer, Microsoft's days would surely be numbered—and some industry observers firmly believe they are.

Then again, for the combination of Navigator and Java to work as a platform for computer users, Netscape and Sun must be able to work together. The writer Karen Southwick reports in her account, *High Noon: The Inside Story of Scott McNealy and the Rise of Sun Microsystems*, that Netscape and Sun had a hard time working together on the creation of "Javigator," Navigator written in "pure" Java. Netscape became highly suspicious of Sun's intentions when Sun licensed its Java programming language to Microsoft so that Microsoft could "optimize" Java for the Windows environment. By 1997, before the Justice Department filed its antitrust charges against Microsoft in which it claimed that Microsoft had prevented the emergence of a "commercially viable" computer platform, the relationship between Netscape and Sun had soured. A Netscape executive said, "[W]e basically concluded that Netscape could no longer view Java as the jihad"—the foundation of an assault on Microsoft's operating system market.

Yes, the Navigator-Java development environment could, if it were ever organized, operate on top of many different computer platforms. But would the advent of that development environment be superior and would it stimulate more innovation than would exist if Windows remained the overwhelmingly dominant operating system? The Justice Department seems to think the answer is clearly yes. But we should not be too quick to agree. The Justice Department and court rave about the extent of the network effects in computer software markets. No doubt, some programmers would benefit from the new platform, for they could write their programs in Java once and have them work with all computers, whether Windows, Apple, OS/2, or Unix-based. But just as surely, the fragmentation of the computer platform markets could undermine the network effects and undercut the gains from having one computing platform standard, Windows, that operates on so many of the world's desktop computers. Would there be more or less innovation in the type of world Sun imagines, and the Justice Department and court endorse? I don't know, but neither do the people at the Justice Department nor Judge Jackson.

THE BROWSER: A SIDESHOW

In assessing the Justice Department's claim that Microsoft has throttled Netscape and, as a consequence, throttled innovation, we should understand that the life or death of Netscape may not be the central concern for many of Microsoft's current industry adversaries—Oracle, Sun, IBM, and everyone else. Netscape's troubles may only provide the adversaries with a convenient case for taking Microsoft to court and slowing down Microsoft's invasion of the adversaries' markets. In fact, as will be argued at length in Chapter 8, until 1993, Microsoft was mainly concerned with dominating the desktop market. The back-office market for computer servers was dominated by other companies—who have become Microsoft's political and legal adversaries.

In the early 1990s, Microsoft was innovative in a way that Microsoft's adversaries didn't like: it developed from scratch a totally new operating system technology, Windows NT, for the express purpose of invading the lucrative server market then dominated by Sun, IBM, Oracle, and several other major firms. In the process of innovating and cutting costs, Microsoft contributed mightily to driving down the prices of servers and server operating systems, for Microsoft started doing what it was good at, underpricing the competition. This meant that firms like Dell and Gateway could get into the server business using the familiar Windows computing environment. The Justice Department's case, if successful, could send an important signal to Microsoft and, by extension, to other aggressive competitors: if you try to take over important markets from your competitors, you can be saddled with substantial legal costs. This would certainly impair innovation.

A MATTER OF EVIDENCE

One of the most fundamental problems with the Microsoft case is that the Justice Department often make a very strong claim, that Microsoft's practices "deter innovation," which however they fail to support. You might think this claim could be empirically supported with data at least in some rough and ready way. The Justice Department's claim could be tested against what has actually been observed in computing markets. "Innovation" could be defined by a variety of measures such as patents, the number and variety of new software programs coming on the market, the spread of personal computers, etc. These measures could be statistically related to Microsoft's growing dominance for operating systems and/or browsers, as measured by Microsoft's "market shares," for example.

But the Justice Department did no such thing, and the court cited no such evidence in its Findings of Fact. The Justice Department provided absolutely *no* evidence of its claim, other than having its expert witnesses, Franklin Fisher and Frederick Warren-Bolton, repeat the deterring-innovation claim almost verbatim. They provided no supporting hard data. It is truly remarkable that in the tens of thousands of pages of documents and court testimony, the Justice Department never produces a shred of data—not even a datum—that independently validates the innovation claim.

In effect, the Justice Department is telling the judge, "Take our word for it. Our arguments are the only way the matter can be reasoned. Hence, we know that Microsoft is guilty of deterring innovation. By extension, it is harming consumers, which is all that needs to be shown to find Microsoft guilty of antitrust violations." And guess what, Judge Jackson took the Justice Department's word for it.

There's probably a good reason why no supporting data have been offered by the Justice Department, its support staff, its witnesses, and the Microsoft critics who in the press have repeated the claim that Microsoft has deterred innovation: the available data either do not support the claim or actually point in the other direction and lead to the inference that the growing dominance of Microsoft has spurred innovation. Most types of data to which researchers might turn to assess the claim—the number of new patents, the number and variety of new software programs coming on the market, the spread of personal computers, employment in software and other technology industries, and other possible measures—do not support the Justice Department's and court's and all others' claims about impaired innovation. Innovation doesn't seem to have been impaired. Consider how rapidly Web browsing has become widespread and reflect on the number of momentous changes in computing just since the trial began; the reemergence of network computing is one such change.

There is no dearth of data on the computer industry, and it does not support the Justice Department's claim. *The Digital Economy Fact Book,* a computer industry statistical abstract, has been published by the Progress and Freedom Foundation, a Washington, D.C., think tank supported, as noted earlier, by Microsoft's adversaries. Without question this statistical booklet is the best short compendium of computer industry data available, and the data series it contains would not appear to support the Justice Department's innovation claim of broad harm done. From this fact book the following points emerge:

- The count of Internet hosts escalated from 1.3 million in 1993 to 9.5 million in 1996, and there is no sign of the growth abating. Indeed, growth is accelerating: the 1999 number is 43.2 million.
- Personal computer sales have marched upward as their prices have fallen dramatically. The percentage of households with personal computers has continued its relentless climb, going from 34.9 percent in 1994 to 53.6 percent in 1999. The percentage of households with access to the Internet has grown from 6 percent in 1994 to 38.1 percent in 1999. If anything, the growth in Internet connections has rapidly accelerated in recent years.
- The growth in shipments of "information appliances" (smart phones, near-PCs, shirt-pocket organizers) has also accelerated, rising from 2.4 million in 1998 to 3.6 million in 1999 (the only years for which data are available), with projected unit sales of 10.5 million in 2002.
- Packaged software sales have grown from $93 billion in 1995 to $135 billion in 1998, a 45 percent increase, again with no apparent abatement in the growth rate, in spite of falling real prices for many programs. During this period, Microsoft's share of software sales expanded only 2 percentage points, from 10 percent in 1995 to 12 percent in 1998, which means the sales of other software firms taken together were also expanding rapidly with no apparent abatement in growth.
- Cellular phone service has spiraled upward, a fact that is self-evident to anyone casually observing how many people on the street have their

cellular phones to their ears. The count of cellular phone subscribers went
from 3.5 million in 1989 to 24 million in 1994 to 69.2 million in 1998.

- The percent of business-to-business e-commerce is expected to explode by
the year 2003.
- Advertising revenues on the Internet have also exploded, rising from a
meager $30 million in the first quarter of 1996 to $656 million in the last
quarter of 1998.
- The economic value added by information technology firms—those
providing communications, software, and hardware—has begun to
escalate. In 1990, the value added by information technology firms totaled
$330 billion. By 1994, the figure was $436 billion, and by 1999, $729 billion.
Plotting the entire data on a graph indicates an acceleration of growth in
the 1990s.
- Venture capitalist funding of new information technology ventures more
than doubled from 1995 ($3.3 billion) to 1998 ($7.8 billion). In 1999, the
initial public offerings of new Internet firms were substantially
outperforming in terms of the increase in the market price of their stocks
than their counterparts in non-information-technology firms.
- Finally, employment in the information technology sector oscillated
between 3.9 million and 4 million between 1990 and 1994, only to start
rising thereafter, reaching 4.7 million by 1997.

Admittedly, these statistical observations do not tell the full story of what has
happened in the country's technology sector. They are presented only because they
are readily available from an organization that also accepts the Justice Department's
contentions about the impact of Microsoft on innovation (the Progress and Freedom Foundation is supported by Microsoft's industry adversaries). The statistics
are useful because they rule out some of the obvious places that Microsoft's impact
might be seen.

Also, the statistics presented are the consequence of myriad economic forces in-
teracting with one another, only one of which is Microsoft's growing dominance of
software markets. It might very well be that the adverse effects of Microsoft's business practices are obscured by the offsetting influence of the other forces at work simultaneously. Sorting out the influence of Microsoft on innovation from all the
other forces would not be easy, but if the Justice Department wants to make its
charges about what Microsoft has done believable, it would seem incumbent upon
it or its expert consultants to do their homework.

What the Justice Department has done in its innovation claim is tantamount to a
county prosecutor claiming that someone has committed a murder but never producing the body. The prosecutor then tells the judge, "Let's assume the accused has

done what my office claims he did. As a consequence, the accused is guilty of what we claim."

"Embrace and Extend," an Industry Strategy

One of the most frequently repeated claims among Microsoft's detractors is that the company has rarely, if ever, innovated anything of consequence. Microsoft is, in the words of Netscape's Jim Clark, the "master copier." Clark argues that Microsoft has built its software library by buying up or duplicating what others, typically smaller firms, have originated. When Microsoft bought the original code for MS-DOS and PC-DOS from Seattle Computer, it consisted of only a few thousand lines of code. But Microsoft added many new features, adding millions of lines of code and pretty much rewriting the whole program in the process. This must be construed as innovative. The "look and feel" of Windows appears to come from the graphic interface on Apple's early computers, which in turn came from Xerox PARC.

No doubt about it, one of Microsoft's guiding strategies, by Gates's own admission, is to "embrace and extend" new software technologies. This means that the company is dedicated to adopting important categories of software that have achieved critical mass in their markets—in other words, adopting technical standards the market has adopted—and then advancing them.

Following this embrace-and-extend strategy for software development, Microsoft has bought from outside vendors a number of key software technologies that have gone into various versions of Windows. For example, in Windows 3.0, Paint, a drawing applet (or small application), was based on ZSoft Corporations's Paintbrush, and Terminal, a telecoms accessory, was based on Future Soft Engineering's DynaComm. In Windows 3.1, Microsoft incorporated the TrueType fonts it bought from Apple Computer. Internet Explorer, incorporated into Windows 95, was originally based on code licensed from Spyglass, and the Windows 95's desktop imaging and object controls were purchased from Wang.

For Windows 98, Microsoft bought the Intel-developed Application Launch Accelerator. In addition, Frontpad was based on Microsoft FrontPage 97, which in turn was based on acquired technology. More recently, Microsoft has invested in Jump Networks, a provider of Web-based calendar services; Qwest Communications, a leader in broadband Internet-based data and voice and image communications for businesses and consumers; LinkExchange, an Internet advertising company; and Firefly Network, a leading maker of Internet privacy software.

However, Microsoft is hardly the only software company that has to one extent or another used the "embrace and extend" approach to product development. Consider the following major products, all of which emerged from the innovative work of others:

- Linux: Essentially another version of the Unix operating system, was developed by the Finnish computer science student Linus Torvalds in 1990, then was refined by other "open-source" programmers, who had access to the Linux code free of charge from the Web.
- Netscape Navigator: Inspired by the Mosaic software developed by the National Center for Supercomputing Applications at the University of Illinois, which built on the work of the computer scientists Ted Nelson and Vannevar Bush.
- Java: Derived from prior interpreted p-code systems, going back at least as far as UCSD Pascal.
- Lotus Notes: In essence a sophisticated adaptation of Usenet newsgroups.
- Apple Mac: Derived (like Windows) in part from several technologies pioneered by Xerox PARC.
- Adobe Photoshop: A notable advance, but Adobe itself didn't invent the application category of photographic image manipulation; a number of companies offered paint-and draw-programs.

Nor is Microsoft the only technology company to buy up other firms for the purpose of exploiting their technologies. Some examples:

- AOL bought Netscape and MovieFone.
- Compaq bought Tandem and Digital.
- IBM bought Lotus and DataBeam.
- Sun bought i-Planet and NetDynamics.
- Oracle bought Concentra and E-Travel.
- Cisco Systems bought GeoTel and Sentient Networks.
- AT&T bought IBM's global data network and MediaOne.
- Intel bought Shiva and Level One Communications.

MICROSOFT, THE INNOVATOR

There is an important grain of truth in the claim that all Microsoft does is copy others, but there is also a ton of misinformation. Microsoft has actually originated a fairly long list of software products since its inception, and it has significantly redeveloped and improved many other products.

For these and other reasons, in January 2000 *PC Magazine UK* awarded Microsoft its "Millennium Award" for Technical Innovation. In announcing the award, the editors stated: "Since we started our Awards for Technical Innovation back in 1992, one company has consistently had its products and technologies nominated.

In eight years, Microsoft has had 48 products as finalists and has won 14 Technical Innovation Awards, including two Product of the Year Awards (Windows 3.1 and Windows 95). No other company has come close to providing so many innovative and groundbreaking products."

But Microsoft's major innovations have not all been products. Microsoft's practice of open licensing its operating system to all hardware vendors was a major business practice innovation. In the early 1980s, this practice ran counter to what virtually every other operating system vendor did. Most vendors followed Apple's practice of tying its proprietary operating system to its own proprietary hardware. By having an open-licensing policy, Microsoft expanded its market for its operating system, but also gave rise to substantial innovative efforts on the part of hordes of software firms who played to the network that Microsoft licensing policy was encouraging, thereby doing exactly what Microsoft wanted them to do: add to the demand for the Microsoft operating system.

In addition to its business innovations, Microsoft has an impressive list of innovative products to its credit:

- Microsoft was one of the pioneers of commercial GUI-based spreadsheets (GUI stands for "graphical user interface"); it produced Excel for the Macintosh.
- Microsoft introduced the first retail mouse.
- Microsoft was one of the first companies to recognize the potential of the CD-ROM, producing many early CD-ROM products, including *Encarta*, the first multimedia encyclopedia.
- Microsoft developed the operating system and applications for the Radio Shack Model 100, the first practical notebook computer.
- Microsoft's Visual Basic created an entirely new software category in the field of visual rapid application development, and transformed Basic from a crude line-number language into an event-oriented, component-based language. With the exception of a small component, Ruby, which was bought from Cooper, all of Visual Basic was developed in-house. Visual Basic remains by far the largest third-party-developer component market, one in which thousands of independent software vendors now compete.
- Microsoft's object technology, OLE, made possible the practical development of commercial, mass-market, componentized application software.
- Microsoft was the first to exploit the concept of wizards and toolbars in its applications to simplify complex tasks and make the power of the PC more accessible. Taskbars, command bars, AutoCorrect, AutoFormat, and

automatic menu customization are just a few examples of features
Microsoft has brought to its application software.

- With Excel, Microsoft pioneered pivot tables, spreadsheet outline, analysis
  tools, and spreadsheet debugging.
- Microsoft integrated Internet protocols, HTML and DHTML, into
  Windows 95 and 98, a major innovation in user-interface design.
- Microsoft developed Windows NT, one of the very few completely new
  commercial operating systems to be developed over the last 20 years. The
  other server operating systems developed during these years developed out
  of the Unix system.
- Microsoft also developed ClearType, which improves LCD-screen text
  clarity up to 300 percent, and this could boost the developing market for
  electronic books.

When the evolution of individual products, like Word, is considered over time,
they have been markedly improved. For example, a list of features in Word 6.0 that
Word 1.0 didn't have includes print preview, background spell-checking, AutoCorrect, AutoFormat, WordMail, tables, mouse-based text selection, ToolTips, drag and
drop, mail merge, OLE support, Format Painter, and Internet Assistant.

Certainly there are many innovative software and technology firms making important contributions to the development of the industry, but it is simply wrong,
unfair, and maybe sour grapes to paint Microsoft as a "me too" firm, or "master
copier," to use Netscape founder Jim Clark's derogatory catch-phrase. If Clark truly
believes that Microsoft has in some significant way "copied" Netscape Navigator, he
should press a copyright infringement lawsuit, not an antitrust lawsuit. As it is,
Clark's words amount to the kettle calling the pot black.

INNOVATION DYNAMICS

Without the antitrust trial, this listing of innovations (see also the comprehensive
list at the end of this chapter) would be of little interest. Does it really matter
whether Microsoft originates a software product or someone else does, so long as
the product emerges and grows better over time? The listing takes on added importance, however, because of the Justice Department's and court's claims that Microsoft has undercut software innovation by its business strategies. If we look only
at what has happened to Netscape and overlook Microsoft's software contributions,
we might be inclined to agree with Microsoft's detractors, that Microsoft's business
practices on balance harm consumers. When we look at Microsoft's innovations,
the conclusion to be drawn about the consequences of Microsoft's business practices for innovation is far more debatable.

Besides, should we expect Microsoft to originate all of the innovative products it distributes? Not very likely. Large firms are notorious for being bureaucratic, which is to say they have a difficult time leaving the creative people in their midst free to do their thing, which is to create. The problem is that large bureaucracies need lots of rules and procedures to ensure employees won't misuse and abuse the resources at their disposal. And the freedom to think and experiment without having to seek the approval of others may be the key attribute of the innovation process.

Microsoft is a very large firm, with over 30,000 employees worldwide and over 16,000 employees housed in the forty-five-plus buildings on the Redmond campus. Even with Microsoft's substantial investment in past and future innovation (it plans to spend $3.8 billion in 2000 on research and development, a greater percentage of its revenues than other key technology companies), its employees could not possibly think of all possible innovations. There are bound to be software breakthroughs that Microsoft employees miss, or don't anticipate as soon as outsiders do. The same is true of other high-tech firms, not the least of which is Lucent Technologies, which has 30,000 scientists at its Bell Labs. Nevertheless, Lucent has set aside $100 million in its own venture capital fund to search for the next "big ideas" devised by smaller outside firms.

Given the complexity of the innovation process, especially in the high-tech arena, it simply may be more cost-effective for the likes of Microsoft and Lucent to sit back and wait for new products to emerge, pick and choose from among the promising innovations, and then "embrace and extend" them, either by buying the products from their originators or by duplicating them (without violating copyrights and patents, of course).

All innovations worthy of the designation add value for consumers. They do this either through savings on costs that must be incurred to get the product to market or through increased usefulness of the products to consumers. The most important innovation Microsoft contributes to software markets might be its "embrace-and-extend" business practice, which many firms had not thought of doing. Such a practice can reduce consumer cost or add usefulness, as would be true of any other innovation.

Sun Microsystems likes to think it is superior to Microsoft because it is far more innovative on a higher level of technical sophistication. Sun's arrogance may or may not be justified (Sun doesn't spend as much on R&D in either absolute dollars or as a percentage of revenues as does Microsoft), but that is no reason for calling on Microsoft to follow Sun's lead, anymore than it would be good to have Sun follow Microsoft. "Different strokes for different folks" is a rule that applies to both Sun and Microsoft. Any requirement that Microsoft generate its "innovations" to the same extent that Sun does might only serve one purpose, to give Sun a competitive advantage, since it would force Microsoft to do more of what it is not good at, creating innovative and sophisticated products, while doing less of what it is good at, identifying promising products and getting them to market at prices lower than the competition. But then, these points are really academic. Contrary to what Microsoft's critics profess ad nauseam, Microsoft has a stellar record of innovations.

SMALL AND BIG IDEAS IN SOFTWARE

Does Microsoft's embrace-and-extend strategy deter innovation? As noted, the strategy probably deters some innovations, maybe those "small" innovations that can be easily duplicated and on which the innovator does not have a marketing and distribution cost advantage over Microsoft. But this doesn't mean that the creative juices of entrepreneurs have been suppressed by Microsoft's presence. It means that their creativity is redirected to avenues of creative development that can't be easily duplicated by a larger, more efficient firm like Microsoft.

The next "big idea" in computing software is not likely to lie dormant for long just because of the cost advantages Microsoft might have in copying, producing, marketing, and distributing the product. Many creative people come up with "big ideas" all the time in all kinds of industries and never seek to put them into production themselves. This is because they understand they have no particular expertise in producing and getting the products to market.

What creative people do is get a patent or copyright on their "big ideas" and then sell them to firms that have the cost advantage in production and distribution. This is exactly what software entrepreneurs can do with their "big ideas": sell them to Microsoft or some other high bidder. This is also what Netscape could have done early on with its "Mosaic killer" (and what it did in 1998 when the whole company was bought by AOL). Microsoft will only be the highest bidder for such proposed products when it has the greatest cost advantage in developing, producing, marketing, and distributing the product.

Then again, Netscape probably didn't try to sell the concept of its "Mosaic killer" to Microsoft in early summer 1994, before it developed the product, simply because the concept of a "Mosaic killer" was not at that time likely to be seen as the kind of really "big idea" that would remain exclusive to Netscape for long. When Netscape had a working program in late fall 1994, it tried to sell an equity interest in Navigator to Microsoft, as Clark reports.

Copying—really, pirating—is a serious problem in the software industry. The prospect of ideas being copied with impunity can undermine incentives to innovate. This problem does need attention by policymakers, but the problem concerns flaws in the nation's patent and copyright laws, and is not the foundation of an antitrust suit. When and where intellectual property rights can be protected, they should be protected from being infringed, no matter who the infringing person or firm is, and Microsoft's infringements, when they occur, should be prosecuted just as any other infringement by any other firm should be prosecuted. This goes also for Netscape.

What is interesting about this case is that Jim Clark feels perfectly comfortable tagging Microsoft pejoratively as the "master copier" for carrying out its embrace-and-extend business strategy. But wasn't that exactly what Netscape set out to do when Clark and Andreesen hit upon the idea of producing a "Mosaic killer"? They basically "embraced" the concept of producing a more useful browser and then set out to "extend" the technology by making their browser ten time faster than Mosaic. For their efforts, they came under the threat of a lawsuit from the University of Illinois that they had infringed on the university's intellectual property rights. It appears that in order to abate Netscape's growing legal and financial problems in late fall 1994, Clark offered the university a stake in Netscape.

In the end, Clark and Andreesen were able to prove that their work was done independent of the actual code written for Mosaic, but still the central point holds: Clark and Andreesen set out to do exactly what they now fault Microsoft for doing to Netscape, "embracing and extending" the browser technology. Any legal problems Microsoft faces because of what it did to the browser technology should not fall under the auspices of the Antitrust Division of the Justice Department. If Microsoft is charged with "copying," it seems reasonable that Netscape should face the same charge for much the same reason.

Besides, Microsoft's embrace-and-extend strategy has had benefits for others besides Microsoft. It can also encourage innovations by people outside Microsoft in several ways.

- First, if Microsoft's embrace-and-extend strategy is more cost-effective than a strategy of originating all or most innovations in-house, Microsoft can offer its products at reduced prices to consumers, decreasing the overall cost of computing and generating all of the benefits of "networks" that the Justice Department touts.
- Second, Microsoft's embrace-and-extend strategy, because it ultimately brings profits to the company, can mean that Microsoft can pay more for outside innovations than it would otherwise be able to do, increasing the incentive outsiders have to innovate.
- Third, Microsoft can use its internal resources to pay more attention to what it does best, improving, marketing, and distributing its software products.

CONCLUDING COMMENTS

Software innovation can be expected to continue apace well into the twenty-first century—in fact, the pace of change will likely speed up. Innovation will also likely become simultaneously both simpler and more complex. Simpler because the resources needed for innovations are easily identified: a good idea, a good computer, and some reasonable intelligence combined with computer skills, as Netscape's Jim Clark reminded us. More and more people will be able individually and in groups to change the sequences of code to improve existing software products and devise new ones that we cannot now imagine.

The innovation process has also become more complex, as a result of the rising demands for power and sophistication by some consumers and for ease and simplicity by others. Product placement in various markets will become much more complicated, as will the problems of trying to optimize software products for targeted market groups. Innovation will continue to become more global in scope. One of the great advantages of computer code is that sequences of 1's and 0's are not stopped by national boundaries. They can be shipped anywhere and everywhere more or less simultaneously. Moreover, the code writers can be anywhere and can work with virtually anyone or any group of other code writers anywhere else in the world.

Few industry experts have more than a vague impression of where the software business will be ten or twenty years from now. It's a safe bet that Gates doesn't know. It's a sure bet that Joel Klein and other lawyers, not to mention Judge Thomas Penfield Jackson, don't know how the software industry will evolve. There are simply too many variables, too many people, and too many opportunities involved in the innovation process. There are too many ways that people can interact to create the future that we will come to know.

These points are worth noting here because they speak to the ability of anyone or any organization, even one the size of Microsoft, to know and control the evolution of innovation as we move into the twenty-first century. There are just too many ways for innovative people to get around efforts to control the process. It would be a shame to allow the government to try to control the evolution of innovation under the guise of an antitrust prosecution, especially when it has made no effort to show how a firm like Microsoft has deterred innovation in the first place.

And make no mistake about it, the government does seek to control the innovation process when it demands that Microsoft not be allowed to integrate, or just bundle, its browser with its operating system, as other firms have done. We need to demand more supporting evidence and even-handedness when the government lobs charges such as "Microsoft has impaired innovation"; we must demand more from the government than it has offered in the Microsoft case. Otherwise, the government may easily do more harm than good to the course of future innovations.

Microsoft per se is incidental to the arguments made here and elsewhere in the book. This book is a defense of the right of people and firms to retain the freedom to innovate, unless there is strong evidence that the identified business practices by identified firms have actually impaired innovation. The government has not done its homework. If anything, the evidence concerning the path of innovations over the past decade or so suggests the contrary, that innovation has not been abated in the least. Microsoft may very well have contributed mightily to speeding up innovation.

APPENDIX: INNOVATIONS FROM MICROSOFT

Here is a year-by-year listing of several of Microsoft's major and minor innovations:

- **1975** Microsoft BASIC: First programming language written for a PC (the Altair 8800)
- **1983** Word 1.0 for MS-DOS: First PC-based word processor to support a mouse
- **1985** Word 3.0 for Networks: First PC-based word processor to support a laser printer
- **1987** Windows/386: First commercial operating system to take advantage of Intel 32-bit 80386 architecture
- **1987** Excel for Windows: First spreadsheet designed for Windows technology
- **1989** Word 4.0 for Mac: First word processor to offer tables
- **1989** Office: First suite of business-productivity applications
- **1991** Works: First business-productivity application to incorporate multimedia
- **1991** Word 2.0 for Windows: First major word processor to offer drag-and-drop
- **1993** IntelliSense: First "intelligent" user-assistance technology
- **1994** Microsoft-Timex DataLink watch: First watch to accept information from a computer
- **1995** Internet Explorer 2.0: First browser to support advanced multimedia and 3D graphics
- **1996** IntelliMouse: First pointing device to add a "wheel" to improve navigation
- **1996** Exchange: First integrated messaging/groupware server with native open and secure Internet access
- **1996** NetMeeting: First integrated standards-based video-conferencing, telephony, and multipoint data-conferencing for real-time collaboration on the Internet or intranets
- **1996** Picture It!: First application to let consumers enhance, create, and share photo-quality images using home PC
- **1997** DirectX: First multimedia architecture to integrate Internet-ready services

- **1998**   Microsoft/Clarion Auto PC: First commercial PC for automobiles
- **1998**   WebTV-Baywatch: First internationally syndicated "Internet-enhanced" season finale
- **1998**   ClearType font technology
- **1999**   Digital/optical mouse

In Windows 2000 (the next version of Windows NT), the following technologies and innovations have been added:

- Text-to-speech engine
- Decision-theory onboard troubleshooting tools
- Reliable multicast protocol algorithms
- Registry performance improvements
- DirectX: Several contributions to graphics algorithms and libraries
- Network monitor IPv6 support
- Network packet classifier and scheduler
- Single Instance Store for ZAW
- Virtual Server Failover
- Vulcan/BBT performance optimizations
- Source-code analysis tools for kernel data structure tuning
- Source-code analysis tools for identifying bugs and security attack vectors
- Public key cryptography library
- PPP extensible authentication protocol design
- Font subset signature design
- Protected store domain controller backup encryption design

Microsoft has a number of futuristic technologies under development, including the following:

- Virtual worlds/telepresence
- Vision-based user interfaces
- Self-administering databases
- Wearable computing
- Multimodal input devices
- Retargetable compilers
- Handwriting recognition
- Distributed operating systems
- Intentional programming
- Ubiquitous computing
- The application of statistical physics to computer networks

- Technology that finds bugs before program code is compiled
- Social user interfaces
- Intelligent agents
- Quantum computing
- Adaptive computing

⚖ CHAPTER 7 ⚖

Mud Farming

Driving into the parking lot at Microsoft's headquarters in Redmond, Washington, is a head-turning experience. The place is massive, larger than many of the nation's largest universities—forty-five sizable buildings on the main campus with two satellite campuses going up a mile or so away. Though there are an ample number of lower-end cars such as Tercels in the parking lot, immaculately waxed Porsches and other high-end automobiles are clearly overrepresented, reflecting the substantial good fortunes of the employees inside. The employees kid each other about being "Microserfs" for what they believe are relatively low hourly rates of pay, given the enormous number of hours they put in, but they also understand that much of their compensation comes in the form of stock options.

No doubt about it, there are probably more young multimillionaires working for Microsoft than there are millionaires of all ages in any other whole industry in the world—in fact, Microsoft might be considered an industry unto itself. Clearly, the people at Microsoft, from the head of the company on down, appreciate making a buck and accumulating the trappings of great wealth.

In bringing its antitrust case, the Justice Department is effectively accusing Microsoft's employees of achieving their fortunes—and buying their Porsches and upscale homes—not so much through well-honed skills of product and market development, or even luck, but through guile: efforts to artificially control the world's software markets with the intent of harming their competitors and consumers for their own personal gain. Paradoxically, therein lies one very good reason that we must all worry about the motives and methods of those who have taken Microsoft to court. The people who work for Microsoft are not a race apart from the rest of us—nor are the people who work at the Justice Department and other software and technology firms. Microsoft's employees did not invent greed, nor are they as a group likely to be any greedier than anyone else. Moreover, they will not likely be the last group that has imagined it could use extramarket means to gain personally at the expense of others, an inherent problem for antitrust enforcement

141

in general for the last hundred years that is being played out in spades in the particulars of the Microsoft charges.

MICROSOFT'S MOTIVES

The Justice Department's case and the court's Findings of Fact against Microsoft are grounded in the time-honored presumption that businesspeople will, when given the slightest chance, exploit every market advantage at their disposal for their personal gain. Even the venerable Adam Smith, author of the free-market tome *The Wealth of Nations*, warned that businesspeople seldom come together "even for merriment and diversion" (or any other purpose) without their attention soon turning to "a conspiracy against the public, or [. . .] some contrivance to raise prices," or to some scheme that will allow them to override their natural inclination to compete. The case is also grounded in established microeconomic theory, specifically, that a firm that does not have to fear the market responses of competitors—a monopolist—can be expected to restrict output for the purpose of raising its prices and profits and redistributing wealth from consumers to its owners and employees. At Microsoft they often are one and the same: the heavy reliance on stock options as compensation means that a quarter of Microsoft's stock is held by the workers.

As the Justice Department worries that Microsoft has developed and used its market power to further its own ends, so we also worry that Microsoft's legal accusers are doing much the same thing with political and governmental power. Is this concern unreasonable? Not really. Indeed, it would be unreasonable not to consider that prospect. After all, Microsoft's employees and accusers are all drawn from the same broad cross-section of humanity, and both groups are subject to the same human failings. Microsoft's employees may not have the intentions of angels, but no one should accept the view that *only* Microsoft's employees have the market morals of devils. Just after Adam Smith fretted about "people of the same trade" conspiring against the public in their social gatherings, he mused that the law "ought to do nothing to facilitate" businesspeople's conspiracies against the public.

THE ACCUSERS' MOTIVES

At one time—more than a century ago, when government's influence in the economy was seriously circumscribed—our worry that Microsoft's accusers are not beyond reproach might have been quickly dismissed, if ever even entertained. People inside and outside government could not then use government powers to pad their own pockets, mainly because there was not much that government could do to redistribute wealth.

In this earlier era, policy commentators blithely thought of the political and market processes as worlds distinct, activated by groups of people who were, at their motivational cores, radically different. Back then, people in markets were assumed to take up their work assignments largely because of their commitment to their own private interests (as Adam Smith reckoned), whereas people in politics were assumed to take up their civic duties because of their commitment to the "greater good." This meant in part that they spent much of their working days correcting the "failures" of markets that were activated by people whose interests were too narrowly conceived. Surely, people in politics did not intend to add to the damage done by markets, or so it was assumed by many political analysts virtually without serious challenge until three or so decades ago.

Then there was the more reasonable view that people in markets and people in politics were not fundamentally different, only that they faced different institutional constraints. The motives of the people in politics in these earlier times might have appeared tolerably pure (at least purer than their counterparts in the private sector), given that there may have been little they could actually do to further their own private gain and/or to cater to the specific private interests of identified constituencies. When government's authority is highly constrained anyway, it doesn't make sense for private groups to spend a lot of money trying to manipulate government policies.

PRIVATE GAINS FROM PUBLIC CHOICES

Over the past several decades political scientists and economists have learned and relearned a very old lesson: power corrupts—not only those who work inside the government power structure, but also those on the outside who might harness governmental power for their own advantage. The growth in the size and scope of government and concomitantly in its influence on the economy have introduced substantial temptations for people in and out of governments to vigorously exploit the authority of government to pursue private ends or to engage in what has come to be known as "rent seeking." This is the hot pursuit of profits by private groups through government-backed market restrictions and wealth transfers.

As Adam Smith recognized all too well, competitors have an incentive to conspire, to voluntarily restrict their collective output in order to boost their prices and collective profits. A basic problem the competitors have is that the incentive that brought them together—profit—can also inspire the breakdown of their voluntary efforts to cartelize the market. Each competitor may reason that it can be better off individually if it cheats on the cartel by not curbing production. The net result of this may be rampant cheating. As a consequence, the market supply is not curbed after all, and the cartel members' prices and profits are not raised.

The competitors can then turn to their political leaders to get the government to do that which they were unable to do: enforce production curbs, which would lead to the achievement of their cartel goals. The growth in private interest groups' political efforts to have the government do their bidding is self-evident in the still-escalating political contributions, which come with policy strings attached.

For example, farmers have always known that if they could collectively curb production of various crops, they could raise their profits, *as if* they were a monopolist. After all, a reduction in market supply can result in higher market prices. However, when the farmers have tried to collude in the past, they quickly realized that the higher market prices would inspire cartel cheating, which meant a greater market supply and a return to the lower (competitive) prices.

Farmers also learned in the early part of the twentieth century that because of their dominant influence in elections, they could enlist the cooperation of their congressmen and senators in their effort to boost their incomes. How? In a variety of ways. For one thing, farmers got the federal government to enter markets as an active buyer of their grains, which caused the prices of grains to rise and, along with them, farmers' profits. The farmers also prevailed on the government to set production quotas on crops from soybeans to tobacco and, better yet, to pay farmers to take land out of production. The purpose of these policies was always to raise market prices, much as a private cartel would *if* the farmers on their own voluntarily got together and made a cartel work without assistance from government.

So what if the government-backed purchases and supply restrictions caused the prices of breads and other products to rise? So what if the farm programs undercut the real incomes of other—even low-income—American consumers? The farmers got their take from higher prices and lower production costs, which they shared with their political supporters in the form of campaign contributions, if not outright bribes.

Similarly, over the years, at one time or another, trucking companies, airlines, utility companies, brokerage houses, television and radio stations and networks, and barber and beauty professionals recognized that if they could not by themselves restrict industry competition and output collusively and voluntarily, then they could turn to government for relief. They got their own industry regulations that were, of course, advocated in the name of the "public good," but all too often yielded nothing more than restrictions on market supply that were tailored to the industry's particular needs.

Again, so what if the general public got skewered in the process? The industry demanders of the regulations and the political suppliers of the regulations were able to come to terms on the division of the newfound government-backed industry spoils, or what economists call "rents."

As this political process became self-evident, economists began talking and writing about how businesspeople would understandably engage in "rent seeking," meaning they would be just as willing to invest their firm's resources in political maneuvering to obtain profits as to invest in plant and equipment to obtain profits. The exact amount and allocation of their investment funds depended on which investment avenue was expected to be most profitable. Indeed, the more profitable the rent seeking, the more rent seeking that should be expected.

Along the way, policy critics learned why it was possible that the larger public's interest in lower-priced goods and higher real incomes seemed so often to give way to the narrow interests of industry groups. The larger public has the votes all right, but they didn't have adequate economic incentives to monitor the political process carefully and negate with informed votes the campaign contributions of the special interest groups (whether representing banks or software firms).

Unfortunately, the profits from the use of governmental powers to manipulate industry supply are often highly concentrated in a relatively small number of firms within special interest industry groupings, each of whom can justify the expenditure of considerable time and money on political activism. Meanwhile, the significant economic benefits to be derived from counteracting the political activities of special interest groups are necessarily diffused among a very large number of consumers (voters), meaning that each person in the larger public has precious little incentive to incur the substantial costs of leaning against the political winds that can be stirred up by special interest groups.

Besides, each voter/representative of the general public understands that if he or she works hard to beat back the efforts of one industry group or another to curry political favors, all that will have been accomplished is that a political vacuum will be opened up, to be filled by some other industry group in hot pursuit of those favors. Hence, there is a tendency for the political process to favor the interests not of the general public but of narrowly defined groups of companies.

Economists have also realized over the course of the past several decades that businesspeople were not always the ones who initiated the proposals, the results of which would be to boost the rents of the firms. Politicians could be expected to propose to firms that market protections could be provided by government—but of course the price would be campaign contributions to the politicians who did the required lobbying in the halls of Congress.

Moreover, the politicians can force the businesspeople to share with them the rents obtained, through a process that the Northwestern University law professor Fred McChesney has dubbed "rent extraction." McChesney equates rent extraction with "mud farming," an extortion scam of farmers in William Faulkner's *The Reivers*. At night, the farmers would plow the dirt roads near their houses and then water them down to ensure that when cars passed the following day, they were certain to get stuck; the farmers with the help of their mules would extract them—at a price, of course.

Mark Melcher and Stephen Soukup, political commentators for Prudential Securities, suggest that the process of rent extraction is as old as the "protection racket," whereby "a mobster would say to a businessman, 'Would you like to buy some insurance against broken windows?' The businessman would say, 'Why, I've never had any trouble with broken windows.' And the mobster would say, 'If you buy this insurance, you won't have any trouble in the future either.' " Perhaps "political shakedown" would be a coarser but more descriptive term for the process of rent extraction.

In the case of government, firms and their leaders can be asked to effectively "buy" protection from various forms of government intrusion on their business. For example, firms can be expected to pay to have the politicians beat back congressional or bureaucratic drives to impose unwarranted and costly new regulations and taxes, or to withdraw existing beneficial regulations and tax deductions and exemptions—or even antitrust suits. No matter, politicians can dip into the firms' coffers, shifting the costs of their campaigns and political lifestyles to consumers through higher prices or to business owners and workers through lower dividends and wages than would otherwise be paid. McChesney says rent extraction amounts to "money for nothing," or payments made to politicians for not doing anything.

Of McChesney's many examples of rent extraction, only two need to be noted. When Congress mandated that the government regulate used-car warranties, it also retained a veto over Federal Trade Commission regulations concerning used cars. The result is that the National Auto Dealers Association substantially expanded its political contributions to members of Congress who worked effectively to veto the FTC regulations that Congress had ordered be devised. Another example: When the Clinton administration set up a commission to propose a radical restructuring of the nation's health-care system, the medical industry began to "shower" Congress with "lobby money," according to the *New York Times*. "While it remains unclear who would benefit and who would suffer under whatever health plan is ultimately adopted," the *New York Times* reporter surmised, "it is apparent that the early winners are members of Congress."

McChesney argues, further, that if regulatory threats are made with the intent and effect of extracting wealth from companies, when the threats are withdrawn or the enacted regulation is overturned, we should expect the affected companies to lose market value. This conclusion has been borne out, according to the limited empirical literature on rent extraction. For example, when the Canadian government concluded in 1981 that consumers there had been "overcharged" for gasoline between 1958 and 1973 to the tune of $12 billion, the stock prices of the affected oil companies dropped. When in 1986 the Restrictive Trade Practices Commission reversed the assessment, the stock prices of the oil companies rose, but not by as much as the prices had fallen in 1981, presumably because some of the affected companies' wealth had been siphoned off into battling the charges.

Similarly, when the Clinton administration health-care commission considered the imposition of price controls on pharmaceutical companies in 1993, the stock market values of the threatened companies tumbled and then only partially recovered in the fall of 1994 when the administration's health-care plans were abandoned. McChesney concluded, "In the end, the threatened firms paid good money for nothing: their wealth was diminished, and no legislation was passed."

Public choice economics is the study of politics using the analytical tools of economics. Public choice economics seem to offer a pessimistic appraisal of governments' ability to do anything right, or rather to do anything for the good of the general public. Clearly, governments are necessary and useful. But public choice economics reminds us to be mindful of the fact that government policies are not always adopted with the best of intentions and may often have perverse effects.

In short, we should not be naïve. We need to be on guard against the government's being used by people who have little or no concern for the public's welfare and employ whatever arguments, data, and rhetoric they have at their disposal to achieve narrow economic and political gains at the expense of the public welfare. The lesson in a nutshell: Just because policies are endorsed by government bodies does not mean that they are efficient, just, right, or fair.

PUBLIC AND PRIVATE GAINS FROM ANTITRUST

For a long time, critics of government-inspired regulations held their fire on the intent and consequences of antitrust prosecutions, preferring to think solely in terms of how antitrust laws really did serve their ostensible purpose, to thwart the evils of monopoly and promote competition. Even as late as the mid-1980s, more than four fifths of the professional economists who were surveyed on their policy views agreed with the statement "Antitrust laws should be used vigorously to reduce monopoly power from its current level." One of the reasons that statement enjoys so much support is that it is hard to be against doing something about true monopoly power that is actually exercised. Richard Posner, a prominent federal judge and professor of law and economics at the University of Chicago and no fan of government involvement in the economy, has reasoned that the goal of economic efficiency "establishes a *prima facie* case for having an antitrust policy."

Another reason for the agreement on this point among economists is that generally speaking, they have taken it for granted that the intent—and the effect—of antitrust laws was to thwart monopoly, not competition. The former federal judge Robert Bork has argued in some detail that the framers of the Sherman Act, most notably Senator John Sherman, clearly aimed the legislation at promoting competition and opposing efforts to monopolize key industries. Judge Bork concluded that the legislative history of the Sherman Act shows that "these statutes [the Sherman Act, Clayton Act, and the FTC Act] were at least primarily intended to protect consumers from exactions of monopolists," thus improving consumer welfare. Bork acknowledged that in the 1970s, when he was writing his book, monopoly power was not the only concern of antitrust scholars. They were also concerned that another antitrust law, the 1936 Robinson-Patman Act (the Federal Anti-Price Discrimination Act), which was aimed primarily at discouraging the favorable pricing of chain stores, was intended to preserve "small merchants from depredation." But Bork quotes approvingly Representative Wright Patman, who argued that the bill was intended to preserve competition and would be "in the interests of wage earners, farmers, and the general welfare of the people."

These glowing defenses notwithstanding, the country's antitrust laws have come under increasing scholarly scrutiny and, over the last two or three decades, have often been found wanting in both intent and consequences. A growing number of economic and legal scholars have come to share the concern of William Baxter, assistant attorney general for antitrust in the Reagan administration, who in an article published before his tenure in the Antitrust Division at the Justice Department voiced his doubts that those responsible for the passage of antitrust laws were actually "public-spirited legislators" or that those responsible for enforcing the laws actually constituted a "public-spirited judiciary."

These scholars led by Baxter also argued that antitrust laws have all too often done exactly what Adam Smith warned against. Instead of discouraging people within an industry from conspiring against the public, antitrust laws have "facilitated" (Smith's word) the conspiracies—and were intended to do so. And this process, these scholars conclude, has been "facilitated" by the FTC and the Antitrust Division of the Justice Department. Indeed, this is precisely the position taken by two prominent economists, William Baumol and Janusz Ordover, who have concluded, "There is a specter that haunts our antitrust institutions. Its threat is that, far from serving as the bulwark of competition, these institutions will become the most powerful instrument in the hands of those who wish to subvert it. . . . We ignore it [this threat] at our peril and would do well to take steps to exorcise it."

Exactly how have the antitrust laws been misused? Let us look at just a few of the ways that have been documented by scholars like Bork, Baxter, Baumol, and Ordover:

•*Firms that have grown in size and market share from internal sources, mainly greater internal efficiency, have been wrongly prosecuted for being monopolies simply because of their size or market share.* This has been the case even though, as the UCLA economics professor Harold Demsetz has noted, "The asserted relationship between market concentration and competition cannot be derived from existing theoretical considerations and . . . is based largely on an incorrect understanding of the concept of competition and rivalry." For example, Alcoa Aluminum was judged to be a monopoly in 1945 simply because it had 90 percent of the aluminum market, a degree of market dominance it had achieved by embracing "each new opportunity as it opened" and, hence had "precluded competition" (the court's words), which is hardly the way a monopolist is supposed to act. Similarly, the United Shoe Machinery Company was accused of antitrust violations in 1953 because of its dominance of the manufacturing and sale of shoe-making machinery. One source of its dominance, the court concluded, was "the superiority of United's products and services."

IBM was attacked by the Justice Department in 1969 in part because of its size. The case was finally terminated in 1982 because of the advent of the Reagan administration, and with it new thinking that mirrored the views of Robert Bork. In his antitrust treatise *The Antitrust Paradox: A Policy at War with Itself*, Bork, reflecting views of many other scholars, wrote: "There was no sensible explanation for IBM's dominance in the computer industry at the time [it was taken to court] other than superior efficiency, and, as the firm's superiority declined, the market began to erode IBM's market position."

Even firms that have had market shares far smaller than IBM's, as low as 20 percent, and that have faced heavily subsidized state-owned rivals, have been found by juries to have "monopolized" their market. The problem is that such antitrust prosecutions and decisions can not only damage the firms directly involved in the suit but also discourage more efficient firms within other industries from taking advantage of their superior efficiency and growing.

•*Firms that have sought to merge and, as a consequence, achieve greater efficiencies in production that could be passed on to consumers in the form of lower prices have been prevented from doing so by the antitrust enforcers and courts at the behest of market rivals on the grounds that the mergers would lead to monopolies. In fact, the newly formed merged firms would pose a more serious competitive threat to market rivals because of the merged firms' reduced costs.* In the 1950s, the Brown Shoe Company, a shoe manufacturer, sought to merge with the G. R. Kinney Company, a shoe retailer. The two firms combined would have had a meager 2.3 percent of sales in a retail shoe market, which at the time was supplied by 800 shoe manufacturers—hardly a market where the absence of competition was a problem. Nevertheless, the Supreme Court ruled the merger illegal; Chief Justice Earl Warren wrote the majority opinion, which was that Congress intended "to promote competition through the protection of viable, small, locally-owned businesses. Congress appreciated that occasional higher costs and prices might result from the maintenance of fragmented industries and markets. It resolved these competitive considerations in favor of decentralization."

Office Depot and Staples, two office supply retailers, were prevented from merging in 1997 on the grounds that their combined sales would account for a large share of all sales of office supplies in some "local markets." Not included in the FTC's concept of the "market" for sales by "office superstores" were people's purchases of office supplies at discount stores like Wal-Mart and Target and also via the Internet. If all these outlets had been accounted for, the merged Office Depot–Staples operations would have had a trivial percentage, perhaps no more than 5 percent, of all sales of office supplies.

•Any number of firms have been charged with predatory pricing tactics by their competitors in private antitrust lawsuits on the grounds that the prices are supposedly below their production costs—or worse, the production costs of their rivals. The classic case of predatory pricing is the 1911 Standard Oil case. The historical record shows that the company did nothing more than engage in competitive pricing that competitors didn't like, for obvious reasons. But genuine predatory pricing—below-cost pricing with the intent of eliminating competitors and then exploiting the resulting monopoly power—is very unlikely to be a sane policy for firms in markets where there are no barriers to entry (and there are precious few enduring entry barriers that aren't maintained by governments). Indeed, the author of a study of 123 antitrust cases involving charges of predatory pricing in which 95 of the firms were found liable as charged found few instances where concrete evidence of predatory pricing was presented in court. There were only seven cases in which predatory pricing was even attempted, and among these there were no cases where all competitors had been eliminated from the market, meaning a monopoly had actually been established. (Thus, the predation was largely futile.)

Despite the lack of evidence of both predatory pricing and of the entry barriers that are part and parcel of the predatory-pricing rationale, charges of predatory pricing have been made to stick. Discount stores like Wal-Mart have repeatedly been taken to court by local merchants on the argument that the store's lower prices are made possible by its "monopoly" market position and thus constitute predatory pricing; in fact such stores' ability to buy in large quantities and obtain favorable discounts from suppliers that cannot be obtained by independent local merchants is not genuine predatory pricing. They are simply cost advantages that come with the economies of scale.

•Firms have been charged with seeking to extend their monopoly into other markets through "tie-in" sales, meaning requiring buyers of some monopoly good to buy another good that would otherwise have to be sold in a competitive market. For example, in the 1930s the Justice Department prosecuted IBM for requiring businesses that leased IBM tabulating machines also to buy IBM punch cards. The presumption was that the tie-in was anticompetitive, since it ruled out competition for punch-card orders by other punch-card suppliers. New thinking suggests that if a firm like IBM tried to tie a good like punch cards to a monopoly good and then raised the price of the punch cards, it would have to lower the price of its monopoly good, thus reducing its overall profits. Besides, IBM had a good business reason for having the tie-in sale that had nothing to do with *extending* any monopoly it might have in tabulating machines. Its purpose was to monitor the lessees' use of the tabulating machines by counting the cards the lessees ordered and then to set the price of the machine according to the use made of it. Moreover, if a monopoly were charging the maximum price it could on its monopoly good and then bundled that product

with another good that, when included in the tie-in sale, made the additional good more expensive than if it were bought separately, the monopoly could charge no more than the original monopoly price on the original good plus the competitive price on the competitive good. The firm simply can't charge more than that; market forces, and the drive of the firm to make as much money as possible, won't allow it.

•*Manufacturers have been prevented from including "retail price maintenance" provisions in their contracts under which the manufacturers would set either maximum or minimum resell prices for retailers.* In one particularly egregious case in the early 1950s, the Supreme Court ruled that Seagram and Calvert could not set a *maximum* price at which wholesalers could resell their liquors, even though the two liquor manufacturers argued that they were trying to squash the wholesalers' efforts to fix prices above competitive levels. Similarly, the Court prevented the *St. Louis Post-Dispatch* from setting maximum prices at which independent carriers could sell papers to home subscribers.

In the 1960s, the Schwinn bicycle company was charged with price fixing on the grounds that it set *minimum* prices that its resellers could charge for its bikes. Although the court did not hold Schwinn in violation of the law (because Schwinn's prices were covered by fair trade laws), Bork suggests that such prosecutions had an impact because "the district court and Supreme Court continued to view resale price maintenance as a per se violation." The presumption was that the only explanation for the retail price agreements was to ensure that the goods were sold at monopoly prices. However, such agreements could have beneficial effects for everyone involved—manufacturers, retailers, *and* consumers. By maintaining the price at a certain level for all retailers, manufacturers could require retailers to provide valuable product information to customers, increasing the market value of the manufacturers products in the process. Without the price agreements, customers could go to one store for the information and then buy the product at another store that sells the product for less, but without the information. All retailers would be discouraged from providing information that customers need and want.

Judge Richard Posner, in an extensive review of antitrust cases that was published in 1969, concluded that one of the main reasons the antitrust prosecutions were so rarely intended to promote the interests of the general public is that they were undertaken "at the behest of corporations, trade associations, and trade unions whose motivation is at best to shift the cost of private litigation to the taxpayer and at worse to harass competitors." The Federal Reserve Board chairman, Alan Greenspan, came to much the same conclusion in the early 1960s, long before he became Fed chairman: "The entire structure of the antitrust statutes in this country is a jumble of economic irrationality and ignorance. It is the product: (a) of a gross misinterpretation of history; and (b) of rather naive, and certainly unrealistic, economic theories."

Even Robert Bork, who believes that the country's antitrust laws were originally intended to promote consumer welfare, lamented in the first edition of *The Antitrust Paradox*, that as a consequence of misguided interpretations of the antitrust laws (particularly by the Warren Court justices), company growth has been made "dangerous," mergers have been made "practically impossible," cooperative ventures among businesses have been "outlawed," the court "has needlessly proliferated rules about pricing behavior that has the effect of making prices higher and markets less effective allocators of society's resources." Judge Bork concluded,

> The theme of this book has been that modern antitrust has so decayed that the policy is no longer intellectually respectable. Some of it is not respectable as law; more of it is not respectable as economics; and now I wish to suggest that, because it pretends to one objective while frequently accomplishing its opposite, and because it too often forwards trends dangerous to our form of government and society, a great deal of antitrust is not even respectable as politics.

William Shughart, a professor of economics at the University of Mississippi and a long-time student of the politics of antitrust intervention, takes issue with Bork on why antitrust enforcement has so often failed to promote competition: "Congress is (rationally) less interested in enhancing wealth than it is in redistributing it" through antitrust enforcement (as well as through the budget and regulatory process).

For these reasons, and others, the venerable free market economist Milton Friedman has had a major change of heart on the efficacy of antitrust laws:

> When I started in this business, as a believer in competition, I was a great supporter of antitrust laws; I thought enforcing them was one of the few desirable things the government could do to promote more competition. But as I watched what actually happened, I saw that, instead of promoting competition, antitrust laws tended to do exactly the opposite, because they tended, like so many government activities, to be taken over by the people they were supposed to regulate and control. And so, over time, I have gradually come to the conclusion that antitrust laws do far more harm than good, and that we would be better off if we didn't have them at all, if we could get rid of them.

Why have so many economic and legal scholars become hostile to antitrust enforcement? Bork grounded his hostility in the way antitrust enforcement was being carried out in the 1970s and before, due mainly, he insisted, to intellectual errors in the economic reasoning of the justices on the Warren Court. (Bork believed that the problems had been largely corrected by the time his *Antitrust Paradox* was re-released in 1993 because of the force of new legal thinking that had emerged from law and economics scholars at the University of Chicago [including George Stigler, Richard Posner, and Ronald Coase] over the preceding two decades.)

Other scholars, perhaps Friedman included, have not been so sanguine. These critics stress that the problems with the antitrust laws are matters not of "mistakes" but of the motivations of those involved in the antitrust process. Companies often have a private economic interest in accusing their competitors of being a monopoly, of seeking to become a monopoly, or of using their presumed monopoly powers to achieve their market goals and then in having the government pay for investigating the claims and bringing suit.

For example, Wal-Mart has been accused of antitrust violations any number of times by local merchants when it announces plans to move into a community. The charges and threats of lawsuits are often made in the hope that they will bring the more efficient firms to drop their expansion plans. They can also serve to divert the attention of the management of the accused firms from actually competing aggressively in the market to defending themselves against the charges in public forums. And antitrust charges are often gratuitously appended to lawsuits intended for other purposes because in antitrust issues attorneys can sue for treble damages on behalf of their clients—and, not incidentally, for "reasonable attorneys fees" for themselves. If the Justice Department and/or the FTC decides to investigate the charges and prosecute, the accused firms can incur substantial legal expenses in mounting their defenses. The net effect can be that the accused firms begin to think that their expanded market share has unexpected legal costs, so they curb growth in production and raise prices in the process— enabling the accusing firms to expand *their* sales and also raise *their* prices.

The accusers get what they want— less aggressive competitors, a greater market share, and higher profits that more than compensate them for the costs incurred in their political activism—though the consumers end up with higher prices. Once again, the "rent seekers" win.

The accusing firms rarely claim that their rivals act like the monopolists described in economics textbooks—understandably so. The monopolies of textbook fame restrict production with the intent of raising prices and profits, in the process increasing demand for its market rivals' products. No rival would be against such monopoly behavior, because such behavior benefits the monopolist's rivals. What the rivals often argue is that a company they accuse of being a monopolist is seeking to further monopolize the market by, say, merging with or buying out one or more firms in its market or by engaging in "predatory" pricing, with the ultimate intent of destroying the existing competition. The accusers often claim that once any firm has monopolized the market, at some unstated point in the future it can and will act like the monopoly described in textbooks. The accused firm is left in a whale of a legal bind, given that it must prove what it *won't* do in the future. It must prove the absence of a prospective negative, which is a difficult legal assignment at best.

Baumol and Ordover point out that when General Motors and Toyota sought to develop a joint venture in automobile production in the early 1980s, Ford and Chrysler objected, arguing to the FTC that the venture would reduce competition. When AT&T tried to bring its long-distance charges into line with their real cost by lowering its charges in some low-cost but prime long-distance markets to forestall MCI from taking advantage of the distortions in the regulated long-distance charges, MCI sued AT&T, charging that the lower prices were anticompetitive.

The problem with these types of charges is that the market actions of the accused can be those of aggressive competitors that the accusing firms don't want to or can't match.

Again, competitors should not be opposed to mergers that lead to restricted production and higher prices by the larger merged firm; those consequences simply open up more market opportunities for the accusing competitors. Very likely, the mergers will be opposed only by competitors because the larger firm will achieve greater economies of scale that will allow it to lower its production costs along with its prices, thus making it difficult for competitors to remain competitive. As Baumol and Ordover note, "Paradoxically, then and only then, when the joint venture is beneficial [to consumers], can those rivals be relied upon to denounce the undertaking as 'anticompetitive.' "

Similarly, competitors can also complain about "predatory" prices not because they believe that the pricing strategy is truly predatory in the legal sense (below-cost prices designed with the intent to eliminate the competition in order to charge higher prices later), but because they either can't or don't want to match the prices. In such cases, the charge of predatory pricing can be a means by which the accusing firms can impose legal costs on their more aggressive competitors, causing them to refrain from such aggressive competitive price cutting. The net effect of the antitrust charges can be that all firms in the industry will end up charging higher prices than would otherwise be the case, an unexpected consequence if the *intent* of antitrust laws were to fight monopolies.

THE INTENT OF ANTITRUST LAWS

The popularly imagined *intent* of the antitrust laws is to thwart the emergence and expansion of monopoly. But is this their true intent? Laws are passed by a group of legislators who constitute a majority in Congress, but who individually face a variety of political forces, which means they likely differ in their reasons for supporting any proposed law. It is likely that the congressional supporters of the 1890 Sherman Act, the nation's first national antitrust law (which received unanimous approval in the Senate), conceived of different intents for the law. No doubt some members of Congress voted for the law because they truly believed that it was necessary to curb the decline in market competition that they believed was accompanying the growing market dominance of trusts (then commonly thought of as large firms, which were not necessarily monopolies) in the late nineteenth century. However, there probably were other members of Congress who supported the law precisely because they saw it as a means of actively throttling the more intense price and product-development competition from the expansion of trusts that, by their size and market dominance, were making life difficult for their smaller, less cost-effective rivals, who happened to have a lot of votes in many political jurisdictions.

Other spheres of government policies have been manipulated by special interest groups out to pad their own pockets and those of their representatives, many of whom see their jobs as being to represent the interests of those who help them get elected in their particular congressional districts or states. In addition, some important research on the political origins of the Sherman Act indicates that the economy did not, in the decade or so before its passage, appear to be operating in the way one would expect if trusts, or monopolies, were the core problem that they were made out to be.

This position is supported by a sizable and still growing scholarly literature. The late University of Chicago economist George Stigler observed that before the passage of the Sherman Act, seventeen states had passed their own antitrust legislation. He reasoned that if these state statutes were intended to thwart monopolies and promote the public welfare, we should expect these laws to tend to be passed in states where the employees of the trusts were concentrated. After all, that's where one would expect the damage from trusts to be concentrated, for as trusts restrict their production, they curb their employment and real incomes fall. But Stigler found that the opposite tended to be the case: in fourteen of the seventeen states with antitrust statutes, the employment in those industries thought to be subject to monopolization was below the national average, which suggests that the demand for antitrust laws was not likely inspired by concern over the damage done by "monopolies." Stigler also found that congressional support for the Sherman Act tended to be concentrated in states where small business employment tended to be dominant, not large. This caused him to conclude somewhat conservatively that his work provides "modest support for the view that the Sherman Act came from small business interests or that opposition came from areas with potential monopolizable industries, or both."

Other economists—Donald Boudreaux, Thomas DiLorenzo, and Steven Parker—who have studied the antitrust movement in the seventeen states that had enacted antitrust statutes before the passage of the Sherman Act have not been as cautious as Stigler in their assessments of the likely intent of antitrust statutes. These economists observed that many of the economies of the seventeen states with state antitrust statutes were based largely on farming and were clustered around Missouri, a fact that caused the economists to pay special attention to the antitrust movement in Missouri. The economists noted that at the time the state statutes were passed, in the 1880s, the prices of farm goods were falling. At the same time, though, the quality of farm products had been rising in the decades preceding the passage of the state antitrust laws. Moreover, the prices of many costs of farming such as freight rates and farm machinery, as well as mortgage interest rates, were falling, not what would be expected if the nonfarm economies of these states were plagued with monopolistic suppliers of farm inputs.

These economists noted that the farm interest groups complained frequently and vociferously about the "evils of 'monopoly,' " but that "the term, as used by the agrarians, referred only to the larger and more efficient firms which were driving small farmers and merchants out of their traditional lines of work and business. They [the agrarians] equated 'monopoly' with bigness, even if 'bigger' firms meant greater economic efficiency and lower prices for consumers." Boudreaux, DiLorenzo, and Parker concluded from their statistical analysis of the driving forces behind the state statutes that "the political impetus for some kind of antitrust law came primarily from the farm lobbies of Midwestern agricultural states such as Missouri. Rural cattlemen and butchers were especially eager for statutes that would thwart competition from newly centralized meat-processing facilities in Chicago. The evidence on price and output in these industries, moreover, does not support any claim that these industries suffered from a monopoly problem in the late nineteenth century, *if 'monopoly' is understood conventionally as an organization of industry that restricts output and raises prices*" (emphasis added).

Similar to Stigler, the economist Thomas DiLorenzo in another study reasoned that if monopoly was the core problem behind the Sherman Act, then key industries—such as steel, coal, oil, zinc, and sugar—that might be subject to monopoly practices should have experienced retarded growth in the 1880s, the decade prior to the passage of the act. However, he found that in the 1880s, the growth of what were thought to be trust-dominated industries seemed to be spurring growth in the economy as a whole, which might explain why a majority of the economists of the day opposed passage of the Sherman Act. Specifically, DiLorenzo found that while the nation's output of goods and services expanded by a healthy 24 percent between 1880 and 1890, the supposed trust-dominated industries grew by much more: steel, 158 percent; coal, 153 percent; zinc, 156 percent; sugar, 75 percent; and oil, 79 percent.

Moreover, prices of the trust-dominated industries were falling relative to other indicators. While the consumer price index fell by 7 percent during the 1880s, the prices of the supposed trust-dominated industries fell substantially more: steel prices, down 53 percent; zinc prices, down 20 percent; and sugar prices, down 22 percent. Coal prices remained more or less constant during the 1880s but dropped 29 percent in the 1890s. Three University of Georgia economists—Charles Delorme, Scott Frame, and David Kamerschen—subjected DiLorenzo's thesis to more rigorous statistical tests and came to much the same conclusion, that the antitrust laws were passed more with private interests in mind than the welfare of the general public.

In his review of the scholarly antitrust record, the journalist James DeLong notes poignantly,

> Even mighty Standard Oil, the great *bête noire* for trustbusters of the late 19th and early 20th centuries, was a symbol more than a true villain. By 1911, when the Standard "monopoly" was broken up by the Supreme Court, eight other large integrated oil companies were competing with it. Before that, Standard never tried to sustain prices at high levels. The history of oil during the late 19th century was one of huge expansion in markets and facilities and steadily falling prices.
>
> Many of the complaints about Standard came from medium-sized refiners that lost cozy local monopolies to Standard's rationalizing and price cutting. The same pattern has been repeated many times. As changes in communications and transportation create possibilities for new forms of business organization that might make things cheaper and better for consumers, firms that are doing well under the old forms fight back. This was true in the late 19th century, and it remains true today.

William Shughart has uncovered court opinions in antitrust cases that give force to the view that the real intent of the antitrust law for many supporters was not so much to fight monopoly as to ensure that smaller, less efficient firms could survive in markets dominated by larger, more efficient firms. In Trans-Missouri Freight (1897), Justice Rufus Peckman, writing the majority opinion, noted the concern that "small dealers and worthy men" would be run out of business by larger and more efficient competitors. Judge Learned Hand in Alcoa (1945) reasoned that the Sherman Act

> . . . was not necessarily activated by economic motives alone. It is possible, because of its indirect or moral effect, to prefer a system of small producers, each independent for his success upon his own skill and character, to one in which the great mass of those engaged must accept the direction of the few. These considerations, which we have suggested only as possible purposes of the Act, we think the decisions prove to have been in fact its purpose.

Judge Hand goes on to add, "Throughout the history of these statutes it has been constantly assumed that one of their purposes was to perpetuate and preserve, for its own sake and in spite of possible cost, an organization of industry in small units which can effectively compete with each other."

In short, according to Judge Hand, the intent of the antitrust laws has always been to preserve the market position of competitors and not the protection of consumer interests, which means that *competitive*—not *monopoly*—behavior can be construed to be against the law. This is one very important reason that if a firm (Microsoft, for example) is ultimately found to have violated the antitrust laws, it does not necessarily follow that the firm has acted like a monopoly. On the contrary, a finding of "wrongdoing" may be intended to preserve and strengthen the market positions of the firm's competitors, whom the Justice Department and courts consider "worthy men."

The net effect of the company's conviction could be that prices rise, but that consumer harm could, the court might reason implicitly, be offset by the greater social good of having an economic "system of small producers, each dependent for his success upon his own skill and character." In fact, Assistant Attorney General Joel Klein may have had this interpretation of the antitrust laws in mind when he complained that computer manufacturers "have no commercially reasonable alternative to Microsoft operating system" and wrote eloquently of preserving consumer "choice."

Clearly, Klein understands that the economies of scale and network effects that he says dominate the software market will lead to the market being dominated by one firm like Microsoft. His emphasis on ensuring that consumers have a "choice" of operating systems and browsers seems to suggest that having more than one producer in key national markets is a goal unto itself, even if consumers must pay more for their software as a consequence. Actually, Klein's talk about preserving "choice" seems to be simply code for preserving competitors from competition. (Besides, it must be stressed that the Justice Department's legal team never showed in court that computer manufacturers did not have "choices." The manufacturers did have choices in the sense that they *could* have installed operating systems other than Windows that were available, and would have, *if their customers had demanded them*. The computer manufacturers only argued that they saw no "viable" alternative operating system because their customers did not want them.)

In short, Microsoft may stand accused not of acting like a real *monopolist* (one that cuts production to raise its prices and profits) but of eliminating "commercially viable alternatives" by its *competitive* behavior. Klein and the state attorneys general in his train simply seek to make sure that Microsoft backs off from its competitive tactics and allows other firms to survive and share the market.

THE EFFECT OF ANTITRUST ENFORCEMENT

All of this leads to a point worth stressing again: if Microsoft or any other firm suffers an antitrust conviction, it doesn't necessarily follow it is a monopoly, or that it has exercised monopoly power.

Furthermore, an array of studies suggests that the *effect* of much antitrust enforcement has been to stifle competition, not monopoly, and economic efficiency and consumer welfare suffer in the process. Consider these findings:

The University of California–Davis economist George Bittlingmayer wondered why there was such an upsurge in mergers in the late 1890s and the first five or so years after the turn of the century. Between 1898 and 1902, over half the country's industrial capacity was involved in one merger or another. Bittlingmayer reasons that in industries that have heavy fixed costs, which means relatively low marginal production costs, producers need to cooperate to maintain price stability and to ensure that everyone doesn't incur losses (which relates to the "natural monopoly" argument discussed earlier). In the 1890s, the Sherman Act was viewed as being *anticartel* (cartels were cooperative arrangements among firms to stabilize prices) but wasn't seen by the courts as *antimerger* until 1904. From his statistical work, Bittlingmayer suggests that the Sherman Act had the effect of encouraging the development of larger firms through mergers, the exact opposite of what was supposedly intended by the Act's framers.

In another study, Bittlingmayer reasoned that if antitrust enforcement had the effect of discouraging firms from restricting production to raise their prices and profits, antitrust enforcement should be expected to encourage firms' increased investment in plant and equipment. However, he found that the waves of antitrust activism that were experienced in the 1947–91 period led to a reduction in firms' investment. In fact, in his study of twenty-one major industries he found that "each extra [antitrust] case overall is associated with a decline in investment of $1.4 billion in non-manufacturing, $370 million in durable goods, and $645 [million] in non-durable goods"—again, the opposite of what one would expect if antitrust laws were used to encourage competition, expand industry production, and lead to lower prices. Bittlingmayer reasoned that investment falls with each extra case because the litigation acts like a kind of uncertain tax on business expansion. Not surprisingly, Bittlingmayer found that in the 1891–1914 era, antitrust case filings against business, especially large businesses that were claimed to have monopoly power, tended to suppress business activity, not expand it as would be expected if the antitrust laws were intended to curb monopolies and expand competition.

Similarly, Shughart and his University of Mississippi economics colleague Robert Tollison, who has also directed the economics bureau at the FTC, found that antitrust enforcement activity between 1947 and 1981 tended to aggravate the country's unemployment problems, especially when there is a sudden unexpected increase in the government's expenditures on more cases. They reason, "If the allegations [of antitrust violations] are correct, then a successful prosecution of the cases by the Antitrust Division will lead to increased competition in the industry, resulting in expanded output and employment." But if the allegations are not correct, antitrust enforcement activities in fact force firms to adopt less efficient organizational structures and pricing strategies, then a lower level of production and employment would be expected. They conclude, "We do not claim that antitrust is responsible for all (or even most) of observed unemployment, nor do we suggest that every antitrust action throws people out of work. Rather, our most conservative results imply that on average an unexpected increase of 1 percent in antitrust case activity leads to about a 0.15 percent increase in the overall unemployment rate."

Shughart and Tollison, with the help of the economist Jon Silverman, also reason that if antitrust enforcement were intended to encourage competition, then it might be expected that the growth in imports, which represents a source of greater competitive pressures in the U.S. market, would be associated with a reduction in antitrust enforcement activity. This is because antitrust enforcement wouldn't be as needed in periods of greater competitive pressures from abroad. However, they found the opposite: "[W]hen foreign producers compete more effectively with domestic firms and consumer welfare losses [from domestic monopolies] are arguably lower than otherwise, Congress appropriates additional funding to support more vigorous antitrust intervention in the economy." However, the FTC's budget expands by .54 percent when import penetration of domestic markets rises by 1 percent (after adjusting for other political and economic variables that likely affect the FTC's funding level). The same 1 percent increase in import penetration leads to a .26 percent increase in the budget of the Justice Department's Antitrust Division. And, of course, the greater the antitrust budgets, the more harm antitrust enforcement can do to economic efficiency, according to Shughart, Tollison, and Silverman.

Not surprisingly, given the empirical findings already noted, Bittlingmayer found in a series of statistical studies a consistent inverse relationship between antitrust enforcement and stock market values (other economic considerations held constant); that is to say, when antitrust enforcement has been aggressive, financial markets have gone into a tailspin (as was the case in 1907, 1929, and 1962). When enforcement has been lax (in, for example, the 1920s and 1980s), the markets have tended to boom. If the overall effect of antitrust enforcement were to stifle monopolies, Bittlingmayer reasons that the opposite relationship between enforcement activity and market swings would be expected. This is because the market fortunes of the monopolies attacked by the Justice Department would have been undercut, but the market fortunes of all other firms would be expected to have risen with antitrust enforcement, given the expected welfare gains for the country as a whole.

Other researchers have examined an array of individual antitrust cases. They have often found that when structural relief is provided against monopoly behavior, the consumer gains were short-lived, since the accused firms were soon back to what they were doing prior to the court decisions. In those cases in which structural relief was provided for claimed antitrust violation, "more than 70 percent presented no likelihood of a substantial lessening of competition" and few cases held out the prospects of welfare gains for consumers.

Do these findings represent "failures" of the antitrust enforcement system? Maybe so in some cases—mistakes happen—but we suspect that the antitrust critics are on target when they suggest that in many other cases "the observed effects—the 'failures'—of antitrust *are* the intended effects." As noted, antitrust enforcement is not— cannot be and will never be—developed in a political vacuum. Congress and the administration are heavily influenced by their constituencies, many of whom have private interests in having antitrust cases brought against their competitors. And these constituents make their complaints known in Congress and the administration and regularly enlist the aid of their representatives in getting the Justice Department and the FTC to bring cases. This has caused researchers to look upon antitrust suits as another form of congressional pork passed out to favored constituents.

How do congressional politics affect antitrust enforcement? In several strategic ways. Congressional and administration views on cases need to be taken seriously by the people at the Department of Justice and the FTC because Congress and the administration have important budgetary and appointment controls over these agencies, and members of Congress and the administration can use these controls for the benefit of identified interest groups, not for the benefit of the broad consuming public. Politics can affect not only the total number of cases brought but also which cases are taken to court. Indeed, researchers have found that members of Congress manipulate antitrust budgets (especially at the FTC) for the purpose of influencing the number of cases brought according to the preferences of members of the congressional committees that oversee the FTC and the Justice Department. From research, it is apparent that members of Congress also affect the number of complaints dismissed by the FTC, suggesting significant political tampering with what appears to be an independent investigatory process designed to seek out the truth of monopoly power in the economy. Other researchers have found that when congressional interest in antitrust activism has waned, the FTC has become less active. Finally, Richard Higgins and Fred McChesney found that the more press a merger gets and the more Congress exhibits interest in it, the more likely the FTC is to challenge it and the more often FTC officials are called to testify before congressional committees around the time the merger is being investigated, which is a way of saying that public relations and politics taint the antitrust process.

No one should overlook the fact that the whole of the antitrust process is also affected by the political and career inclinations of the attorneys who investigate complaints and decide to pursue cases in administrative hearings and in court, and there is no reason to believe that their motives are always the most noble. Many of the attorneys involved in antitrust cases take their government jobs in the first place at relatively low pay for short periods of time for the purpose of gaining experience in investigating and trying antitrust cases. The trial experience gained can mean lucrative jobs in the practice of antitrust law when they return to the private sector.

Posner notes that one FTC lawyer admitted, "For me, each complaint is an opportunity, a vehicle which someday could take me into the courtroom. I want to go to trial so badly that there are times when I overstate the possibilities which the particular matter might offer." Judge Posner adds, "The principal attraction of [FTC] service to lawyers who wish to use it as a stepping stone to private practice lies in the opportunities it affords to gain trial experience. . . . It is the experience of trying cases, the more the better, not the social payoff from the litigation, that improves the professional skills and earning prospects of FTC lawyers."

Shughart concludes his survey of bureaucratic incentives in the antitrust process: "Taken as a group, these few studies of organizational behavior point to the conclusion that the antitrust bureaucracy does not select cases to prosecute on the basis of their potential net benefit to society. Instead, the managers and staff of the Antitrust Division and the FTC use the discretion at their disposal partly to further their own private interests rather than those of the public at large." The antitrust case against Microsoft is, no doubt, viewed by attorneys at the Justice Department as a career-shaping and career-capping opportunity, given Microsoft's relative size and importance in the U.S. and world economy.

It might also come as a surprise that state attorneys general do not always have high-minded goals when they pursue antitrust cases. The offices of state attorneys general are widely recognized as "profit centers" for state governments, which means they are expected to turn a profit on the various legal actions they take. Antitrust suits against major companies that harbor the potential for substantial damages paid to state coffers, and the potential for elevating the national visibility of the state attorneys general, invite abuse of the antitrust laws. This is especially true when legal action can be brought against Microsoft, the largest and richest company in the world. Many state attorneys general who did not pursue legal action against the tobacco industry years ago and as a consequence will not share in the substantial spoils those suits have brought have a special reason to jump on the antitrust bandwagon: they want to avoid "being tobacco'd," an expression that is now used widely within state attorney general circles to indicate that they don't want to miss out on the next round of legal awards that, as in the tobacco cases, could run into the tens of billions of dollars.

CONCLUDING COMMENTS

The conclusions that researchers have drawn from their studies relating to the political taint of antitrust cases should not come as any big surprise. All antitrust work is tied to and dependent upon the political process, which offers the people in that process broad discretion for action or inaction. The people who work in antitrust will exploit the opportunities for private gains at their disposal as much or as little as the people who work in companies that are the objects of antitrust complaints.

Firms should be expected to take advantage of their market discretion, given any monopoly position they might have. Antitrust agencies should be expected to take advantage of their political positions and the discretion at their disposal, given the even more powerful monopoly positions of these agencies.

The next chapter is concerned with how the antitrust enforcement process has once again been tainted with politics. The story behind the Microsoft antitrust case is the one that tells how Microsoft's competitors used the political and legal processes to slow down Microsoft's competitive invasion of the market that until the mid-1990s had been their stronghold. This market was not the market for browsers. Microsoft's competitors knew that there wasn't much money to be made in browsers. Browsers were too easily duplicated. The critical money-making market they wanted to protect from invasion by Microsoft was the back-office market for servers and their operating systems. This story is also about "rent extraction," as Microsoft has learned to play the political game in order to fend off the political assaults of its competitors.

CHAPTER 8

Politics 101

Politics is fundamentally about choosing policies that will guide the economy, as well as the broader society. All too often, however, the economy—most notably changes in the economy—drives politics. This is because well-positioned and well-heeled interest groups have a stake in using politics to shore up their economic positions with government policies that favor them. Much politicking is tame, founded on polite point-counterpoint debates by policy opponents who respect each other's political and ideological differences and who truly seek reasoned compromises.

But much of modern politicking is counterproductive, even destructive, as representatives of interest groups bar no holds in how they seek their own gain at the expense of targeted individuals and companies or the broader pubic. This destructive interest group–based politics, under which the powers of government are misused and abused for private ends under the guise of the pursuit of public goals, has undermined the public's trust in much of what goes on in the seats of government power. This part of the political process has become highly competitive. With so much at stake, given how public policies can realign competitive advantages and redistribute wealth, the rules of competition have radically shifted. Prominent market rivals must compete as aggressively in the political arena as they do in markets. Woe unto the company that stands aloof from political competition. Regrettably, with growing frequency, the political competition has become intensely brutal.

No wonder the public has such a low opinion of politicians and has a craving for campaign finance reform—a craving that few politicians, understandably, share.

The process whereby special interest groups seek to gain political advantage by denigrating, even smearing, people, companies, and whole industries in the media by means of innuendo, misleading arguments, half-truths, lies, and name-calling has a long and dishonorable history in the annals of American politics. But recently, this process—in which special-interest advocates, many of them hired guns, throw out just enough truths to give their campaigns a patina of credibility—has acquired a new name: Borking.

Successful Borking generally requires a coordinated campaign, sometimes orchestrated by Washington-based public relations firms, in which the truth of the matter is deliberately obfuscated by critical comments coming from a variety of sources and places at more or less the same time. The editors at the *Wall Street Journal*, in reference to the hearings on Clarence Thomas's nomination to the Supreme Court, described Borking as a strategy of hurling a plethora of "mud balls in the hope that some will stick."

The term "Borking," as many readers will immediately realize, has its origins in another hearing on a Supreme Court nominee, Judge Robert H. Bork. His 1987 nomination was effectively quashed with an avalanche of criticisms from a broad range of interest groups—from Planned Parenthood and the NAACP to the National Organization of Women and the National Abortion Rights Action League—as well as from a host of congressional detractors. Within hours of the nomination announcement, Senator Ted Kennedy had lambasted Judge Bork on the floor of the Senate: "Robert Bork's America is a land in which women would be forced into back-alley abortions." In addition, "blacks would sit at segregated lunch counters, rogue police could break down citizens' doors in midnight raids, schoolchildren could not be taught about evolution."

By the end of the campaign against Judge Bork, he had been charged with being racist, antiwomen, and antiabortion. He had been branded as an ultraconservative in his judicial philosophy, mainly because he interpreted the Constitution strictly. "From the tone of his inquisition," wrote a *Los Angeles Times* reporter, "one would think he had committed serious crimes as a traitor or a wife beater." Yet Bork was eminently qualified to serve on the Supreme Court. By the time of his nomination, he had been a longtime and distinguished Yale Law School professor and had written extensively as a legal scholar. He had also been solicitor general of the United States, acting attorney general of the United States, and a judge for several years in the Circuit Court of the U.S. District Court of Appeals for the District of Columbia.

Borking was perfected and taken to a new level of shrillness during the Senate hearings for Clarence Thomas. NOW's Florence Kennedy coined a new phrase as she flatly stated her group's goal: "We're going to Bork him. We're going to kill him politically." In those hearings, critics castigated Thomas for various infractions: for being Catholic, for being black, for being not black, for being an affirmative-action ingrate, for being anti-Semitic, and for living what his detractors believed was a weird lifestyle. Never mind that the criticisms may not have been true or may have been only tangentially related to his nomination; even unfounded charges can be effective in causing a nominee to withdraw. (In Thomas's case, however, that didn't happen.)

In recent years and in Washington and other quarters, Borking has evolved into a highly sophisticated long-term political strategy not restricted to a single event like a congressional hearing. Now these campaigns are carried out in a more tempered way, with more guarded language, than were the campaigns against Bork and Thomas. But their essence remains unchanged: the Borking process involves a broad-based, concerted effort by members of an interest group to discredit—if possible, demonize—people and firms with invective, and with the same old objective: to use the power of the state against the targeted party or parties. A modern Borking campaign uses the standard techniques of discrediting in which various members of the interest group pass off rehearsed sound bites to the media. In addition it may include several other frequently used methods of scoring political points:

- Running ads in major news publications that are designed more to excite emotions against the targeted parties than to offer useful information
- Hiring consultants and front men whose political, academic, and business pedigrees and celebrity status give them ready access to the print media and the television and radio talk-show circuit
- Paying for and then distributing commentaries to major regional newspapers, to be used as Op-Eds, editorials, or background information without identifying the organizations that have commissioned and funded or otherwise sponsored their creation
- Contributing to think-tanks in the D.C. area and elsewhere with the intent of having them redirect their research efforts to distributing reports that invariably serve the goals of the special interest group
- Funding conferences that offer the pretense of studied consideration of the issue, but that are designed to provide another public forum for supposedly neutral parties to attack the targeted person or organization
- Orchestrating campaigns to have petitions signed by disinterested experts (for example, academics) and then have the petition published as an ad containing an "open letter" to, say, the President or all members of the Congress
- Hiring lobbyists who have access to members of Congress, who in turn can hold hearings that allow members of the special interest group to vent their ill will toward the targeted person or company
- Last but not least, contributing to the political campaigns of all the politicians who lead the Borking charge

There are, naturally, myriad ways Borking can be pursued, but whatever the ways employed, Borking stands apart from ordinary lobbying, which can be done with decorum and constructive ends in mind. Borking is public lobbying with a mean-spirited edge and a destructive aim. As will be seen, to a great extent the campaign to have Microsoft sued for violating antitrust laws has been Borking at its most effective. This can only erode our trust in antitrust enforcement.

The sad truth of modern Borking is that it has come full circle, as Judge Robert H. Bork has lent his name, credentials, and fame to an orchestrated political campaign to "get Microsoft" by political means. But Microsoft's adversaries may have aroused a sleeping giant to the realities of modern-day politics. Microsoft has now begun to follow the lead of others with a political strategy of counter-Borking. In this process of political punch and counterpunch, it looks as though Microsoft has woken up to the fact that it can and must play politics as well as—better than—its adversaries. Gates and Microsoft have a bankroll that can more than match the bankrolls of whole industries. And therein lies a new threat to the public's and their own well-being that the Borkers may not have anticipated.

THE EMPTY POLITICAL RADAR SCREEN

At one time, circa 1995, Bill Gates could boast that political concerns were not "on our radar screen." By all accounts, Gates truly despised playing the Washington political game then, and he still despises it now. As late as 1995, Microsoft had only one full-time lobbyist in Washington, and this was a person who had no secretary and whose office was out in the remote Chevy Chase section of the nation's capital, not near the K Street corridor renowned as the locus of a high concentration of the lobbying offices of major American corporations and trade associations. The company's political action committee had a total of $16,000 to distribute to politicians, mainly for reforming the country's copyright and encryption laws.

Back in the early and mid-1990s, maybe Gates saw political activity as a waste of company resources, time, and money. Maybe he believed that Microsoft could outcompete all market rivals with superior products and better prices. Maybe he believed that Microsoft was so powerful in its markets that his company need not pay attention to politics, and that his business strategies were beyond legal assault. Or maybe Gates was just politically naïve and inept. Whatever the reason, his insistence on remaining aloof and detached from politics as Microsoft grew in market prominence probably cost the company tens, if not hundreds, of millions of dollars.

Gates probably should have known better. Perhaps he should have understood that Microsoft's business strategy in the early and mid-1990s was widely equated with the approach taken by the female praying mantis—first she would have sex with her partner and then turn around and devour him bite by bite. Gates should have also recognized that Microsoft's strategy—to dominate personal computing with cheap but good software and then to enter the back-office market—was, at its core, a radical competitive assault on the established business computing model of that time. That was reason enough for Microsoft's rivals—led by people whose egos may have been just as inflated as Gates's—to try first to demonize Microsoft as the

"Evil Empire" or "Godzilla" and then to work cooperatively (or should we say "collusively"?) to stop Microsoft, through either market or political means, whichever held out the prospect of being more cost-effective.

Perhaps Gates should have recognized then that the personal disdain and envy his rivals openly expressed in the media for him and his company would eventually translate into cooperative efforts and motivate their political crusade to get Gates and get Microsoft. A lot of money and industry status was at stake in the wars for software-industry dominance. Perhaps he should have done a few simple calculations to estimate the gains to his market rivals if they had the good fortune only to slow Microsoft down in its conquest of new markets by a few months (not to mention to win an antitrust case and force a breakup of Microsoft, as has been proposed). The numbers are quite substantial, and can easily justify Microsoft's rivals spending a minor fortune on a political campaign.

As will be seen, Gates has learned a valuable lesson in a practicum for what Senator Slade Gorton of Washington, Gates's home state, calls Political Science 101: a true-to-life course taught daily to reluctant students in the streets of Washington and the halls of Congress. Gates is a fast learner and is responding accordingly.

But why should anyone be out to get Gates, or Microsoft? What is the market backdrop to the political campaign?

THE MARKET BACKDROP

To understand the politics of the Microsoft antitrust case, you must understand the radical change in the economics of computing that Microsoft helped to forge during the 1980s. Before the 1980s, centralized mainframe computers overwhelmingly dominated virtually all computing. Personal computers were a novelty. If people needed computing for their office work, they did it by way of "dumb" terminals connecting them directly to the mainframe. (Before that, they walked to the computer center and entered their programs and data on punch cards.) Those dumb terminals rapidly gave way to smarter and smarter personal computers for home and office work. By the early 1990s, personal computers–the biggest manufacturers were IBM, Compaq, Dell, Gateway, and Apple—dominated home computing and office desktop work. Nevertheless, the overwhelming preponderance of business transactions of large enterprises—recording sale and purchasing transactions, managing inventories, making payroll—were still conducted by large, expensive mainframe computers and, increasingly, midrange and minicomputers. These down-sized versions of the mainframes had been made possible by the miniaturization technology of the 1950s and 1960s, including the development of integrated circuits, or "chips."

In the late 1970s and early 1980s, IBM was the overwhelmingly dominant player in the computer industry, accounting for perhaps 80 percent of all information technology expenditures by businesses. IBM controlled the "server stack," the full range of computer system components: the hardware, the operating system, the database programs, the middleware programs (software used to write applications or to mediate between separate preexisting programs), and actual applications used by people sitting at terminals. The battle that would shape up among Microsoft and its rivals—and ultimately between Microsoft and its rivals—was about who would profit from different parts of the server stack.

The battle started with Microsoft's rivals trying to consort in an attempt to re-align their industry assets and roles, with the intent of more effectively thwarting Microsoft's assault on their markets; it ended with a political campaign to have the Justice Department take up the antitrust case against Microsoft.

IBM's dominance resulted partly from its successful expansion of its customer base through its managers, who—while remaining dedicated IBM-ers—frequently moved on to take high-ranking positions in firms that bought from IBM. Two decades ago, IBM was so dominant in the computer market and faced such a strong demand for its mainframe that it was able to hold lotteries when new versions were introduced, to see which lucky winners would take home a new computer. For ex-ample, when the 303X was introduced, IBM had an eighteen-month backlog, ne-cessitating a lottery to determine whose orders would be filled first. Given the then market dynamic, the profit margins at IBM were, according to insiders, often in the range of 300 to 400 percent of cost. You can imagine that those kinds of profit mar-gins inspired competition.

In the 1980s, growth in the market for enterprise, or business, computing sys-tems used throughout companies began to shift from being driven by hardware to being driven by software, and the aphorism "he who controls the database controls the customer" was heard widely in the industry. Oracle's and Infomix's database ap-plications ran on dozens of computer platforms cheaper than IBM's, and soon these two software firms began taking accounts away from IBM, cutting into IBM's earnings.

The changes were not only in applications. Now there were new operating sys-tems competing with IBM's MVS system, particularly versions of Unix, an operat-ing system used on servers and high-end workstations. Unix systems were manufactured by Sun Microsystems, Hewlett-Packard, and a dozen or so other companies, and these companies began to grow at an exponential rate, causing a further deterioration of IBM's market position. These new rapidly expanding en-terprise-computing firms, following the IBM model, tended to be highly vertically integrated, meaning that the companies sold both hardware and software comput-ing products that worked together.

This was important because it meant that if a firm could capture a customer on the benefits of its hardware, it could also sell its software packages at, of course, in-flated prices. With the development of relatively cheap microprocessors by firms like Intel, the personal computer rapidly undercut many people's need to be tethered to a mainframe computer. People could do their computer work at their own desks and could store their work on disks—first, floppy disks, then hard disks.

The rapidly growing power and economic efficiency of personal computers in the late 1970s and all of the 80s made it possible for more and more firms in all industries to use them in lieu of the larger computers dominant under the "old" business computing model, which was based on large computers with integrated software packages. Under the new, personal computing, model, businesses did not have to buy all of their computing components (for example, hardware, middleware, and applications) from the same vertically integrated firm, for example, IBM or Sun. Firms in need of computing services could obtain the benefits of greater market competition by buying their personal computers and servers (a computer used in a network) from any number of new computer manufacturers such as Dell, Gateway, and Compaq.

Moreover, under the new model, firms in need of computing services could make use of a sequence of relatively cheap versions of Microsoft's MS-DOS and Windows operating system programs for the desktops that they could spread among the employees in their front offices.

Things were fine in the computer industry until the early 1990s. By then, however, it had become obvious to everyone, including Microsoft, that the real money to be made was in the enterprise-computing market, including hardware and attendant software products. By the early 1990s, this market included the rapidly developing sector made up of Internet servers dedicated to what would become known as e-commerce.

Even as late as 1994, computing and hardware firms like Oracle, Compaq, Hewlett-Packard, and IBM saw themselves competing against one another for all or a part of the "server stack," the full range of computing hardware and software. They did not recognize that Microsoft was plotting to take over much of the entire stack, yet perhaps they should have suspected this in the very early 1990s. In the late 1980s, Microsoft had hired David Cutler from DEC. Cutler was responsible for DEC's server operating system, VMS. At Microsoft, his responsibility was to develop Windows NT, an operating system designed not for the desktop, heretofore the locus of Microsoft's market dominance, but for back-office servers (computers that tie together networks of desktop computers or terminals, run Web sites, or provide Internet services or applications to all the computers on the network). This market had gigantic potential in the early and mid-nineties because of the advent of the Internet.

Windows NT (for "new thing," Cutler's new program's nickname at Microsoft), introduced in mid-1993, was a direct competitive challenge to a variety of firms, including IBM and Sun, that had built their computer business around their own Unix-based server operating systems. Sun had only recently introduced its Solaris operating system, designed to run sophisticated workstations (used in, say, manufacturing and construction firms' computer-aided design work), which sold at premium prices. (Windows NT has been revised, upgraded, and renamed Windows 2000.)

A new computing model had begun to emerge. Under the old model, companies tended to rely on a single supplier for their hardware and software needs. The new computing model was far more dependent on a fragmentation of the server stack. Under the new model for database management firms could use Microsoft's Back-Office (a bundle of server software, introduced in 1994, that included Windows NT, Exchange, and other programs) and for business applications they could get software from firms that, like SAP and Baan, had decided to write their business programs for the Windows platform. In no small way, Microsoft's BackOffice was designed to be a competitive challenge to the dominant position in database management and communications then held by Oracle and Lotus. Gates and company foresaw that the equipment would become a low-priced commodity just as desktop computers had and would likely get much cheaper. Accordingly, Microsoft was developing products that would compete in every component of the server stack besides hardware.

Firms adopting the new model could gain the considerable business bonus of synergies from networking their burgeoning stock of desktop computers with their back-office computers, all using much the same familiar Windows interface. As many computer experts understand, Microsoft may not always produce the "perfect" software, but it does do two things well: it integrates its products so that they work well together (as Microsoft had done with the applications in Microsoft Office); and it drives down market price by means of its more cost-effective marketing and distribution channels. Microsoft's competitors in the server market were at a decided disadvantage because there were seventeen different versions of Unix (a multi-user, multitasking operating system originally developed at Bell Laboratories in 1969 to help scientists share data), not all of which worked together. This meant that Microsoft was offering a unified computer platform that its competitors very likely could not match without working together.

By the mid-1990s, Microsoft reigned supreme over the personal computer operating system market, having beaten all comers for market share, most notably IBM. Having been outsmarted and humbled by Microsoft on a couple of major personal computing fronts in the 1980s and early 1990s, IBM was ripe for a fight with Microsoft over the remaining major back-office computer market. In the very early 1980s, IBM had been king of practically all computing hills, aside from the newly emerging personal computer market, which it was, as noted earlier in the book, late to see as a powerful threat to its mainframe market. Still, in spite of its faltering mainframe business, IBM saw itself as the industry standard setter, as did Gates and

Microsoft's cofounder, Paul Allen, and a lot of other computer people. IBM's major mistake was to assume that its market position was impregnable.

When IBM finally recognized the threat of personal computers, it believed that it could quickly catch up and use its franchise name to establish the industry standard for operating systems in personal computers. This is why IBM was willing to hire young Gates and Allen to develop the DOS operating system, which IBM called PC-DOS, and to pay Gates and Allen a flat fee of about $80,000 with no royalties. At the same time, IBM was willing to allow Gates and Allen to license their own version of DOS, dubbed MS-DOS, to other personal computer manufacturers at a per unit licensing fee. These fees gave Microsoft the cash flow it desperately needed to stay afloat while it developed other software products.

Little did IBM understand in 1981, when the first IBM personal computer was shipped, that it had handed Gates and Allen a virtual gold mine in that initial contract. IBM helped establish DOS as the operating system standard for personal computers and then effectively gave Gates and Allen the right to trade on that standard. That was all the incentive they needed to encourage a host of budding personal computer firms—the soon-to-be-called "clone makers"—to go into competition with IBM. When Gates and Allen licensed MS-DOS to IBM competitors, they made money on each non-IBM computer sold and lost nothing in royalties from any reduction in IBM sales. Remember that IBM's contract with Gates and Allen had no provision for royalties. No doubt IBM began to wish it had given Gates and Allen a share in IBM's income stream. That was IBM's first really misguided personal computer play; it cost the company dearly and probably gave rise to some hostility within IBM toward Microsoft.

Later in the 1980s, IBM once again teamed up with Gates and Microsoft, to develop a new 32-bit, graphics-based operating system. After unsuccessful attempts to blend their corporate cultures, IBM and Microsoft parted company in 1989, after which IBM finalized the development of OS/2 and Microsoft finalized a major upgrade of Windows (version 3.0), launched in 1990, and Windows NT, launched in 1993 (which has since become Windows 2000). When IBM and Microsoft agreed to work together again in the late 1980s, IBM assumed again, as did Microsoft, that it could use its franchise name and its computer manufacturing and distribution channels to make OS/2 the dominant operating system for personal computers. This is a central reason IBM dismissed Gates's 1987 offer to give IBM a 30 percent stake in Microsoft to ensure the continuing working relationship (a decision that by 1999 had cost IBM nearly $150 billion in equity in Microsoft).

By the mid-1990s, IBM was smarting from having been soundly outsmarted and badly beaten by Microsoft's Windows for the desktop market. Only 300,000 copies of OS/2 had been sold in the first three years, whereas 3 million copies of Windows versions 1.0 and 2.0 were sold. The net effect was that Microsoft's market capitalization surpassed IBM's as early as 1993, although IBM still had far greater sales and far more tangible assets on its balance sheet.

So by the mid-1990s, Windows was the undisputed king of the personal computer operating system hill. During the first half of the 1990s, OS/2 had a very small fraction of the operating system market (less than 4 percent), and then mainly because IBM installed OS/2 on its own desktops and laptops without giving its customers a choice of Windows. By early 1995, after seeing its market cap fall by half from its 1991 high, once-almighty IBM was forced by the dictates of the market to humble itself and include Windows as an option on its personal computers. IBM's executives no doubt had a tough time in 1993 and 1994 (when the company was in even worse trouble with the financial markets) justifying to their board of directors and stockholders the company's poor market performance for its personal computers. One easy solution: Blame Microsoft!

Novell, a Utah-based company best known for its company-based networking software, NetWare, was another major firm that by the mid-1990s understood the harsh reality of working with and simultaneously competing against Microsoft. Novell's then aging chairman, Ray Noorda, had long claimed that Microsoft had torpedoed the success of DR-DOS, which Novell had bought from Digital Research in the early 1990s, by writing code into Windows that caused Windows to work poorly when running on top of DR-DOS. By 1994 the two companies were also poised to invade each other's software strongholds. Novell was intent on combining NetWare with the other software products it owned, the most important being UnixWare, which it had purchased from AT&T; offering a new program, AppWare, which would allow Windows applications to run on UnixWare as well as other versions of Unix sold by Sun, Hewlett-Packard, and IBM; and selling its own suite of productivity applications, which included WordPerfect (purchased in early 1994 for $1.4 billion) and the spreadsheet software Quattro Pro (bought at about the same time for $145 million), which would put it in direct competition with Microsoft Office, a suite of productivity applications. In 1993, Microsoft went into the networking business with Windows NT at the same time that it was working diligently to improve LAN Manager, a program that when combined with Windows NT offered the prospects of unseating NetWare's dominance in the server market. Like Microsoft and IBM, Microsoft and Novell were headed for competition over a layer of the server stack.

In 1990, WordPerfect had a nearly 50 percent share of the word-processing market (as measured by revenues generated), while Microsoft's Word had slightly more than 10 percent of the market. However, by the time Novell was ready to challenge Microsoft in the suite market in 1994, Microsoft Word's market share had jumped to more than 60 percent. WordPerfect had plunged to a market share of less than 10 percent. Two years later, the duel between WordPerfect and Word had been settled, since by then Word had a market share of close to 90 percent, more than twice the market share that WordPerfect had in the late 1980s. Novell's effort to counter Microsoft's Office suite with PerfectOffice was a miserable miscalculation and a financial failure.

Novell's chairman, Ray Noorda, saw his company's market losses again as a consequence of Microsoft's foul play, mainly, he charged, because Microsoft supposedly was able to use its knowledge of new versions of Windows to give it a market edge. Analysts, however, attributed Novell's failure to business decisions motivated more by Noorda's antipathy for everything connected to Microsoft and Bill Gates, who didn't seem to live by Noorda's live-and-let-live principle of "coopetition," than by good business judgment. In addition, industry watchers attributed WordPerfect's market share losses to the fact that Novell was slow to market with a Windows 95 version of WordPerfect and its spreadsheet software, Quattro Pro. Furthermore, when WordPerfect reached the market it was full of bugs (to which this author, who until then was a WordPerfect devotee, can attest from miserable experience).

Noorda was replaced in 1995, and Novell finally sold DR-DOS to Caldera and sold off WordPerfect to Corel for what amounted to pennies on the company's mega-investment dollars. In July 1996, Noorda used his financial stake in Caldera, and Caldera's newly acquired control of DR-DOS, to file a private antitrust suit against Microsoft for "predatory acts and practices," which Caldera lost. It is hard to see how any court could award Caldera damages, for the fire-sale price Caldera paid for DR-DOS must have reflected the damages already inflicted. If Microsoft damaged anyone, it was DR-DOS's former owners, not Caldera, which got DR-DOS on the cheap.

But of course, Noorda's aim may have been not recovery of damages but carrying forward his vendetta against Microsoft. As one industry watcher observed, Ray Noorda "likes suing Microsoft so much that he'll even buy a company for the purpose of suing Microsoft again."

By 1995, Silicon Valley and other high-tech areas of the country were strewn with the corpses of companies that had tried to make it big with a new software program; a number of them had fallen prey to the competitiveness of the "Evil Empire," the "Godzilla from Redmond." Microsoft killed off any number of competitors by picking off their markets one after another. In some cases, Microsoft eliminated markets altogether by integrating "applets," small specialized programs such as disk compression and fax programs, within Windows. As discussed in earlier chapters, many of the Windows enhancements started out as product lines developed by other software companies.

Microsoft is one of the companies most admired by the general business community, but it came to be intensely disliked by some of its competitors for following a different competitive drummer and either eliminating them or threatening to do so. In his book, Jim Clark variously caricatures Bill Gates as "Lord Gates," "Machiavellian Prince," and "Emperor" and refers to Microsoft as "Godzilla," the "eight-hundred-pound gorilla," "Monster," and "Evil Empire." Similarly, Sun's Scott Mc-Nealy has thought nothing of belittling Gates as "Butt-head" or talking about "killing Microsoft" in public and suggesting that Gates really can't be trusted: "He'll shake your hand until he's ready, and then put what you've done in his own operating system." This turn of words suggests that McNealy believes companies in competitive industries should keep to their own markets and take a more live-and-let-live approach to product development.

There seemed to be a feeling among successful high-tech Silicon Valley entrepreneurs that they had developed or, better yet, created their markets and therefore in some sense owned them, in much the same sense that they owned their programs; thus Microsoft was invading and usurping what was *theirs*. Certainly Netscape's Clark was concerned about Microsoft's restrictive business practices, which made life difficult for Netscape, but he also seems to be charging throughout his book that Microsoft's prominence in the industry and its cash reserves enabled it to bully its way into any markets it wished to enter, even though Microsoft may have contributed nothing to the identification and development of those markets.

A similar feeling was best put by a Lotus Corporation attorney in September 1993, after a day of pressing the Justice Department to undertake an antitrust investigation of "the broad range of Microsoft's practices in the application software and related markets." He said, "We hope that all competing firms in the software industry will be able to thrive in coming years." Loosely translated, the lawyer seemed to mean that antitrust laws must ensure that no firm like Microsoft should be allowed to overtake other people's markets with aggressively competitive market strategies. The attorney's feelings seem to be shared by a number of operators of high-tech firms who have complained that Microsoft should not be allowed to buy everything.

Many people in the software business may have grown to resent Microsoft because its forte might not be the development of new and path-breaking software (although it spends billions of dollars each year on research and development) or even in the production of the software, but in combining it, and marketing it, and exploiting the famed network effects. All software firms have access to the scale economies of third-party manufacturers of CDs and shrink-wrapped boxes, and all software firms can transmit their software to computer manufacturers for installation on the machines that the computer manufacturers sell directly to buyers over the web. Microsoft's decisive advantage may be in improving software, rapidly upgrading the software with its massive staff of programmers, and getting the software to customers through its vast worldwide marketing and distribution channels.

Netscape's Clark may have been right (though only to a degree) when he derided Microsoft for being the "master copier." And Gates admits that one of his company's primary goals must be to "embrace and extend" software technologies, which is another source of Clark's problems with Microsoft. But given that role and its marketing and distribution advantage, Microsoft can understandably be seen as a threat to entrepreneurs who seek to identify new software markets. This is because, in spite of Microsoft's size, "Microsoft time" appears to be faster than "Netscape time," or any other time.

People in the industry understandably resent Microsoft because, as became evident to Clark as he tried to develop Netscape, Microsoft is in an enviable bargaining position when it seeks to buy out firms that have identified new markets. Microsoft can put take-it-or-leave-it offers on the table, and such offers will tend to reflect Microsoft's costs of copying and taking over the new market for the product, not necessarily the cost firms like Netscape have to incur to identify the markets. Indeed, in his book Clark bemoans the fact that in the fall of 1994, after Netscape had released its first version of Navigator (then called Mosaic Netscape), Microsoft proposed to buy Netscape's browser technology for $1 million when Clark had already sunk by that time about $5 million of his own money into the project over the first six months of Netscape's existence. (Of course, some of Clark's initial outlays went to warding off legal problems with the University of Illinois, which was claiming that Netscape had pirated its Mosaic technology.) Do such offers reflect the position of a "monopolist"? Not really. They are the type of offer any lower-cost producer should make.

No doubt many other operatives in the high-tech field came to resent Microsoft because its growing dominance made life more difficult for them. If you are a computer programmer, or just a geek, who believes that some version of Unix or OS/2 is superior to Windows (and many techies and others do swear by Unix and OS/2), then Windows' growing dominance means that your preferred operating system is less valuable to you than it could be, because of the much vaunted network effects central to the discussions in earlier chapters: as Windows sucks away customers from your preferred system through attractive pricing and the addition of valuable features, it decreases the incentive of programmers to write applications for your preferred system.

You may feel justified in resenting Microsoft's fierce market portion, but not because it occupies a monopolistic position. If Microsoft acted monopolistically, your preferred operating system would become more valuable. As Microsoft hiked its price and lowered its sales, playing a monopoly strategy, the network for your preferred operating system could be expected to expand (because it would then be relatively cheaper), making it all the more valuable to you and others, because there would be more applications written for your preferred operating system. If, on the other hand, Microsoft acted competitively, increasing its market dominance by aggressively pricing its products, you could be made worse off as the variety of applications shrink for your preferred operating system.

This problem of shrinking applications may have been a growing one for high-tech devotees of alternative operating systems, since by the mid-1990s, the various versions of Windows NT were beginning to pick up steam in the back-office market as their prices fell and features expanded. During the first year after it was introduced, 1993, Windows NT sold only 300,000 copies (far below Gates's sales target of a million copies). In 1994, NT sales rose to a respectable 700,000 copies. Even then, NT had a fraction of 1 percent of the market for servers and work stations, but its market share was obviously going to increase. It looked as though the feat Microsoft had pulled off in the desktop market—total dominance—would be duplicated in the back-office market, which the old-guard computer companies still viewed as their stronghold. All the while, the prices of servers began to fall dramatically for everyone, including Microsoft's competitors, in large measure because of Microsoft's venture into the server market. Microsoft had two great advantages, price and uniformity (which Unix suppliers had trouble providing).

No wonder Oracle and IBM began to see Microsoft as a growing threat to their market positions. As a consequence, they led efforts to bring the old-line principals—Hewlett-Packard, Sun, Oracle, Novell, Data General, Compaq, Digital Equipment, and Infomix—together in an attempt to stop the Microsoft takeover of the market for the entire server stack, as well as other markets—most notably the emerging Internet market. As Sun's Scott McNealy told a *Wall Street Journal* reporter, "Those who can, do. Those who can't, consort." This is exactly what the anti-Microsoft group did.

In order to have any chance of stopping Microsoft's growing dominance on all software fronts, Oracle and IBM and the other principals of the anti-Microsoft group understood that they had to first suppress their infighting over which of the several versions of the Unix-based operating systems would become an industry standard. This meant the group would have to agree on a single version of the Unix operating system, so more applications could be written for Unix, which would undercut the attractiveness of Windows NT.

Ultimately, Digital and Compaq chose to stay with the Windows platform. The rest of the old guard agreed to use Novell's UnixWare as the foundation for the new standard operating system, to be called Global Unix, toward which everyone in the group would begin to steer their Unix-based work.

A number of companies coming together to set an industry standard is not an antitrust problem per se. Setting an industry standard offers opportunities for all sorts of efficiency gains, not the least of which is that computer hardware and software can work together and achieve greater network benefits. What makes the efforts of the IBM-led group troublesome is that there also seemed to be an effort by group members to coordinate their public attacks on Microsoft in an attempt to vilify Gates and his company. IBM's John Thompson declared in July 1996 that Microsoft "has a stranglehold on distribution. It's called pre-load." Ray Noorda was ever ready to cast aspersions on his nemesis on the order of "Bill Gates's behavior is an insult to the industry and the world."

Such public attacks were no doubt a part of the rivals' strategy of undermining the public's devotion to Microsoft products. At the same time, the consortium began pressuring the Justice Department to launch its investigation. It also laid the groundwork for an escalating political attack on Microsoft by way of the group's well-positioned operatives in Washington, a campaign to which we will return in the next chapter.

FALSE START FOR NETWORK COMPUTING

During the first half of the 1990s, the anti-Microsoft group seemed to take heart from the fact that the then burgeoning World Wide Web and the prospects it offered for a return to network computing would fundamentally change the way the world does business and, perhaps more important, might bring an end to Microsoft's dominance. The rhetoric certainly began to heat up by the mid-1990s. In September 1995, a month after Windows 95 was released and the Microsoft Network was launched, Larry Ellison, head of Oracle, which played second fiddle to Microsoft in terms of size within the software industry, told a European communications conference with his usual confidence, "A major paradigm shift is occurring as we speak. We're going from a desktop-centric view to a network-centric view." He also mused that Microsoft's future did not look promising because it was still wedded to personal computers that were "expensive and complicated." In the future, Ellison asserted, "All users will want is something that plugs into the wall to get electrons for power and plugs into the wall for data. Personal computers are ridiculous machines."

Gates was none too respectful and gentle in his response: "People who think dumb terminals will completely replace PCs in the world of [the] Internet are wrong." He suggested that in the future there would, no doubt, be "network computers," but personal computers would represent a major share of all network computers in use. Nonetheless, David Moschella, the senior research consultant for International Data Group, which sponsored the conference at which Ellison spoke, suggested, "Microsoft could be at its peak. Windows 95 could be the high-water mark." He then added that Mosaic, the precursor to Netscape's Navigator, "can be seen as a window to the Internet."

At the same time, beginning in mid-1994, Netscape intended to conquer the Internet with Navigator (originally called "Mosaic Netscape"), which Netscape cofounder Marc Andreesen had described as the "Mosaic killer" because it was easier to use and ran ten times faster than Mosaic. Hugh Hemple, Netscape's electronic marketing director, summarized the company's grand strategy: "We intend to be the leading supplier of the enabling technologies of the Internet. What does that mean? That means we want to be to the Internet what xerography was to the printed communications, what PostScript is to desktop publishing, what Windows is to the PC."

In 1995, it looked to some observers as though the ground might be moving with tectonic force from under the personal computer. A University of Maryland computer professor began pressing for a "Webtop" device that would be about the size of a magazine, have a "virtual keyboard" on the screen, and cost $100 to $300. Later that year, Scott McNealy, head of Sun Microsystems, announced that his company would develop a cheap network access device that would use Sun's network programming language Java and would allow for the downloading of programs from the Net.

Lou Gerstner, the newly appointed head of IBM, chimed in at the 1995 Las Vegas Comdex, the largest trade show for computer software and hardware developers and vendors in the world, agreeing with Ellison that the computer industry was on the threshold of a "network-centric" era and announcing that IBM would be developing "network appliances." John Thompson, an IBM vice president, later estimated that network appliances could reduce the price of computing by 25 percent or more and would then be a viable replacement for the 30 million "green screens" (Thompson's description of personal computers) used by businesses around the globe.

By 1996, McNealy had become convinced that the Internet would undermine Microsoft: "The planet will not have to go to one lousy place for desktop operating systems and productivity tools. We dream of millions of Java applets available over the Internet, bringing it to life." He rhetorically asked later in 1996, with even more obvious disdain for Microsoft, which had by then become the Redmond beast to be slain, "What is this stuff [operating systems] but a language?" to which he gave his own answer: "It's like English. Nobody owns English," and then concluded that if Microsoft owned English, "They [Gates and company] would issue it as English 3.0 and then sell you upgrades for the letters N and T."

Similarly, Ellison started talking about how "the center of gravity" in computing first migrated from the mainframe to the personal computer and was at that time migrating to the Internet, which is why Oracle would be developing its "network computer," which would sell for less than $500. He also began comparing Gates unfavorably with the reputed robber baron John D. Rockefeller, claiming that, because of the advent of the Internet, Microsoft's "monopoly on the computer" would not last long: "I guess I always resent other people's monopolies. But the laws of business don't like vacuums and they don't like monopolies. Even IBM's monopoly only lasted for twenty-five years. Rockefeller's monopoly didn't last that long. Nor will Bill Gates's and Microsoft's." Ironically, this position stands in sharp contrast to Ellison's urgent appeals to the Justice Department to file an antitrust suit against Microsoft and to bring its reign to a premature end.

When a *Forbes* editor suggested to Ellison in an interview that Microsoft did not share Oracle's vision of network computing—under which there would be "thin clients" and "fat servers"—and that Gates had demonstrated "brilliance" in his business strategy, Ellison derisively responded, "Bill Gates, brilliant? Really? Uh-huh [Ellison laughs for several seconds]. Let me start by saying that intelligence, like love, is one of those words that have no real meaning. Let me leave it there." At the Spring Comdex/Windows World 1996, held in Chicago, McNealy heated up the verbal feud he and others had with Microsoft and Gates by giving what he mocked as the "Top Ten Reasons for Owning a PC" to the laughter of his audience: "It's the only CD player they allow in the office. . . . It makes a good step aerobics plate. . . . We WANT to add photographs and music to our spreadsheets. . . . Because it says Intel Inside on the outside. . . . You can use the reboot time for a [bathroom] break."

According to Netscape's Jim Clark, Netscape began talks with Sun in the fall of 1994 to combine the browser technology with the Java language, which the two firms saw as a "virtual operating system" and as a potential alternative platform to Windows. Seeing the promise of the Web, Netscape joined in with its support of network computers in 1996, with Marc Andreesen, who was by then being touted in the media as "the next Bill Gates," acknowledging that network computing represented a "major new business opportunity. There are thirty to forty million copies of Netscape Navigator in use today. Over the next five to ten years, network computers could expand the user base to hundreds of millions, or even billions."

THE FIRST PASSING OF NETWORK COMPUTING

Unfortunately for the anti-Microsoft group, their best-laid plans and dreams began to unravel (at least for the next two years) with a series of market events that undermined the raison d'être for network computing.

A Waking Giant

First and foremost, beginning in 1995, Microsoft demonstrated remarkable nimbleness in its ability to radically shift the direction of its future product development, this in spite of its size (it had 20,000 employees at the time). Microsoft was clearly aware of the Internet before 1995 and had working groups watching its development, but all very tentatively, given the attention the company was devoting to providing content on CDs and to developing MSN, its network access to rival AOL. However, it had not yet made a company-wide commitment to making its products Internet-ready, or developing its product lines for the express purpose of taking advantage of the Internet.

In late 1994 or maybe early 1995, Gates seemed to wake up to the full reality of the Internet's importance to personal computing. In his book *The Road Ahead,* released in November 1995 (so the final manuscript was probably completed in late 1994), Gates recognized in a number of places the importance of the Internet, contrary to what his critics have often claimed. He wrote, "The popularity of the Internet is the most important single development in the world of computing since the IBM PC was introduced in 1981." By early 1995, a change in direction was clearly in the works: Microsoft had by then already licensed the Spyglass browser technology (for $1.4 million) from the University of Illinois; it formed the basis of Internet Explorer, the first version of which was released in the summer of 1995.

Microsoft claims that its browser plans began taking shape at a retreat for executives held in April 1994, about the time Clark and Andreesen were plotting to set up Netscape. Though Gates had not made the Internet a top priority for the company before the spring of 1995, things were about to change, dramatically. Perhaps, Gates had been watching the growing publicity swirling around Netscape's progress over the previous ten months. As Clark boasts, few start-ups have ever attracted as much press attention as Netscape. A 1994 cover of *Red Herring* showed Gates and Clark as chess pieces and had the headline "The Once and Future Kings," while *Forbes ASAP* carried a 1995 cover story on Netscape and Marc Andreesen titled "This Kid Can Topple Gates."

Whatever the impetus, in a long May 1995 memorandum to his executive staff ominously titled "The Internet Tidal Wave" that was then marked "confidential," Gates radically upgraded company-wide interest in and commitment to the Internet, outlining both the threats and opportunities the Internet presented Microsoft. He insisted that his executive staff give the Internet the "highest level of importance." Indeed, in that memo, as in his 1995 book, Gates equated the importance of the Internet to Microsoft with the development of the first IBM PC and asked all company divisions to rethink and redesign their products with the Internet in mind, indicating with force the problems Microsoft would face in playing catch-up to existing Internet players and noting that the proposed network computer was a "scary possibility."

In making the moves he did in such short order, Gates demonstrated for the entire world, including his competitors, to see that Microsoft could turn on the proverbial dime the software behemoth that the rivals dismissed as a "software Titanic" on course for a collision with the Internet iceberg. Moreover, Gates's version of "Internet time" could be ticks faster than "Netscape time," which Clark has described as "life lived in a blur."

By the time Gates's book *The Road Ahead* was released, in late November 1995, Microsoft had released version 2.0 of Internet Explorer. Two weeks later, on Pearl Harbor Day, Gates started his talk at the company's "Internet Strategy Workshop," attended mainly by Microsoft workers but widely reported around the world, by saying that in his preparation for the talk, he had searched for "parallels" between that day in history fifty-four years before and the day of his talk. He concluded that the most intelligent comment made on that "Day of Infamy" was actually delivered by "Admiral Yamomoto, who observed that he feared they had awakened a sleeping giant." This image probably caused more than one executive in the anti-Microsoft group to want to take back their earlier taunts of Gates and Microsoft for not being Internet-savvy.

Gates then proceeded to outline Microsoft's historical strategy of waiting until new markets reached "critical mass" before software projects were commercially viable, possibly because he knew his company's advantage was serving the mass market at mass market prices, even if the products might not always be up to the standards of competitors. He then explained how winning the Internet would depend critically upon the company's being able to "embrace and extend" known technology and indicated that the outcome of the competition to come would turn on which company could "embrace and extend" the browser technology the fastest.

Gates acknowledged that industry seers had predicted the Internet would radically undermine the demand for software tied to personal computers, because people could fill their software needs from Web sites. This could lead to Microsoft's demise. Gates, however, disagreed with this prognosis. He believed that the burgeoning Internet would have the same impact on Microsoft's software sales as the burgeoning market for low-cost personal computers had done previously: namely, because the Internet would increase the usefulness of and market demand for personal computers, which would require operating systems and applications. As competition had driven down the price of personal computers, the expansion of the Internet would drive down the prices of Internet services and content, leaving software "the only element in the value chain." In other words, since Windows would soon be the only profitable product related to the Internet market—so long as Microsoft catered to the demand for Internet-ready computers by integrating its browser into Windows and giving it away, as well as by making all other Microsoft software products Internet-functional. The fact of the matter was that the development of the browser had been unbelievably cheap, given how little Microsoft and twenty other firms had paid to Spyglass for licenses and how little time Microsoft and Netscape took to develop their browsers. He may have also observed that Netscape could get a band of seven recent college graduates from the University of Illinois to write Navigator from scratch in less than four months, as Jim Clark attests with pride.

Version 3.0 of Internet Explorer was released in April 1996, eight months after version 1.0. The rapid-fire release of a series of upgrades to Internet Explorer paid off: Microsoft's browser technology went from being judged (by computer magazines) inferior to Netscape's Navigator in the spring of 1996 and earlier to on par with or superior to Navigator before the end of 1996. Clearly, the "giant from Redmond" was no longer sleeping, if that had ever been the case. The zest with which Microsoft thereafter pursued its Internet strategy no doubt busted the plans of the anti-Microsoft group to have the Web market to themselves. It was obvious to them and everyone else that Gates intended consumers to see personal computers as "network computers" that would continue to use the Windows platform.

Falling PC Prices

The second development in the passing of network computing concerned pricing for the proposed machines. In the early nineties, when the backers of network computers began to estimate costs of their proposed network devices, it became clear that they could not then be sold at retail for less than $500, as Oracle's Larry Ellison had promised. At the time, a modem alone cost $300, and the entire machine would likely cost the consumer upwards of $1,000. As the network computer camp struggled to develop the requisite software and get their devices to market, the price of personal computers continued to fall. In 1996, AST was the first computer manufacturer to announce plans to introduce a personal computer priced below $1,000, with even deeper price cuts to come (now down to $300), undermining much of the advertised economic advantage on hardware of the network computer.

New Central-Server Software

Third, by the time network computers appeared toward the end of 1996, several companies had developed software that allowed large businesses to put their Windows software on central servers and then buy low-end personal computers and make use of all of the existing Windows applications. More than two dozen companies were selling network management programs that took away another argument for the network computer, all of which caused one reporter to start his assessment of the future of network computing with "Thin client. Fat chance."

The Intel/Microsoft Response

Fourth, Intel and Microsoft responded to the threat of cheap network computers with new products that were end-runs around the necessity for a new computer. Intel developed the less expensive Celeron microprocessor, which made moving to network computers less attractive. Microsoft developed Windows CE, a stripped-down operating system that could be used on a wide range of computing "appliances," including network computers. If there was going to be a network computing revolution, Intel and Microsoft would be there to help migrate users to these new devices, many of which would continue to run on their products. Thus, Intel and Microsoft undercut the gains of network computing.

The Emperor's Clothes

Fifth, analysts began to see the network computing movement for what it seemed to be, a "vision of the world sans Microsoft." In 1996, the software specifications for machines that could be used as network computers supported Sun's Java language but not Microsoft's Windows. This may have prompted Stephen Auditore, president of the marketing group Zona Research, to comment, "This initiative has much more to do with power and greed than it does with customer need. Sun is attempting to substitute its products for Microsoft's. Instead of paying a tax to Microsoft for Windows, Sun wants people to pay them a tax for Java."

Meanwhile the decibel level and intensity of the rhetoric coming from key participants in the get-Gates and get-Microsoft movement continued to rise. And no wonder. Some very big business egos had been repeatedly bruised by Microsoft's winning ways in the market. Holman Jenkins, a regular *Wall Street Journal* columnist and critic of Microsoft's critics, noted that Ellison regularly denounced Microsoft as the "Death Star" during 1996, and "in the presence of reporters . . . has launched into strident second-person tirades against an absent Bill Gates." Moreover, "Scott McNealy, CEO of Sun Microsystems, has made a habit of going before trade show audiences and deriding Windows as 'whipped cream on a road apple.' He portrays Bill Gates as some kind of freakish perversion of capitalism, though 'throwing him in jail is not the answer,' Mr. McNealy generously added. 'I would put a bronze statue of him in front of the Commerce Department and make him the head.' "

Gates was not above going on the counterattack; he once dismissed the network computer as "Larry's silly idea." He also impugned the motives of the backers of network computing, suggesting that their goal was simply to "kill the movement toward powerful personal machines, and recentralize computing," with the none-too-subtle implication that consumers would then be under the market control of the likes of Ellison, as they had been under IBM's control in the pre–personal computer era.

In short, by the end of 1996, there were two clear visions of the future of personal computing:

1. The Microsoft vision. In this vision the personal computer becomes ubiquitous, and Windows and all of the attendant applications, many of which would be supplied by Microsoft, are the mainstay of the computing universe.
2. The Anti-Microsoft view. A vision sans the personal computer—and sans Microsoft.

It is safe to say that the principals had locked horns in something of an intra-industry death struggle, with no apparent holds barred. The goal for the combatants seemed to be to "win" in whatever way was the most cost-effective.

THE PLOT TO RESHUFFLE INDUSTRY ASSETS

Before May 1994, it is doubtful that the companies that had begun to rally around the network-computing concept saw Microsoft as the serious competitor they saw in one another. After all, they were watching each other. Oracle was carefully watching Sybase, Infomix, and IBM, since they had database management programs with which they could organize, update, and expand huge volumes of business information; they in turn were watching Oracle for much the same reason: they were going after many of the same business customers.

But along about mid-1994, Microsoft's scheme to take over much of the server stack, especially the operating system component, was becoming apparent. In mid-1994 they decided to fight back by working together to realign industry assets and roles. Each party to the consortium was assigned a component of the server stack, and on this front it would fight Microsoft. If they didn't divide up the server stack, the members' prior record of wasting company resources in competing with each other meant that the whole stack might be at risk from developments in Redmond.

The consortium of Microsoft detractors went further than coordinating their verbal attacks on Microsoft. During the summer of 1994, the consortium members began working out a reshuffling of industry assets to accomplish their goal, according to sources who were involved in the development of the strategy. The meetings were secret, understandably so, for if the plans came to light, they might not only have been in violation of antitrust laws but might also have provoked a response from Redmond. Oracle was going to buy Lotus Development Corporation, keep Lotus Notes but sell off Lotus's SmartSuite of business applications to Novell, which at the time owned WordPerfect. This would position Novell to challenge Microsoft on the office suite front. In return for the office applications, Oracle was to get Novell's Unix International division. If Sun and IBM would rewrite their version of Unix to match the Oracle-backed standard, Unix could then become an effective challenger to Microsoft's Windows NT in the server market. The principals in the group may not have liked each other, but they apparently disliked Gates even more.

By the first of September 1994, the group was set to make a big announcement of its plans the day before the start of the Oracle User Group convention, which was to be held at the Mosconi Center in San Francisco. According to insiders, their press briefing was to include representatives of the consortium's major participants on stage—Larry Ellison of Oracle, John Thompson of IBM, Scott McNealy of Sun Microsystems, Ronald Skates of Data General, and Wim Rolandte of Hewlett-Packard. Intel, Compaq, and Dell were invited to participate, but turned down the overtures on the grounds that they did not want to displease Microsoft, especially since their computer models were firmly tied to Microsoft operating systems and applications. Oracle's Ellison was set to be master of ceremonies.

The consortium had planned a fairly elaborate stage production for the members of the media in attendance, according to insiders who helped draw up the program. They were to start by giving Bill Gates an award for having the best operating system for the desktop market. They would acknowledge the problems customers had with the various versions of Unix and with the importance of uniformity in operating systems within firms and across firms. They would then fault Windows NT for lack of scalability—the ability to run on different-sized back-office computers and different databases of large and small firms—and for its lack of dependability, which initial users of NT had reported. This part of the program was planned to set the stage for their announcement of the unified version of Unix—Universal Unix—which of course would be far more scalable and dependable than Windows NT. With it they expected to be able to stop Microsoft's invasion of the back-office market.

Unfortunately for the principals in the consortium, they were not a single firm—nor even a tight cartel—and could not act like one. Just before the planned event, Oracle's Ellison met socially with his good friend Steve Jobs, who understood all too well the struggle Apple had faced fending off Microsoft in the desktop market and who needed a capital infusion. That evening Jobs apparently convinced Ellison that it was a serious tactical blunder to concede the desktop market to Microsoft and go after only the back-office market. As a consequence Ellison pulled out, refused to buy Lotus, and basically told the group, "To hell with you." Also, as noted, Ellison decided to try to undermine Microsoft's grip on the personal computer market by creating a whole new class of computers, network computers, that would not use Windows at all but would get their Oracle-supplied operating instructions and applications via the Net. In Ellison's view of the future of computing, Windows would be made irrelevant.

McNealy took a different tack, pushing Sun's version of Unix. According to Hasso Plattner, cochairman of SAP, a major international business software firm based in Germany, McNealy believed that Sun had a "better Unix." Later in 1995, a former HP employee hired by Microsoft spilled the beans to Bill Gates about the plans of the consortium. When HP executives learned that Microsoft was aware of the consortium's plans, HP formally pulled out of the group and agreed to build servers that would run Windows NT.

In 1995, IBM bought Lotus, because it thought the firm's programs were a good business deal that Ellison had left on the table. In 1996, Novell sold WordPerfect. By the end of 1997, Novell, Data General, and Infomix had decided to provide Windows NT–based systems. According to the *Wall Street Journal*, Netscape "became suspicious when Sun introduced its own browser, named HotJava. Netscape's distrust grew when Sun licensed Java to Microsoft, which was adapting its own strategy to the Internet." Netscape probably also did not take kindly to Ellison's 1996 assessment of Netscape's future: "I think their stuff is very, very thin. We can blow their doors off with our server technology. Right now their real value is based on Web browsers that take you to the Netscape home page. No one will tolerate that. You think everyone will start their day with the Netscape logo? No way. It's not going to happen." When pressed to explain his view, Ellison added, "Because when you have major Internet service providers—and there will be major Internet service providers—they will make sure that the browser starts on their home page, not Netscape's. Then what has Netscape got?"

Jim Barksdale, who had taken over from Jim Clark as head of Netscape, responded to Ellison's repeated attacks by suggesting that Ellison was simply seeking to talk down Netscape's stock "because he wants to acquire the company." Tensions within the anti-Microsoft forces grew even greater when Netscape began to compete directly with IBM's Lotus Notes.

More important, Microsoft played competitive cards that the rivals, individually and as a group, may not have anticipated, especially with quite the force and energy it did. With the rise of the Internet, Microsoft decided to make sure that its own operating system was network-capable by bundling its Internet Explorer browser with Windows, thus totally busting the dreams of the rivals that Microsoft would be dethroned and that computing would be recentralized, via network computing, into mainframe computers with ease. They would then be the new kings of all computing hills.

Was Microsoft acting like a monopolist when it did this? No way. Microsoft responded competitively to a competitive threat. The government sees the Microsoft browser move as one by a monopolist acting badly. Actually, Microsoft's browser move was a no-brainer for a competitor: if you are in a highly competitive, rapidly changing market, you move with the computer/software market forces, and at the time it looked to virtually all participants and observers that in the not-too-distant future, the action would rely extensively on the Internet.

As has so often been true in the history of federal and state regulations, companies that are unable to successfully cooperate in achieving collective goals often turn to the government for assistance. Its plans for a unified industry-organized assault busted, IBM could not by itself seek to regain the upper hand in its battle with Microsoft by claiming that Microsoft was a big bad monopolist and appealing to the government for relief under the antitrust laws. After all, in 1996, IBM had six times Microsoft's revenues. However, IBM and other principals could, with some potential for believability, claim that Microsoft had played its monopoly hand with regard to upstart Netscape, which had proposed to unseat Microsoft's market dominance with a net-based strategy that combined Navigator with Java.

The efforts of Microsoft's market rivals to work together to unseat Microsoft in the market may not have worked quite as well as planned, but they were able to make their arrangements sufficiently operational that a *Wall Street Journal* reporter stated that "this anti-Microsoft cabal represents an experiment in cooperation against a single enemy that may be unprecedented in modern American industry." The rivals' failure to pull off the reshuffling of industry assets was not the end of their efforts; they were just redirected. The Microsoft rivals even coined its own acronym, NOISE, for Netscape, Oracle, IBM, Sun, and "everyone else." Their ostensible purpose as a group was to work for the development of a shared operating system standard that would allow them to compete effectively with Microsoft, as several key players have publicly acknowledged. John Thompson, an IBM software executive, mused in 1998, "We must work together using all of our collective contacts to establish Java as the standard." Similarly, James Barksdale said, "We must move quickly to preempt Microsoft," and Scott McNealy admitted in 1999, "We meet regularly, we talk regularly. If we don't set the standards, we lose."

CONCLUDING COMMENTS

There is nothing illegal or improper about cooperating for the purpose of setting industry standards. After all, widely adopted standards for software that can be sold by a number of vendors promise a lowering of production costs and product prices, all of which can be beneficial to consumers. There's no problem with companies in a given industry ganging up on the dominant player in their industry if the intent is to improve their collective product, lower their prices, and outcompete the dominant player for customers. That's good old-fashioned competition at work in the marketplace.

But the NOISE principals' arguments are disturbingly inconsistent. They seek to collectively supplant Microsoft and, at the same time, accuse Microsoft of wrongly doing what they are trying to do. They suggest to any and everyone who will listen that Microsoft should not be allowed to play by the rules that they themselves are playing by. NOISE members maintain with straight faces that Microsoft should be penalized for trying to supplant them—and they will be rewarded by supplanting Microsoft. This is rank hypocrisy. It is doubly hypocritical for David Boies, the government's lead trial attorney on the case, to dismiss the collective NOISE efforts on the grounds that small companies should legally be allowed to collude, but large companies should not be able to do the same. It is definitely a stretch to view IBM, whose sales remain close to five times Microsoft's, as a "small" firm under any circumstances.

Microsoft's adversaries also should be called to task for conducting the antitrust debate with the kind of taunts more usually heard in schoolyards. Should we allow those taunts to be taken seriously and become factors in the country's political and judicial processes?

As we have seen, the history of antitrust trials has been a history of misuse and abuse of the antitrust laws, mainly because of the role politics has played in determining which firms are prosecuted. All too often the government has done the bidding of disgruntled competitors who would like nothing more than to see their more aggressive rivals throttled with the expense of defending against an antitrust suit. Microsoft's rivals have done what Judge Bork faulted antitrust prosecutors for in his book and more recently in interviews: they have politicized the process, thus throwing into doubt the Justice Department's real reasons for taking Microsoft to court.

⚖️ CHAPTER 9 ⚖️

Politicizing Antitrust

ANTITRUST LAW ENFORCEMENT IS *supposed* to be about thwarting the market power of firms that act like monopolies, who restrict their production in order to raise their prices and increase their profits. As Judge Robert Bork insisted throughout his classic 1978 treatise on antitrust law, antitrust enforcement is supposed to have the welfare of consumers at heart, not the welfare of market rivals who might be harmed by competition from a strong competitor. Actually, market rivals should be delighted when one or more firms in their midst tries to act like a monopoly, because as a monopolist restricts production to raise its prices, the market is opened to expansion by rivals. That is a theme of this book.

Market rivals who are being beaten by a strong competitor have an incentive to use the country's antitrust laws to their advantage, especially when they are unable to control market forces by means of consortiums. Offended rivals may claim with much self-righteousness that competitors will monopolize markets if they are allowed to merge or that the low prices of much more efficient producers are "predatory." Even the threat of an antitrust lawsuit can work to the advantage of weaker competitors because the actual or threatened legal expenses incurred in an antitrust defense could encourage companies with the potential to become more dominant than they already are to instead curb production and raise their prices. This would benefit the rivals who make the bogus claims of antitrust violations.

What's remarkable about the history of antitrust enforcement is how often the political system has heeded the chants of offended market rivals for antitrust prosecutions. This is reason enough to scrutinize the political maneuvering of market rivals in the Microsoft case. There's a lot of evidence that Microsoft's rivals worked together to try to stop Microsoft, and it is clear that their collusive efforts didn't work. Furthermore, Microsoft's rivals have good reason to want to work the political system: just slowing Microsoft down from invading their markets, will increase the return on their political investments.

Demonstrating cause-and-effect connections between what industry and political operatives do to exploit the powers of government for the operatives' mutual benefit is a tough assignment under the best of circumstances. Operatives of all stripes are smart enough to know that they need to keep their political deals hidden as much as possible from public scrutiny. Few people in industry will ever likely admit that they make contributions to politicians, or lend them their moral support, for the express purpose of skewering the public or their competitors with tailor-made changes in government policies for their own private gain. Few politicians will ever likely admit that they take money from contributors with the intent of padding the pockets of the contributors in some direct or indirect way. Few politicians will admit that they initiate deals with businesspeople with the intent of padding their own pockets. Few people who work for government will openly admit that they bend to political pressures. Virtually all conversations that occur in the process of political deal making will be invisible to the public—held "off the record," out of range of cameras, microphones, and reporters' notepads. Even worse, operatives on both sides intentionally mislead the public by surrounding their visible activity with a cloud of sanctimonious rhetoric to the effect that their actions serve the greater public interest, not special interests.

So it is with the Microsoft case. We should not expect Microsoft's adversaries ever to admit openly that they have made contributions to political campaigns for the express purpose of throttling Microsoft's competitiveness by way of an antitrust suit and, in the process, improving their bottom lines. We should, on the other hand, expect the rivals to argue that their political efforts are ultimately designed in some way to improve the welfare of the consuming public. The rivals can also be expected to intimate that they are merely giving of their own personal or company resources to serve the greater good of the country. Any increase in their own profits is incidental to their more noble social goals. Similarly, we should not expect the Clinton administration to admit that contributors to its past campaigns have influenced in any way how antitrust enforcement is conducted or who is prosecuted. In short, there will always be an apparent disconnect between political words and contributions and political actions.

However, we would be naïve to assume that companies are willing to make substantial political payments and engage in significant political maneuvering without expecting some return on their investment. Most people in Washington and the state capitals know that industry money and endorsements count for a great deal in politics; otherwise they wouldn't pay so much attention to them. Political maneuvering must also pay off because if it didn't, the financial markets would punish companies that made such payments and got no return on their money. Bottom lines of such foolishly wasteful companies would suffer, along with their stock prices. Worsening bottom lines would give rise to opportunities for investors to buy the companies' stock at low prices, change management, eliminate the wasted political payments, and then resell the stock at prices that reflect the company's financial prospects. The fact that many companies make significant campaign contributions and fund expensive lobbying efforts suggests that playing politics is a paying proposition for these companies.

Because antitrust enforcement in the past has been corrupted by politics and because, as the arguments of this book suggest, Microsoft's competitors stand to benefit from the antitrust suit, we are naturally inclined to look for evidence that the Microsoft case has been influenced, if not corrupted, by politics. We might not find the proverbial "smoking gun" that proves that the actual legal deliberations in the case have been tainted by special interest politics, but we might find some definite smoke from political guns that have been fired with a discernible target in mind. We might find circumstantial evidence that the Justice Department has been pressured by industry operatives and their political allies to take up the case for their own benefit and has yielded to the pressure both in the decision to pursue the case and in the development of the arguments presented to the court.

The record shows fairly clearly that as Microsoft grew in products, sales, and market dominance in the late 1980s and early 1990s, its competitors became progressively more openly hostile, critical, and envious. This is understandable, for their livelihoods and dreams of greater prosperity were in progressively greater jeopardy as Microsoft's market successes mounted. Microsoft's rivals seem to have followed a tried-and-true market and political path worn bare in the past by many other business groups. First, the rivals try to compete individually on the merits of their products. When some rivals are soundly beaten by one or more of the others, the losers individually vilify the market victors and blame their market hardships on the victor's market shenanigans, never conceding to themselves or anyone else that they—the losers—ever did anything wrong or failed to develop their business strategies as well as the victor. Then, the losers seek to form a cartel with the intent of collectively overriding the victor's market successes. When their collusive efforts begin to break down, they turn to government for market relief through some form of government regulation—including some antitrust remedy—drawing on their well-groomed political connections to do so.

PRESIDENTIAL CONNECTIONS

Microsoft's political and antitrust troubles can probably be traced to the 1992 presidential election, which pitted George Bush against Bill Clinton. Microsoft was then not yet the object of open hatred by others in the industry, but it was a company on the move with obvious intentions of achieving nothing short of domination in whatever market it entered. Microsoft's executives were doing precious little as members of the company team or as private individuals to foster the company's political contacts in Washington and elsewhere.

As noted earlier, the company had only a single lobbyist in the nation's capital, and the lobbyist's office was physically far removed from the day-to-day hubbub of downtown Washington politics. The company passed out only a few thousand dollars a year to politicians. As a *Washington Post* reporter noted, for two decades "Microsoft had all the visibility in Washington of a Third World republic," causing many Washington policymakers who have met Gates to view him as not only arrogant but also "politically tone deaf." Indeed, as late as the fall of 1997, when the Justice Department filed a suit against Microsoft alleging the company had violated a previous court order and seeking millions of dollars in fines (a case which the Justice Department ultimately lost after spending millions of dollars), Microsoft's president, Steve Ballmer, stunned the Washington establishment by arrogantly quipping in public, "To heck with Janet Reno." In the 1992 presidential election, Ballmer did come out publicly in favor of a candidate—Clinton—but he kept a fairly low profile and was the only Microsoft executive to do so. Gates and the other Microsoft executives expressed no support of either presidential candidate.

In 1992, Gates had not yet learned two important lessons in the school of hard political knocks, possibly to his later regret. The first one is that businesses can buy important "friends" in Washington who can work government policies to their company's advantage—in other words, businesses can engage in "rent seeking"; this friendly help is relatively cheap, in light of the private gains the expenditures can lead to. Second, businesses can buy off their political enemies to keep them from doing their companies harm—in other words, they can fend off the threat of "rent extraction" at their expense. Either way, a company's political "investments" can improve the company's bottom line as much as or more than investments in a new building or office applications.

For a variety of reasons, Microsoft's Silicon Valley–based competitors were not as politically shy as Bill Gates in 1992, and thereafter. During the presidential election cycle, the country was sluggishly emerging from a recession that had begun in 1990. In California, the home state for the all-important high-tech epicenter, Silicon Valley, the economy had been especially hard hit by the recession, in part because of the ongoing defense cutbacks in a state that was heavily dependent upon the defense budget. Though the evidence of the country's recovery in 1999 was there to be seen in economic statistics, much of the public and business community—especially in California—remained convinced that the previous twelve years had been an epoch of significant national economic decay, a theme Clinton repeatedly sounded. Many Americans were convinced that the American Dream was dead and that the next generation would live less well than past generations.

George Bush demonstrated in 1991 that he could successfully lead a coalition of twenty-seven of the world's most formidable military powers in an all-out assault against Iraq, a small country the size of Kentucky, but he seemed to be clueless to devise and articulate an imaginative economic policy for the country (other than raising tax rates and expanding government expenditures at a rate not seen since the Nixon administration). Moreover, he seemed at times totally out of touch with the growing ubiquity of computer technology. His deficiency on that score appeared self-evident when he went through a checkout line at a grocery store to provide the accompanying media with a photo opportunity—perhaps a show of how he was an ordinary guy—and asked the clerk a question about the scanner. It came across on television as though he did not know what the scanner was.

In 1992, businesspeople were looking to the two major candidates, plus the Reform Party candidate, Ross Perot, for signs that they had the "vision thing" (Bush's turn of phrase). An unusual percentage of them—especially the high-tech elites— found that Clinton had a more plausible vision than Bush, especially since Clinton cast himself as a "New Democrat," someone who would look for workable solutions regardless of their ideological grounding.

Bush may have had more supporters among the broad executive ranks of American business than Clinton—mainly because business executives have traditionally supported Republican candidates—but there were significant Republican defections to the Clinton camp. High-tech business leaders seemed to be especially impressed with Clinton's talk about working with their industry to computerize the nation's schools and to increase basic technology research.

Lawrence Perlman, the head of Ceridian Corp., a data-processing firm headquartered in Minneapolis, felt compelled in 1992 to explain the Clinton campaign button in his lapel to his workers and the media, given that he had supported Bush in 1988: "It's the first campaign button I've worn in a long time. Business has become much more pragmatic about the need for active programs, and we're not seeing it in the Republicans." In spite of voting Republican for the previous twenty years, Ben Rosen, chairman of Houston's Compaq Computers, supported Clinton simply because he felt the government needed a management change, much like the one he had orchestrated at Compaq in 1991: "It's not so much what Mr. Clinton is saying, but given the state of the economy, I really think we need some fresh thinking."

When asked why he was supporting Clinton, John Sculley, then CEO at Apple, explained to a *Forbes* reporter that he preferred a more proactive government than Bush would likely provide:

> Well, I'm still a Republican, so I haven't changed parties. When you sit on the edge of the Pacific Rim, you start to realize that the world really is changing a lot faster than our political leaders in Washington realize. . . . We are going through a fundamental change from an industrial-based economy to a knowledge-based economy. . . . We're at a time when there has to be a lot more cooperation between the private sector and the public sector. . . . I know Bill Clinton. I think he's bright. I think he's a centrist.

Sculley acknowledged that there wasn't much difference between Clinton and Bush, other than "Clinton does believe that the government should have a proactive role."

At a press conference held in San Jose where a hundred high-tech executives endorsed Clinton, who was present for the event, Oracle's Larry Ellison announced, "Bill Clinton and Al Gore have embraced the need for a national policy to help invigorate the economy, create jobs, and stimulate other sectors with the fruits of high-tech invention. It is a reasonable and balanced approach and the reason why I am joining with other high-tech CEOs today to endorse the plan. It is also why I am departing this year from my lifelong support of the Republican Party to endorse the Clinton-Gore ticket."

The list of other high-tech business executives endorsing Clinton included John Young of Hewlett-Packard, Gil Amelio of National Semiconductor, Ed McCracken of Silicon Graphics, Bill Miller of SRI International, and Mitch Kapor of Lotus. Clinton probably greatly appreciated the executives' endorsements, which were worth more than the money they contributed to his campaign. They gave credence to his claim that he was a "New Democrat" prepared to address the needs of the "New Economy" with forward-looking policies that would serve the country well and move it into the next millennium.

Money flowed during the 1992 presidential election as never before. When all was said and done, more than $100 million was spent on the Bush-Quayle and Clinton-Gore campaigns, 20 percent more than had been spent in the 1988 campaign. Contrary to the experience of past presidential campaigns, the Clinton-Gore campaign was able more or less to match the Bush-Quayle Republican fundraising. (Actually, the incumbent, Bush, was reported to be having fundraising problems in the months just prior to the campaign.) As usual, the Republican candidates had the edge in support from the business community overall, but what is important here is that many high-tech executives did more in 1992 than offer Clinton a handshake and a few nice supporting words for public consumption. They put their money where their mouths were, often giving the limit for individual contributions, and then hosting receptions and other events in Silicon Valley with Clinton and Gore to bring in funds from industry associates.

In 1992, the high-tech contributors' main purpose in helping Clinton was, most likely, to ensure they had a modicum of access to the administration on an array of high-tech policy issues, and they might also have wanted to make sure they had a chance to be visitors at White House functions, if Clinton were elected. It probably had little to do with pressing the government for an antitrust suit against Microsoft. No one could have known in the months leading up to the 1992 election that the FTC commissioners would be deadlocked the following year on what to do about Microsoft's growing industry dominance and pricing strategies.

Many of Microsoft's competitors would not have to face the threat of competition from Windows NT until May 1993; even as late as the spring of 1995, NT had only 1 percent of the server market. Anyway, at election time 1992, Marc Andreesen of Netscape fame was still a senior at the University of Illinois. He would not make his university's browser software, Mosaic (from which Navigator was developed), available free on the Web until March 1993. He and Jim Clark would not meet to form the company that came to be known as Netscape until a year after that.

At election time 1992, Gates had no obvious plans to take over the server market. Moreover, Gates had no announced designs on or apparent interest in the browser market, and his plans to move on the browser market would not be fully known for two and a half years. Finally, in 1992, the high-tech executives and would-be Microsoft critics were then mainly concerned with competing with one another and were by and large worried about more narrow legal and policy matters, for example, the pirating of software, stockholder class action suits against companies for allegedly purveying inaccurate information that gave rise to stockholder losses, and the coming telecommunications deregulation.

Nevertheless, the support the computer-company executives gave the Clinton-Gore campaign meant that the executives could possibly use the access they had "purchased" for a range of issues that might come up in the future. And it also meant that Clinton was to some extent beholden to them because of their contributions to his campaign and their public pledges of support.

Lobbying Justice

Within a year of the 1992 election, the anti-Microsoft group's political maneuvering against Microsoft's business practices, within the Clinton administration and Congress via the Justice Department, began in earnest. The previous year the Federal Trade Commission had initiated an investigation of Microsoft that focused mainly on Microsoft's practice of giving computer manufacturers discounts on copies of the operating system if the manufacturer would pay a royalty for each processor, or computer, shipped. The FTC dropped its case against Microsoft in midsummer 1993, but at this point the Justice Department took up its own investigation, with the encouragement and perhaps even at the behest of people in the high-tech industry.

In late September 1993, representatives from Microsoft rivals Novell, Lotus, and WordPerfect met with Justice Department officials in Washington, D.C., to lay out what they considered Microsoft's monopoly practices that were in violation of the country's antitrust laws (note that this was long before the "browser war" began). At that time, they encouraged the Justice Department to revisit the central issue in the FTC's investigation of Microsoft, the discounts Microsoft offered computer manufacturers in exchange for a royalty calculated on the basis of each processor shipped (even when the computer was not loaded with a Microsoft operating system). They also asserted that Microsoft had an unfair competitive advantage in the applications market because of its early knowledge of the code in forthcoming versions of Windows, and that Microsoft was stifling competition by repeatedly announcing product upgrades months, if not years, in advance (such software notices have come to be known as "vaporware"). These notices, so it was argued, caused buyers to hold off buying non-Microsoft products.

By midsummer 1994, the Justice Department had issued its complaint on Microsoft's per-processor licensing practice, declaring that Microsoft was a "monopoly" and that it had "unlawfully maintained its monopoly of personal computer ('PC') operating systems and has unreasonably restrained trade." Microsoft agreed to stop offering discounts to computer manufacturers in exchange for per-processor licensing fees and to abandon contracts that committed computer manufacturers to licensing software for two-to-three-year terms.

While these events were transpiring, Joel Klein, the assistant attorney general for antitrust who in May 1998 filed the antitrust complaint against Microsoft, was serving the Clinton White House as deputy counsel to the President. He had been brought into the White House after Vince Foster's suicide, but had known Clinton for years through their attendance at Renaissance Weekends, an annual gathering in Hilton Head, South Carolina, of business, academic, and political elites interested in discussing mostly a wide range of cultural and societal issues. Klein's duties as deputy counsel included improving the administration's relationship with Congress and dealing with a growing array of scandals, for example, the Whitewater land deal and the Paula Jones affair.

The 1994 agreement may have satisfied Microsoft's competitors, but not for very long—especially not after January 1995, when Microsoft took out a license from the University of Illinois for Spyglass Mosaic, a Web browser. In May Gates told his executive staff that the "Internet tidal wave" posed an imminent threat to the company's future and told them to radically accelerate their efforts to convert Microsoft into an Internet company. By the summer of 1995, Microsoft was well on its way with the development of its own browser, Internet Explorer.

By 1995, the anti-Microsoft camp had grown by one very important player, Netscape, which during the previous October had begun to offer, for free, "Mosaic Netscape," which according to Netscape's founder, Jim Clark, was ten times faster than the original version of Mosaic that could be downloaded for free from the Web. The company's purpose in giving away its browser, which had previously sold for a list price of $99, was to grow its market and to take advantage of what it perceived to be network economies. Jim Clark also saw the value of a browser as a "viewport," because "anyplace you go on the Web, any information you access, anything you buy, when you do it, what you spent—anything related to the Internet—goes through [the browser]."

In February 1995, Joel Klein was moved from the deputy counsel's office in the White House to the Justice Department, where he became the principal deputy to the then assistant attorney general for antitrust, Anne Bingaman. It was at best a lateral career move, even possibly a downward move, but one that held the prospect of a move up at a later date. At the Justice Department Klein handled the appeals on the 1994 settlement between the Justice Department and Microsoft on the per-processor licensing arrangement. Although Klein's motives in pursuing the antitrust case might have been pure, his move from the White House to the Justice Department suggests a possibly suspicious link between presidential politics and antitrust enforcement, especially since his initial position at the Justice Department could not be construed as a promotion. The shift would also enable the White House to claim that the administration and the Justice Department never communicated on pending antitrust cases.

Microsoft's rivals were not satisfied with the remedies in the settlement of the first investigation. In April 1995, Gary Reback, an attorney with the Palo Alto, California, law firm of Wilson, Sonnini, Goodrich & Rosati, argued in a letter to the Justice Department that the proposed settlement "does not undo the damage" that supposedly had been caused by Microsoft's monopoly position with MS-DOS and Windows. He insisted that the Justice Department should have pursued other antitrust charges against Microsoft. The parties Reback was representing were unnamed at the time he wrote the letter.

In June 1995, Netscape and Microsoft agreed to talk about the possibility of cooperative efforts in developing browser technology, which resulted in a meeting on June 21. Two days later attorney Reback, now openly representing Netscape, sent a four-page, single-spaced letter, stamped "confidential," to Jon Jacobs in the Antitrust Division of the Justice Department (it became exhibit 1259 in the Justice Department's case). In it he accused Microsoft of a variety of anticompetitive practices, including the withholding of "critical technical information"—the APIs (application programming interfaces) that would enable Netscape's software to connect with Internet service providers and would allow Netscape to upgrade its browser and run on the forthcoming Windows 95. Supposedly, Microsoft had been stalling on providing the APIs since March; at the June meeting, it refused again to provide the requested information unless Microsoft got an "equity interest in Netscape." In addition, Reback claimed that during the meeting, Microsoft had threatened to "harm" Netscape if Netscape sought to compete with Microsoft in any way, by, for example, building its own personal computer platform that would allow computer users to bypass Windows. Reback appended to his letter the notes that Marc Andreesen said he had taken at the meeting as support for their (Reback's and Andreesen's) contentions.

There was no mention in Reback's letter of a division of the operating system and browser markets, which, it was later charged, had been proposed by Microsoft at the June 21 meeting. This suggests that the division proposal might have been an afterthought of Andreesen's or Reback's.

There also was no mention in Reback's letter of crucially important information about why the issue of Microsoft's getting an equity interest in Netscape may have come up. In his book *Netscape Time* Jim Clark reveals the context. During the previous December Netscape was apparently somewhat strapped for cash, because of normal start-up costs and the legal costs associated with the threatened lawsuit by the University of Illinois over possible property rights infringement. In its cash-strapped state, Clark had proposed to Gates that Microsoft take an equity interest in the firm. Clark recounts the substance of a December 1994 phone call between him and Gates: "'I'm wondering,' I said, 'whether you'd consider going with Netscape instead of Spyglass.' Taking a cautious step forward, I reminded him that he'd been interested in licensing our software a few months before." In the next paragraph Clark says, "To get past an awkward moment, cut to the chase, and sweeten the deal all at once, I said that Microsoft could have an equity position and a seat on the board. I was opening the door a crack, confident that I could keep Microsoft's share of stock small enough to prevent any future meddling." It is conceivable that the discussion of an equity interest for Microsoft in Netscape at the June 21 meeting, if it occurred, could have been prompted by this earlier offer Clark made. Who's to know?

If Microsoft did what Reback charged—stalling on the APIs and threatening to harm Netscape—Microsoft would be in violation of antitrust law, which prohibits attempts to collude and divide markets. But Microsoft has denied the charges, which were never brought to Microsoft's attention until 1998. Nevertheless, Klein seemed to accept the charges as reason enough to pursue the Justice Department's investigation. When the charges were first leveled, and later, in the trial, Microsoft effectively challenged this interpretation, asking in effect, "Where's the evidence that such deals were tendered at that meeting?"

The lengthy letter was composed and sent two days after the June 21, 1995, meeting. Is it possible that Reback's letter had already been contemplated before the meeting and that the meeting was something of a setup, designed to lead Microsoft to incriminate itself? There is no real way to know who is telling the truth about what was said at that meeting.

What we do know is that Microsoft was still writing the APIs as of the June 21 meeting, and that no other firm got the APIs before Netscape. We also know that after the meeting, the markets were not divided and Netscape got the "critical information" it needed to produce a new version of its browser for Windows 95 when it appeared, and Netscape representatives attended the big launch party in August 1995 on the Microsoft campus for the release of Windows 95, which suggests that the strain between Microsoft and Netscape may not then have been as great as is now claimed. If Netscape was damaged by Microsoft, the markets didn't show it. The company went public on August 9, 1995, just before the Windows 95 launch, for $28 per share, but the stock began trading that first day at $71 a share. Clark was instantly worth $663 million; not bad for someone who had started the company sixteen months before and had invested only about $5 million of his own money, plus his time. The stock climbed skyward for the rest of the year, making just about everyone Clark had hired that first year a millionaire (Clark's own net worth peaked at $1.4 billion). The market didn't seem to be saying that Netscape had been damaged by being denied the critical information needed for the development of Navigator for Windows 95.

Microsoft executives may or may not have said at the June 1995 meeting what Reback and Andreesen insist they said, but the stock price data do indicate that if Microsoft attempted to harm Netscape by withholding information, it failed miserably. Two months later, in August, Microsoft invaded the browser market and then worked aggressively to rapidly dominate it by doing what Netscape had been doing, giving away its browser. Netscape then held this market strategy against Microsoft in the claims of "predatory" pricing by Microsoft that it presented to the Justice Department. In any event, Microsoft's Internet strategy must have begun taking shape months before the June meeting; otherwise it is doubtful that the company could have had Internet Explorer ready to emerge in August 1995 along with Windows 95.

In August 1996, Reback wrote another letter to the deputy assistant attorney general, a position by then filled by Joel Klein. This time the letter was eight single-spaced pages long. In it, Reback beseeched Klein to investigate Microsoft's alleged violations of the 1994 consent decree concerning the per-processor-shipped pricing and the bundling of Internet Explorer with Windows. He also tacked on demands that the Justice Department launch a new investigation of Microsoft's violations of "substantive antitrust laws." Reback argued that the investigation was required because "Internet software vendors face the threat of elimination from the market by reason of Microsoft's illegal conduct."

Reback laid out a theory of monopoly that served as a basis for his cataloguing of Microsoft's wrongs. (In her 1999 book, *High Noon: The Inside Story of Scott McNealy and the Rise of Sun Microsoft System*, Karen Southwick writes that it had been rumored in Silicon Valley for years that Sun Microsystems had supported the legal research Reback did to develop the monopoly theory that he sent to the Justice Department.) His letter was basically rolled over with new words and extensions to become the complaint against Microsoft that Joel Klein filed in the spring of 1998. But Reback's central complaint should be noted. He charged that Microsoft's strategy of giving away its browser and giving discounts, which he tagged as "clandestine side payments" when Internet Explorer was adopted as the preferred browser, was necessarily illegal because it was "predatory." From Reback's letter one can infer that Reback viewed give-aways as necessarily and by definition "predatory" by dint of the fact that Microsoft had already been declared by the Justice Department to be a "monopolist" and other Internet browser companies faced the "threat of elimination."

Even though companies that give away their products are not labeled monopolists by economists who understand the concept of monopoly, Reback's letter had its intended effect: Klein, who had by then been promoted to acting assistant attorney general for antitrust, wrote to William H. Neukom, Microsoft's chief counsel, in September 1996 asking for a substantial number of documents that had to be submitted within a month.

All the while, the members of the anti-Microsoft consortium put their considerable Washington resources in overdrive. John Doerr—a Silicon Valley venture capitalist legendary for having the foresight to invest early in Compaq, Sun, AOL, Amazon, @Home, and Intuit—took a significant financial stake in Netscape and a seat on Netscape's small board. When Netscape went public in August 1995, Doerr's investment in Netscape was worth about a quarter of a billion dollars. Of course, a successful prosecution of Microsoft that weakened it could be helpful to many of his investments and his partners, a number of whom have publicly supported the government's case against Microsoft.

Doerr also began to work diligently to get the principals in the consortium involved in a $100-million "Java fund," which would finance software start-ups that used Sun's Java. One of his investment ventures is Red Hat, a North Carolina–based firm that produces a version of Linux that is sold, with documentation and services, in retail stores. Red Hat has been supported by Oracle, Netscape, Sun, and IBM. Doerr also worked closely with Vice President Al Gore on Gore's efforts to improve the country's technology policy and infrastructure. Indeed, by the time *Netscape Time* was completed, Doerr's work with the administration had become so close that Clark freely described Doerr as a "fixture" in Washington and mused about how Doerr's colleagues often joked that a future Democratic presidential campaign slogan might very well be "Gore and Doerr in 2004."

MOVING ON CONGRESS

Throughout 1996, contributions from the anti-Microsoft group began to flow to the Clinton reelection campaign and other candidates for federal office. Total 1996 presidential campaign expenditures exceeded $150 million, nearly 40 percent more than the 1992 presidential campaign. Clinton's support within the high-tech industries had abated somewhat because he had vetoed a bill that would have curbed shareholder lawsuits. Nonetheless, he did pick up more high-tech supporters than Bob Dole (57 percent for Clinton versus 43 percent for Dole in one poll of 600 technology executives), and at one event he was able to get endorsements from seventy-five Silicon Valley executives. According to the Center for Responsive Politics, which tracks campaign contributions for federal candidates and issues frequent "Money in Politics Alerts," Sun Microsystems gave just under $36,000 to federal candidates in the 1995–96 election cycle, nearly four times what it gave in the 1991–92 election cycle. Oracle distributed nearly $120,000 in the 1995–96 election cycle, a quarter more than it did in the 1991–92 cycle. Netscape, which did not exist in the 1991–92 election cycle, gave almost $35,000 in 1995–96. By then, Microsoft had begun to counter its adversaries by doling out in 1996 nearly a quarter million dollars in contributions to federal candidates and party committees.

During the latter part of 1996 and all of the next year, Microsoft's industry accusers began to broaden their campaign to rally bipartisan political support for an antitrust assault against Microsoft at both the FTC and the Justice Department. In August 1996, Netscape hired Mike Pettit, who was at the time serving as an aide in Bob Dole's presidential campaign. In June 1997, Microsoft's critics went to Senator Conrad Burns of Montana, Wyoming's Senator Greg Thomas, and Alabama's Senator Ted Stevens and got them to write to the FTC, saying that the information they had received about Microsoft's business practices was "very troubling" and that the FTC should "investigate thoroughly," mainly because they had received reports that Microsoft was not living up to the 1994 consent decree and suggested that the FTC had the authority to investigate antitrust decrees, "particularly where, as here, the continued monitoring of an important decree by the Department of Justice has been called into question." The senators then insisted that the FTC extend its investigation to "any business practices that are alleged to run afoul of the Nation's antitrust laws, and to make a complete report to the Attorney General, which report could then be made available both to members of Congress and the public." Four days after the letter was written, Netscape's Jim Barksdale gave the keynote address at the Conrad Burns Telecommunications Center at Montana State University, which Barksdale had helped to fund. In July 1997, Pitofsky rejected the senators' request for an FTC investigation on the grounds the FTC's efforts might duplicate the investigation at the Justice Department (which Pitofsky refused to confirm was under way).

In their effort to expand their political support in Congress, several accusers went to California's Democratic senator Barbara Boxer in July 1997 and asked her to appeal to the FTC to initiate an investigation into Microsoft's compliance with the consent decree. She subsequently wrote a letter to Robert Pitofsky, the FTC chairman, in which she requested the FTC to "investigate whether Microsoft is in compliance with the Consent Decree ... I have been contacted by several companies who allege that Microsoft is not in compliance with that Decree. I find these allegations extremely serious ..." They also went to South Dakota's Democratic senator, Tom Daschle, and were successful in getting him to express concern to Joel Klein in September 1997 that the Justice Department's "investigation has not been sufficiently aggressive" and that the "assigned attorneys are not sufficiently experienced to handle the review." Daschle noted that his letter was "not intended to alter or influence your investigation in any way." At the same time, he asked Klein for a "status report," which is a way of exerting congressional pressure, and for any indication on "whether you believe congressional assistance or additional resources are necessary," which is a none-too-subtle way of telling Klein, "Tell us what you need"—or maybe it was a gentle reminder that the people on the Hill controlled his budget.

The most important political ally in the U.S. Senate of Microsoft's critics has surely been Orin Hatch, a Republican from Utah, the home state of Novell, who is also chairman of the Senate Judiciary Committee. He not only appealed to the chairman of the FTC in the summer of 1997 to do what his Senate colleagues had requested, investigate Microsoft's alleged monopoly practices, but he also went on a public campaign against Microsoft, pressing the Justice Department to take up the Microsoft case and then supporting the Justice Department when, in October 1997, it filed suit against Microsoft for violating the 1995 court decree that forbade Microsoft from bundling its browser with its Windows operating system. In a news release, Hatch commended Assistant Attorney General Joel Klein for filing the suit, "given Microsoft's apparent strategy to position itself as a gateway or 'toll taker' through which all users access the internet." He added, "I would also hope that the Department continues to vigorously pursue other aspects of its ongoing Microsoft investigation. . . . I am concerned that Microsoft is abusing its Windows monopoly to coerce companies not to distribute or promote competitive internet products." He indicated that he intended to use the Judiciary Committee as a forum for examining Microsoft's business practices.

Sure enough, two weeks later, on November 4, Senator Hatch convened a hearing of the Senate Judiciary Committee. He declared at the start, "I would like to emphasis that this is not a hearing on Microsoft. This committee may well hold such hearings down the road. Today's hearing, however, is meant to explore a broad set of issues emerging in our new economy," mainly issues related to "competition, innovation, and public policy in the digital age." However, the day before, Hatch had already tipped his card on how he viewed the hearings, having told a reporter that "Microsoft now has the ability to virtually annihilate any competitive product it wants by bringing it into the next version of Windows" and that there was evidence that Microsoft was seeking to extend its monopoly to the Internet. There were eight witnesses at the hearings, and seven of the eight were hostile toward Microsoft, all making many of the charges that the Justice Department has, since that hearing, made against Microsoft. In spite of the claimed broader objective of the hearing, one reporter noted that "much of the discussion was, in fact, aimed squarely at the software behemoth, with Hatch leading the attack." No wonder Silicon Valley executives were happy to attend a December 1999 fundraiser for Hatch that raised $60,000 for his then long-shot presidential campaign. The list of e-economy executives attending his fundraiser at the Palo Alto restaurant—almost all of whom supported the government's case against Microsoft—included Eric Schmidt of Novell, Inc.; Scott McNealy of Sun Microsystems, Inc.; Jeff Henley of Oracle Corp.; George Vradenburg of AOL; Larry Wolfe of Intuit Inc.; and Andrew Steinberg of Sabre Inc. (an airline reservation company).

The criticisms from Microsoft's rivals rose to their shrillest yet a week after the Hatch hearings, when the consumer activist Ralph Nader organized a two-day conference in Washington, D.C., called "Appraising Microsoft and Its Global Strategy." Now the Borking began in earnest. Nader had already sounded a theme of the conference when he published an article called "The Microsoft Menace" in the preceding month's edition of Microsoft's on-line magazine, *Slate,* about the Channel Bar technology included in Internet Explorer 4.0. This technology included links to chosen Web sites. Nader charged, "Not content with its enormous market share in PC software, Microsoft wants to hold our hand as we navigate the information superhighway, and to push us—not so subtly—toward its own partners or subsidiaries." (Ironically, the Channel Bar bombed with customers.)

Thirty of Microsoft's harshest critics, including Scott McNealy, spoke at the conference, which was attended by 500 other industry players, most of whom—for example, Gary Reback—were there to bathe in the Microsoft complaint session at the steep entrance price of $1,000. In his keynote address, titled "No One Should Own the Alphabet," McNealy suggested that Microsoft's grand strategy was to use its Web browser to establish what the *Wall Street Journal* loosely interpreted to be a "hegemony over on-line commerce," meaning that Microsoft would become the gatekeeper for the entire economy. As McNealy put it, "How are you going to compete if Microsoft won't put you on the Microsoft Shopping Center—which will be the opening screen on everyone's computer?" He concluded that the Justice Department's efforts to date had "done nothing but accelerate the market value of Microsoft." Netscape's general counsel, Roberta Katz, was there to warn ominously, "Our society is in a precarious position, because we have so much control of a vital resource, software, in the control of a single company, Microsoft." The self-styled "futurologist" Ray Hammon, in a paper that was distributed by the Nader organization as a part of the conference literature, suggested, "Perhaps only a Roman emperor could have surpassed the influence Gates will have over individual lives in the early twenty-first century—if he and his company continue unchecked."

The relationship between Klein and Microsoft's critics began to take on a new degree of coziness. In the fall of 1997, according to a *Wall Street Journal* reporter, "Netscape's Mr. Barksdale hosted Assistant Attorney General Joel Klein [who had recently been confirmed in this position] for breakfast at his home and both Netscape and Sun fed government lawyers a steady diet of complaints. Netscape, Sun, and Oracle also helped finance an anti-Microsoft lobbying group called Pro-Comp [the Project to Promote Competition in the Digital Age]." ProComp members include Sybase, Sabre, American Airlines, Software Publishers Association, the Computer and Communications Industry Association, and worldweb.net; a number of ProComp members prefer to remain anonymous.

Obviously, the anti-Microsoft group needed no convincing that antitrust suits are influenced by politics. In December 1997, Microsoft's political foes began to expand the scope of their political efforts. They appealed to the former congressman Jack Kemp, who has served on Oracle's board of directors, to join with other con-

servatives who are not beholden "to the Microsoft line in this issue." Kemp resisted
the invitation. That same month the Microsoft foes enlisted the help of the Washington, D.C., firm of Cassidy, Powell, and Tate Public Relations, which is headed by
Jody Powell (President Jimmy Carter's press secretary). The former U.S. senator
and 1998 Republican presidential candidate Bob Dole also signed on with the anti-
Microsoft group to push the case in the media with a series of columns and letters
to the editor in leading national newspapers, and to lend the effort an enhanced bipartisan look and feel.

By the end of the year, members of the anti-Microsoft group, notably Oracle
and Novell, had also begun contributing to the Progress & Freedom Foundation, a Washington-area think tank specializing in technology issues. Subsequently, the foundation began commissioning studies and developing
conferences that would purvey the anti-Microsoft message among academics
and policy thinkers.

In February 1998 the foundation sponsored a conference in Washington, D.C.,
called "Competition, Innovation and the Microsoft Monopoly: Antitrust in the
Digital Marketplace," that brought together scholars to address issues related to
the appropriateness of antitrust laws in the digital age. The head of the Progress
& Freedom Foundation, Jeffrey Eisenach, a former Newt Gingrich aide, stated in
a contribution to the conference volume that it was *not* the organization's goal
"to draw conclusions about whether Microsoft has violated the antitrust laws,"
but he seemed to "protest too much." It is clear from just about everything else in
the conference volume (coedited by Eisenach and Thomas Lenard, a senior fel-
low at the foundation) that that was exactly what the organization did: it drew
some pretty strong conclusions for Microsoft's prosecution. No doubt about it,
the volume makes clear, Microsoft was a monopolist that should, because of its
predatory pricing and restrictive contracts, be subject to antitrust prosecution.
For example, Lenard states flatly in a paper based on one read in the conference
that "Microsoft's restrictions have little apparent business justification." This line
has been repeated with only minor variations by Klein and the members of the
anti-Microsoft coalition. But no matter how often the claim is repeated, it remains totally without foundation and is evidence of a lack of understanding by
the critics of the pricing implications of the "network effects" they constantly
harp upon.

The anti-Microsoft group's efforts to enlist the cooperation of conservatives
didn't stop with Hatch, Dole, and Kemp. In March 1998, Jim Miller and Dan Oliver,
former chairmen of the FTC during the Reagan administration, wrote Orrin Hatch
applauding him for pressing the investigation of Microsoft in Senate Judiciary
Committee hearings. That month ProComp also incorporated; its main purpose
was to work for government actions against Microsoft and to disseminate anti-
Microsoft materials. By November 1998, Miller and Oliver had shifted their posi-

tion from simply agreeing that the case was worthy of investigation to suggesting that "enough is known already to justify the government in going forward with the current case." These comments were included in a letter sent to Trent Lott, the Senate Majority Leader from Mississippi, who is a friend of Netscape's Jim Barksdale from the days when both were students at the University of Mississippi. Miller became actively involved in asking economists, friends, and colleagues (the author included) to sign a petition supporting the government's case, to be used in a variety of public relations efforts.

BORK'S ENLISTMENT

In April 1998, the distinguished antitrust scholar Robert Bork, whom I have repeatedly quoted in these pages, became a consultant for Netscape and joined Bob Dole in pressing the anti-Microsoft case in the media and on Capitol Hill. Judge Bork and Dole held a press conference organized by ProComp at the National Press Club in Washington, D.C., on April 21 to announce their joint lobbying effort.

As a former presidential candidate Dole brought an important measure of political cachet to the campaign to have Microsoft sued for antitrust violations. But Bork's willingness to take up the anti-Microsoft position was an unusually important plum for Netscape and other ProComp members because he had in the past, through his widely acclaimed 1978 book, *The Antitrust Paradox*, broadly condemned antitrust in no uncertain terms as no longer "intellectually respectable."

Why was Bork's enlistment so important? A *Washington Post* columnist gave a good answer. "Bork's key contribution might be his very presence. It's a savvy update of the old only-Nixon-can-go-to-China theory of statesmanship, say critics. Who better to tag Microsoft as a predator, after all, than one of the intellectual godfathers of the hands-off school of antitrust thinking?"

Bork took his campaign public with a series of interviews, television appearances, columns, and letters to editors of newspapers, all backed up with an extended position paper posted on ProComp's Web site, "The Case Against Microsoft." His *Wall Street Journal* column summarized the major points he made at practically every media stop:

> The two greatest threats to Microsoft's chokehold on operating systems are Netscape's Web browser and Sun Microsystems' Java, a language that works on any operating system. An even worse nightmare for Mr. Gates is the possible cooperation of Netscape and Sun to create a product that would bypass Windows altogether, making his company a mere competitor rather than a monopolist. To prevent that from happening, Microsoft employs a minefield of restrictive agreements that make it hard for rivals to attack, coupled with direct assaults upon Netscape and Sun.

Bork was soundly criticized by conservative-leaning columnists and law and economics scholars for what they believed were blatant contradictions between what he was charging in the Microsoft case and what he had written in his 1978 book. For example, in his *Wall Street Journal* column (and elsewhere), Bork insisted that the core of the case stands on one statistic: "Microsoft now ships 97% of the personal computer operating systems on the market. That is the source of its extraordinary wealth. Not surprisingly, the company will do whatever it takes to keep that monopoly." However, in *The Antitrust Paradox*, he insists that "any size a company achieves by internal growth is the most efficient size for that company, and dissolution would always impose a significant efficiency cost." Elsewhere, he flatly argued, "No firm size created by internal growth should be attacked by antitrust."

In his book, Bork does sometimes qualify his conclusions about the efficiency gains from large size by suggesting that growth obtained by "predation" is subject to antitrust prosecution, and he does now argue that Microsoft has engaged in "predatory pricing" and what can only be described as "predatory product development": "Microsoft's insistence upon integrating its own browser with its operating system is a tactic deliberately chosen to bury Netscape." However, in *The Antitrust Paradox*, Judge Bork notes that, for any number of reasons, as we saw in earlier chapters, cases of "predation" are "rare" and that, because of the complexity of the economic theories involved, "victory often goes to the party whose lawyer and economic expert are more adept at demagoguery." James Miller, the Reagan administration chairman of the FTC who has endorsed efforts to put Microsoft on trial, had also concluded in an earlier article, "If the historical literature is to be believed, cases of successful predation are rare. And if the theoretical literature is to be believed, this is no accident."

Bork also charges in his position paper that Microsoft has engaged in "exclusive dealing" with Internet service providers, computer manufacturers, and others, and has thus injured its competition by keeping them out of its markets. In fact, many of the contracts Bork cites were not exclusive. For example, Earthlink, which was thought to have a contract that required it to ship only Internet Explorer, actually shipped more copies of Navigator than of Internet Explorer. Besides, Bork's charge of Microsoft's exclusive dealing and harming competitors appears to contradict his statement in *The Antitrust Paradox*: "The truth appears to be that there has never been a case in which exclusive dealing or requirements contracts were shown to injure competition. A seller who wants exclusivity must give the buyer something for it. If he gives a lower price, the reason must be that the seller expects the arrangement to create efficiencies that justify the lower price."

Bork seemed to get testy because of criticisms of his position in a letter published in the *Wall Street Journal*. He grumbled back, "Holman Jenkins's attack on me for representing Netscape . . . is both false in its facts and gratuitously insulting in its comments." Bork then insisted in absolute terms that Microsoft's "bundling" of Internet Explorer with Windows "produces *no* significant efficiencies of itself." Bork's self-professed limited knowledge of computers and software should lead one to seriously doubt the value of his assessment. He also reiterated that the "sole function" of Microsoft's "highly restrictive contracts with customers and suppliers" is "to exclude rivals that might undercut Microsoft's monopoly of operating systems (97% of those currently shipped)."

Clearly, Bork has consistently argued that antitrust laws can be applied to restrictive contracts. But he makes it equally clear in his book that he would be the first to argue that "bundling" can produce efficiencies not recognized by courts in the past and that "restrictive contracts" do not always have as their "*sole* function" the preservation of a monopoly. In his own letter to the editor, the Loyola College economist Thomas DiLorenzo reminded Bork and *Journal* readers of the potential benefits of bundling and restrictive contracts, many of which Bork covers in his book. These benefits include the fact that consumers prefer bundled products and can buy them with lower transaction costs and at a lower combined price. DiLorenzo adds that exclusive-dealing contracts, under which a retailer commits to buy only from one producer, can reduce the cost of record keeping and inventory, can increase the retailer's incentives to promote the producer's products, can increase the producer's incentive to provide the retailer with specialized training, can improve the producer's return on advertising and thereby can increase advertising and sales of the retailers, and can give producers the benefits of vertical integration without their having to invest capital in retail outlets.

Concerning the benefits of vertical integration, in his book Bork came out against using antitrust laws to thwart "vertical integration." This suggests that he would be in favor of alternative, improved means of achieving the efficiency benefits of vertical integration: "[I]n the absence of a most unlikely proved predatory power and purpose, antitrust should *never* object to the verticality of any merger." Moreover, let's face the fact that Microsoft probably wants to integrate Internet Explorer into Windows because the integration makes Windows a better operating system, which means it will sell better.

Bork asserts in his ProComp position paper that Microsoft's monopoly is self-evident from the fact that the company has "the power to charge above competitive prices," . . . and the fact that "the company's profits are among the highest of any American businesses. Its own financial statements show a profit margin of about 47%. Though profit levels are viewed by some as ambiguous indicators of monopoly power, this profit margin is so high that many commentators would think it raises a strong inference of monopolistic pricing." This directly contradicts Bork's stance in 1978, when he was one commentator who approvingly reprinted the UCLA professor Harold Demsetz's statement that economists "*have no theory that allows us to deduce from the observable degree of concentration in a particular market whether or not price and output are competitive"* (emphasis in the original).

As noted earlier, Bork himself also deduced from lengthy theoretical discussions of cost issues that "high rates of return" are "utterly ambiguous" because they "are consistent with other factors besides restriction of output, primarily superior efficiency, so that if these debatable correlations [for example, high rates of return imply monopoly] could be made to stand up, they would prove *nothing* of interest to antitrust policy" (emphasis added). And he was right on target when he stated repeatedly throughout his book that "antitrust should not interfere with any firm size created by internal growth."

When it comes to specific concerns relating to Microsoft, Bork seems not to be in control of the facts. For example, in his ProComp position paper and elsewhere he expresses great concern that "Microsoft's licenses for Windows 98 prohibit computer manufacturers from modifying the screen first seen when users turn on their personal computer. This enforced uniformity prevents computer manufacturers from offering customers a choice of first screens." Actually, computer manufacturers have always had the right to modify the desktop, which is the only "first screen" of any consequence, by adding their own preferred icons, including a Netscape icon, which they regularly do. The only thing that Microsoft prevents manufacturers from doing is taking off icons that come with Windows, or changing their appearance so that, say, the Netscape icon is more prominent than the Internet Explorer icon. Perhaps Bork, with his limited understanding of computers, doesn't understand how easy it is for customers to modify the desktop (any computer user can delete any icon on the desktop with a couple of clicks of the mouse). The Yale Law School professor George Priest reminded his former colleague, "[T]he competitive harm from Microsoft's domination of the first screen is no greater than the trouble all Americans face when they have to dial an 800 number to reach an AT&T, MCI or Sprint telephone charge line, and actually less since any even moderately competent computer user can change the initial screen once and for all (or have a friend do it) in a matter of minutes. Microsoft's other restrictions on licensees are no worse."

On the issue of prices, Bork agrees that antitrust laws were designed to protect consumers, not competitors. However, he now adds, "the way to protect consumers is to say there is a variety of choices and also low prices. Microsoft is saying that low prices have dominated the industry. But the impression that Microsoft has something to do with those low prices is [wrong]. Those are due to chip manufacturers. [Microsoft's] Windows prices haven't gone down. They have stayed the same." The dollar price of succeeding versions of Windows has stayed more or less the same, but Bork surely knows that *real* prices are what count in monopoly/antitrust discussions. As was shown in Chapter 2, the real price of Windows trended downward during the 1990s, and today's *real* price is less than half of what it was in the early

1990s. Also, succeeding versions of Windows have been even better deals for the consumer because of all of the enhancements made to Windows over the years. Moreover, the fact that Windows is licensed to so many computer manufacturers has meant that more of them were in the market, competing for sales, and driving down prices. This price competition in personal computers in thus attributable at least in part to Microsoft's licensing policy, which involves holding the price of Windows down and making Windows available to a variety of computer vendors.

On the subject of breaking up large firms, Bork reasoned in *The Antitrust Paradox* that "advocates of large firm dissolution must demonstrate that the process will not destroy significant amounts of efficiency. Otherwise, they ask us to risk doing consumers more harm than good." When he began his lobbying for Netscape in April 1998, he was reluctant to advocate a breakup of Microsoft: "I wouldn't say break up the company. They ought to ban these restrictive [contract] practices. Beyond that, you have to have a lot of thinking to do yet." By the start of 1999, however, Bork had substantially changed his position on remedies, saying, "The single, most efficient remedy may be three companies," but adding the quip "One school of thought says that whoever gets Gates [becomes] a monopoly again."

Unfortunately, Bork provides not even a shred of evidence that a breakup would work to the betterment of the broad sweep of computer users—the kind of hard data that he demanded of advocates of breakups in his earlier writings. More important, he ignores the many arguments that a breakup of Microsoft can lead to higher prices for consumers because of the breakdown of network effects and scale economies. He simply speculates that a breakup *might* add unnamed efficiency gains.

These are just a few of the disconnects between what Bork wrote years ago and the opinions he has expressed since becoming a lobbyist for Netscape. To give Bork the benefit of the doubt, he does seem to be convinced that the government has a strong case against Microsoft, and that there are adequate precedents: "You have the monopoly. You have the expressed intent to stifle competition, you have the practices that are not necessary for consumers but to crush rivals." When challenged on his principles, he says he never wrote that "there was no role for antitrust to play." He told a group of reporters, "Only a knee-jerk conservative would say there's never a case for antitrust. A monopolization case ought to be a rare thing, and this is one of those rare cases." He has also professed, "I did not become involved in this one because Netscape 'showed up waving a fee.' Microsoft . . . has stated that it also offered me a retainer. I chose to go with Netscape because its position is sound and Microsoft's is not." Microsoft denies that such an offer was ever made. Despite these assertions, Bork cannot escape the fact that years ago, he proclaimed himself the consummate legal advocate for consumers. Now, he is an advocate for a market rival, and he really has to torture the words in his claims to make out consumers, not Netscape, to be the ultimate beneficiaries of this lawsuit.

Bork is also inconsistent in his stance on the politicization of the antitrust process. He recently reminded reporters of one factor in his earlier opposition to antitrust enforcement: "I just thought that in the past [antitrust enforcement] was overdone and politicized." Now his personal media and lobbying campaign on behalf of Netscape have helped to repoliticize the antitrust process.

Bork must be aware that he is being paid to make his public comments not merely for the power of his words, but because his comments enhance the influence of the words of other Microsoft critics, with the press, Congress, and the Justice Department. Bork has become a figurehead for a much broader political campaign directed against Microsoft and Bill Gates, that has incorporated inflammatory name-calling reminiscent of the Borking the eponymous Bork got years ago.

Bork and Dole took their public stand against Microsoft on April 22, 1998, and the Justice Department filed its formal antitrust complaint against Microsoft a month later, on May 20, 1998. Were the two events connected? A direct connection could be that the Justice Department was working with the anti-Microsoft coalition to justify each other's positions and actions with the media and general public. Or the connection could have been more indirect: the broad-based political and media campaign could have had its intended effect, to move the Justice Department to legal action. Either way, it's not a pretty picture to contemplate. It undermines trust in the legal process, and the Justice Department's integral role in that process.

THE ESCALATING DOLLAR WAR

The political punches and counterpunches in the "get Microsoft" campaign have meant that more and more computer industry money and talent are being sucked into politics, not into building better programs and computers. Microsoft's political activity was virtually nil in 1992. As can be seen in Table 9.1, by 1996, Microsoft's lobbying expenditures had reached nearly $1.2 million, according to estimates reported by the *Washington Post*. The total lobbying expenditures for Microsoft's chief attackers—ProComp, Netscape, Oracle, IBM, America Online, and Sun—were close to twice what Microsoft spent that year. Over the next two years, Microsoft's lobbying expenditures more than tripled, to more than $3.7 million in 1998. But that year Microsoft's rivals spent $5.8 million, 55 percent more than Microsoft. And all the expenditures by the various public relations firms employed by all of the firms most likely are not captured in these figures.

The figures escalate at an ever-increasing rate in a negative spiral. If the anti-Microsoft group spends more money on lobbying and public relations, then Microsoft must spend more, and vice versa. All the while, the people who are on the receiving end of the dollars—members of Congress and lobbyists—see their incomes going up.

TABLE 9.1   Rising Lobbying Expenditures by Microsoft and Its Chief Rivals

Company	1996	1997	1998
Microsoft	$1,180,000	$2,120,000	$3,740,000
Microsoft's Chief Rivals			
ProComp	0	0	$700,000*
Netscape	$960,000	$724,000	840,000
America Online	165,000	784,000	1,180,000
Sun	600,000	420,000	1,180,000
Oracle	600,000	900,000	1,900,000
Total of Chief Rivals	$2,325,000	$2,828,000	$5,800,000

*Includes funds reported separately by Netscape, Sun, and Oracle.
SOURCE: Rajiv Chandrasekaran, "Microsoft's Window of Influence; Intensive Lobbying Aims to Neutralize Antitrust Efforts," *Washington Post*, May 7, 1999, p. A1.

Significant political expenditures are also made for the Borking and counter-Borking campaigns of the two sides, and the ways these funds are spent may not always stand up to critical scrutiny in the light of day. In September 1999, the *Los Angeles Times* reported that in 1998, reporters had "obtained documents that showed that Microsoft was considering a range of behind-the-scenes public relations maneuvers, including submitting letters to the editor and opinion pieces presented as independent testimonials but solicited and paid for by Microsoft." Both sides were actively working to get columnists, reporters, academics, and researchers to publicly support their arguments and to enlist organizations to develop conferences. The *Times* reported that as many as a dozen think tanks may be receiving funding from the Microsoft and anti-Microsoft sides. Both sides were urging economists and other academics to sign petitions supporting their position in the dispute. (I have received fax and e-mail petitions from both sides; I signed neither, but I did accept invitations to two conferences, one organized by a pro-Microsoft group and one organized by an anti-Microsoft group.)

They were also paying for ads placed by supposedly independent research groups. Microsoft got nailed in the *New York Times* in September 1999 for having surreptitiously paid for ads in the *Times* and the *Washington Post* the previous June in which the Independent Institute posted an open letter to President Bill Clinton that made the case against Microsoft's prosecution and that was endorsed by 240 of the "country's leading economists." The ads never mentioned Microsoft's support of the institute, even though Microsoft reimbursed the institute for the cost of the ads, plus the first-class travel expenses of the institute's head and a colleague to attend a Washington, D.C., press conference organized around the letter and ads. Microsoft's total cost was nearly $154,000, but it should be pointed out that the letter signers themselves were paid nothing.

In October 1999, Microsoft mounted a campaign to have its stockholders and Web site visitors write their congressmen on how Microsoft should be left alone to innovate in the future, unencumbered with the kind of antitrust constraint the Justice Department had been seeking. When he sent out the company's 1999 annual report to its two million stockholders, Robert Herbold, Microsoft's chief operating officer, included a letter warning that "litigation and government intervention . . . could choke off innovation and threatened the vitality of our industry as a whole." He urged them to write their members of Congress and to join with hundreds of thousands of Microsoft's Web site visitors to join the company's newly established "Freedom to Innovate Network," with its own Web site, through which visitors could express their views to both Microsoft and their members of Congress.[10]

Is there anything really wrong with such tactics? In one sense the answer is clearly no. Microsoft is simply defending itself against similar tactics used by its political adversaries, and the company has a clear right to appeal its case to the American public and their representatives. Its efforts are politics as usual; they are democracy at work. The expenditures to date are not outlandish. Then again, these are the sorts of tactics Microsoft would likely have studiously eschewed in the early 1990s when the company's executives were politically tone-deaf. By the logic of the workaday world in the nation's capital, Microsoft's current political maneuvering can be seen as "productive," given that its maneuvers might avert even more serious political assaults on the company's fortunes.

Then again, from a broader perspective, one that comes naturally to ordinary people outside the Washington Beltway, Microsoft's expenditures of time and money (as well as the expenditures of its adversaries) on political maneuvers are an unmitigated waste. What is particularly egregious and is evident in the political maneuvering surrounding the Microsoft antitrust case is that the rules of competition have clearly shifted for technology industries: you can't compete solely in product markets; you must compete in the streets of Washington and the Halls of Congress. Fortunately for those who benefit from the political infighting, the waste will go unrealized, literally, since the wasteful political expenditures will show up in software products not produced and not upgraded with the care they might have been.

Unfortunately, the internal logic of so many political battles for the hearts and minds of the public, and maybe the judicial process, is to do what comes naturally: *escalate.* As in fights, you had better counter what the other side does. Better yet, do what you expect your opponent to do, only do it sooner and do more of it. There are often first-mover advantages in public relations campaigns, just as there are first-mover advantages in the software business. What does this mean? Very simply, that the political arms race between the two sides will continue for years into the future. Even if Microsoft were a monopoly, one wonders whether the efficiency gains from any remedy the court might fashion could make up for the waste that will likely mount from the political arms race the case has inspired.

THE INDEPENDENT JUDICIARY

The Microsoft case is not being tried in the court of public opinion. It is being tried in a federal district court before a judge, not a jury, and the rules of law apply. However, we can't be completely sanguine that Microsoft will get the kind of hearing it deserves as a defendant against the full force of the United States government.

We have shown in earlier chapters how antitrust enforcement has contributed to the obstruction of competition, reduced economic efficiency, and adversely affected labor and financial markets (see Chapter 7). Robert Bork has also shown in great detail that for a long time the courts were swayed by flawed economic arguments when it came to antitrust enforcement, especially when cases were politically popular. Judges were also prone to err on the side of obstructing competitive practices that could have yielded significant consumer benefits. While we might like to think the judiciary is independent because judges may be appointed for life, we have to acknowledge that the judiciary has been a part of the legal process that has enforced antitrust laws wrongly, and many of the cases brought have had a political grounding.

In recent years, Bork has determined (as noted in the second edition of *The Antitrust Paradox*) that the courts have by and large corrected the errors of their past ways. That's the good news. The bad news is that they are still capable of returning to the errors of the past. This is an especially big danger in the Microsoft case because it turns on some fairly new concepts—"network effects," "tipping," and "switching costs"—whose relevance to Microsoft's business practices is not clear, but may be less than the government claims.

CONCLUDING COMMENTS

Every schoolchild learns that justice is blind. At least, it should be. In the pursuit of justice, the Framers of the Constitution separated the country's legal system from the political system. The reasoning was simple: if our political system is allowed to fuse with our legal system, then justice will all too readily be put up for sale to the highest bidder by politicians attempting to accommodate the special interests they serve. Our reverence for this institutional divide tempts us to believe that the government's legal efforts are necessarily and always based on an unadulterated search for truth and justice.

However, the separation between the legal and political systems is hardly complete, and the quest for legal truth sometimes succumbs to other objectives that all too often reflect human frailties, not the least of which might be personal gain. Unfortunately, there remain important direct avenues by which politics can influence the way and extent to which justice is pursued. Special interest groups hold the purse strings for politicians, and the politicians hold the purse strings for those in government who work for the legal system. Special interest groups and politicians cannot always control who is convicted, but to a considerable extent they can define what constitutes an offense and, therefore, who is prosecuted and for how long and at what expense. The courts, regrettably, have shown that they can seriously err in their evaluation of novel antitrust arguments, as Robert Bork has shown, which is all the encouragement special interests need to press their case in political forums.

There are also indirect avenues by which the legal system can be tainted by politics. The media play an important role in conveying to politicians and the people within the legal system notions of who are wrongdoers and should be prosecuted and convicted for alleged offenses. This has become especially true in the information age, for information—and misinformation—can speed through society and to decision makers faster than ever before, along electronic superhighways on Internet time.

We cannot prove definitively that Microsoft's critics have worked their will on the legal system for their own ends. As indicated early in the chapter, we haven't found the "smoking gun" that would constitute conclusive proof that Microsoft's rivals and critics have had undue influence on the Justice Department's case. But political operatives are too smart to let a smoking gun be found. They know how to play the political game, which requires the pretense of legitimacy as to how their funds are spent. The evidence may be circumstantial. Nevertheless, the patterns of political expenditures and maneuvers that have surrounded the charges of Microsoft's alleged monopoly power since 1992 should be disconcerting to those who believe that the pursuit of justice should be immune from politics.

⚖ CHAPTER 10 ⚖

Antitrust Ironies

THE MICROSOFT ANTITRUST CASE IS HISTORIC in proportion. It has pitted the legal power of the United States government against the legal power of the Microsoft Corporation, which also has the highest market capitalization of any company in the world.

The case is a test of how the country's antitrust laws will be enforced in an era that is vastly different from the one in which those laws were conceived. It tests some novel economic concepts and theories—such as "network effects," "tipping," and "switching costs"—that have not been major issues in other antitrust cases. Without question, the case will likely redefine "monopoly" for legal purposes in the modern information technology era, in which, by many accounts, business is—and must be—done on "Internet time." And the case will also determine the extent to which the Justice Department and/or courts will be allowed to become involved in structuring, or, rather, restructuring, companies and industries in the information technology age.

However, the case also raises the specter of the legal process being misdirected by serious errors in economic thinking and tarnished, if not subverted, by politics. Clearly, Microsoft's competitors have much to gain if Microsoft's market position is ultimately checked by a court ruling (or by a settlement made under the threat of an adverse decision for Microsoft). The redistribution of tens of billions of dollars of company and individual wealth is at stake. Just as clearly, Microsoft's competitors have waged a prolonged, high-profile, and sophisticated political and media campaign to press the Justice Department into suing Microsoft. The evolutionary future of critically important software products and their prices hangs on the outcome.

What makes the political campaign troubling is that the history of antitrust enforcement is replete with instances in which competitors—through their influence over Congress and the administration—have used antitrust laws to their own advantage, not to thwart monopoly, but to relieve competitive pressures on them-

selves. The net effect of these intrusions has often been the impairment, not en-
hancement, of the efficiency of the American economy. This is a conclusion that
even the staunchest free-market (and antimonopoly) advocates have ultimately
come to, albeit perhaps reluctantly. For example, the longtime free-marketer Milton
Friedman told a Washington, D.C., audience at the Cato Institute while the trial was
under way, "My own views about the antitrust laws have changed greatly over time.
When I started in this business, as a believer in competition, I was a great supporter
of antitrust laws; I thought enforcing them was one of the few desirable things that
the government could do to promote more competition. But as I watched what actually happened, I saw that, instead of promoting competition, antitrust laws
tended to do exactly the opposite, because they tended, like so many government
activities, to be taken over by the people they were supposed to regulate and control. And so over time I have gradually come to the conclusion that antitrust laws
do far more harm than good and that we would be better off if we didn't have them
at all, if we could get rid of them."

Indeed, one of the reasons Robert Bork's antitrust views have played such a
prominent role in this book is that he also once railed, with scholarly detachment
and allegiance to the validity of antitrust laws in principle, against the misuse of
those laws, the enforcement of which he concluded had been "overdone and politicized." In the second edition of his landmark book he did declare the "crisis" he had
seen in antitrust litigation to be over, but he also warned that the recent improvement in court decisions could be reversed. The country must now face the very possibility that the Microsoft case will usher in a return to the sordid way things were
done in the 1970s and before. The damage of such a policy reversal will be far
greater now than in the 1970s, for the potential impairment of the economy's dynamism is greater. One of the signal antitrust ironies is that Bork has helped to repoliticize the antitrust enforcement process after making a career of decrying it. To
that extent, he has contributed to undermining the trust we can have in antitrust.

The charge that the legal attack on Microsoft amounts to prosecution for hire has
to be taken seriously: Microsoft's critics obviously believe that politicking works—
how else can one explain their extensive and expensive campaign?

The public must demand that the case the government is bringing against Microsoft in the public's name be demonstrably clear, strong, and beyond reproach.
But it is not. Key economic arguments of the government's case often don't square
well with the theory of how monopolists are expected to behave. The government
must show strong evidence that a company accused of being a monopolist has actually restricted production for the purpose of raising its prices. Yet Microsoft stands
accused by the Justice Department of trying to expand its market by lowering the
price of its browser to zero (and beyond). This is classic competitive behavior.

In fact, in their more venturesome moments, Microsoft's accusers in and out of
the Justice Department not only deride Microsoft for attempting to expand its mar-

ket but also accuse it of having a pathological will to dominate everything. Like many of Bill Gates's critics, Netscape's Jim Clark repeatedly points to Gates's (and by extension, Microsoft's) aggressiveness. In his book he observes, "I, for one, had no doubt about what lay beneath Bill Gates's jolly nerd exterior—a killer instinct and sheer relentless aggression. I knew that when he reacted, it would be with ferocity. Gates was like the evil Lord Sauron in J. R. R. Tolkien's Hobbit fable *The Fellowship of the Rings,* whose all-seeing eye searched ceaselessly for any threat to his tyranny." In another place, Clark adds, "But Gates's Microsoft constantly operates as if it's under siege by enemies that threaten its existence. If survival and paranoia are intimately linked, as Intel's Andy Grove has said, then the empire of Microsoft is going to be around for a very long time." And, finally, he concludes, "Microsoft doesn't go to sleep for five or ten minutes." Perhaps Microsoft's paranoia is justified.

According to the Justice Department, Microsoft is a monopolist protected by insurmountable entry barriers. Yet if you look past some of Clark's inflammatory language, his comments about Gates and company do not describe a self-assured, protected monopolist.

Monopolists raise prices. Yet Microsoft has lowered its prices. As shown earlier with reference to data and a variety of studies, as Microsoft's market share has moved upward its prices have trended downward. The price of Internet Explorer is down to zero. Clark points to the fact that Microsoft charged $5 a copy for MS-DOS in the early 1990s, but now charges $125 for a copy of Windows 98. This might seem to suggest that there has been a dramatic price increase in the cost of the operating system. But such numbers include the effects of inflation and program enhancements, and are grossly misleading; they are not what economists call "real" prices—as Clark and anyone familiar with market pricing knows perfectly well. By integrating its browser into Windows, Microsoft dropped the *real* price of Windows even further. The Justice Department claims and the court accepted the claim that the integration had no conceivable consumer benefits and was purely "predatory." If this is so, then why do all other major operating systems now bundle browsers with their operating systems? To believe the critics' claims, you would have to assume that only the Justice Department's lawyers, expert witnesses, and court know how to build the kind of operating systems consumers want.

The government tells us that Microsoft stands alone as the sole producer of commercially viable operating systems, and that the barriers to entry in software are prohibitive for outside firms. But as shown in earlier chapters, there are already more than a dozen operating systems actually *in* the market, despite the supposedly impenetrable barriers to entry.

When it filed its complaint against Microsoft, the Justice Department stated in no uncertain terms that the emergence of operating systems like Linux and FreeBSD as competitors to Windows was impossible. Yet those operating systems *did* emerge and *did* expand while the trial proceeded. You can see large special displays of the Linux operating system on sale at Staples and CompUSA. And it looks for all the world as though AOL bought Netscape for billions because it thought Netscape was worth billions; and it is apparent that AOL intends to use Navigator along with its customer base to establish an alternative computing platform. Similarly, in late 1999, Sun Microsystems began making another stab at establishing network computing as an alternative platform that drastically lowers major costs of computing, system service, and software upgrades. Also, in the first quarter of its fiscal year 2000 (July through September 1999), Sun reported a stellar 25 percent increase in its revenues and a nearly 40 percent increase in its net income over first quarter 1999 (after one-time adjustments), mainly because it was able to ride the Internet wave for its powerful computers and scalable operating system. Sun's performance will probably temper Scott McNealy's enthusiasm for claiming that an unchecked Microsoft will eventually have the Internet economy under its control. In October, not to be left behind by Sun in the emerging network computing market, Oracle launched its new business system, called "Oracle Business Online," under which it proposed to offer "top-tier business applications" over the Internet with subscribers paying a monthly fee based on usage.

As might be expected in ever-changing competitive markets, Microsoft fairly quickly matched Sun's and Oracle's new business moves, redirecting its own business strategy toward the prospects that its software products would inevitably be sold not always as "packages," as previously done, but as "services" that could be rented on-line. Microsoft even introduced its own line of network computers, called a "MSN Web Companion," which would compete with Sun's previously announced network computer, "Sun Ray."

In December 1999, Dell and Compaq introduced their own versions of Web-ready personal computers, WebPC (starting at under $1,000) and iPaq (starting at under $500), respectively, that appeared intended to serve as a bridge between old personal computers that rely mainly on the computer's internal mechanisms for computing capacity and that have Internet access as an addendum and network computers (like the Sun Ray) that will rely exclusively on external mechanisms for computing capacity. Moreover, at the fall 1999 Comdex convention in Las Vegas, there were at least 150 various forms of new "information (or Internet) appliances"—allowing for e-mailing, Web surfing, and on-line computing—on display that did not use Windows and that should hit the market in 2000. Among these new devices is the "i-Opener" from Netpliance, which costs $199 and only allows for e-mailing and Web browsing; the machine, which comes with a ten-inch flat-panel display, is programmed to log on automatically six times a day to check for e-mails and turn on a light when new e-mails are found. Then there is the "iBrow," from Boundless Technologies, which has many of the same capabilities as the "i-Opener."

The main difference is that the "iBrow" has been developed primarily for sale to businesses who will give it away, or sell or rent it, to their customers, because it will have a window that can't be obscured and that can contain ads.

With these kinds of software and hardware developments coming on top of one another, *PC Magazine* ran a cover story in its November 2, 1999, issue that was headlined: "Throw Out Your Software; Run Your Applications Over the Web." (The article stressed that Web-based applications would not likely work for everyone and would not be practical without very fast Internet connections.)

In light of all that has happened in technology industries that was totally unanticipated even when the Justice Department filed its antitrust suit, does anyone believe the country needs the Justice Department to direct or supplant the very active market forces that are working relentlessly on Microsoft and every other company in the industry? The Justice Department's attempt to throttle the integration of Internet Explorer with Windows speaks volumes about the Justice Department's foresight and understanding of the technology market: a year later, even grade-school children have become Internet-savvy and -reliant.

From all that has happened just while the trial was under way, the conclusion is inescapable that the entry barriers are not what the Justice Department and court have made them out to be. As stressed, software is made from a resource abundantly available worldwide, various sequences of *1*'s and *0*'s. Even Netscape's Clark made this point with considerable eloquence: "In comparison [to industrial-age goods], the manufacture of software is no big deal. The idea, the design, and the engineering are all done in the same place, by the same people. The basic materials are laughably cheap. No spot-welding robots need apply. All you need is a good brain and an okay computer (though some people have managed surprisingly well by reversing those adjectives)." As noted earlier, Netscape was able to develop Navigator from scratch—without borrowing a line of code from Mosaic, Jim Clark assures us—in just four months. How could anyone monopolize such a market? It is absurd to imagine that anyone could corner such a digit-based market and act for long like a monopolist. The Justice Department and court don't seem to realize that a monopolist acting badly in new-age markets sows the seeds of its own (rapid) destruction.

Both the Justice Department and court stress that Microsoft *could* easily raise the price of Windows and not have to worry that its market will materially erode. That may be true for the *near term*, the government's myopic time horizon, but not necessarily for the *long term*, the time horizon of financial markets, which Gates and company must steer by. Microsoft has to worry that any increase in profits achieved today from price increases can be more than negated by profit reductions in the future from the erosion of its market by new entrants and by the unraveling of the "net effects" at the core of the government's case. Seen from this perspective, the *ability* of a firm to raise current prices implies nothing about the firm's monopoly. The fact of the matter is that Microsoft's prices are, by and large, in line with or lower than the prices other software producers charge. As shown earlier, whenever Microsoft has entered a market, the prices in that market have tended to fall.

The Justice Department has made much of the Microsoft e-mails it has unearthed that contain some tough words of executives sounding off about "killing" the company's competitors. But how should we interpret such e-mails? As the "locker-room" talk of monopolists or competitors? (Bear in mind that these executives did not imagine that their words would be used later as legal documents.) The e-mails could mean nothing more than the locker-room blustering of politically naïve young executives who haven't learned to guard what they say and who haven't put their words to a market test. For these types of reasons, one of the government's chief economic experts, Franklin Fisher, argued forcefully years ago in his defense of IBM against antitrust charges that practically no weight should be given to evidence of intent (in contrast to his testimony in the Microsoft case).

Let's be realistic: "killing"—beating market rivals with better prices and products—is what competition is all about. If Microsoft "kills" Netscape, which it has yet to do, it is doing no more than what Netscape set out to do to Mosaic. In relating the story about how he and Marc Andreesen stirred around for the next "big idea" software, Jim Clark recalls in his book, "Marc leaned back in his chair, thought for a few minutes, then said . . . 'Well, we could always build a Mosaic killer,' " to which Clark snapped, " 'A what?' " Andreesen elaborated: " 'You know, build a browser that's better than Mosaic, put it out there, let it take over instead of Mosaic. Right now, the University [of Illinois] is spreading a copy of this program that my friends and I worked our butts off writing, and they're trying to make a business of it. We need to take it over. We gotta kill it." If Netscape can "kill" Mosaic, then shouldn't Microsoft be allowed to "kill" Netscape?

But, then, all this emphasis on "killing" talk is misplaced. After only four and a half years in operation, Netscape wasn't buried. Netscape was sold for the tidy sum of $4.3 billion at the time the AOL deal was signed in November 1998. Recall that this deal was worth over $10 billion by the time it was closed, in March 1999. AOL could have walked away from the deal at the closing; that it didn't means that Netscape must have been worth that much to AOL. Not bad. Netscape is still here—but where is Mosaic? If "killing" is the crime, the Justice Department is surely barking up the wrong tree, and Netscape should be prosecuted. This obvious conclusion makes the outrage over "killing" talk in Microsoft e-mails silly.

Of course, there never was any real reason for Netscape to fear being "killed" by Microsoft or anyone else—*if* Netscape and Sun really could pull off what the government claims they intended to do, combine Navigator with Java into an alternative computing platform that was truly superior to and carry a lower price than Windows. To assume that consumers would not migrate to the better system is to believe that consumers—including some very big businesses with sophisticated in-formation technology managers—would be content to suffer into the distant future at the hands of Microsoft—the same company that has duped them into buying re-peatedly an inferior product at a higher price than the alternative. No recounting of the QWERTY story can obscure the total untenability of the presumption at the foundation of the government's case: that Justice Department lawyers, their expert witnesses, and the court are the only ones smart enough to figure out the raw deal people are enduring at the hands of Microsoft.

Dubbing Microsoft "Godzilla" and Bill Gates as "Butthead" may be easier for Mi-crosoft's critics than doing what you have to do to succeed in markets: offer buyers a truly better computing platform at a more attractive price, and let the network ef-fects pile up. As it is, the market verdict on the superiority of a Web-based comput-ing platform is still out. Java is not the universal programming language that Sun claims it to be. One Java expert reckons that Java is the "80 percent solution"—pretty good, but not *universal*. Web-based computing might or might not be cheaper than personal computer–based computing. Many consumers may shun Web-based computing simply because it harbors a potential loss of control over programs and files and could lead to some loss of privacy. Moreover, Web-based computing could be slower, depending on the extent of Web traffic and bandwidth. Some other users might not want to install a second telephone line and would not want to do all their computing on-line. What is needed is a serious market test of Sun's computing concept, not a courthouse test.

The Justice Department and court tell us that Microsoft's treatment of Netscape shows how innovation can be undermined by the unfettered business practices of a dominant firm. The presumption is that if a firm like Netscape can be "crushed" by powerful Microsoft, then Microsoft's very presence, backed up by the threat of crushing, could deter many other computer programmers from innovating. But that argument ignores the fact that Microsoft's "power" came from an old source, a lower price, which suggests that Microsoft's power to override market forces isn't what it is cracked up to be. It also ignores the extent to which Netscape caused Mi-crosoft to create its browser and see the competitive usefulness of making its oper-ating system Internet-ready by integrating its browser into Windows. Thus, Microsoft responded to the market pressure represented by Netscape and the po-tential for other Web-based operating systems.

The critics' argument regarding impaired innovation fails to take account of the prospects that Microsoft's willingness to buy up new companies can spur innova-tion among a host of companies, only some of which Microsoft will ultimately be interested in buying. And the argument totally ignores the billions of dollars Mi-crosoft spends each year on R&D and the substantial stream of innovations that have come out of Redmond over the last two decades. What is extraordinary is the fact that the Justice Department has not been able to provide a shred of evidence that innovation in this country has been undercut by Microsoft's growing dominance, and it hasn't been willing to consider the prospects that its own operations may be impairing innovation far more than Microsoft could ever do.

Perhaps Robert Scheer, a liberal columnist for the *Los Angeles Times,* was right when he observed after reading the judge's Findings of Fact, "Nowhere in the Justice Department filing is there a compelling case that the power of Microsoft undermines consumer freedom. Instead, what should be called into question is the outdated model of antitrust being pursued by the government. In the Information Age, the concern of the regulators should focus not on size but rather the power of a company or industry over the lives of ordinary citizen-consumers."

Actually, all the legal and media focus on Netscape is what Microsoft's critics want. They understand also that Netscape and its browser technology, whether combined with Java or not, is largely a computer industry sideshow. They understand that the working relationship between Netscape and Sun had been strained so severely as late as 1997 that there would not likely be a Navigator-Java computer platform. Besides, there are other browser technologies that Sun could combine with Java in order to market an alternative network-centric computer platform to compete with the Windows platform. Sun has always believed, as it advertises, that "The Network Is The Computer," and that would not have changed even if Netscape had been crushed, which it has not been. Sun probably doesn't care about Netscape's fate per se. What it does care about is not having to compete head to head with another dominant computer platform, Windows, that is also Internet-ready.

The critics also understand that Netscape—the "little start-up that could"—is being used as a stalking horse to divert media and analytical attention from a much more important competitive drama in the computer industry: the lucrative markets that make up the server stack and enterprise computing, or back-office computing. This is where all of the major critics—IBM, Sun, Oracle, AOL, and Netscape—had, by the mid-1990s, locked horns with Microsoft in what they perceived to be something of an industry death dance for dominance in that market. That dance continued as this book went to press. The dance also acquired new steps as Microsoft, Sun, and other firms began to reorganize in order to "rent" applications as a service over the Web.

Ironically, Netscape and the Justice Department have become pawns of the critic-competitors who want nothing more than for the antitrust suit to slow Microsoft down in its invasion of their prize territory, which for several key players covers the whole server stack. They want to bury Microsoft in legal costs in the hope that Microsoft will have to raise its prices, will curb its innovation, and will think twice about stretching its competitive arms further into what they think of as *their* markets. Microsoft's critics would like nothing better than to have Microsoft broken up into three companies because, in a world rife with network effects and scale economies, the three "Baby Bills" would be less competitive than the one "Big Bill." Such a change would immediately raise the market value of their proposed alternative computing platforms, though it wouldn't necessarily make those platforms more efficient or more cost-effective.

The government wants the public to believe that Microsoft's monopoly is self-evident in its "superhigh" profits and its low "predatory" prices. This kind of reasoning has nothing to do with actual economic thought and concepts. On the question of the meaning of Microsoft's high profitability and Gates's great personal wealth, the Justice Department lawyers should remember Robert Bork's words (written before he became a lobbyist for Netscape): high company profitability is "utterly ambiguous" in an antitrust case, for all the reasons Bork gave (and that have been recounted in this book). Remember also that the government founded its case on software markets being rife with "network effects" and "scale economies" that occur when the marginal cost of producing another copy of a program is zero, or close to it. As argued earlier, those conditions often imply that software products and Internet content and services *should be* given away, as many software and Internet companies are doing. Indeed, as also argued, these market conditions can imply that some firms should pay their customers to take their products.

There's a good chance that companies like IBM, AOL, Sun, and Oracle will regret their efforts to have the Justice Department get Microsoft on the grounds that Microsoft dominates its markets. All four firms have major shares of their markets. The old adage "What goes around often comes around" may well apply here. The Justice Department can take its pursuit of "equal justice for all" very seriously, which means IBM, AOL, Sun, or Oracle could very well be the next target of litigation for the crime of dominating its markets.

This isn't to say that the country's antitrust laws should be jettisoned. Adam Smith was right when he noted how people of the same trade rarely get together without some interest in how they might override competitive market forces. If it can be proved that Microsoft sought to divide the market with Netscape (and the evidence presented is suspect), then Microsoft should be severely penalized, just to deter such efforts in the future. That would be an appropriate application of antitrust law. But to make sure that all enforcement of antitrust law is undertaken with great care, the enforcement needs to be subjected to intense scrutiny by a skeptical eye. We need to acknowledge the conflict of interest companies have when they go begging the government for antitrust suits against their competitors. We need assurance that the Justice Department is not working, out of political obligations, at the behest of those competitors who stand to gain market advantage at the expense of the accused. We need to ensure that consumer gains, not competitor gains, drive antitrust prosecutions. The Microsoft case has put antitrust on trial because it shows how politics can corrupt the legal process. And this has put trust in antitrust litigation on trial.

No one should expect perfection in antitrust enforcement, but certainly more should be demanded of those who enforce antitrust laws than has been achieved in the past. Perhaps Milton Friedman, in his criticism of the historical record of antitrust enforcement, is suggesting a productive route for reform—let's call it "the Friedman test." Perhaps the Antitrust Division of the Justice Department should be made accountable, meaning that it should be required to show over a span of cases and with hard data and argumentation that its enforcement efforts have actually done more good than harm to the economy. And maybe in twenty years the overall record of antitrust enforcement ought to be weighed by disinterested outside observers of antitrust law enforcement who have no industry ties, with an eye toward determining whether the Friedman test has been passed. If the enforcers are given a passing grade, meaning more good than harm was done over the review period, then we keep them. If not, then we substantially reform the law and its enforcement.

At the very least, at the time it files an antitrust suit, the Justice Department should be required to lay out the remedies it will actually seek, if it wins, in order that the companies' alleged market transgressions can be weighed against the likely consequences of having the proposed remedies given legal force. What is really criminal about the Microsoft case is that the Justice Department pursued it in spite of the fact that from the start it had only a foggy notion of what it would do if it won. As this book was going to press, Justice Department lawyers were clearly in a quandary over what remedies they should recommend, and had been seeking outside consultants for help in appraising the economic impacts of alternative remedies.

Similarly, the reason Judge Jackson took the unusual step of appointing Judge Richard Posner, a distinguished antitrust scholar and lecturer at the University of Chicago Law School, as mediator in any settlement talks between Microsoft and the Justice Department is obviously because he very much wants a settlement, and for good reason: he understands that he has put himself in a very uncomfortable legal bind. Given the strength of his condemnation of Microsoft as a monopoly scourge on the software industry in his Findings of Fact, any remedy he might fashion must be substantially more than a slap on Microsoft's financial wrist, or else the credibility of his Findings would be undermined. If Judge Jackson hands down a harsh remedy that matches the strength of his Findings—such as breaking up Microsoft, as Microsoft's rivals recommend—he will likely go down in history as another jurist who has used the antitrust laws to impose more harm on consumers than Microsoft ever contemplated. His best hope in the absence of a settlement is for the case to drag on through the courts for years until, as in the IBM antitrust case (which lasted for thirteen years and was dropped by the government in 1982), technological and market developments have made the case moot.

Whatever the outcome of the Microsoft case, we should expect that over the coming decades, the antitrust enforcers should be less inclined to impose their authority over the economy for obvious reasons: Capital continues to become more mobile. A consequence of this is that businesses are increasing their ability to cross national borders and market boundaries. Accordingly, the world economy is becoming more fluid and more competitive. Accordingly, there should be progressively less need for antitrust enforcement.

The core line of argument developed in this book should be disconcerting. The arguments that the government offers in support of its suit don't stand up to close scrutiny, which leads to the question "Then why is Microsoft in court?" The answer given in this book can be crystallized in a story that is all too familiar in the annals of government regulation of industry: Microsoft's competitors wanted it that way. Microsoft's competitors were being soundly beaten in the desktop marketplace by Microsoft. They feared that Microsoft might be even more successful in its plans to dominate other markets. They wanted to be able to dominate the emerging Internet economy without being challenged by an Internet-ready Microsoft. Initially they tried to respond by consorting to reorganize and divide up the market. When that effort fell apart, they went to the Justice Department to get the government to do what they could not do, slow down, if not stop, Microsoft's invasion of their markets and the burgeoning Internet world. The Justice Department's lawyers have done the bidding of Microsoft's competitors, although the lawyers might honestly think they were doing otherwise.

Clearly, Microsoft's critics have orchestrated a broad-based campaign with the public, politicians, and even Justice Department officials that has one overriding theme: "Stop Microsoft." When the "pattern" of events is seen, it now looks as though the country's political system has listened attentively, and the legal system appears to have buckled under, adopting almost verbatim the arguments of Microsoft's critics without regard to the fact that the critics' arguments may amount to nothing more than special pleading for relief from a highly aggressive competitor.

Taking a close look at and dissecting the critics' charges against Microsoft does not mean that Microsoft has always operated with the best of business intentions and manners. Microsoft does seem to be an aggressive competitor operating under the influence of business steroids. It drives hard bargains with its suppliers and buyers, apparently not always leaving much on the table for the firms with which it deals, which is hardly all bad for consumers. Gates and company don't seem to suffer fools gladly. Members of Microsoft's executive team seem to use language that could be more guarded and less abrasive and abusive of people with whom they must deal. (Though some of Jim Clark's formulations lead one to suspect that Microsoft's business manners and e-mail may not be any worse than its competitors'.) But these problems should hardly be of concern to the Justice Department. As another judge in a federal appeals court ruled in a private antitrust case against Intel on the very day that Judge Jackson handed down his Findings of Fact, "[The] Sherman act does not convert all harsh commercial actions into antitrust violations." The antitrust laws were never intended to ensure good business manners, only a healthy competitive environment. The legal system is simply not capable of fine-tuning people's everyday behavior with any degree of precision—and might very well do considerable harm in the process of trying. Where would this all stop? Whose sense of manners should rule? Can a substantive case be made that the top executives at Microsoft behave any worse than the top people at Sun or Oracle?

What is most distressing about this case is that there is a good chance that Microsoft would not be in this legal fix if Gates and other Microsoft executives had not, early in the 1990s, been so politically self-assured (and maybe naïve) and had guarded their political flanks better by padding the pockets of politicians. This is an unfortunate commentary on the trial for a couple of important reasons: First, people in business should not have to waste their company's resources fending off political attacks in court by unhappy competitors, especially when the competitors' argument that they need market protection doesn't square with economic logic.

Second, and much more important, the political success of Microsoft's critics raises a new specter: We may now have to fear Microsoft in ways and to a degree never before imagined. In markets unfettered by political payoffs for protection from competition, if Microsoft acted like a feared monopolist, driving up prices and driving down the quality of its products, we are confident that its efforts would be soundly rebuked by market forces in a relatively short time. Competitors would enter and take over Microsoft's markets.

However, when companies are able to use politics to achieve their market goals, as Microsoft's critics have shown, once again, is possible, it also follows that Microsoft can use politics to pursue its own goals.

We now have to fear that with its newfound political savvy, Microsoft will do just that, easily swamping the political efforts of its critics or anyone else. After all, Microsoft has a market cap close to a half trillion dollars, more than the combined value of several of its major competitors. It has billions in cash reserves and is headed by the wealthiest man in the universe, one who is acknowledged to be a "fierce" competitor. Moreover, all that wealth is concentrated in one company that can coordinate its political deployment in a way that can't be matched by several firms acting collectively (but who are also competitors) in the political arena. And the kind of money Microsoft can tap can do major damage through politics, mainly because the firm has proved its adeptness at outcompeting its rivals. Those who doubt that politics can affect—or rather, infect—antitrust enforcement need only reflect that as this book went to press, it was reported in the *Wall Street Journal* that Senator Slade Gorton, Microsoft's home-state senator, was working diligently to hold down the budget of the Antitrust Division. One of the senator's aides noted, "He wants to send a message about this case."

Microsoft's critics seem to think that competitiveness stops at the edges of their market, or perhaps the city limits of Washington, D.C. That is hardly the case. If anything, the competition there heats up—and becomes destructive of firms and people. There is every reason to believe that a company's market prowess can be transformed into political prowess, when the firm has been awakened to the realities of modern politics and the advantages of political competition.

Thus, another great irony in the trial lies in the fact that prosecuting Microsoft may have the ultimate result of heightening its power and influence in the country, if not the world. Even if Microsoft were a monopolist, which has been disputed in this book time and again, the Justice Department probably should have let the sleeping (political) giant lie. Companies can use the political process to enhance their existing power, a consequence that perverts the original intent of antitrust law.

There is no need to call for a total hands-off policy on the part of the Justice Department. But it must be made to understand that in the new information technology age into which the world is rapidly moving, its vigilance against the threat of monopoly is needed less than ever. At the same time, we all must realize that as markets become increasingly competitive, we must become more vigilant of what the antitrust enforcers do, lest they become political pawns of competitors who would like nothing more than to abate the growing market pressures they face.

APPENDIX I
MICROSOFT'S
LEGAL TROUBLES

1990

May 30—The Federal Trade Commission starts an investigation of Microsoft's business practices—specifically, Microsoft's possible collusion with IBM in the development of OS/2, its pricing policy on Windows, and its competitive advantage in markets for Windows applications resulting from its knowledge of changes in forthcoming versions of Windows.

1993

August 21—FTC commissioners are deadlocked 2–2 on filing charges, and the FTC drops its investigation, but the Justice Department announces that it is taking up its own investigation of the charges.

1994

July 15—Microsoft and the Justice Department sign a consent decree in U.S. District Court, Washington, D.C., that prohibits Microsoft from calculating its licensing fees on the basis of the number of personal computers a manufacturer ships, and also prevents Microsoft from requiring personal computer makers to take any other software product as a condition of their license for the Windows operating system. The consent decree does allow Microsoft to develop "integrated products."

1995

February 14—Judge Stanley Sporkin of the district court throws out the consent degree on the ground that it is too lenient on Microsoft.

April 27—The Justice Department sues Microsoft in U.S. District Court to block its proposed $1.5 billion acquisition of Intuit, the developer of Quicken, the leading personal finance program. The Justice Department charges that Microsoft, which owns Money, Quicken's main competitor, would have a monopoly in the personal finance software market.

May 22—Microsoft discontinues its Intuit acquisition.

June 16—At the request of both the Justice Department and Microsoft, a judge in the D.C. federal court of appeals upholds the July 15 consent decree, thus reversing Judge Sporkin's decision, and removes Judge Sporkin from the case.

August 21—Judge Thomas Penfield Jackson approves the consent decree.

1996

September 19—The Justice Department starts a probe of the bundling of Internet Explorer with Windows 95, which it thinks may be an extension of Microsoft's monopoly in the operating system market into the browser market.

1997

August 18—The Justice Department announces its investigation of Microsoft's $150 investment in Apple Computers and in three firms that provide video and sound over the Internet.

October 20—The Justice Department sues Microsoft in U.S. District Court for illegally bundling Internet Explorer with Windows, in violation of the 1995 consent decree, and asks for a $1 million-a-day fine.

November 7—The state of Texas sues Microsoft for impeding its antitrust investigation of Microsoft.

December 11—Judge Jackson issues a preliminary injunction that prevents Microsoft from requiring personal computer manufacturers to install Internet Explorer as a condition for their use of Windows 95.

December 16—Microsoft appeals Judge Jackson's injunction and offers two versions of Windows 95, one with and one without Internet Explorer. The Justice Department asks Judge Jackson to hold Microsoft in contempt for failing to abide by his December 16 order.

1998

January 22—Microsoft signs an agreement with the Justice Department, according to which personal computer manufacturers are not required to place an Internet Explorer icon on the Windows 95 desktop.

May 12—A judge in the D.C. federal court of appeals rules that Judge Jackson's December 11 injunction did not apply to Windows 98. This allows Microsoft to proceed with its June 25 launch of Windows 98, which has an integrated Internet Explorer browser.

May 18—Attorney General Janet Reno announces that the Justice Department is bringing suit in U.S. District Court against Microsoft for using its monopoly power in the operating system market to stifle competition in the Internet browser market (United States v. Microsoft Corporation, civil action no. 98-1232).

May 20—Assistant Attorney General Joel Klein and twenty state attorneys general file a joint antitrust suit against Microsoft in U.S. District Court, Washington, D.C. (State of New York *ex rel.* Attorney General Dennis C. Vacco *et al.* v. Microsoft Corporation, civil action no. 98–1233).

June 23—A judge of the D.C. federal appeals court overturns Judge Jackson's December 11 injunction, which prohibited requiring manufacturers to take Internet Explorer along with Windows 95.

September 24—Judge Jackson rejects Microsoft's motion to dismiss the Justice Department's antitrust case against it (United States v. Microsoft).

October 19—The trial begins.

November 24—America Online announces its intention to buy Netscape.

1999

June 26—After 76 days of trial, the testimony ends.

November 5—Judge Jackson issues his Findings of Fact in United States v. Microsoft, in which he states that Microsoft is a monopoly that has abused its market powers to stifle competition in the operating system and Internet browser markets.

December 6—The Justice Department files its proposed Conclusions of Law—its interpretation of how the nation's antitrust laws apply in the case, given the judge's Findings of Fact. Microsoft has until January 31, 2000, to file its Conclusions of Law. Then the judge will render his decision in the form of his own Conclusions of Law.

— Appendix II —
Summary of the
Major Antitrust Cases
the Justice Department
Has Brought
Against Microsoft

United States v. Microsoft:
Licensing (or Consent Decree) Case

*Justice Department Complaint for Violations of Sections 1 and 2
of the Sherman Act, July 15, 1994*

"Virtually all major PC manufacturers find it necessary to offer Microsoft operating systems on most of their PCs. Microsoft's monopoly power allows it to induce these manufacturers to enter into anticompetitive, long-term licenses under which they must pay royalties to Microsoft not only when they sell PCs containing Microsoft's operating systems, but also when they sell PCs containing non-Microsoft operating systems."

*Final Judgment as Agreed to by the Justice Department and Microsoft,
July 15, 1994*

"Microsoft is enjoined and restrained as follows:
  A. Microsoft shall not enter into any License Agreement for any Covered Product that has a total Duration that exceeds one year . . .
  B. Microsoft shall not enter into any License Agreement that by its terms prohibits or restricts the OEM's licensing, sale or distribution of any non-Microsoft Operating System Software product.
  C. Microsoft shall not enter into any Per Processor License.

D. Except to the extent permitted by Section IV (G) below,

E. Microsoft shall not enter into any License Agreement other than a Per

F. Copy License.

G. Microsoft shall not enter into any License Agreement in which the terms of that
   agreement are expressly or impliedly conditioned upon:

   1. the licensing of any other Covered Product, Operating System Software product
      or other product (provided, however, that this provision in and of itself shall not
      be construed to prohibit Microsoft from developing integrated products); or

   2. the OEM not licensing, purchasing, using or distributing any non-Microsoft
      product.

H. Microsoft shall not enter into any License Agreement containing a Minimum
   Commitment. However, nothing contained herein shall prohibit Microsoft and any
   OEM from developing non-binding estimates of projected sales of Microsoft's
   Covered Products for use in calculating royalty payments. . . ."

Disposition of the Case

On February 14, 1995, U.S. District Judge Stanley Sporkin threw out the consent degree on
the grounds that it was too lenient on Microsoft. However, later that year in June, an appellate court upholds the consent decree, reversing Judge Sporkin's decision and removes Judge
Sporkin from the case, and in August, U.S. District Judge Thomas Penfield Jackson approves
the consent decree.

UNITED STATES V. MICROSOFT: INTUIT CASE

*Justice Department Complaint for Violating Section 7 of
the Clayton Act, April 27, 1995*

"The United States brings this antitrust action to prevent the proposed acquisition by Microsoft Corporation, the world's largest and most powerful personal computer software
company, of Intuit, Inc., the dominant producer of Personal Finance/Checkbook
("PF/Checkbook") software. Microsoft is Intuit's most significant competitor. The proposed
acquisition would eliminate competition between Microsoft and Intuit, which has benefited,
consumers by leading to high quality, innovative products at low prices."

Requested Relief

"The United States requests (a) adjudication that Microsoft's proposed acquisition of Intuit
would violate Section 7 of the Clayton Act, (b) preliminary and permanent injunctive relief
preventing consummation of the proposed acquisition, (c) an award to the United States of
the costs of this action, and (d) such other relief as is just and proper."

Disposition of the Case

Microsoft terminated its efforts to acquire Intuit on May 22, 1995.

UNITED STATES V. MICROSOFT:
THE TYING AND EXCLUSIONARY AGREEMENT CASE

Justice Department Complaint for Violating Sections 1 and 2 of the Sherman Act, May 18, 1998

1. "This is an action under Sections 1 and 2 of the Sherman Act to restrain anticompetitive conduct by defendant Microsoft Corporation ("Microsoft"), the world's largest supplier of computer software for personal computers ("PCs"), and to remedy the effects of its past unlawful conduct."

2. "Microsoft possesses (and for several years has possessed) monopoly power in the market for personal computer operating systems. Microsoft's "Windows" operating systems are used on over 80% of Intel-based PCs, the dominant type of PC in the United States. More than 90% of new Intel-based PCs are shipped with a version of Windows pre-installed. PC manufacturers (often referred to as Original Equipment Manufacturers, or "OEMs") have no commercially reasonable alternative to Microsoft operating systems for the PCs that they distribute."

3. "There are high barriers to entry in the market for PC operating systems. One of the most important barriers to entry is the barrier created by the number of software applications that must run on an operating system in order to make the operating system attractive to end users. Because end users want a large number of applications available, because most applications today are written to run on Windows, and because it would be prohibitively difficult, time-consuming, and expensive to create an alternative operating system that would run the programs that run on Windows, a potential new operating system entrant faces a high barrier to successful entry."

4. "Accordingly, the most significant potential threat to Microsoft's operating system monopoly is not from a direct, frontal assault by existing or new operating systems, but from new software products that may support, or themselves become, alternative "platforms" to which applications can be written, and which can be used in conjunction with multiple operating systems, including but not limited to Windows."

5. "To protect its valuable Windows monopoly against such potential competitive threats, and to extend its operating system monopoly into other software markets, Microsoft has engaged in a series of anticompetitive activities. Microsoft's conduct includes agreements tying other Microsoft software products to Microsoft's

Windows operating system; exclusionary agreements precluding companies from distributing, promoting, buying, or using products of Microsoft's software competitors or potential competitors; and exclusionary agreements restricting the right of companies to provide services or resources to Microsoft's software competitors or potential competitors."

Findings of Fact by Judge Thomas Penfield Jackson, November 5, 1999

Microsoft's Monopoly Power

"33. Microsoft enjoys so much power in the market for Intel-compatible PC operating systems that if it wished to exercise this power solely in terms of price, it could charge a price for Windows substantially above that which could be charged in a competitive market. Moreover, it could do so for a significant period of time without losing an unacceptable amount of business to competitors. In other words, Microsoft enjoys monopoly power in the relevant market.

"34. Viewed together, three main facts indicate that Microsoft enjoys monopoly power. First, Microsoft's share of the market for Intel-compatible PC operating systems is extremely large and stable. Second, Microsoft's dominant market share is protected by a high barrier to entry. Third, and largely as a result of that barrier, Microsoft's customers lack a commercially viable alternative to Windows.

Microsoft's Harm to Consumers

"408. The debut of Internet Explorer and its rapid improvement gave Netscape an incentive to improve Navigator's quality at a competitive rate. The inclusion of Internet Explorer with Windows at no separate charge increased general familiarity with the Internet and reduced the cost to the public of gaining access to it, at least in part because it compelled Netscape to stop charging for Navigator. These actions thus contributed to improving the quality of Web browsing software, lowering its cost, and increasing its availability, thereby benefiting consumers.

"409. To the detriment of consumers, however, Microsoft has done much more than develop innovative browsing software of commendable quality and offer it bundled with Windows at no additional charge. As has been shown, Microsoft also engaged in a concerted series of actions designed to protect the applications barrier to entry, and hence its monopoly power, from a variety of middleware threats, including Netscape's Web browser and Sun's implementation of Java. Many of these actions have harmed consumers in ways that are immediate and easily discernible. They have also caused less direct, but nevertheless serious and far-reaching, consumer harm by distorting competition.

"410. By refusing to offer those OEMs who requested it a version of Windows without Web browsing software, and by preventing OEMs from removing Internet Explorer — or even the most obvious means of invoking it — prior to shipment, Microsoft forced OEMs to ignore consumer demand for a browserless version of Windows. The same actions forced OEMs either to ignore consumer preferences for Navigator or to give them a Hobson's choice of both browser products at the cost of increased confusion, degraded system performance, and restricted memory. By ensuring that Internet Explorer would launch in certain circumstances in Windows 98 even if Navigator were set as the default, and even if the consumer had removed all conspicuous means of invoking Internet Explorer, Microsoft created confusion and frustration for consumers, and increased technical support costs for business customers. Those Windows purchasers who did not want browsing software — businesses, or parents and teachers, for example, concerned with the potential for irresponsible Web browsing on PC systems — not only had to undertake the effort necessary to remove the visible means of invoking Internet Explorer and then contend with the fact that Internet Explorer would nevertheless launch in certain cases; they also had to (assuming they needed new, non-browsing features not available in earlier versions of Windows) content themselves with a PC system that ran slower and provided less available memory than if the newest version of Windows came without browsing software.

"By constraining the freedom of OEMs to implement certain software programs in the Windows boot sequence, Microsoft foreclosed an opportunity for OEMs to make Windows PC systems less confusing and more user-friendly, as consumers desired. By taking the actions listed above, and by enticing firms into exclusivity arrangements with valuable inducements that only Microsoft could offer and that the firms reasonably believed they could not do without, Microsoft forced those consumers who otherwise would have elected Navigator as their browser to either pay a substantial price (in the forms of downloading, installation, confusion, degraded system performance, and diminished memory capacity) or content themselves with Internet Explorer.

"Finally, by pressuring Intel to drop the development of platform-level NSP software, and otherwise to cut back on its software development efforts, Microsoft deprived consumers of software innovation that they very well may have found valuable, had the innovation been allowed to reach the marketplace. None of these actions had pro-competitive justifications.

"411. Many of the tactics that Microsoft has employed have also harmed consumers indirectly by unjustifiably distorting competition. The actions that Microsoft took against Navigator hobbled a form of innovation that had shown the potential to depress the applications barrier to entry sufficiently to enable other firms to compete effectively against Microsoft in the market for Intel-compatible PC operating systems. That competition would have conduced to consumer choice and nurtured innovation. The campaign against Navigator also retarded widespread acceptance of Sun's Java implementation.

"This campaign, together with actions that Microsoft took with the sole purpose of making it difficult for developers to write Java applications with technologies that would allow them to be ported between Windows and other platforms, impeded another form of innovation that bore the potential to diminish the applications barrier to entry. There is insufficient evidence to find that, absent Microsoft's actions, Navigator and Java already would have ignited genuine competition in the market for Intel-compatible PC operating systems. It is clear, however, that Microsoft has retarded, and perhaps altogether extinguished, the process by which these two middleware technologies could have facilitated the introduction of competition into an important market.

"412. Most harmful of all is the message that Microsoft's actions have conveyed to every enterprise with the potential to innovate in the computer industry. Through its conduct toward Netscape, IBM, Compaq, Intel, and others, Microsoft has demonstrated that it will use its prodigious market power and immense profits to harm any firm that insists on pursuing initiatives that could intensify competition against one of Microsoft's core products. Microsoft's past success in hurting such companies and stifling innovation deters investment in technologies and businesses that exhibit the potential to threaten Microsoft. The ultimate result is that some innovations that would truly benefit consumers never occur for the sole reason that they do not coincide with Microsoft's self-interest."

Disposition of the Case

At this writing, Judge Jackson has received the government's proposed Conclusions of Law and has appointed Judge Richard Posner to mediate settlement talks between the Justice Department and Microsoft. If a settlement is not reached, the judge will receive Microsoft's view of what the Conclusions of Law should be by the end of January 2000. The judge will thereafter draw up his own Conclusions of Law, which will amount to a verdict. The case can then be appealed.

NOTES

PREFACE

xii **Even deny Microsoft the right . . .** : Ashley Dunn, "Sun's CEO Urges 'Chain Saw' for Microsoft," *Los Angeles Times*, November 19, 1999, p. C4.

xii **What these critics seem to want . . .** : See Mike France, "Does a Breakup Make Sense?," *Business Week*, November 22, 1999, pp. 38–41.

1 FROM RAILWAY TIME TO INTERNET TIME

2 **The antitrust suit that the Department of Justice . . .** : United States v. Microsoft Corporation, First District Court, civil action no. 98–1232, Thomas Penfield Jackson, Findings of Fact, November 5, 1999.

5 **In a real sense goods . . .** : Tom Peters, *Tom Peters Seminar: Crazy Times Call for Crazy Organizations* (New York: Vintage Books, 1994), p. 13.

6 **The nature of capital has changed . . .** : See Richard B. McKenzie and Dwight R. Lee, *Quicksilver Capital: How the Rapid Movement of Wealth Has Changed the World* (New York: Free Press, 1991); and Richard B. McKenzie, *The Paradox of Progress: Can Americans Regain Their Confidence in a Prosperous Future?* (New York: Oxford University Press, 1997).

6 **Over the past hundred years . . .** : See McKenzie and Lee, *Quicksilver Capital.*

6 **In this new economic universe . . .** : George Gilder, *Microcosm: The Quantum Revolution in Economics and Technology* (New York: Simon and Schuster, 1989), p. 63.

8 **The company is also . . .** : For a survey of what Microsoft does and how it operates, see Michael A. Cusumano and Richard W. Selby, *Microsoft Secrets: How the World's Most Powerful Software Company Creates Technology, Shapes Markets, and Manages People* (New York: Free Press, 1995).

9   ... the lawyers in the Antitrust Division ... : The state attorneys general who are participating in the Justice Department's antitrust suit are Dan Lungren, California; Richard Blumenthal, Connecticut; Bob Butterworth, Florida; Jim Ryan, Illinois; Tom Miller, Iowa; Carla Stovall, Kansas; Frank Kelley, Michigan; Mike Easley, North Carolina; Betty D. Montgomery, Ohio; Jan Graham, Utah; James Doyle, Wisconsin; Ben Chandler, Kentucky; Richard Ieyoub, Louisiana; Tom Reilly, Massachusetts; Carrell V. McGraw, West Virginia; J. Joseph Curran, Jr., Maryland; Mike Hatch, Minnesota; and Dennis Vacco, New York.

9   **They see Microsoft ...** : United States v. Microsoft, Jackson, Findings of Fact; ibid., Joel I. Klein *et al.,* Complaint, May 20, 1998, p. 4.

9   **It is interesting to note ...** : Both types of characterizations are used together freely by many reporters and commentators, including Bruce Headlam, "What's Funny at Microsoft? Blocking Netscape's Web Site," *New York Times,* April 8, 1999, p. C3.

9   **The 30 million–plus lines of code ...** : Those programmers even had a substantial effect on both the Justice Department's case and the writing and editing of this book, mainly because both in-house Justice Department lawyers and I do our work on personal computers running some version of Windows, although the Justice Department in-house lawyers apparently use WordPerfect, whereas I use Word.

10   **After IBM and Microsoft parted ...** : William F. Zachmann, "Blue Believer: Why I Still Think OS/2 Is a Winner," *PC Magazine,* February 25, 1992, p. 107.

10   **In its fiscal year ending ...** : David Bank, "Microsoft Profit Jumped in Quarter," *Wall Street Journal,* April 21, 1999, p. A3.

11   **In 1999 ...** : Available at Microsoft Web site, December 5, 1999: www.microsoft.com/presspass/fastfacts.htm.

11   **As Microsoft's legal ...** : Tony Jackson, "World's Most Respected Companies, GE, Microsoft Top Survey of Most Admired Businesses," *Financial Times* (U.S.A. edition), November 30, 1998.

11   **In early 1999 ...** : Eryn Brown and Len A. Costa, "America's Most Admired Companies: We Tell You Why the Two New Companies in the Top Ten, Dell and Wal-Mart, Are Just Alike—Sort Of," *Fortune,* March 1, 1999, p. 68.

12   **Its *Fortune* ranking ...** : Bank, "Microsoft Profit Jumped in Quarter," p. A6.

12   **In the fall of 1999 ...** : Jake Kirchner, "100 Most Influential Companies," *PC Magazine,* October 19, 1999, pp. 94–132.

12   **In November 1999, the publicity ...** : Ronald Alsop, "The Best Reputations in High Tech," *Wall Street Journal,* November 18, 1999, p. B1.

12   **It should be little wonder that ...** : In announcing the award, the editors of *PC Magazine UK* wrote, "Since we started our awards for Technical Innovation back in 1992, one company has consistently had its products and technologies nominated. In eight years, Microsoft has had 48 products as finalists and has won 14 Technical Innovation Awards, including two Product of the Year awards (Windows 3.1 and Windows 95). No other company has come close to providing so many innovative and groundbreaking products" ("Technical Innovations Awards, 1999: Millennium Award Winner, Microsoft," *PC Magazine UK,* January 1999).

12   ... **an assault for which ...** : "Quick Takes," *Windows,* March 1999, p. 40.

13 **In early September 1999 . . .** : Verlyn Klinkenborg, "The Man at Microsoft; or How High the Moon," *New York Times*, p. A12.

14 **The Justice Department's spin . . .** : See John R. Wilke, "Browser-Beaten: As Microsoft Struggles with Antitrust Case, Tactical Errors Emerge," *Wall Street Journal*, February 18, 1999, p. A1.

14 **The conclusion . . .** : Klinkenborg, "The Man at Microsoft," p. A12.

15 **If an "incident" is defined . . .** : Joel Brinkley, "If Microsoft Loses Suit, 19 States Plan to Seek a Radical Overhaul," *New York Times*, March 16, 1999, p. C1.

17 **They have written e-mails . . .** : United States v. Microsoft, Klein *et al.*, Complaint, p. 4.

17 **. . . comments that Microsoft . . .** : United States v. Microsoft, Defendant Microsoft Corporation's Answer to the Complaint filed by the U.S. Department of Justice, paragraph 9, Microsoft Web site, November 25, 1999: http://www.microsoft.com/press-pass/doj/7–28answerdoj.htm.

17 **Indeed, one of the founding technicians . . .** : Bob Metcalfe, "From the Ether: Without Case of Vapors, Netscape's Tools Will Give Blackbird Reason to Squawk," *InfoWorld*, September 18, 1995.

17 **Similarly, Netscape chairman Jim Clark . . .** : Michael A. Cusumano and David B. Yoffie, *Competing on Internet Time: Lessons from Netscape and Its Battle with Microsoft* (New York: Free Press, 1998), p. 105.

17 **Scott McNealy, head of Sun Microsystems . . .** : Karen Southwick, *High Noon: The Inside Story of Scott McNealy and the Rise of Sun Microsystems* (New York: John Wiley, 1999), p. 57.

17 **Perhaps it's important . . .** : Daniel Lyons, "Slay Your Rivals," *Forbes*, December 14, 1998, pp. 55.

17 **Microsoft has not been kind . . .** : Leslie Helm, "E-Mails Show Gates, Others Plotting to Thwart OS Rivals," *Los Angeles Times*, April 29, 1999, p. C1,

17 **Similarly, IBM charges that Microsoft . . .** : United States v. Microsoft, Transcript of Proceedings, June 7, 1999 (A.M. session), p. 16.

18 **He explained that Microsoft . . .** : Ibid., pp. 41, 49. Norris also introduced (p. 49) his notes of the meeting in which he had indicated that the Microsoft negotiator was also concerned about IBM competing with them in the browser market. "After we exchanged niceties, the first thing Bengt [a Microsoft negotiator] said was, 'We have a problem if you load Netscape.'" If IBM did not promote Internet Explorer there would be "MDA repercussions," meaning there would be a reduction in the discount Microsoft would give IBM in its "market development agreement," meaning the price of Windows would rise for IBM (ibid., p. 32).

18 **According to Norris . . .** : Ibid., p. 67.

18 **Then, according to Norris . . .** : Ibid., p. 63.

18 **If Norris's recollections . . .** : If the statements are correct, the Justice Department's lead trial attorney on the case, David Boies, was probably correct when he pointed out to reporters on the courthouse steps, "This is some of the most important evidence in the case. It shows Microsoft, once again, going to a competitor and trying to persuade it or pressure it not to compete. This conduct is a clear violation of the antitrust laws."

See Steve Lohr, "I.B.M. Official Has Harsh Words for Microsoft," *New York Times*, June 8, 1999, p. C1.

18   **Norris has acknowledged . . .** : John R. Wilke, "IBM Official Says Microsoft Pressed Firm," *Wall Street Journal*, June 8, 1999, p. A3.

18   **When Baber was asked . . .** : Lohr, "I.B.M. Official Has Harsh Words for Microsoft."

18   **Microsoft introduced documents . . .** : At the close of the court day, June 8, 1999, William Neukom, Microsoft's attorney, stressed at a press conference, "There's nothing in the documents [introduced in court that day] about exclusive promotion of Microsoft's possessive technology." See John R. Wilke, "Microsoft Responds to Allegations That It Employed Pressure Tactics," *Wall Street Journal*, June 9, 1999, p. B6.

19   **As this book went to press . . .** : Steve Lohr, "Plaintiffs' Rift Disturbs Microsoft Judge," *New York Times*, November 24, 1999, p. C2.

20   **The *Wall Street Journal*'s chief . . .** : Walter S. Mossberg, "New Microsoft Browser Adds Some Nice Details for Simpler Use of Web," *Wall Street Journal*, March 18, 1999, p. B1.

21   **His credibility with the press . . .** : United States v. Microsoft, Richard L. Schmalensee, Direct Testimony, January 3, 1999.

21   **Jake Kirchner, a columnist . . .** : Jake Kirchner, "Microsoft Is Bloodied but Still on Its Feet," *PC Magazine*, April 20, 1999, p. 30.

21   **Toward the end of the trial phase . . .** : Joel Brinkley, "Gates' Memo Deals a Blow to Microsoft," *New York Times*, June 25, 1999, p. C4.

21   **Even Microsoft's attorney . . .** : Steve Lohr, "Testimony Over, Microsoft Judge Awaits Motions," *New York Times*, June 25, 1999, p. A1.

22   **The proposed remedies would . . .** : John R. Wilke, "Microsoft Peers Urge Restructuring If Firm Loses Trial," *Wall Street Journal*, March 3, 1999, p. B8.

22   **Even Microsoft feels compelled . . .** : Bill Gates, *Business @ the Speed of Thought: Using a Digital Nervous System* (New York: Warner Books, 1999), p. 182.

24   **The *PC Magazine* columnist Jake Kirchner . . .** : Kirchner, "Microsoft Is Bloodied but Still on Its Feet," p. 30.

24   **And it should be noted . . .** : "U.S. Department of Microsoft," editorial, *Wall Street Journal*, November 8, 1999, p. A50.

2   MONOPOLY MANTRA

27   **U.S. Attorney General . . .** : These remarks were made by Attorney General Janet Reno at a press conference she held to explain her request that a federal judge impose a fine of $1 million a day on Microsoft for as long as Microsoft requires computer manufacturers to bundle Internet Explorer with Windows 95. The Justice Department lost. See "Pipeline," *PC Magazine*, December 16, 1997, p. 9.

27   **According to the attorney general . . .** : Ibid.

28   ***New York Times* columnist . . .** : Maureen Dowd, "Liberties: Revenge of the Nerds," *New York Times*, January 21, 1998, p. A17.

28   **Gary Reback, a Silicon Valley . . .** : Ibid. Early this century, the American Banana Company complained that its leading rival, United Fruit, had undertaken a variety of

anticompetitive acts, including blowing up some of American Banana's Central American facilities, in order to preserve its domination of the banana export business. See American Banana Co. v. United Fruit Co., 213 US 347 (1909).

28   **No wonder Jacob Weisberg . . .** : Quoted in Dowd, "Liberties: Revenge of the Nerds."

28   **He declared in the *Los Angeles Times* . . .** : Bob Dole, "Microsoft Must Obey the Law," *Los Angeles Times*, November 24, 1997, p. B9.

29   **The *Wall Street Journal* reporter . . .** : Alan Murray, "It's Time Gates Placed Trust in Trustbusters," *Wall Street Journal*, March 9, 1998, p. A1. Murray adds, "The most important question being debated in Washington now isn't whether Microsoft is a monopoly, or even whether it stifles some competition. It is whether the government can do anything about it without causing more harm than good."

29   **New York Attorney General Dennis Vacco . . .** : Quoted in David Bank, "Subpoenas Issued in Probe of Microsoft," *Wall Street Journal*, February 3, 1998, p. A3.

29   **Clearly, if Microsoft has become . . .** : United States v. Microsoft Corporation, U.S. District Court, civil action no. 98–1232, Joel I. Klein *et al.*, Complaint, May 20, 1998, p. 19, at Department of Justice Web site: www.usdoj.gov/atr/cases/micros/1763.htm.

29   **. . . and Judge Jackson concurred . . .** : Ibid., Thomas Penfield Jackson, Findings of Fact, November 5, 1999, p. 21.

29   **Because, according to the Justice Department . . .** : Ibid., p. 20.

29   **The Gateway executive John Von Holle . . .** : Ibid., p. 20.

29   **In the rebuttal phase . . .** : Ibid., Transcript of Proceedings before the Honorable Thomas P. Jackson, June 1, 1999 (A.M. session), p. 9. See also Patrick Thibodeau, "Microsoft Trial Resumes, Economist Retakes Stand," *InfoWorld Electric*, June 1, 1999, at: http://cnnfn.com/digitaljam/9906/01/microsoft/.

29   **Similarly, the former judge Robert Bork . . .** : Robert H. Bork, "The Case Against Microsoft," downloaded from ProComp's Web site, July 12, 1999, p. 2: http://www.pro-competition.org/research/bork.html.

30   **Fisher explains the tie . . .** : United States v. Microsoft, Franklin M. Fisher, Direct Testimony, filed October 14, 1998, p. 10, at Department of Justice Web site: http://www.usdoj.gov/atr/cases/f2000/2057.pdf.

30   **Fisher believes . . .** : Ibid., p. 10.

30   **. . . which he equates with . . .** : Ibid., p. 12.

30   **He then suggests . . .** : Ibid., p. 14.

30   **Fisher points out . . .** : Ibid., pp. 15–16.

30   **Hence, "Microsoft possesses . . . ":** Ibid., p. 22.

30   **Like the Justice Department . . .** : Ibid., pp. 22–25.30 **However, Warren-Boulton . . .** : State of New York *ex rel.* Attorney General Dennis C. Vacco *et al.* v. Microsoft Corporation, civil action no. 98–1233 (TPJ), Frederick R. Warren-Boulton, Direct Testimony, p. 16, at Department of Justice Web site: http://www.usdoj.gov/atr/cases/f2000/2079.htm.

30   **Moreover, he adds that . . .** : Ibid., p. 17.

31   **This implies, he maintains . . .** : Ibid.

31   **This is because the monopolist . . .** : For example, suppose that the price of a product is raised by nearly 24 percent, from $89 to $110. If the quantity sold decreases by only 5 percent, from 1 million copies sold to 950,000, then total revenues would rise from

$89 million ($89 times 1 million copies) to $104.5 million ($110 times 950,000 copies). Revenues would rise by 17.4 percent.

31   **The reduction in sales would . . .** : Actually, a monopolist would tend to continue to raise its price into the elastic range, in spite of falling revenues. This is because initially costs would likely fall by more than revenues. The monopolist would only stop raising its price when the drop in revenues was greater than the drop in costs, at which point its profits would be falling.

31   **Second, by describing the price . . .** : Another way of saying the same thing is that as a firm moves up its demand curve, its elasticity coefficient tends to rise. It follows that the lower the coefficient, the further down the demand curve the firm is, meaning the lower its price must be.

32   **Indeed, Judge Richard Posner . . .** : Richard A. Posner, *Antitrust Law: An Economic Perspective* (Chicago: University of Chicago Press, 1976), p. 69.

32   **Warren-Boulton admits that . . .** : Warren-Boulton testified, "The evidence I have seen supports the inference that Microsoft took exclusionary actions and incurred costs without regard to whether its actions were profit-maximizing—or even profitable—absent the future revenue gains from weakening rival browsers and thereby preserving its Windows operating system monopoly and from gaining monopoly power in the browser market. Instead Microsoft viewed winning browser share at almost any cost as being of overwhelming strategic importance. Accordingly, on the basis of the available evidence, I conclude that Microsoft's conduct, in the aggregate, was not expected to be profitable except for the market power Microsoft expected to gain from the exclusion of browser rivals and therefore was predatory" (United States v. Microsoft, Warren-Boulton, Direct Testimony, pp. 84–85).

33   **Like his colleague Fisher . . .** : Warren-Boulton reasons, "The first step in determining whether a firm has monopoly power is usually to determine the level and stability of its share of the relevant market. According to Microsoft's figures, 80.8 percent out of the estimated 209.2 million PCs shipped worldwide since July of 1995 include a Microsoft operating system. During this period, naked PCs, e.g., PCs shipped without any operating system at all, accounted for 31.5 million units, or 15 percent of the total PCs shipped. In other words, of the PCs shipped with an operating system, Microsoft's share was 95.1 percent. This high market share has been remarkably stable. As shown in Pl. Ex. 1, Microsoft's share of PCs shipped with an operating system has been above 90 percent since at least the early 1990s and this dominance is forecast through at least 2001" (ibid., p. 20). Judge Jackson repeats the conclusion about Microsoft's market dominance this way: "Every year for the last decade, Microsoft's share of the market for Intel-compatible PC operating systems has stood above ninety percent. For the last couple of years the figure has been at least ninety-five percent, and analysts project that the share will climb even higher over the next few years" (United States v. Microsoft, Jackson, Findings of Fact, p. 13).

33   **Fisher refers to the government's . . .** : The Justice Department's exhibit 1 can be found at http://www.usdoj.gov/atr/cases/exhibits/1.pdf.

34   **It's true that basic microeconomics . . .** : More precisely, textbooks tend to define a monopoly as a market structure that is a single producer that produces a product that

has no close available substitute made by another producer in that market and that is protected by barriers to entry.

36 **The government gives no evidence . . .** : Friedrich Hayek made this point at various times throughout his long and illustrious career. See one of his more important articles, F. A. Hayek, "The Use of Knowledge in Society," *American Economic Review* 35, no. 4 (September 1945): 519–530.

36 **Judge Jackson tries . . .** : United States v. Microsoft, Jackson, Findings of Fact, p. 24.

36 **Microsoft's average revenue . . .** : As computed by Chris E. Hall and Robert E. Hall, "National Policy on Microsoft: A Neutral Perspective," available at the Web site: http://www.NetEcon.com.

36 **Indeed, one of the government's . . .** : Ibid., p. 17.

37 **Second, Judge Bork suggests . . .** : Bork, "The Case Against Microsoft," p. 2.

37 **Even Judge Bork argues . . .** : Robert H. Bork, *The Antitrust Paradox: A Policy at War with Itself* (New York: Free Press, 1978), p. 181.

38 **This, says the Justice Department . . .** : Ibid., p. 21.

38 **These costs can translate . . .** : United States v. Microsoft, Jackson, Findings of Fact, pp. 54–55.

41 **The price of Microsoft's Excel . . .** : The history of Microsoft's prices compared with those of its major competitors is covered in detail by Stan J. Liebowitz and Stephen E. Margolis, *Winners, Losers, and Microsoft: How Technology Markets Choose Products* (Oakland, Calif.: Independent Institute, 1999), especially chapters 8 and 9.

44 **One producer—a so-called monopolist . . .** : For an example of the way "natural monopoly" is taught in economics courses, see Edgar K. Browning and Mark A. Zupan, *Microeconomics, Theory and Practice*, 5th ed. (New York: HarperCollins, 1996), pp. 437–443.

44 **There is every reason to believe . . .** : After scoffing on June 1 at the argument of Microsoft's economist, Richard Schmalensee, that Microsoft was not a monopoly and calling his analysis "peculiar," "ridiculous," and "credulous," the government's economist Franklin Fisher had to concede the next day that Microsoft did face competitive threats. Microsoft lawyers produced an AOL document, called "The Strategic Rationale: The Plan," which lays out the plan for the AOL-Netscape merger: "to be a more comprehensive desktop application . . . with the goal of becoming users' *de facto* [computing] environment." See Joel Brinkley, "After Three-Month Recess, Microsoft Trial Resumes," *New York Times*, June 2, 1999, p. C2, and Jube Schiver, Jr., "U.S. Antitrust Witness' View Challenged," *Los Angeles Times*, June 3, 1999, p. C3.

45 **Supposedly, other firms can't compete . . .** : United States v. Microsoft, Jackson, Findings of Fact, p. 12.

45 **First, a "few years" . . .** : Ibid., p. 15.

46 **Finally, economists have long . . .** : For an extensive critique of the natural monopoly theory, see the early work of one of the country's leading law and economic experts and jurists, Richard A. Posner, *Natural Monopoly and Its Regulation* (Washington, D.C.: Cato Institute, 1999; first published in 1969).

47 **In his classic treatise . . .** : Harold Demsetz, "Why Regulate Utilities," *Journal of Law and Economics* 55 (1968), cited in Bork, *The Antitrust Paradox*, p. 180.

47 **Bork was also right . . .** : Bork, *The Antitrust Paradox*, p. 181.

47   And Bork was right on target . . . : Ibid., p. 178.

47   Instead, the government's case . . . : United States v. Microsoft, Jackson, Findings of
      Fact, p. 13.

3   Little Linux

49   It is, according to Clark . . . : Jim Clark with Owen Edwards, *Netscape Time: The Mak-
      ing of a Billion-Dollar Start-up That Took On Microsoft* (New York: St. Martin's Press,
      1999), p. 156.

50   But never mind, the trial judge . . . : United States v. Microsoft Corporation, U.S. Dis-
      trict Court, civil action no. 98–1232, Thomas Penfield Jackson, Findings of Fact, No-
      vember 5, 1999, pp. 8, 11, 12, 13, 21, 23, and 24.

50   Even a year later . . . : United States v. Microsoft, June 1, 1999, pp. 13–14.

51   As late as November 1999 . . . : Ibid., Jackson, Findings of Fact, p. 21.

51   Linus Torvalds, the original . . . : Steve Hamm et al., "Microsoft, How Vulnerable?"
      Business Week, February 22, 1999, p. 60.

51   The International Data Corporation . . . : At International Data Corporation Web
      site: http://www.idc.com/Data/Software/default.htm.

51   By mid-1999, users . . . : At Red Hat's Web site: http://www.redhat.com/
      corp/about_facts.html.

51   Germany's Star Division . . . : Stephen H. Wildstrom, "Watch Yourself, Microsoft,"
      Business Week, July 12, 1999, p. 18.

51   One of the factors . . . : Ashley Dunn, "Linux Gets Past Front Door," *Los Angeles
      Times*, September 16, 1999, p. B1.

52   According to speed tests . . . : Speed tests also gave NT a similar edge on computer
      servers with four microprocessors communicating with desktop computers running
      Windows 95, according to International Data Corporation, which tracks worldwide
      sales in the computer and software industries. Lee Gomes, "Upstart Linux Draws a
      Microsoft Attack Team," *Wall Street Journal*, May 21, 1999, p. B1.

52   This turnaround in Linux's . . . : Wildstrom, "Watch Yourself, Microsoft."

52   Instead, the judge kept his head buried . . . : United States v. Microsoft, Jackson,
      Findings of Fact, p. 25.

53   But the really interesting story . . . : Lee Gomes, "You Just Can't Beat This Price: Be-
      yond Linux, Free Systems Help Build the Web," *Wall Street Journal*, September 10,
      1999, p. B1.

53   After all the evidence . . . : Steve Lohr, "As Testimony Ends, Microsoft's Judge Waits
      for Motions," *New York Times*, June 25, 1999, p. 1.

54   By the time this book . . . : Walter S. Mossberg, "Using a PC Got Harder in 1999, but a
      New Age Is About to Dawn," *Wall Street Journal*, October 28, 1999, p. B1.

55   "Well, let's look at the facts" . . . : Holman W. Jenkins, Jr., "What We Learned in the
      Microsoft Trial," *Wall Street Journal*, June 30, 1999, p. A27.

55   "We added in Netscape" . . . : Ibid.

000   McNealy's intent . . . : John Markoff, "Sun to Introduce an Even More Basic Network
      Computer Today," *New York Times*, September 8, 1999, p. C6.

55   According to Mark Templeton . . . : Don Clark, "Citrix Helps Lead Drive to Rent Software," *Wall Street Journal*, September 9, 1999, p. B8.

56   The efforts of such as McNealy . . . : John R. Wilke, Gary McWilliams, and David Bank, "PPC Makers to Launch 'Window-Less' Products," *Wall Street Journal*, October 28, 1999, p. B6.

56   The *Wall Street Journal*'s legal columnist, Holman Jenkins . . . : Jenkins, "What We Learned in the Microsoft Trial."

57   Should Gates be miffed . . . : Donald J. Boudreaux and Burton W. Folsom, "Microsoft and Standard Oil: Radical Lessons for Antitrust Reform," working paper (New York: Mackinac Center for Public Policy, 1999), p. 4. For more on the myths of the robber barons and other problems in the history of antitrust, see also John S. McGee, "Predatory Price Cutting: The Standard Oil (N.J.) Case," *Journal of Law and Economics* 1 (1958): 137–169; Dominick T. Armentano, *The Myths of Antitrust* (New Rochelle, N.Y.: Arlington House, 1972); and Burtom W. Folsom, Jr., *The Myth of the Robber Barons* (New York: Young American Foundation, 1993).

58   "We had vision," Rockefeller later said: Boudreaux and Folsom, "Microsoft and Standard Oil," p. 6; Allan Nivens, *Study in Power: John D. Rockefeller,* vol. 1 (New York: Scribner, 1959), p. 666, quoted in Boudreaux and Folsom, "Microsoft and Standard Oil."

58   Boudreaux and Folsom cite . . . : Ibid., p. 7.

58   When Rockefeller refused . . . : Ibid., p. 8.

58   The Justice Department, court . . . : See Robert P. Merges, "Who Owns the Charles River Bridge? Intellectual Property and Competition in the Software Industry," unplublished paper, presented at "Competition and Innovation in the Personal Computer Industry," Carlsbad, California, April 24, 1999.

63   The University of Chicago professor of law and economics . . . : Ronald H. Coase, "Durability and Monopoly," *Journal of Law and Economics* 15 (April 1972): 143–149.

64   "In a competitive market," . . . : United States v. Microsoft, Jackson, Findings of Fact, p. 24.

64   As the Hudson Institute economist . . . : Alan Reynolds, "US vs Microsoft: The Monopoly Myth," *Wall Street Journal*, April 9, 1999, p. A12.

65   As Reynolds observes . . . : Ibid.

65   Microsoft Windows CE, a stripped-down . . . : Ibid.

65   The projections for Microsoft's market share . . . : Ibid.

65   He concludes, "Exhibit One . . . " : Ibid.

4   DIGITAL PREDATION

68   The economics professor Stan Liebowitz . . . : Stan Liebowitz, "U.S. v. Microsoft: Bill Gates' Secret? Build Better Products," *Wall Street Journal*, October 10, 1998, p. 10. See also Stan J. Liebowitz and Stephen E. Margolis, *Winners, Losers, and Microsoft: How Technology Markets Choose Products* (Oakland, Calif.: Independent Institute, 1999), in which the studies in the column are discussed at length.

68   Liebowitz and Margolis also found . . . : Ibid.

69   **Microsoft's application prices . . . :** Ibid.

69   **But when Microsoft's Word began . . . :** Ibid.

69   **Internet Explorer's improved performance . . . :** State of New York *ex rel.* Attorney
      General Dennis C. Vacco *et al.* v. Microsoft Corporation, U.S. District Court, civil ac-
      tion no. 98–1233, Richard L. Schmalensee, Direct Testimony, pp. E–15, exhibit 4, and
      p. 132.

69   **These facts were presented in court . . . :** Ibid. This information comes from the re-
      search of Richard Schmalensee, the MIT economics professor who also serves as Mi-
      crosoft's economics expert at the trial, and was part of his direct trial testimony. This
      testimony has never been disputed by anyone, not even the government's lawyers, and
      it can be verified by anyone.

69   **In early 1999, the chief technology columnist . . . :** Walter S. Mossberg, "New Mi-
      crosoft Browser Adds Some Nice Details for Simpler Use of Web," *Wall Street Journal*,
      March 18, 1999, p. B1.

69   **Similarly, the *New York Times* . . . :** Peter H. Lewis, "Listen to This Browser," *New York
      Times*, March 18, 1999, p. D1; and Matt Richtel, "Slimmer Version of Browser Is Rolled
      Out," *New York Times*, March 19, 1999, p. C2. Interestingly, Microsoft stands accused
      of illegally integrating its browser with Windows. With Internet Explorer 5.0, it is inte-
      grating radio capabilities, supplanting many Windows users' need for a radio card and
      program, which were once sold separately by other vendors.

70   **Even though Judge Jackson accepted . . . :** Judge Thomas Jackson put his question to
      Edward Felten this way: "It seems self-evident to me, but maybe it's not, that the pres-
      ence of a browser increases the risks of penetration by a virus or something like that"
      (United States v. Microsoft, U.S. District Court, civil action no. 98–1232, Transcript of
      Proceedings, June 10, 1999 [A.M. session], p. 39).

70   **Felten responded by noting . . . :** Ibid., p. 40.

71   **The Microsoft legal team showed the court . . . :** For his demonstration, the Mi-
      crosoft attorney brought to court a laptop computer that he had bought that morning
      at a local computer store and was still in its original box, which had not been opened
      outside of court. The Microsoft attorney asked Professor Felten to run his browser-
      removal program and then had him make a few clicks of the mouse that eventually
      opened Internet Explorer (ibid. [P.M. session], p. 27ff.).

73   **At the close of the century . . . :** Frank J. Derfler, Jr., "Future Technology: Networking
      Will Be Ubiquitous," *PC Magazine*, June 22, 1999, p. 114.

73   **Okay, the judge is right . . . :** United States v. Microsoft, Thomas Penfield Jackson,
      Findings of Fact, November 5, 1999, pp. 56 and 57.

75   **"It is not possible with . . . " :** Ibid., p. 33.

75   **In other words . . . :** United States v. Microsoft, Transcript of Proceedings, June 1,
      1999 (A.M. session), p. 39. See also Patrick Thibodeau, "Microsoft Trial Resumes,
      Economist Retakes Stand," *InfoWorld Electric*, June 1, 1999, at: http://cmnfn.com/digi-
      taljam/9906/microsoft.

76   **The Justice Department economic consultant . . . :** Vacco *et al.* v. Microsoft, civil ac-
      tion no. 98-1233, Franklin M. Fisher, Direct Testimony, p. 15, at: http://www.usdoj.
      gov/atr/cases/f2000/2057.pdf.

77   **In networks, just the opposite . . .** : See Kevin Kelly, *New Rules for the New Economy* (New York: Viking/Penguin Group, 1998), chapter 3.

79   **This discussion might have . . .** : David S. Evans, Albert Nichols, and Bernard Reddy, "The Rise and Fall of Leaders in Personal Computer Software," report (Cambridge, Mass.: National Economic Research Associates, January 7, 1999), p. 4.

79   **At that time, 90 percent . . .** : Ibid.

79   **CP/M's market dominance . . .** : Ibid.

79   **"It's only through volume . . . "**: Charles Wright, "Bill's World," *Australian Financial Review,* November 24, 1995, p. 1.

79   **Gates advised Sculley . . .** : Memorandum from Bill Gates and Jeff Raikes to John Sculley and Jean Louis Gassee, "Apple Licensing of Mac Technology," June 25, 1985; and letter from Bill Gates to John Sculley, July 29, 1995.

80   **Gates took his own advice . . .** : See, for example, Virginia I. Postrel, "Creative Insecurity: The Complicated Truth Behind the Rise of Microsoft," *Reason,* January 1998, p. 4ff.

81   **By pricing low . . .** : United States v. Microsoft, Jackson, Findings of Fact, November 5, 1999, pp. 33–34.

5 DIGITAL SWITCHING

84   **Assistant Attorney General Joel Klein introduced . . .** : United States v. Microsoft Corporation, U.S. District Court, civil action no. 98-1232, Joel I. Klein *et al.*, Complaint, May 20, 1998, p. 38, at: http://www.usdoj.gov/atr/cases3/1763.htm.

84   **"Where network effects are present . . . "**: State of New York *ex rel.* Attorney General Dennis C. Vacco *et al.* v. Microsoft Corporation, U.S. District Court, civil action no. 98–1233, Franklin M. Fisher, Direct Testimony, filed October 14, 1998, pp. 15–16, at: http://www.usdoj.gov/atr/cases/f2000/2057.pdf.

84   **"As a result of scale . . . "**: Ibid., p. 27.

84   **. . . further, Microsoft is protected . . .** : United States v. Microsoft, Thomas Penfield Jackson, Findings of Fact, November 5, 1999, p. 15.

84   **" 'Network' effects, in which . . . "**: "Lessons from Microsoft," *The Economist,* March 6, 1999, p. 21.

86   **Frederick Warren-Boulton, the lead economist . . .** : Vacco *et al.* v. Microsoft, Frederick R. Warren-Boulton, Direct Testimony, p. 21, at: http://www.usdoj.gov/atr/cases/f2000/2079.htm. Warren-Boulton adds, "Often, switching operating systems also means replacing or modifying hardware. Businesses can face even greater switching costs, as they must integrate PCs using the new operating systems and application software within their PC networks and train their employees to use the new software. Accordingly, both personal and corporate consumers are extremely reluctant to change PC operating systems" (ibid., p. 22).

86   **Fisher concedes . . .** : Vacco *et al.* v. Microsoft, Fisher, Direct Testimony, p. 16.

87   **The Justice Department argued . . .** : United States v. Microsoft, U.S. Department of Justice, Plaintiff's Joint Proposed Findings of Fact, August 10, 1999, p. 8, at: http://www.usdoj.gov/atr/cases/f2600/2613.htm.

87   **Indeed, at the time . . .** : Benjamin Klein, "Microsoft's Use of Zero Price Bundling to
       Fight the 'Browser Wars,' " in *Competition, Innovation and the Microsoft Monopoly:
       Antitrust in the Digital Marketplace*, proceedings of a conference held by the Progress
       and Freedom Foundation in Washington, D.C., February 5, 1998 (Boston: Kluwer
       Academic Publishers, 1999), pp. 217–254.

87   **Indeed, at the time it wrote . . .** : This line of argument is supported by two articles
       that appear to have little to do with network effects, but are very much related. Dwight
       Lee and David Kreutzer explain how the long-run elasticity of demands for goods
       with "lagged demands" is much higher than the elasticity of the short-run demand
       ("Lagged Demands and a 'Perverse' Response to Threatened Property Rights," *Eco-
       nomic Inquiry* 20 [October 1982]: 579–588). Gary Becker and Kevin Murphy develop
       a theory of "rational addiction," which is grounded in the proposition that the de-
       mand for "addictive goods" (drugs, for example) may be highly "inelastic" ("A Theory
       of Rational Addiction," *Journal of Political Economy* 96, no. 4 [August 1988]: 675–700).
       However, because the consumption of addictive goods in the future is very much re-
       lated to how much is currently consumed, the long-run elasticity of demand for ad-
       dictive goods must be highly elastic, because, as with network goods, the consumption
       of addictive goods builds on itself. Hence, a price reduction for an addictive good
       might lead to few addiction sales in the short run. However, the response can be quite
       substantial over the long run as the addiction builds. Both papers explain why drug
       dealers and cigarette companies often give away their products to first-time users and
       why the elasticity of demand for "lagged demand goods" and "addictive goods" should
       be much higher than the short-run elasticity of demand, and maybe much higher
       than other more "normal" goods that don't have the "lagged" or "addictive" attributes.
       Becker and Murphy did indeed find that the long-run demand for cigarettes is "elas-
       tic," not "inelastic" as conventionally thought

89   **When Microsoft's market share . . .** : B. Klein, "Microsoft's Use of Zero Price
       Bundling to Fight the 'Browser Wars,' " p. 225.

90   **Some of the benefits generated . . .** : Ibid., pp. 227–230. Klein uses this line of argu-
       ment to explain why Microsoft's business application prices are so much higher than
       the price for Windows, and tend to be higher than their competitors' application
       prices. He notes, "For example, Microsoft Office has a suggested retail price of $499 or
       $599 (for the professional version that includes Access) while Windows 95 has a sug-
       gested retail price of only $209."

90   **Assistant Attorney General Klein . . .** : United States v. Microsoft, Klein *et al.*, Com-
       plaint, p. 6.

90   **Franklin Fisher maintained . . .** : Vacco *et al.* v. Microsoft, Fisher, Direct Testimony, p.
       19.

90   **This conviction led Fisher . . .** : Ibid., p. 7.

91   **Throughout its arguments . . .** : In fact, Microsoft needn't actually be broken up in
       order for prices to be pushed up across the board in software markets. A breakup need
       only be threatened. One of the reasons Microsoft, or any other network firm, will sup-
       press its prices is that the suppressed prices will lead to a growing market dominance
       and gains in the future from the escalating increase in demand. If Microsoft begins to
       fear that its current and/or future dominance will be cause for an antitrust assault and

a future breakup, the expected gains from current suppressed prices will decrease, and Microsoft can be expected to raise its prices. Interestingly, such an antitrust threat can have an effect exactly the opposite from the one expected from antitrust action: prices will rise, not fall. But then again, the price effects of such a threat are exactly what the Justice Department may want. It may be taking the antitrust action to benefit Microsoft's market rivals, not consumers that the Justice Department claims to be protecting with much legal self-righteousness.

92   **Franklin Fisher acknowledges that . . .** : Ibid., p. 16.

92   **This is why, in Fisher's view . . .** : Ibid.

92   **. . . Netscape's Marc Andreesen seemed . . .** : Michael A. Cusumano and David B. Yoffie, *Competing on Internet Time: Lessons from Netscape and Its Battle with Microsoft* (New York: Free Press, 1998), p. 105.

93   **Warren-Boulton was right . . .** : Vacco *et al.* v. Microsoft, Warren-Boulton, Direct Testimony, p. 22.

97   **Phil Lemmons, the editorial director . . .** : Charles Piller, "Gates' Rivals Force Improved Performance," *Los Angeles Times*, April 5, 1999, p. C2.

97   **The Justice Department also argues . . .** : United States v. Microsoft, Klein *et al.*, Complaint, p. 46.

98   **According to economic historian . . .** : Paul A. David. "Clio and the Economics of QWERTY," *American Economic Review* 75 (1985): 332–337.

98   **"The occurrence of this 'lock in' . . . ":** Ibid., pp. 335–336.

98   **According to this view . . .** : Ibid. p. 336.

98   **The legend . . .** : Ibid., p. 332.

98   **Moreover, experiments . . .** : Ibid., p. 332.

98   **The author of the QWERTY story . . .** : Ibid., p. 336.

99   **Even then, Dvorak's own . . .** : Stan J. Liebowitz and Stephen E. Margolis, "The Fable of the Keys," *Journal of Law and Economics* 33 (April): 1–25; reprinted in Stan J. Liebowitz and Stephen E. Margolis, *Winners, Losers, and Microsoft: How Technology Markets Choose Products* (Oakland, Calif.: Independent Institute, 1999), pp. 19–44.

99   **The claimed benefits . . .** : Ibid., p. 37.

100   **Another similar legend . . .** : Stan J. Liebowitz and Stephen E. Margolis, "Path Dependence, Lock-in and History," *Journal of Law, Economics, and Organization* 11 (1995): 205–226.

102   **In the case of network goods . . .** : For the details of the argument, see Lee and Kreutzer, "A Theory of Lagged Demand," and Becker and Murphy, "A Theory of Rational Addiction."

102   **When Frederick Warren-Boulton testified . . .** : Vacco *et al.* v. Microsoft, Warren-Boulton, Direct Testimony, p. 17.

102   **He based his deductions . . .** : Ibid.

102   **This means that . . .** : See Becker and Murphy, "A Theory of Rational Addiction."

103   **The fact of the matter . . .** : As economists have long argued, the greater the elasticity of demand facing a monopolist, the smaller will be the gap between the monopoly and competitive prices. And the lower will be the dead weight or efficiency loss from the monopolist's charging the monopoly price. Hence, network effects that increase

the elasticity of long-run demand lower the inefficiency from the exercise of monopoly power.

103   **Warren-Boulton believes . . .** : Vacco *et al.* v. Microsoft, Warren-Boulton, Direct Testimony, p. 21.

104   **According to the court . . .** : United States v. Microsoft, Jackson, Findings of Fact, p. 50.

105   **The court also includes . . .** : Ibid., p. 55.

105   **The history of antitrust enforcement . . .** : Robert H. Bork, *The Antitrust Paradox: A Policy at War with Itself* (New York: Free Press, 1978).

106   **The court goes on . . .** : Ibid., p. 50.

106   **But then the court . . .** : Ibid., p. 145.

106   **The judge goes on . . .** : Ibid., pp. 50, 121.

106   **Twenty-five hundred Internet . . .** : Ibid., pp. 122–123.

107   **But the judge chides Microsoft . . .** : Ibid., p. 129.

107   **The court also found . . .** : Ibid., pp. 56–65.

107   **Because IBM would not concede . . .** : Ibid, p. 64.

107   **For example, the court finds . . .** : Ibid., p. 22.

108   **According to the *Byte* magazine . . .** : Jerry Pournelle, "Jerry's Take on the Microsoft Decision: Wrong! Decision Neglects Industry History," *Byte,* November 8, 1999, at: http://www.byte.com/column/BYT19991108S0001.

109   **Netscape refused to do this . . .** : United States v. Microsoft, Jackson, Findings of Fact, p. 46.

109   **According to the court . . .** : Ibid., pp. 168–171.

109   **This will be especially true . . .** : Ibid., p. 72.

110   **Many of the other . . .** : Ibid., p. 76.

111   **Another consumer harm . . .** : Ibid.

111   **The court suggests . . .** : Ibid., p. 85.

111   **Imagine if Microsoft . . .** : Ibid., pp. 203 and 204.

6   INNOVATIVE THINKING

115   **The most remarkable characteristic . . .** : W. Michael Cox and Richard Alm, *Myths of Rich and Poor* (New York: Basic Books, 1999), p. 158.

115   **Throughout the last hundred . . .** : Ibid., p. 162, Figure 8.1.

116   **Assistant Attorney General for Antitrust Joel Klein . . .** : United States v. Microsoft Corporation, U.S. District Court, civil action no. 98-1232, Joel I. Klein *et al.,* Complaint, May 20, 1998, p. 12.

116   **In two separate places in his Findings of Fact . . .** : Ibid., Thomas Penfield Jackson, Findings of Fact, November 5, 1999, p 84.

116   **And "Microsoft's past success in hurting . . . "**: Ibid., p. 207.

116   **How does this happen?:** Ibid.

116   **Consequently, he asserts . . .** : Ibid., pp. 12–13.

116   **For example, Thomas Lenard . . .** : Thomas M. Lenard, "Who's Afraid of Microsoft?" in *Progress on Point,* policy paper (Washington, D.C.: Progress and Freedom Foundation, September 1998), p. 4.

116   **Consequently, it is clear to Lenard . . .** : Ibid.

116   **Lenard and many others . . .** : Ibid., p. 7.

117   **At the time the deal was struck . . .** : Bill Alpert, "Plugged In: AOL's Purchase of Netscape Fills a Void by Providing a Yardstick for 'Net Stock Values," *Barron's,* November 30, 1998, p. 49.

118   **According to Jim Clark's story . . .** : Jim Clark with Owen Edwards, *Netscape Time: The Making of the Billion-Dollar Start-up That Took On Microsoft* (New York: St. Martin's Press, 1999), p. 49.

118   **Indeed, Clark says that he . . .** : Ibid., p. 79.

118   **In fact, Clark reports . . .** : Ibid., pp. 232–233.

119   **In addition, by Jim Clark's . . .** : Ibid., p. 83.

121   **Indeed, in one of the very few . . .** : United States v. Microsoft, Jackson, Findings of Fact, p. 142.

121   **Jim Clark worries . . .** : Ibid., p. 243.

122   **Without hesitation Clark adds . . .** : Ibid.

124   **Technical experts have raised . . .** : See Karen Southwick, *High Noon: The Inside Story of Scott McNealy* (New York: John Wiley, 1999), p. 150.

124   **If Navigator-Java were a real improvement . . .** : See "83 Reasons Why Bill Gates's Reign Is Over," *Wired,* December 1998, pp. 194–202, 254.

125   **The writer Karen Southwick reports . . .** : Southwick, *High Noon,* p. 169.

126   **A Netscape executive said . . .** : Ibid.

127   **There is no dearth of data . . .** : Erran Carmel, Jeffrey A. Eisenbach, and Thomas M. Lenard, *The Digital Economy Fact Book* (Washington, D.C.: Progress and Freedom Foundation, 1999).

129   **One of the most frequently repeated . . .** : Clark/O. Edwards, *Netscape Time,* p. 110.

129   **When Microsoft bought the original code . . .** : After buying DOS from Seattle Computer Products in 1980, Microsoft added device independence, relocatable program files, automatic update of memory information about a disk when it is changed, and date and time stamping of disk files. In MS-DOS 2.0, Microsoft added a hierarchical file system and print spooling. In MS-DOS 3.1 and 3.2, the company offered support for IBM's networking hardware and support for three-and-a-half-inch floppy disks. By popularizing the personal computer, Microsoft helped make DOS the operating system of choice for application programmers, thus spurring an explosion of innovation among third-party software developers.

129   **No doubt about it . . .** : Bill Gates, "Internet Strategy Workshop Keynote," internal Microsoft memorandum, December 7, 1995.

130   **For these and other reasons . . .** : "Technical Innovations Awards, 1999: Millennium Award Winner, Microsoft," *PC Magazine UK,* January 1999.

133   **Even with Microsoft's substantial investment . . .** : During its 1999 fiscal year, Microsoft spent 15 percent of its revenues on research and development. By contrast, IBM spent 6 percent, Intel spent 10 percent, and Oracle and Sun spent 12 percent each.

133   The same is true of other high-tech firms . . . : Chris Edwards, *Entrepreneurial Dy-
       namism and the Success of U.S. High Tech* (Washington, D.C.: Joint Economic Com-
       mittee, U.S. Congress, October 1999), p. 18.
134   When Netscape had . . . : Clark/O. Edwards, *Netscape Time*, pp. 232–233.
135   What is interesting . . . : Ibid., p. 110.
135   It appears that . . . : Ibid., pp. 164–165. It should be noted that Clark describes the
       stock offer as a "donation" to the University of Illinois, not as an attempt to negotiate a
       settlement out of the growing legal conflict between the university and Netscape.

7   MUD FARMING

142   Even the venerable Adam Smith . . . : Adam Smith, *Wealth of Nations* (New York:
       Modern Library, 1937), p. 128.
142   Just after Adam Smith . . . : Ibid.
143   The growth in the size . . . : Robert D. Tollison and Charles K. Rowley, eds., *The Polit-
       ical Economy of Rent-Seeking* (Boston: Kluwer Academic Publishers, 1988); Robert B.
       Ekelund and Robert D. Tollison, *Mercantilism As Rent-Seeking Society: Economic Regu-
       lations in Historical Perspective* (College Station, Tex.: Texas A&M University Press,
       1981).
144   Farmers also learned . . . : For a survey of various farm programs and their perverse
       economic consequences for consumers, see Clifton B. Luttrell, *The High Cost of Farm
       Welfare* (Washington, D.C.: Cato Institute, 1989).
144   Similarly, over the years . . . : For surveys of the impact of interest-group politics on
       the regulatory and deregulatory political processes, see Murray L. Weidenbaum, *The
       Future of Business Regulation* (New York: AMACOM, 1980); and Roger G. Noll and
       Bruce M. Owen, *The Political Economy of Deregulation* (Washington, D.C.: American
       Enterprise Institute, 1983).
144   The industry demanders . . . : Regulation as a product of the interaction of interest-
       group demanders of regulations and political suppliers of regulation is developed by
       George J. Stigler, "The Theory of Economic Regulation," *Bell Journal of Economics and
       Management* 2 (1971): 3–21, included in *The Citizen and the State: Essays on Regula-
       tion* (Chicago: University of Chicago Press, 1975). See also Sam Peltzman, "Towards a
       More General Theory of Regulation," *Journal of Law and Economics* 19 (1976):
       211–240. For a discussion of how the interest-group theory of politics applies to an-
       titrust, see William F. Shughart, *Antitrust Policy and Interest Group Politics* (New York:
       Quorum Books, 1990), chapter 2.
145   Meanwhile, the significant economic . . . : One of the better books that explains the
       imbalance in political incentives of the general population and private interest groups
       is Mancur Olson's *The Logic of Collective Action: Public Goods and the Theory of Groups*
       (Cambridge, Mass.: Harvard University Press, 1971). For an explanation of why the
       general public has impaired incentives to even be informed of the harm done by spe-
       cial interest groups, see Gordon Tullock, *Toward a Mathematics of Politics* (Ann Arbor,
       Mich.: University of Michigan Press, 1972).

145   Moreover, the politicians . . . : Fred McChesney, *Money for Nothing: Politicians, Rent Extraction and Political Extortion* (Cambridge, Mass.: Harvard University Press, 1997), p. 3.

145   **Mark Melcher and Stephen Soukup** . . . : Mark L. Melcher and Stephen R. Soukup, "Potomac Perspective: The Man in Cement Shoes," *Investor Weekly* (published by Prudential Securities), July 15, 1998, n.p.

146   **The result is that** . . . : McChesney, *Money for Nothing*, pp. 55–56.

146   **When the Clinton administration** . . . : Neil A. Lewis, "Medical Industry Showers Congress with Lobby Money," *New York Times*, December 13, 1993, p. A1, cited in McChesney, *Money for Nothing*, p. 57.

146   **When in 1986** . . . : Roger Beck, Colin Hoskins, and J. Martin Connolly, "Rent Extraction Through Political Extortion: An Empirical Examination," *Journal of Legal Studies* 21 (1992): pp. 217ff., cited in McChesney, *Money for Nothing*, p. 74.

147   **McChesney concluded** . . . : McChesney, *Money for Nothing*, pp. 77–78.

147   **Even as late as the mid-1980s** . . . : Bruno S. Frey et al., "Consensus and Dissension Among Economists: An Empirical Inquiry," *American Economic Review* 74 (December 1984): 986–994.

147   **Richard Posner, a prominent federal judge** . . . : Richard A. Posner, *Antitrust Law: An Economic Perspective* (Chicago: University of Chicago Press, 1976), p. 4.

147   **The former federal judge Robert Bork** . . . : Robert H. Bork, *The Antitrust Paradox: A Policy at War with Itself* (New York: Basic Books, 1978).

147   **Judge Bork concluded** . . . : Ibid., p. 63.

148   **But Bork quotes approvingly** . . . : Ibid.

148   **A growing number of economic** . . . : William F. Baxter, "The Political Economy of Antitrust," in Robert D. Tollison, ed., *The Political Economy of Antitrust: Principal Papers by William Baxter* (Lexington, Mass.: Lexington Books, 1980), p. 3.

148   **Indeed, this is precisely** . . . : William J. Baumol and Janusz Ordover, "Use of Antitrust to Subvert Competition," *Journal of Law and Economics* 28 (May 1985): 247.

148   **This has been the case** . . . : Harold Demsetz, "Why Regulate Utilities," *Journal of Law and Economics* 55 (1968).

148   **For example, Alcoa Aluminum** . . . : United States v. Aluminum Co. of America, 148 F. 2d 416, 422–23 (2nd Cir. 1945). Reviews of this case and other cases cited in the course of this discussion can be found in Dominick T. Armentano, *The Myths of Antitrust* (New Rochelle, N.Y.: Arlington House, 1972); Bork, *The Antitrust Paradox;* and Posner, *Antitrust Law: An Economic Perspective.*

148   **Similarly, the United Shoe Machinery** . . . : United States v. United Shoe Machinery Corp., 110 F. Supp. 295 (D. Mass. 1953).

149   **In his antitrust treatise** . . . : Bork, *The Antitrust Paradox*, p. 431.

149   **Even firms that have** . . . : Ibid., pp. 433–434.

149   **In the 1950s** . . . : Brown Shoe Co. v. United States, 370 U.S. 294 (1962).

149   **Nevertheless, the Supreme Court** . . . : Bork, *The Antitrust Paradox*, pp. 215–216.

150   **The classic case of predatory pricing** . . . : The classic article on the subject was written by John McGee, "Predatory Price Cutting: The Standard Oil (N.J.) Case," *Journal of Law and Economics* 1 (1958): 13769. For a review of the cases and arguments, see

Thomas DiLorenzo, "The Myth of Predatory Pricing," *Policy Analysis*, no. 169 (Cato Institute, Washington, D.C.), February 28, 1992.

150   **But genuine predatory pricing . . .** : Predatory pricing is unlikely because (1) it is costly, especially for large firms (and the larger the firm the greater the cost from price reductions); (2) it has uncertain prospects of gain; (3) it may spread to other markets, increasing the cost to the "predator"; (4) it requires monopoly profits that can't be achieved in competitive environments; (5) it assumes that the rate of return on the firm's predation is higher than the rate of return on alternative investments; and (6) it assumes that competitors will not wait out the predatory period, reentering when prices are once again raised; and (7) it assumes that consumers can't stock up on the good when the price is low. See Harold Demsetz, "Barriers to Entry," *American Economic Review* 72 (May 1982): 52–56; and Frank Easterbrook, "Predatory Strategies and Counterstrategies," *University of Chicago Law Review* 48 (1981): 334. For a review of the cases and arguments, see DiLorenzo, "The Myth of Predatory Pricing."

150   **There were only seven cases . . .** : Ronald H. Koller, "The Myth of Predatory Pricing: An Empirical Study," *Antitrust Law and Economics Review* 4 (Summer 1971): 223.

150   **For example, in the 1930s . . .** : International Business Machines v. United States, 293 U.S. 131 (1936).

150   **New thinking suggests . . .** : Aaron Director and Edward H. Levi, "Law and the Future: Trade Regulation," *Northwestern University Law Review*, 281, 286 (1956): 281–317; and Bork, *The Antitrust Paradox*, chapter 19.

150   **Its purpose was to monitor . . .** : International Business Machines v. United States, 293 U.S. 131 (1936).

151   **In one particularly egregious . . .** : Kiefer-Stewart Co. v. Joseph E. Seagram & Sons, Inc., 340 U.S. 211 (1951).

151   **Similarly, the Court . . .** : Albrecht v. Herald Co. 390 U.S. 145 (1968).

151   **In the 1960s . . .** : United States v. Arnold Schwinn & Co., 388 U.S. 365, 372, 378–70, 379–80, 380 (1967).

151   **Although the court . . .** : Bork, *The Antitrust Paradox*, p. 283.

151   **Judge Richard Posner . . .** : Richard A. Posner, "The Federal Trade Commission," *University of Chicago Law Review* 37 (1969): 47–89.

151   **The Federal Reserve Board chairman . . .** : Alan Greenspan, writing in a 1961 paper published in Ayn Rand's *Capitalism*, quoted by James V. DeLong, "The New Trustbusters," *Reason*, March 1, 1999, p. 36.

152   **Even Robert Bork . . .** : Bork, *The Antitrust Paradox*, p. 4.

152   **"The theme of this book . . . "**: Ibid., p. 418.

152   **William Shughart, a professor . . .** : Shughart, *Antitrust Policy and Interest Group Politics*, p. 117.

152   **"When I started . . . "**: Milton Friedman, "The Risky Road to Regulation," *National Post*, July 5, 1999, p. C6.

154   **Baumol and Ordover point out . . .** : Baumol and Ordover, "Use of Antitrust to Subvert Competition," pp. 256–257.

154   **When AT&T tried . . .** : Ibid., pp. 257–258.

154   **As Baumol and Ordover note . . .** : Ibid., p. 257.

155   **Other spheres of government . . .** : For a discussion of the influence of members of Congress on antitrust enforcement, see Shughart, *Antitrust Policy and Interest Group Politics*, chapter 5.

155   **The late University of Chicago . . .** : George J. Stigler, "The Origins of the Sherman Act," *Journal of Legal Studies* 14 (January 1985): 1–12. The seventeen states, in chronological order of passage of the state antitrust statute, were Maryland (1867), Tennessee (1870), Arkansas (1876), Texas (1876), Georgia (1877), Indiana (1889), Iowa (1889), Kansas (1889), Maine (1889), Michigan (1889), Missouri (1889), Montana (1889), Nebraska (1889), North Carolina (1889), North Dakota (1889), Washington (1889). In addition, Kentucky, Louisiana, and Mississippi passed laws in 1890.

155   **This caused him to conclude . . .** : Ibid., p. 7. Stigler suggests that the empirical support is "modest" because the Sherman Act was actually a "modest, not major, change in public policy," for common law was also hostile to restraint of trade by monopolies. It's worth noting that if states that passed their own statutes were making economic life less efficient within their boundaries, they would be put at a competitive disadvantage vis-a-vis states that did not have such antitrust statutes. These seventeen states and their representatives would understandably have a political and economic interest in getting a national antitrust law passed: such a law would re-level the proverbial playing field. The law might extend the harm done to the national boundaries, but it would have its intended effect, that of increasing the *relative* competitive advantage of the states that had statutes in place.

155   **These economists observed . . .** : Donald J. Boudreaux, Thomas J. DiLorenzo, and Steven Parker, "Antitrust Before the Sherman Act," in *The Causes and Consequences of Antitrust*, ed. Fred S. McChesney and William F. Shughart (Chicago: University of Chicago Press, 1995), pp. 255–270.

156   **These economists noted . . .** : Ibid., p. 262.

156   **Boudreaux, DiLorenzo, and Parker . . .** : Ibid., p. 270. This conclusion is shared by Gary D. Libecap, "The Rise of the Chicago Packers and the Origins of Meat Inspection and Antitrust," *Economic Inquiry* 30: 242–262.

156   **Similar to Stigler . . .** : Thomas J. DiLorenzo, "The Origins of Antitrust: An Interest Group Perspective," *International Review of Law and Economics* 5 (1985): 73–90.

156   **However, he found that . . .** : See Sanford D. Gordon, "Attitudes Toward Trusts Prior to the Sherman Act," *Southern Economic Journal* 30 (October 1963): 156–167. Richard Ely, who founded the American Economics Association, probably captured the prevailing view of economists of the 1880s when he wrote, "The so-called trusts are not a bad thing, unless business on a large scale is a bad thing. On the contrary, when they come about as the result of free development, they are a good thing, and it is a bad thing to attempt to break them up" ("The Future of Trusts," *Harper's*, July 1887, p. 265).

156   **While the consumer price . . .** : DiLorenzo, "The Origins of Antitrust," p. 80.

156   **Three University of Georgia economists . . .** : See Charles D. Delorme, W. Scott Frame, and David R. Kamerschen, "Special Interest Group Perspective Before and After the Clayton and FTC Acts," *Applied Economics* 28 (1996): 773–777; and "Empirical Evidence on a Special-Interest-Group Perspective to Antitrust," *Public Choice* 92, no. 3–4 (September 1997): 317–335. This fall in commodity prices, caused by growing

output and an inelastic supply of gold, spurred populist agitation for bimetalism, which the good Senator Sherman helped promote by sponsoring the Silver Purchase Act, also passed in 1990.

157   **"Even mighty Standard Oil . . . ":** DeLong, "The New Trustbusters," p. 36.

157   **William Shughart has . . . :** Shughart, *Antitrust Policy and Interest Group Politics*, pp. 18–20.

157   **In Trans-Missouri Freight . . . :** Ibid., p. 18.

157   **". . . was not necessarily . . . ":** Ibid., p. 19.

157   **Judge Hand goes on . . . :** Ibid.

158   **The net effect . . . :** United States of America v. Microsoft, U.S. District Court, civil action no. 98-1232, Joel I. Klein et al., Complaint, May 20, 1998, p. 1.

158   **Clearly, Klein understands . . . :** Ibid., p. 46.

159   **From his statistical work . . . :** George Bittlingmayer, "Did Antitrust Cause the Great Merger Wave?" *Journal of Law and Economics* 28 (April 1985): 77–118; included in Fred S. McChesney and William F. Shughart, eds., *The Causes and Consequences of Antitrust* (Chicago: University of Chicago Press, 1995), pp. 127–163.

159   **In another study . . . :** Ibid., "Investment and Antitrust Enforcement," unpublished paper, University of California–Davis, Graduate School of Management, March 1999.

159   **In fact, in his study . . . :** Ibid., p. 18.

159   **Not surprisingly, Bittlingmayer found . . . :** George Bittlingmayer, "Antitrust and Business Activity: The First Quarter Century," *Business History Review* 70 (Autumn 1996): 363–401.

159   **Similarly, Shughart . . . :** William F. Shughart and Robert D. Tollison, "The Employment Consequences of the Sherman and Clayton Acts," *Journal of Institutional and Theoretical Economics* 147 (March 1991): 38–52; also in McChesney and Shughart, *The Causes and Consequences of Antitrust*, pp. 165–177.

159   **They reason . . . :** Ibid., p. 177.

159   **They conclude . . . :** Ibid., p. 177.

160   **Shughart and Tollison . . . :** William F. Shughart, Jon D. Silverman, and Robert D. Tollison, "Antitrust Enforcement and Foreign Competition," in McChesney and Shughart, *The Causes and Consequences of Antitrust*, pp. 179–187.

160   **However, they found . . . :** Ibid., p. 187.

160   **The same 1 percent increase . . . :** Ibid., p. 185.

160   **Not surprisingly . . . :** George Bittlingmayer, "Stock Returns, Real Activity, and the Trust Question," *Journal of Finance* 57 (1992): 1701–1730; ibid., "The Stock Market and Early Antitrust Enforcement," *Journal of Law and Economics* 36 (1993): 1–32; ibid., "Government and the Stock Market: The Effects of Antitrust," unpublished paper, University of Chicago, Center for the Study of the State, 1993; and ibid., "The 1920s and the Great Crash," unpublished paper, University of Chicago, Center for the Study of the State, 1993.

160   **They have often found . . . :** See George H. Hay and Daniel Kelley, "An Empirical Study of Price-Fixing Conspiracies," *Journal of Law and Economics* 17 (April 1974): 13–18.

160   **In those cases . . . :** See Robert A. Rogowsky, "The Economic Effectiveness of Section 7 Relief," *Antitrust Bulletin* 31 (Spring 1986): 187–233.

161   Do these findings . . . : Shughart, *Antitrust Policy and Interest Group Politics*, p. 4.

161   This has caused researchers . . . : Posner, "The Federal Trade Commission"; and Roger L. Faith, William F. Long, and Robert D. Tollison, "Antitrust Pork Barrel," *Journal of Law and Economics* 25 (October 1982): 329–342, in McChesney and Shughart, *The Causes and Consequences of Antitrust*, pp. 201–212.

161   Indeed, researchers have found . . . : Faith, Long, and Tollison, "Antitrust Pork Barrel."

161   From research . . . : Ibid.

161   Other researchers have found . . . : Barry R. Weingast and Mark J. Moran, "Bureaucratic Discretion or Congressional Control? Regulatory Policymaking by the Federal Trade Commission," *Journal of Political Economy* 91 (October 1983): 765–800.

161   Finally, Richard Higgins . . . : Malcolm B. Coate, Richard S. Higgins, and Fred S. McChesney, "Bureaucracy and Politics in FTC Merger Challenges," in McChesney and Shughart, *The Causes and Consequences of Antitrust*, pp. 213–230.

161   Many of the attorneys . . . : According to one study, in the 1970s 90 percent of the FTC lawyers had been with the FTC for four or fewer years. See Kenneth W. Clarkson and Timothy J. Muris, "Commission Performance, Incentives, and Behavior," in Kenneth W. Clarkson and Timothy J. Muris, eds., *The Federal Trade Commission Since 1970: Economic Regulation and Bureaucratic Behavior* (Cambridge, U.K.: Cambridge University Press, 1981), p. 300.

162   Posner notes . . . : As cited by Shughart, *Antitrust Policy and Interest Group Politics*, p. 99.

162   Shughart concludes . . . : Ibid., p. 100.

8   POLITICS 101

165   The process whereby . . . : "Bork" is recognized as a verb in William Safire, *Safire's Political Dictionary* (New York: Random House, 1993): to "attack viciously a candidate or appointee, especially by misrepresentation in the media."

166   The editors at the *Wall Street Journal* . . . : "Toward Justice Thomas" (editorial), *Wall Street Journal*, July 25, 1991, p. A8.

166   Within hours of the nomination . . . : Charles Krauthammer, "Back to Bork," *Washington Post*, February 9, 1999, p. A17.

166   "From the tone . . . ": "Judiciary Committee Hearings on Judge Robert Bork," *Los Angeles Times*, September 20, 1987, p. 4.

166   NOW's Florence Kennedy . . . : Quoted in L. Gordon Crovitz, "Rule of Borking Begins, but Mudballs Bounce off Judge Thomas," *Wall Street Journal*, July 17, 1991, p. A9.

166   In those hearings . . . : Ibid.

167   But their essence . . . : To understand how elaborate and organized a Borking campaign can be, see Michael Pertschuk and Wendy Schaetzel, *The People Rising: The Campaign Against the Bork Nomination* (New York: Thunder's Mouth Press, 1989). See also Paul Simon, *Advice and Consent: Clarence Thomas, Robert Bork and the Intriguing History of the Supreme Court's Nomination Battles* (Washington, D.C.: National Press Books, 1992).

168   **At one time, circa 1995 . . .** : Rajiv Chandrasekaran, "Microsoft's Window of Influence; Intensive Lobbying Aims to Neutralize Antitrust Efforts," *Washington Post*, May 7, 1999, p. A1.

168   **Gates probably should . . .** : Praying mantis image from Gary Rivlin, *The Plot to Get Bill Gates: An Irreverent Investigation of the World's Richest Man . . . and the People Who Hate Him* (New York: Random House, 1999), p. 63.

169   **As will be seen . . .** : See Paul A. Gigot, "Potomac Watch: The Political Re-education of Bill Gates," *Wall Street Journal*, March 6, 1998, p. A14.

173   **The net effect was . . .** : In early 1993, IBM's stock price dropped to an eleven-year low, making its market cap $26.4 billion, while Microsoft's market cap was $26.8 billion and rising. By 1996, however, IBM's market cap had recovered and surpassed Microsoft's. By 1999, Microsoft's market cap had once again surpassed IBM's (as well as that of every other company in the country, and the world).

174   **During the first half . . .** : OS/2 had 3 percent of the market in 1992 and 1993, 4 percent in 1994, and 7 percent in 1995, when Microsoft raised its average street price for Windows 44 percent; see Figure 2.1 (the Justice Department's exhibit 1) in Chapter 2. The market share fell back to 3 percent after Microsoft introduced Windows 95 and began lowering its price. The Justice Department's exhibit 1 can be found at http://www.usdoj.gov/atr/cases/exhibits/1.pdf.

174   **In 1990, WordPerfect . . .** : See Stan J. Liebowitz and Stephen E. Margolis, *Winners, Losers, and Microsoft: Competition and Antitrust Technology* (Oakland, Calif.: Independent Institute, 1999), p. 181.

175   **Novell's chairman . . .** : See Richard Morochove, "The Perils of Doing Battle with Mr. Bill," *Toronto Star*, November 9, 1995, p. K6. One good argument for bundling applications with the operating system is illustrated in the WordPerfect experience. If the application and operating system are sold separately and some kind of problem arises, it is hard to attribute blame, which means both sides can blame the other. When one firm produces both, blame is clearer.

175   **But of course, Noorda's . . .** : "Novell Founder Noorda Pushes Antitrust Suit Against Microsoft Computers," *Los Angeles Times*, July 25, 1996, p. D1.

175   **In his book, Jim Clark . . .** : Jim Clark with Owen Edwards, *Netscape Time: The Making of the Billion-Dollar Start-up that Took On Microsoft* (New York: St. Martin's Press, 1999), pp. 115, 131, 225, 226, 227, and 230.

176   **This turn of words suggests . . .** : Brian O'Reilly, "Novell Faces the Battle of Its Life," *Fortune*, August 9, 1993, p. 81.

176   **A similar feeling . . .** : Wendy Goldman Rohm, "Microsoft Rivals Take Tales to Justice Officials," *Chicago Tribune*, September 23, 1993, p. A3.

176   **Netscape's Clark . . .** : Clark, *Netscape Time*, p. 110.

176   **And Gates admits . . .** : Ibid., p. 230.

177   **Indeed, in his book . . .** : Ibid., p. 130.

177   **This problem of shrinking . . .** : Michael A. Cusumano and Richard W. Selby, *Microsoft Secrets: How the World's Most Powerful Software Company Creates Technology, Shapes Markets, and Manages People* (New York: Free Press, 1995), pp. 144–145.

178   **As Sun's Scott McNealy . . .** : David Bank, "Noise Inhibitor: Rivals of Microsoft Find Collaboration Is Easier Said Than Done; When the Chips Are Down, Factions Often Rise Up and Squabbles Ensue," *Wall Street Journal*, November 19, 1998, p. A1.

178   **IBM's John Thompson . . .** : Julie Robotham, "Different Horses for Market Courses," *Sydney Morning Herald*, July 30, 1996, p. 2.

178   **Ray Noorda was ever ready . . .** : Rohm, "Microsoft's Rivals Take Tales to Justice Officials," p. 3.

179   **In September 1995 . . .** : "Oracle Predicts the Demise of Desktops," *The Financial Post*, September 5, 1995, p. 7.

179   **In the future, Ellison asserted . . .** : Ibid.

179   **Gates was none . . .** : Ibid.

179   **Nonetheless, David Moschella . . .** : Ibid.

179   **At the same time . . .** : Clark, *Netscape Time*, p. 49.

179   **Hugh Hemple . . .** : Neil McManus, "The Browser Wars: Netscape and Microsoft Battle to Control World Wide Web Formatting Standards," *Digital Media*, November 6, 1995, p. 11.

180   **Later that year . . .** : Gary Chapman, "Is the PC Becoming Passé?" *Los Angeles Times*, September 28, 1995, p. B2.

180   **Lou Gerstner . . .** : "IBM's Gerstner Foresees New Computer Revolution," *Financial Times*, November 14, 1995, p. 51.

180   **John Thompson . . .** : Louise Kehoe, "Network Computers: High Tech Companies Hoping to Profit from Oracle's War on the PC, Everybody Against Microsoft," *Financial Times*, May 23, 1996, p. 12.

180   **By 1996, McNealy . . .** : Louise Kehoe, "Sun Microsystems' Chief Takes No Prisoners: Scott McNealy, the Man Behind the Leading Supplier of Internet Services, Likes to 'Kick Butt and Have Fun,' " *Financial Times*, February 6, 1996, p. 102.

180   **He rhetorically asked . . .** : James Coates, "Sun Microsystems Scorches Microsoft, Giant Is Again Target as Comdex Show Ends," *Chicago Tribune*, June 7, 1996, p. A1.

180   **Similarly, Ellison . . .** : Nils Blythe, "The Prophet of 'Less Is More,' " *The Independent* (London), February 5, 1996, p. 10.

180   **When a *Forbes* editor . . .** : Ellison continued, softening his caustic comments somewhat, "I think Bill is a very bright guy, but I don't think his strength is in his intellect at all. It's in his relentlessness. Bill is indefatigable about thinking something through to a solution that profits Microsoft. It is that intellectual endurance that singles him out far more than his computational capacity. There are lots of bright guys in this world" (Mark Harper and Rich Karlgaard, "Larry Ellison: Samurai Interview," *Forbes*, April 8, 1996, p. S54).

181   **At the Spring Comdex/Windows World 1996 . . .** : Coates, "Sun Microsystems Exec Scorches Microsoft."

181   **According to Netscape's Jim Clark . . .** : Clark/Edwards, *Netscape Time*, p. 199.

181   **Seeing the promise of the Web . . .** : Kehoe, "Network Computers: High Tech Companies Hoping to Profit from Oracle's War on the PC," p. 12.

181   **In his book *The Road Ahead* . . .** : Bill Gates, *The Road Ahead* (New York: Viking Books, 1995), p. 91. Gary Rivlin suggests that many, if not most, reviewers of *The Road Ahead* "skewered" Gates for having "missed the Internet." Supposedly, according to

Rivlin, Gates was a "laughingstock" for the Internet oversight and admitted to Lotus founder Mitch Kapor that the Internet had "blind-sided him" (Rivlin, *The Plot to Get Bill Gates*, p. 130). One reviewer of *The Road Ahead* noted, "The World Wide Web gets only passing mention" (Paul Andrews, "Dollar Bill's Dog and Pony Show: Microsoft's Master Is Strongly Absent from His Book About the Digital Future," book review, *Barron's*, December 25, 1995, p. 40).

182   **Microsoft claims . . .** : Steve Lohr, "Microsoft Says Internet Browser Idea Arose Long before Netscape," *New York Times*, August 6, 1998, p. A1.

182   **As Clark boasts . . .** : Clark/Edwards, *Netscape Time*, p. 100.

182   **He insisted . . .** : Bill Gates, "The Internet Tidal Wave," memorandum, May 26, 1995, the Department of Justice's exhibit 20, p. 1, at: http://www.usdoj.gov/atr/cases/ms_exhibits.htm.

182   **Indeed, in that memo . . .** : Ibid., pp. 1 and 4.

182   **Moreover, Gates's version . . .** : Clark/Edwards, *Netscape Time*, p. 156.

182   **He concluded that the most intelligent . . .** : Bill Gates, "Internet Strategy Workshop Keynote," speech, Seattle, December 7, 1995.

183   **He then explained . . .** : Ibid.

183   **Gates acknowledged . . .** : Ibid., p. 2.

183   **The fact of the matter . . .** : Clark/Edwards, *Netscape Time*, p. 169.

183   **He may have also observed . . .** : Ibid., p. 163.

183   **The rapid-fire release . . .** : See Liebowitz and Margolis, *Winners, Losers, and Microsoft*, pp. 219–220.

184   **More than two dozen . . .** : Lee Gomes, "PC Industry Is Underwhelmed by Network Machines—Feared Onslaught Is Hardly in Evidence at Comdex Computer Show," *Wall Street Journal*, November 22, 1996, p. B4 (and found through the *Wall Street Journal* Interactive Web site).

185   **Fifth, analysts began . . .** : Ibid.

185   **This may have prompted . . .** : Ibid.

185   **Holman Jenkins . . .** : Holman W. Jenkins, Jr., "Don't Hate Me Because I'm Beautiful," *Wall Street Journal*, December 31, 1996, p. A7.

185   **Moreover, "Scott McNealy . . .** ": Ibid.

185   **Gates was not above . . .** : Roger Ridey, "Bill and Larry's War of Words," *The Independent* (London), September 23, 1996, p. 16.

185   **He also impugned . . .** : Kehoe, "Network Computers," p. 12.

186   **The consortium of Microsoft detractors . . .** : David Bank, "Noise Inhibitor: Rivals of Microsoft Find Collaboration Is Easier Said Than Done, When the Chips Are Down, Factions Often Rise Up and Squabbles Ensue," *Wall Street Journal*, November 19, 1998, p. A1.

187   **According to Hasso Plattner . . .** : Ibid.

187   **According to the *Wall Street Journal* . . .** : Ibid.

188   **Netscape probably also . . .** : Harper and Karlgaard, "Larry Ellison: Samurai Interview," p. S54.

188   **When pressed . . .** : Ibid.

188   **Jim Barksdale . . .** : "Anti-Microsoft Front Cracks as Netscape and Oracle Quarrel," *Financial Times*, October 3, 1996, p. 18.

189   The efforts of Microsoft's . . . : Bank, "Noise Inhibitor."

189   Their ostensible purpose . . . : Ibid.

189   It is doubly hypocritical . . . : Ibid. When asked about the ongoing talks between Netscape and AOL in 1995, David Boies reacted by suggesting that small and large companies can legally play by different rules. "Small companies get together all the time, and especially when they are facing monopolies."

190   Microsoft's rivals have done . . . : David Segal, "In Netscape's Corner Free-Marketeer Robert Bork Is Going Against Microsoft. But Not His Principles," *Washington Post*, June 25, 1998, p. B1.

9   POLITICIZING ANTITRUST

193   As Judge Robert Bork insisted . . . : Robert H. Bork, *The Antitrust Paradox: A Policy at War with Itself* (New York: Free Press, 1978), p. 418.

194   As a *Washington Post* reporter . . . : David Segal, "In Netscape's Corner Free-Marketeer Robert Bork Is Going Against Microsoft. But Not His Principles," *Washington Post*, June 25, 1998, p. B1.

194   Indeed, as late as . . . : Laton McCartney, "Microsoft Takes Lessons in Lobbying," *Upside*, June 1, 1998, n.p.

194   Many Americans were convinced . . . : I have written extensively on the "gloom and doom" views of the Reagan-Bush critics in the 1980s and 1990s. See Richard B. McKenzie, *What Went Right in the 1980s* (San Francisco: Pacific Research Institute, 1994); and, *The Paradox of Progress: Growing Pessimism in an Era of Unbounded Opportunities* (New York: Oxford University Press, 1997).

195   Lawrence Perlman . . . : Rick Wartman and Dana Milbank, "Crossing Over: Clinton's Strength with Business Leaders Is Rare for a Democrat," *Wall Street Journal*, September 24, 1992, p. A1.

195   In spite of voting . . . : Ibid.

196   Sculley acknowledged that . . . : Rich Karlgaard, "ASAP Interview: John Sculley," *Forbes*, December 7, 1992, p. 93.

196   At a press conference . . . : "High-Tech Business Leaders Endorse Clinton-Gore Strategy," *U.S. Newswire*, September 15, 1992.

196   The list of other . . . : The extended list of executives supporting Clinton-Gore at the September 1992 conference at which Ellison and others spoke included Gerry Beemiller, Infant Advantage; Chuck Boesenberg, Central Point Software; Dick Brass, Oracle Data Publishing; Chuck Comiso, Link Technologies; John Freidenric, Bay Partners; Regis McKenna, Regis McKenna Inc.; Gloria Rose, Ott GO Strategies; Sandy Robertson, Robertson, Coleman & Stephens; Keith Sorenson, RasterOps; Robert Goldman, AI Corp.; John Cullinane, Cullinane Group; Charles Cohen, Creative Biomolecules; Kenneth Fallan, American Surgical Technologies; Mitchell Kertzman, Powersoft Corp.; Ramish Kapur, Medical Technical Gases Inc.; Howard Salwen, Porteon Inc.; Alan Solomont, ADS Management Inc.; Phillipe Villers, Compt-Vision Corp.; Robert Weiss, Physical Sciences Inc.; Richard Wurtman, Interneuron Pharmaceuticals; Ken Marshall, Object Design Inc.; and Ronald Cape, Cetus.

197   **Many of Microsoft's competitors . . .** : Jube Shiver, Jr., "Microsoft, Justice Defend Antitrust Pact Software: They Tell Appeals Panel That Judge Exceeded His Authority in Rejecting Deal," *Los Angeles Times*, April 25, 1995, p. A2.

198   **By midsummer 1994 . . .** : As can be found at: http://www.usdoj.gov/atr/cases/f0000/0046.htm

198   **By 1995 . . .** : Jim Clark with Owen Edwards, *Netscape Time: The Making of the Billion-Dollar Start-up that Took On Microsoft* (New York: St. Martin's Press, 1999), p. 204.

199   **Microsoft's rivals were . . .** : Shiver, "Microsoft, Justice Defend Antitrust Pact Software."

200   **In his book *Netscape Time* . . .** : Clark, *Netscape Time*, p. 233.

200   **In August 1996 . . .** : Gary L. Reback, letter to Joel Klein, deputy assistant attorney general, Department of Justice, August 12, 1996, p. 1.

201   **(In her 1999 book . . .** : Karen Southwick, *High Noon: The Inside Story of Scott McNealy and the Rise of Sun Microsystems* (New York: John Wiley, 1999), p. 183.

202   **Klein, who had by then . . .** : Joel I. Klein, acting assistant attorney general for antitrust, U.S. Department of Justice, letter to William H. Neukom, senior vice president for law and corporate affairs at Microsoft, September 20, 1996.

202   **When Netscape went public . . .** : Clark, *Netscape Time*, p. 221.

202   **Indeed, by the time . . .** : Ibid., p. 260.

202   **Nonetheless, he did pick up . . .** : Tom Foremski, *Electronic Weekly*, September 25, 1996, p. 22.

202   **According to the Center . . .** : Jennifer Shecter, Center for Responsive Politics, *Money in Politics Alert* (Center for Responsive Politics, Washington, D.C.), May 26, 1998, at: http://www.opensecrets.orp/alerts/v4/alrtv4n20.htm.

203   **By then, Microsoft . . .** : Segal, "In Netscape's Corner Free-Marketeer Robert Bork Is Going Against Microsoft."

203   **In June 1997 . . .** : Senators Conrad Burns, Ted Stevens, and Craig Thomas, letter to Robert Pitofsky, chairman, Federal Trade Commission, June 1997.

203   **Four days after the letter . . .** : Robert Pitofsky, chairman, Federal Trade Commission, letter to Senator Conrad Burns, July 28, 1999.

203   **In their effort to expand . . .** : Senator Barbara Boxer, letter to Robert Pitofsky, July 8, 1997.

203   **They also went to . . .** : Senator Tom Daschle, letter to Joel Klein, assistant attorney general for antitrust, U.S. Department of Justice, September 24, 1997.

204   **In a news release, Hatch . . .** : Senator Orrin Hatch, news release: Statement on the Department of Justice Microsoft Charges, October 20, 1997.

204   **Sure enough . . .** : Frank James, "Attack Proceeds Against Microsoft," *Chicago Tribune*, November 5, 1997, p. A1.

204   **However, the day before . . .** : John R. Wilke, "Senate Internet Panel to Probe Microsoft's Power," *Wall Street Journal*, November 3, 1997, p. B2.

204   **In spite of the claimed . . .** : James, "Attack Proceeds Against Microsoft."

204   **The list of e-economy . . .** : John Mintz, "Microsoft Foes Team Up for Hatch Fund-Raiser," *Washington Post*, December 9, 1999, p. A26.

204 **The criticisms from Microsoft's . . .** : Scott Sonner, "Nader Leads Anti-Microsoft Conference," *Portland Oregonian*, November 13, 1997, p. E1.

205 **Thirty of Microsoft's harshest . . .** : James Taranto, "Nader's Raiders Try to Storm Bill's Gates," *Wall Street Journal*, November 18, 1997, p. A22.

205 **He concluded that . . .** : Michael Paulson, "Critics Pummel Microsoft and It Gets Feisty," *Seattle Post-Intelligencer*, November 14, 1997, p. A1.

205 **Netscape's general counsel . . .** : Ibid.

205 **The self-styled "futurologist" . . .** : Carolyn Lochhead, "Millionaires Rally to Check Microsoft Clout; Ralph Nader Joins Fight to End Firm's Dominance," *San Francisco Chronicle*, November 14, 1997, p. A1. The speakers may not have had the impact on the media that they intended, mainly because they may have gone "over the top" in the harshness of their criticisms. The *Wall Street Journal* reporter covering the conference asked for a reader "reality check" in the middle of his story, editorializing that "the conference laid out a case against Microsoft that is largely science fiction. Some of its less fanciful elements could come true someday—but mere speculation is no justification for activating that most fearsome monopoly of all, the U.S. government" (Sonner, "Nader leads Anti-Microsoft Conference," p. E1).

205 **The relationship between Klein . . .** : David Bank, "Noise Inhibitor: Rivals of Microsoft Find Collaboration Is Easier Said Than Done," *Wall Street Journal*, November 19, 1998, p. A1.

205 **ProComp members include . . .** : On its Web site, ProComp announced in late November 1999, "There are a number of companies and associations involved, some of whom prefer to remain anonymous. This speaks volumes about the power of Microsoft. People are very concerned about how the power wielded by a single company could dramatically impact their businesses, now and in the future."

Part of ProComp's strategic mission is this statement on Microsoft: "ProComp advocates the basic rules of competition, which favor the many over the few, and which will ensure that Americans, for whom freedom of choice has always been essential, will continue to have that freedom in the 21st century. This is our principal message as we educate policymakers and the public about developments in technology and related markets. At the same time, it must be said that we are literally at the fork in the road with regard to these policies. We frankly acknowledge the structural conflict of interest that exists within Microsoft. Through its control of the operating system, Microsoft controls not only the computer screens that are consumers' conduit to the Internet, but the company also owns and controls much of the software-based Internet content as well. Given that structural conflict, it would be unrealistic to expect Microsoft NOT to promote its own content products to the extent it can. We are saying that this structural conflict exists, and policymakers must examine all of the ramifications of this and decide what policy response may be appropriate—before it is too late." (http://www.procompetition.org/procomp/faq.html#members).

ProComp says it does not advocate specific remedies for the Microsoft antitrust case, but does support the following premises on which actual remedies should be constructed: (1) "Computer manufacturers and users must have the freedom to install whatever software they wish on the computers they make and use." (2) "The basic laws of antitrust must be enforced to insure that an operating system monopoly is not used to preference the dominant company's own software products over those provided by competitors, or that monopoly power is not used to extend the monopoly into other markets."(3) "Software developers must be given complete information about the monopoly operating system at the same time and in the same manner as it is given to software developers working with or aligned with the company having monopoly power."

Premises 1 and 3 actually describe conditions and practices in the software industry today.

All the above information is available at ProComp's Web site, at: http://www.pro-competition.org/procomp/faq.html#members.

205   **They appealed to . . .** : E. Floyd Kvamme, of Kleiner, Perkins, Caufield & Byers, memorandum to Jack Kemp, December 22, 1997.

206   **Subsequently, the foundation . . .** : See the Progress and Freedom Foundation anti-Microsoft literature on the foundation's Web site: http://www.pff.org.

206   **In February 1998 . . .** : Jeffrey A. Eisenach and Thomas M. Lenard, *Competition, Innovation, and the Microsoft Monopoly: Antitrust in the Digital Marketplace* (Boston: Kluwer Academic Publishers, 1999), p. ix.

206   **For example, Lenard states . . .** : Thomas M. Lenard, "Who's Afraid of Microsoft?" in *Progress on Point* (Washington, D.C.: Progress and Freedom Foundation, September 1998), p. 6.

206   **That month ProComp also . . .** : For the various commentaries on Microsoft, Bill Gates, and the trial, see ProComp's Web site, at: http://www.procompetition.org/xp/p-headlines/i-current/top.view.

206   **By November 1998 . . .** : Kevin Arquit, Tom Campbell, Jeffrey A. Eisenach, James C. Miller III, Daniel Oliver, James F. Hill, Lawrence J. White, and Robert D. Willig, letter to Senator Trent Lott, November 12, 1998.

207   **But Bork's willingness . . .** : Bork, *The Antitrust Paradox*, p. 418.

207   **A *Washington Post* columnist . . .** : Ibid.

207   **Bork took his campaign public . . .** : Robert H. Bork, "The Case Against Microsoft," available at the ProComp Web site, at: http://www.procompetition.org/research/bork.htm.

207   **"The two greatest threats . . . "**: Ibid., "The Most Misunderstood Antitrust Case," *Wall Street Journal*, May 22, 1998, p. A16. Bork also produced a longer defense of his position taking on the complaints of his critics. See Bork, "The Case Against Microsoft."

208   **Bork was soundly criticized . . .** : For example, see George L. Priest, "U.S. v. Microsoft: A Case Built on Wild Speculation, Dubious Theories," *Wall Street Journal*, May 19, 1995, p. A22.

208   **For example, in his . . .** : Bork, "The Most Misunderstood Antitrust Case."

208   **However, in *The Antitrust Paradox* . . .** : Ibid., p. 192.

208   **Elsewhere, he flatly . . .** : Bork, *The Antitrust Paradox*, p. 430.

208   **In his book, Bork does . . .** : Bork, "The Most Misunderstood Antitrust Case."

208   **However, in *The Antitrust Paradox*, Judge Bork notes . . .** : Bork, *The Antitrust Paradox*, p. 432.

208   **. . . because of the complexity . . .** : Ibid., p. 433.

208   James Miller, the Reagan . . . : James C. Miller III and Paul A. Pautler, "Predation: The Changing View in Economics and the Law," *Journal of Law and Economics* 28 (May 1985): 498:

208   Bork also charges . . . : Bork, "The Case Against Microsoft," p. 1.

208   Besides, Bork's charge . . . : Bork, *The Antitrust Paradox*, p. 309.

208   Bork seemed to get testy . . . : Holman W. Jenkins, Jr., "An Antitrust War Horse Comes In from the Pasture," *Wall Street Journal*, July 15, 1998, p. A17.

209   He grumbled back . . . : Robert H. Bork, "Don't Insult Me or My Intelligence," letter to the editor, *Wall Street Journal*, July 22, 1998, p. A15.

209   He also reiterated . . . : Ibid.

209   In his own letter . . . : Bork, *The Antitrust Paradox*, chapters 15 and 19.

209   DiLorenzo adds that . . . : Thomas J. DiLorenzo, "The Economic Joy of Bundling," letter to the editor, *Wall Street Journal*, July 29, 1998, p. A15.

209   This suggests that he . . . : Bork, *The Antitrust Paradox*, p. 245.

209   Bork asserts in his ProComp . . . : Bork, "The Case Against Microsoft," p. 2.

209   This directly contradicts . . . : Harold Demsetz, "Why Regulate Utilities," *Journal of Law and Economics*, vol. 55 (1968), cited in Bork, *The Antitrust Paradox*, p. 180.

210   As noted earlier . . . : Bork, *The Antitrust Paradox*, p. 181.

210   And he was right on target . . . : Ibid., p. 178.

210   For example, in his ProComp . . . : Bork, "The Case Against Microsoft," p. 6.

210   The Yale Law School professor . . . : George L. Priest, letter to the editor, "The Dangers of Attack on Microsoft," *Wall Street Journal Europe*, p. 11.

210   However, he now adds . . . : "Bork Urges Action Against Microsoft Software: Conservative Jurist, Now a Lobbyist for Netscape, Asserts 'Clear Attempt to Monopolize,'" *Los Angeles Times*, April 27, 1998, p. D2.

211   On the subject of breaking up . . . : Bork, *The Antitrust Paradox*, p. 192.

211   When he began . . . : "Bork Says U.S. Has a Tight Antitrust Case Against Microsoft," Dow Jones Online News, April 27, 1998. To another reporter, Bork elaborated on the limited state of his thinking on remedies: "Well, I think that requires a great deal of thought. And I'm just starting on this. I have a variety of ideas, but I'm not ready to float them. I think the government certainly can prove a Section Two case, a Sherman Act case. But the question is, once they've proved it, what's the relief? You have to have an effective remedy and a remedy that increases consumer welfare. . . . But this is a new industry, and it poses problems that we haven't seen before in antitrust" (Lisa Wirthman, "Computers & Technology Antitrust Jurist Says Microsoft Hurts Consumer," *Investor's Business Daily*, April 27, 1998, p. A8).

211   By the start of 1999 . . . : Robert MacMillan, "Bork: Break Up Microsoft," Newsbytes News Network, January 17, 1999. During the first week of March, the Software and Information Industry Association, which has 1,400 members (including Microsoft), came out in favor of breaking up Microsoft into three firms (John R. Wilke, "Microsoft Peers Urge Restructuring If Firm Loses Trial," *Wall Street Journal*, March 3, 1999, p. B8).

211   To give Bork the benefit . . . : "Bork Says U.S. Has a Tight Antitrust Case Against Microsoft," Dow Jones Online News, April 27, 1998.

211   **When challenged . . .** : Segal, "In Netscape's Court Free-Marketeer Robert Bork Is Going Against Microsoft, but Not His Principles."

211   **He told a group of reporters . . .** : "Bork Urges Action," *Los Angeles Times*, p. D2.

211   **He has also professed . . .** : Bork, "Don't Insult Me."

212   **He recently reminded reporters . . .** : "Bork Urges Action."

212   **As can be seen . . .** : Rajiv Chandrasekaran, "Microsoft's Window of Influence; Intensive Lobbying Aims to Neutralize Antitrust Efforts," *Washington Post*, May 7, 1999, p. A1.

213   **In September 1999 . . .** : Gregg Miller, "Pro-Microsoft Ads Were Funded by Software Giant," *Los Angeles Times*, September 18, 1999, p. C1.

213   **The *Times* reported . . .** : Ibid.

213   **Microsoft got nailed . . .** : Joel Brinkley, "Microsoft Covered Cost of Ads Backing It in Antitrust Suit," *New York Times*, September 18, 1999, p. A1.

214   **When he sent out . . .** : John R. Wilke, "Microsoft Seeks Help of Holders," *Wall Street Journal*, November 1, 1999, p. A56.

214   **He urged them to write . . .** : http://www.microsoft.com/freedomtoinnovate/default.htm.

215   **Judges were also prone . . .** : Bork, *The Antitrust Paradox*.

215   **While we might like . . .** : See William F. Shughart II, *Antitrust Policy and Interest-Group Politics* (New York: Quorum Books, 1990), chapter 6.

10   ANTITRUST IRONIES

218   **For example, the longtime free-marketer Milton Friedman . . .** : Milton Friedman, "The Business Community's Suicidal Impulse," Web site of the Cato Institute, September 23, at: http://www.cato.org/pubs/policy_report/v21n2/friedman.html.

218   **Indeed, one of the reasons . . .** : "Bork Urges Action Against Microsoft Software: Conservative Jurist, Now a Lobbyist for Netscape, Asserts 'Clear Attempt to Monopolize.' " *Los Angeles Times*, April 27, 1998, p. D2.

218   **In the second edition of his landmark book . . .** : Robert H. Bork, *The Antitrust Paradox: A Policy at War with Itself* (New York: Free Press, 1993), pp. ix-xv.

219   **In his book he observes . . .** : Jim Clark with Owen Edwards, *Netscape Time: The Making of the Billion-Dollar Start-up that Took On Microsoft* (New York: St. Martin's Press, 1999), p. 79.

219   **In another place . . .** : Ibid., p. 224.

219   **And, finally, he concludes . . .** : Ibid., p. 227.

219   **Clark points to the fact . . .** : Ibid., p. 243.

220   **Also, in the first quarter . . .** : Sun Microsystems' revenues rose from $2.5 billion in the first quarter of fiscal year 1999 to $3.1 billion in the first quarter fiscal year 2000. Its net income after adjusting for one-time charges went from $198 million in first quarter 1999 to $275 million in first quarter 2000 (David P. Hamilton, "Sun Microsoft's Net More than Doubles," *Wall Street Journal*, October 15, 1999, p. B4).

220   **In October . . .** : Full-page advertisement placed by Oracle in the *Wall Street Journal*, October 5, 1999, p. A13.

220 **Microsoft even introduced . . .** : John Markoff, "Microsoft Sets Shift in Internet Strategy," *New York Times*, September 24, 1999, p. C2.

220 **Moreover, at the fall 1999 Comdex . . .** : Lawrence J. Magid, "Internet Appliances Ease Visits to Web," *Los Angeles Times,* November 22, 1999, p. C6.

221 **With these kinds of software . . .** : Jim Seymour, "Send Out for Software," *PC Magazine*, November 2, 1999, pp. 100–121.

221 **Even Netscape's Clark . . .** : Ibid., p. 83.

221 **As noted earlier, Netscape . . .** : Ibid., p. 163.

222 **For these types of reasons . . .** : In Franklin M. Fisher et al., *Folded, Spindled and Mutilated: Economic Analysis and the U.S. v. IBM* (Cambridge, Mass.: MIT Press, 1983), it was stated, "The subjective intent of a company is difficult to determine and will usually reflect nothing more than a determination to win all possible business from rivals—a determination consistent with competition. . . . To premise their legality on an inquiry into the specific motivations of subjective intent of the firms that engage in such conduct (when it is clear that all firms engaged in competition attempt and intend to win as much business as they can) or on retrospective evaluation of whether there were more 'desirable' alternative actions that could have been chosen, would be to elevate competitors above competition and threaten the entire competitive process for the sake of those who are not intended to be its beneficiaries and at the expense of those who are" (p. 272).

222 **Let's be realistic . . .** : Clark/Edwards, *Netscape Time*, p. 49.

223 **One Java expert reckons . . .** : John Mitchell, president of Non Incorporated, a Java consulting firm, quoted in Karen Southwick, *High Noon: The Inside Story of Scott McNealy* (New York: John Wiley, 1999), p. 150.

224 **Perhaps Robert Scheer . . .** : Robert Scheer, "Microsoft Should Be Our Last Worry," *Los Angeles Times,* November 9, 1999, p. B15.

225 **Robert Bork's words . . .** : Bork, *The Antitrust Paradox*, p. 181.

226 **As this book was going to press . . .** : The Justice Department hired Greenhill & Co. mainly because the company is headed by Robert F. Greenhill, who is renowned for his work on difficult acquisition and merger cases and for his ability to financially evaluate companies' structuring strategies (Joel Brinkley, "U.S. Hires Advisory Firm in Microsoft Case," *New York Times*, December 3, 1999, p. A2).

228 **As another judge . . .** : "U.S. Department of Microsoft?" *Wall Street Journal*, editorial, November 8, 1999, p. A50.

228 **One of the senator's aides . . .** : Ronald G. Shafer, "Washington Wire: Pro-Microsoft Lobbying to Limit Antitrust Funding Irks Top Lawmakers," *Wall Street Journal*, October 10, 1999, p. A1.

APPENDIX II:
SUMMARY OF THE MAJOR ANTITRUST CASES

235 **Justice Department Complaint for Violations of Sections 1 and 2 . . .**: Anne K. Bingaman, et al., Complaint, United States of America vs. Microsoft Corporation, civil action no. 94–1564, July 15, 1994 (which may be found at http://www.usdoj.gov/atr/cases/f0000/0047.htm).

235 **Final Judgment as Agreed ...:** Charles R. Richey, U.S. District Court for the District of Columbia, U.S. Government vs. Microsoft Corporation, civil action no. 94–1564 (which can be found at http://usdoj.gov/atr/cases/f0000/0047.htm).

236 **Justice Department Complaint for Violating Section 7 ...:** Anne K. Bingaman, et al., Complaint, United States of America vs. Microsoft Corporation, civil action (not given), April 27, 1995 (which may be found at http://www.usdoj.gov/atr/cases/f0100/0184.htm).

237 **Justice Department Complaint for Violating Sections 1 and 2 of the Sherman Act ...:** Joel I. Klein, et al., Complaint, United States of America vs. Microsoft Corporation, civil action no. 98–1232, May 18, 1998 (which may be found at http://www.usdoj.gov/atr/cases/f1700/1763.htm).

238 **Findings of Fact by Judge Thomas Penfield Jackson...:** Thomas Penfield Jackson, U.S. District Court, Findings of Fact, U.S. Government v. Microsoft Corporation civil action 98–1232, November 5, 1999 (which can be found at http://www.usdoj.gov/atr/cases/f3800/msjudgex.htm).

INDEX

Adobe Photoshop, 130
Alcoa Aluminum, 148, 157
Allen, Paul, 173
Alm, Richard, 115
Amazon.com, 101
Amelio, Gil, 196
America Online (AOL), 2, 18, 44, 46
  and Java, 2, 55
  and operating systems, 54, 92
  and the Microsoft desktop, 105–106
  back office computing, 224–225
  customer base, 54
  lobbying, 213
  purchase of Netscape, 54, 117, 123, 220
  TV, 54
American Airlines, 206
Andreesen, Marc, 17, 92, 117–119, 121–122,
  135, 179, 181, 199–201, 222
Antitrust law
  and competition, 17, 47, 91, 160
  and consumers, 13, 19, 160, 191
  and market dominance, 95
  and politics, 161, 212, 215–216
  and property rights, 86
  and the digital economy, 2, 6–7, 13–14,
    23, 50, 72–74, 191, 193, 217, 224, 226,
    229
  criticism of, 152–153
  early U.S., 4, 22, 58, 155–157, 249n, 259n

  enforcement of, 2, 5, 7, 67, 95–96,
    158–161, 227
  misuse of, 147–154, 162–163, 190,
    217–218
  purpose of, 147–148, 154–155, 157–158,
    228
  See also Sherman Act; Clayton Act;
    Federal Trade Commission Act
Antitrust Paradox, 37, 47, 149, 152, 207–209,
  211, 215
Apple
  applications, 46
  as a monopoly, 16
  browsers, 108–109
  competition from, 10
  CP/M, 79
  dispute with Microsoft, 108–109
  Excel, 131
  iMac, 52
  MAC Office, 108–109
  Macintosh, 30, 79–80
  operating system, 10, 41, 44, 79–80
  PCs, 169
  sales restrictions, 103
  share of market, 54–65, 80
Application Launch Accelerator, 129
"Appraising Microsoft and Its Global
    Strategy" conference, 205, 267n
AST, 184

AT&T, 21, 44, 154
Attorneys general, 9, 15, 29, 30, 162, 242n
Auditore, Stephen, 185

Baber, Mark, 18
Ballmer, Steve, 194
Barksdale, Jim, 2, 188–189, 203, 205
Barriers to entry, 23, 30, 37–38, 44–45, 75,
    81, 83–84, 86, 107
Baumol, William, 148, 154
Baxter, William, 148
Be, 44
Bennett, Rob, 84
Bingaman, Anne, 199
Bittlingmayer, George, 159–160
Bliss, Megan, 84
Boies, David, 73, 189
Bork, Robert
    and antitrust law, 47, 105, 147–149,
        151–152, 190–191, 215–216, 218, 225,
        269n
    anti-Microsoft efforts, 29–30, 37,
        207–212
    Borking, 165–168, 213
    consultant to Netscape, 207
    Supreme Court nomination, 166
Borking, 165–168, 213
Boudreaux, Donald, 57–58, 155–156
Boundless Technologies, 220
Boxer, Barbara, 203
Brinkley, Joel, 21
Brown Shoe Company, 149
Browning, Eric, 29
Browsers, 29, 32, 89, 34, 61, 70–73, 88–89,
    250n. *See also* specific browser
Burns, Conrad, 201
Bush, George, 193–196
Bush, Vannevar, 130
Business Week, 51–52
Byte, 107–108

Caldera, 8, 17, 52, 175
Capital, 3, 6, 7
Cartels, 143–144, 159

Cassidy, Powell and Tate Public Relations,
    206
Cato Institute, 218
CD-ROM, 131
Celler-Kefauver Act, xv
Cellular phone service, 127–128
Center for Responsive Politics, 202
Ceridian Corporation, 195
Chase Bank, 101
Chrysler Corporation, 154
Citrix, 55–56
Clark, Jim, 2, 17, 34, 49, 117–119, 121–122,
    129, 132, 135, 175–177, 181–182, 188,
    200–201, 219, 221
Clayton Act, xv-xvi, 147
Clinton, Bill, 192–198, 214
Coase, Ronald, 63, 153
Coca-Cola, 11
Collusion, 9
Comdex, 56, 180–181, 220
Compaq, 18, 44, 51, 56, 107, 178, 195, 220
Competition
    and coopetition, 175
    and mergers, 154
    and pricing, 35–37, 47
    in the software industry, 17–18, 22, 25,
        247n
    perfect, 19, 35
    potential, 34–35, 37, 45–46
"Competition, Innovation and the
    Microsoft Monopoly" conference,
    206
CompUSA, 38, 52, 220
Computer Shopper, 69
Computer virus, 70, 250n
Cook, Scott, 90
Corel, 51, 175
Cox, Michael, 115
Cutler, David, 171

Daschle, Tom, 203
Data General, 44, 178
David, Paul, 98–99
Dealey, W.L., 98

DEDC, 44

Dell Computers, 46, 51, 56, 107, 126, 169, 220

DeLong, James, 157

Delorme, Charles, 156

Demsetz, Harold, 47, 148, 210

Department of Justice
  accountability, 226
  and consumer welfare, 70, 94, 110–111, 119
  and monopoly power, 59–60, 74, 89
  and technology markets, 20, 32, 37, 41, 74, 94, 221
  budget, 229
  charges against Microsoft, 9, 20–21, 23–24, 27, 35, 37, 46, 198–199, 235–240
  filing of Microsoft suit, 2, 27
  inconsistencies, 71–72, 87, 92–94, 102–103, 218–219
  legal strategy, 14, 21
  meeting with Microsoft rivals, 197–198
  political pressure on, 203–207, 212, 217, 226–228
  potential remedies in Microsoft suit, 21–22, 91, 110, 226
  private interests of, 162
  view of Microsoft, 9, 11, 16

Digital Economy Fact Book, 127

Digital Equipment Corporation (DEC), 17, 51, 171, 178

Digital Research, 174

DiLorenzo, Thomas, 155–156, 209

Diminishing returns, law of, 3, 5

Doerr, John, 53, 202

Dole, Bob, 28, 202–203, 206–207, 212

DOS, 8, 10, 17, 68, 79, 171, 173–175, 255n.
  See also Operating systems

Dowd, Maureen, 28, 51

Drugstore.com, 101

Dvorak, August, 98–99

Earthlink, 209

E-commerce, 9, 128, 171

Economies of scale, 23, 30, 32, 38, 41, 44–45, 53, 74

Economist, The, 84

Eisenach, Jeffrey, 206

Ellison, Larry, 2, 54, 56, 179–181, 184–186, 188, 196, 263n

E-mail, 72

Encarta, 131

Enterprise computing, 224–225

Excite, 55, 122

Federal Anti-Price Discrimination Act, 147–148

Federal Reserve Board, 151

Federal Trade Commission, 197, 203

Federal Trade Commission Act, xvi, 95, 46–147, 160

Felten, Edward, 70–72

Financial Times, 11

Findings of Fact
  alternatives to Microsoft, 51–53, 158
  and barriers to entry, 29, 45–46, 60, 81, 84
  and consumer choice, 224
  and opportunistic behavior, 104–105
  and pricing, 36, 38, 64, 75
  legal meaning, 18
  Microsoft's contributions, 67, 120
  possible remedies, xii, 50, 71
  security, 70
  validity of, 8, 227

Fisher, Franklin, 29–30, 32–33, 50–52, 75–76, 84, 86, 90, 92, 126, 222

Folsom, Burton, 57–58

Forbes, 17, 182

Ford Motor Company, 154

Fortune, 11

Frame, Scott, 156

FreeBSD, 44, 53

Freedom to Innovate Network, 214

Friedman, Milton, 152, 218, 226

Frontpad, 129

Frye's, 52

Future Soft Engineering, 129

Gates, Bill
  and industry standards, 79–80
  and network computing, 179, 185
  and politics, 168–169, 194
  criticism of, 12, 14, 28, 118, 175–176, 181, 185, 223
  deal with IBM, 173
  net worth, 12–13
  reputation, 12
  Road Ahead, 181–182, 263–264n
  testimony, 14, 21
Gateway, 29, 56, 107, 126, 169
GEM, 44
General Electric, 11, 34, 46
General Motors, 154
Geos, 44
Gerstner, Lou, 180
Gilder, George, 6
Gore, Al, 196, 202
Gorton, Slade, 169, 229
Graphical user interface (GUI), 131
Greenspan, Alan, 151

Hammon, Ray, 205
Hand, Learned, 157
Handheld computers, 65
Harris Interactive, Inc., 12
Hatch, Orrin, 204–205
Hemple, Hugh, 179
Henley, Jeff, 205
Herbold, Robert, 214
Hewlett-Packard, 29, 44, 51, 107, 170, 178, 196
High Noon: The Inside Story of Scott McNealy and the Rise of Sun Microsystems, 125, 201
Hotmail, 53

IBM
  Ami Pro, 11
  and licensing, 17–18, 173
  and network computing, 126, 169, 171, 178, 186
  antitrust violations, 149–151
  back office computing, 224–225

  competition with Microsoft, 10, 43, 172–173
  contract with Microsoft, 17–18, 80, 107, 173
  Lotus purchase, 187
  market power of, 8, 169–170, 262n
  operating systems, 11, 33, 44, 46, 51, 79–80
  OS/2, 10, 17, 35, 41, 59, 107, 173–174, 262n
  Smart Suite, 107
  Work Pad, 65
Independent Institute, 214
Infomix, 170, 178, 186
Information appliances, 127
Infoseek, 122
Infoworld, 69
Innovation. *See* Microsoft, effect on innovation
Intel, 33, 42, 45, 64–65, 104–105, 170–171, 184
Interactive television, 9
International Data Corporation, 33, 51–52, 62, 64
International Data Group, 179
Internet
  access services, 8–9, 171
  advertising on, 128
  and monopoly power, 28
  and network computing, 56, 180
  commerce, 5
  controlling access to, 29
  early days of, 72
  growth of, 54- 127
Internet Explorer. *See* Microsoft, Internet Explorer
Internet time, 6–7, 49, 217, 223
Intuit, 68, 90

Jackson, Thomas Penfield, 9, 14, 18, 27, 32, 36, 38, 47, 50–53, 64, 67, 70–71, 75, 81, 84, 120, 158. *See also* Findings of Fact
Jacobs, Jon, 199
Java, 2, 55. *See also* Sun Microsystems, Java
Jenkins, Holman, 56, 185, 209

Jobs, Steve, 79, 109, 187
Justice Department. *See* Department of
    Justice

Kamerschen, David, 156
Kapor, Mitch, 196
Katz, Roberta, 205
Kemp, Jack, 206
Kennedy, Florence, 166
Kennedy, Ted, 166
Kinney, G.R., Company, 149
Kirchner, Jake, 21, 24
Klein, Joel I., 9, 53–54, 84, 90, 116, 158,
    198–205

Laptop computing, 72
Law of demand, 76, 101
Lemmons, Phil, 97
Lenard, Thomas, 116, 206
Liebowitz, Stan, 68–69, 99
Linux
    applications, 51, 55
    operating system, 44, 51, 130
    pricing, 39, 41, 52
    sales, 51–53
    servers, 51, 65–66
Lobbying, 143–146, 167–168, 192, 213–214
Lock-ins, 2, 83–84, 86, 92, 94, 96–99, 112
Loki, 51
Los Angeles Times, 28, 166, 213, 224
Lott, Trent, 207
Lotus
    database management, 172
    meetings with Justice Department, 176,
        197
    Notes, 51, 130
    1–2–3, 41, 44, 68–69
    political involvement, 196
    sale of, 186–187
    Smart Suite, 17–18
Lucent Technologies, 133
Lycos, 55
Lyons, Daniel, 17

Margolis, Stephen, 68, 69, 99

Markets, 5–7
McChesney, Fred, 145–147
McCracken, Ed, 196
MCI, 154
McNealy, Scott, xii, 2, 17, 55–56, 92, 176,
    178, 180–181, 185–187, 205, 220
Melcher, Mark, 145
Micro Center, 52
Micron, 29
Microsoft
    and politics, 168–169, 193–194, 203,
        228–229, 212–213
    awards and rankings, 11–12, 68–69, 130,
        242n, 248n
    browser integration, 70–73, 111,
        120–121, 172, 219, 224
    browser war, 17, 34, 58, 117, 118–122,
        177, 201–202
    consortium against, 186–189, 193,
        202–203, 205, 207, 218
    criticisms of, 15, 27–29, 58, 175–176, 180,
        185, 205, 223
    defense strategy, 13, 20–21, 24
    effect on innovation, 116–117, 119–123,
        125–129, 136–139, 224
    embrace and extend strategy, 129,
        133–135, 176, 183
    employees, 133, 141–142
    legal action against, 231–233, 235–240,
        244n
    licensing agreements, 79–80, 103, 125,
        131
    market evaluation, 11, 173–174, 217, 229
    market power of, 8, 11, 19–20, 27, 32–34,
        41, 65–66, 69, 97, 223
    market strategies, 16–18, 24–25, 60, 70,
        87, 103
    operating systems, 10, 23–24, 29–34,
        36–37, 70–73. *See also* Windows
    opportunistic behavior, 104–105, 108,
        110, 112–113, 177, 228
    personal computing, 1, 29–30
    pricing strategies, 31–32, 35–42, 46,
        62–64, 69, 75, 86–91, 211, 219,
        221–222

products. *See* Microsoft Products
profit, 10–11, 29–30, 37, 94
proposed breakup, 21–22, 211, 225, 252–253n
research and development, 85–86, 133, 138–139, 224, 255n
Microsoft products, 137–138
  Back Office, 172
  Clear Type, 132
  Excel, 41, 44, 68–69, 131–132
  Internet Explorer, 60–61, 63, 69–71, 73, 84, 89, 182–183, 198, 250n
  Money, 68
  MSN, 8, 81, 220
  Office Suite, 107, 175
  Office, 41, 174
  Visual Basic, 131
  Windows. *See* Windows
  Word Pad, 111
  Word, 11, 41, 68–69, 132, 174–175
Miller, Bill, 196
Miller, Jim, 207–208
Modems, 72
Monopoly
  actions of a, 15, 19–20, 23–24, 27, 31–32, 66, 153
  and firm size, 156
  defined, 27, 30, 34, 191, 246–247n
  in the digital age, 23, 217
  natural, 38, 41, 44–47, 159
  pricing, 29–32, 36–39, 45, 80, 95, 151, 245–246n, 253–254n
  protecting consumers from, 27, 59
  See also Antitrust law
Mosaic, 58, 118–120, 122, 130, 179
Moschella, David, 179
Mossberg, Walter, 69
Murray, Alan, 29, 245n

Nader, Ralph, 205
National Auto Dealers Association, 146
National Center for Supercomputing Applications, 130
National Semiconductor, 196
Nelson, Ted, 130

Netpliance, 220
Netscape
  and ProComp, 206
  AOL purchase, 54, 220, 222–223
  browser war, 17, 34, 58, 118–122, 201–202
  charges against Microsoft, 199–201
  competition with Microsoft, xi, 17, 24, 32, 44, 50, 53, 120, 177, 223–224
  Mosaic killer, 118–119, 122, 134–135, 179, 222
  Navigator, 15, 18, 24, 34, 60, 69, 74, 89, 92, 105–108
  stock price, 118–119, 201
Netscape Time, 34, 49–50, 122, 200, 202
Network computing, 55–56, 73, 179–181, 184, 186, 220–221
Network effects
  and demand, 252n, 253–254n
  and monopoly power, 84, 95–96, 101–103
  and network goods, 6, 76, 102
  and path dependency, 97–98
  and pricing, 81, 87–89, 91, 95
  defined, 76, 84–85
  in the software industry, 23, 32, 53, 74–75, 78–79, 122
Neukom, William, 21, 202, 244n
New York Times, 13, 18, 21, 28, 146, 214
New Yorker, 28
Next, 44
NOISE, 15, 189
Noorda, Ray, 174, 175, 178
Norris, Gary, 18, 243–244n
Novell, 174, 175, 178, 186–187, 197

OEM (original equipment manufacturer), 29
Office Depot, 149
Oliver, Dan, 207
Operating systems
  competition in, 30, 219–220
  market, 29–30, 32–34, 42, 59, 78–80, 100–101

pricing, 31, 36, 41–42, 75, 80–81, 87–88, 102
producers, 44
virtual, 181
See also Windows; DOS; OS/2
Oracle, 2, 15, 44, 53, 56, 126, 170, 172, 178
and ProComp, 206
and the Internet, 54–55
back office computing, 224–225
Business Online, 220
network computing, 180, 186
Ordover, Janusz, 148, 154

Parker, Steven, 155–156
Path dependency, 2
Patman, Wright, 148
PC Magazine, 10, 12, 21, 24, 69, 73, 130
PC World, 97
Peckman, Rufus, 157
Perlman, Lawrence, 195
Perot, Ross, 195
Personal computing
birth of, 1, 3–4, 22, 169–171
changes in, 5–6, 56, 185–86
prices, 184
sales, 127
total cost of ownership (TCO), 55
Peters, Tom, 5
Pettit, Mike, 203
Pitofsky, Robert, 203
Plattner, Hasso, 187
Politics, 165, 167–168, 192–193, 202, 205, 216. *See also* Microsoft, and politics; Lobbying; *and* Presidential election campaigns
Posner, Richard, 32, 147, 151, 153, 162, 227
Pournelle, Jerry, 107
Powell, Jody, 206
Predatory business practices, 9, 24, 70, 86–87, 90, 150, 153–154, 258n. *See also* Monopoly, pricing
Presidential election campaigns, 194–197, 202, 265n. *See also* Politics
Price elasticity, 31–32, 246n
Priest, George, 210

ProComp, 206–207, 210, 213, 267–268n
Productivity applications, 8
Progress and Freedom Foundation, 116, 127–128, 206
Psion, 44, 65
Public choice economics, 147

Quatro Pro, 174–175
Quayle, Dan, 196
QUERTY, 98–100, 223

Radio Shack Model 100, 131
Railway time, 4, 7, 23
Real Networks, 105
Reback, Gary, 28, 199–201
Red Hat, 39, 41, 52–53, 202. *See also* Linux
Red Herring, 182
Reno, Janet, 27, 194, 244n
Rent extraction, 145–146, 163, 194
Rent seeking, 143–145, 153, 194
Reynolds, Alan, 64–66
Road Ahead, 181–182, 263–264n
Robinson-Patman Act, 147–148
Rockefeller, John D., 57–58, 180
Rockwell International, 46
Rolandte, Wim, 186
Romano, John, 29
Rosen, Ben, 195

Sabre, 206
SAP, 187
Scheer, Robert, 224
Schmalensee, Richard, 21, 69
Schmidt, Eric, 205
Schwinn, 151
Sculley, John, 79, 195
Seagram and Calvert, 151
Seattle Computer, 129
Secure Internet Programming Laboratory, 70
Senate Judiciary Committee, 204
Sherman Act, xiv, xvi, 4–5, 25, 147, 154–157, 159, 228, 259n. *See also* Antitrust law
Shughart, William, 152, 157, 159–160, 162
Signature Software, 34

Silicon Graphics, 196
Silicon Valley, 17, 194, 196
Silverman, Jon, 160
Skates, Ronald, 186
Slate, 28, 205
Smith, Adam, 142–143, 148, 225–226
Software and Information Industry
    Association, 21, 65, 269n
Software industry
    and pirating, 134–135
    attributes of, 16, 22–23, 74–75, 78–79, 83
    competition in, 17–18, 22, 25
    innovation, 24, 115–116, 135–137, 184
    market, 19, 22, 127
Software Publishers Association, 206
Soukup, Stephen, 145
Southwick, Karen, 125, 201
Spyglass, 34, 119, 129
SRI International, 196
Standard Oil, 57–58, 150, 157
Staples, 149, 220
Star Division, 51, 55–56
Steinberg, Andrew, 205
Stevens, Ted, 203
Stigler, George, 153, 155–156
St. Louis Post Dispatch, 151
Sub-notebook computers, 65
Sun Microsystems, 2, 8, 15, 17, 65, 74, 133,
    201–203, 213, 220, 270n
    and network computing, 55–56, 92,
    180–181, 220, 224
    and ProComp, 206
    competition with Microsoft, xi, 53, 55,
    171
    Java, 116, 125, 130, 185, 187, 223
    operating systems, 44, 46, 51, 170
    servers, 53, 126, 178
    Solaris, 41, 65, 171–172
Sunk costs, 38
Switching costs, 30–31, 62, 251n
    and the QUERTY keyboard, 98–100
    and videocassette recorders, 100
    defined, 83–84,
    extent of, 86, 91–94
    overcoming, 101, 106, 112, 123

Sybase, 186, 206

Target, 149
Technology, 54, 56–57, 67, 115, 128
Templeton, Mark, 55–56
Thomas, Clarence, 166
Thomas, Greg, 203
Thompson, John, 178, 180, 186, 189
3Com, 44
Tipping, 2, 79–80, 97
Tollison, Robert, 159–160
Torvalds, Linus, 51, 130
Toyota, 154
Trans-Missouri Freight, 157

United Shoe Machinery Company, 148–149
U.S. District Court for the District of
    Columbia, 20
University of Illinois, 34, 200, 222, 256n
Unix, 33, 44, 170, 172, 174, 178, 187, 186

Vacco, Dennis, 29
Vaporware, 198
Vertical integration, 209
Von Holle, John, 29
Vradenburg, George, 205
Vxtreme, 105

Wal-Mart, 11, 34, 38, 149–150, 153
Wall Street Journal, 12, 14, 20, 29, 56, 64, 66,
    69, 166, 185, 187, 189, 205, 229
Wang, 44, 129
Warren-Boulton, Frederick, 30–33, 35, 86,
    93, 102–103, 126, 246n
Warren, Earl, 149, 152
Washington Post, 194, 214
Wealth of Nations, 142
Web-based computing, 221, 223
Weisberg, Jacob, 28
Wheeler-Lea Act, xvi
Wildstrom, Stephen, 52
Wilson, Sonnini, Goodrich, and Rosati, 199
Windows
    alternatives to, 23, 29–30, 34, 52, 56,
    59–60, 107, 124, 158

development of, 9, 10, 38
market, 8, 27, 29, 64–66, 80, 174
price, 31, 35–36, 38–42, 44, 211, 219
upgrades to, 39–41, 43, 62–64, 85, 129,
 138, 173, 198
versions, 43, 51, 61, 63, 65, 71, 110, 126,
 129, 132, 171–172, 174, 178, 187, 197
Wireless communication, 9
Wolfe, Larry, 205
Word Perfect, 11, 41, 44, 51, 68–69,
 174–175, 187, 197

Worldweb.net, 206
World Wide Web, 8, 72–73, 179

Xerox, 44, 129–130

Yahoo, 8, 53, 55, 122
Young, John, 196

Zona Research, 185
ZSoft Corporation, 129